FLY-FISHING
Heresies

FLY-FISHING
Heresies

A new gospel
for American anglers

Leonard M. Wright, Jr.
foreword by Nick Lyons

Winchester Press

Some of the material in this book has been printed previously in *American Sportsman*, *Esquire*, *Field & Stream*, *Fishing World*, *Random Casts*, *Signature*, *Sports Afield*, and *The Anglers' Club of New York Bulletin*.

The author wishes to thank the following for their contributions of photographs: William Aller, Wesley Balz, Bob Elman, Andrew Kner, and Shirley Wright.

Library of Congress Catalog Card Number: 75–9260
ISBN: 0–87691–203–X

Library of Congress Cataloging in Publication Data

Wright, Leonard M.
  Fly-fishing heresies.

  Includes index.
  1. Fly-fishing. I. Title.
SH456.W73   799.1′2   75–9260
ISBN 0–87691–203–X

Book and jacket design by Marcy J. Katz

Published by Winchester Press
205 East 42nd Street, New York 10017

Contents

FOREWORD

Leonard Wright:
The Angler as Iconoclast
by Nick Lyons

In the midst of debunking one or the other of fly-fishing's hallowed traditions, Leonard Wright asks simply: "But shouldn't fly-fishing be a joy as well as a challenge?" Not one or the other but both—for a challenge unleavened by pleasure becomes a stale mania, and a joy without a challenge wears as thin as hedonism. Part of both, for Wright, is being radically independent—taking one's joys and challenges on one's own terms, free from what one has read, free from the shackles of what someone else has legislated as the only "right" way.

If one of the abiding pleasures of fly-fishing has been its discrete traditions, an equally delicious sport, when supported by common sense, is breaking them. Wright does so with relish. The saints—Halford and Walton—short rods, dead drift, and a host of other sacred cows and mores and techniques draw his fearless blows. But Wright is not merely pugnacious: He is brilliant, full of common sense and uncommon ingenuity, and he is one of the happiest and most thorough-going iconoclasts in the tradition of angling.

Consider his attack on one of the newer orthodoxies: that it is sportier to fish with a short, light rod than with a long, heavier one. Heading briskly wrongwards down what might seem a one-way street, and blithely referring to a "36-ounce beauty" of a rod with a "light, flexible tip," Wright calls the short rod "the least effective, least comfortable, least 'sporting' fly-fishing tool ever invented for fishing running water. I know it's risky to knock another man's woman, dog, or favorite rod, but look at the evidence." And then he proceeds to show precisely *how* the short rod is ineffective and uncomfortable, and your doubts turn to intense interest as he eloquently extols the virtues of the longer rods he uses.

Nothing is sacrosanct before Wright's penetrating eye. He even scores the revered Walton — whose influence, he says, "is almost as strong and all-pervading as original sin"—for his *style* as well as his angling ability and ethics. And labels him a plagiarist, to boot. He pushes not only the "sudden inch" for caddis but also jiggled mayflies—and the logic of casting dry flies across and *down*stream. He sees many modern nymphal imitations as being "as realistic as the figures in Mme. Tussaud's waxworks" but "as stiff as boards," and asks us to reconsider the recently discarded wet-fly patterns as more effective. Invariably, his suggestions are the product of careful observation; the Quill Gordon, he notes, "leaves its nymphal shuck on the river floor and ascends through the water to the surface as a winged adult"—making any nymph a poor choice.

Admirers of Wright's first book, *Fishing the Dry Fly as a Living Insect,* will welcome his additional information on the now-much-less-neglected fluttering caddis. There are more tying instructions, more valuable suggestions on technique. But he is more than an Apostle for Trichoptera. There is some marvelous information here on increasing trout populations by improving rivers; some memorable glimpses of the once-extraordinary fly-fishing on Austria's Traun River as well as the intriguing pleasures of "backyard fishing"; a convincing invitation to fish "slower and lower" for big salmon and to use imitations of crane flies, house-flies, wasps, bees, and flying ants for summer trout; and a glorious paean to "the perfect fish," the Salmo family.

Leonard Wright admits that he's been a "compulsive fisherman" ever since he could walk. He's also become a uniquely observant, and articulate fisherman. He's come to recognize that, "Obviously, trout aren't as gullible as people. You can't fool all of the fish some of the time or even some of the fish all of the time."

Fly-Fishing Heresies, for all its hard looks at past and reigning orthodoxies, remains devoted to sharing the fruit of very real trial-and-error experimentation. It *will* help you catch more of the trout more of the time.

Happily, the ways of trout and salmon will always remain something of a mystery; we'll never be able to gull them all the time. That's the source of both the joy and the challenge of fly-fishing. But fishing through this book with Len Wright will make flyfishermen less gullible and more observant—and hopefully encourage more of that independent, iconoclastic spirit which is his.

Nick Lyons
New York City
September 1, 1975

PREFACE

"Heresies" is a strong word. It smacks of blasphemy, sacrilege, and worse. How could it possibly be applied to what Walton called "the blameless sport"? Especially in these days of "do-your-own-thing" values?

Easily.

Perhaps the only solid establishment left today is made up of the fly-fishing followers of the nearly sainted Frederick M. Halford. They still believe unswervingly in three major tenets proclaimed by the Master from England nearly ninety years ago.

The first of these was that dry-fly fishing is an enjoyable and productive way to take brown trout. To this, I can only say "Amen."

But the corollary pontifications seem suspect to me. The two most influential were that the artificial fly must be fished without any motion (or absolutely "dead drift") and that the artificial is increasingly more effective as it nears the exact photographic imitation of the natural fly.

Several years ago I wrote a book questioning the dead-drift dogma. In *Fishing the Dry Fly as a Living Insect* I attempted to prove that a little carefully controlled manipulation increased the appeal of a dry fly much, perhaps most, of the time.

Reactions were mixed. A few wrote that they already knew

this. Many said that this technique and the recommended "fluttering caddis" imitations had increased their catches considerably. But the establishment was not moved.

Shortly after publication I bumped into Sparse Grey Hackle — dean of American fly-fishing authors and Boswell of the purist fraternity. "Congratulations, Len," he said. "I see you've written an entire book devoted to the ancient art of trolling." I could see the twinkle behind his glasses, but I could also feel the needle in the words of this, one of the kindest of men.

In the *Fly-Fishing Heresies* launched on the following pages I add arguments against the "dead-drift" doctrine, challenge "exact imitation," and attempt to topple some neo-Halfordian beliefs—ones that have since been added by the faithful. After you've read them, perhaps you will reflect and experiment. If these chapters open your mind to new suppositions and start you theorizing on why a trout does, indeed, take a counterfeit fly, then angling will be the richer for it.

Consider this book, then, as opening remarks to a jury. Not as a verdict. That last word will always come from the final judge, the fish.

Leonard M. Wright, Jr.
New York City
September 1, 1975

FLY-FISHING
Heresies

1

A Dry-Fly Heresy

Fishing for trout with the floating fly, as it is practiced and preached in America today, has become as highly ritualized a performance as bullfighting. Both pursuits are straitjacketed by rigid rules, hobbled by out-of-date choreography, and bear little relevance to the final downfall of the quarry.

I'm not an expert on the efficient slaughter of beef cattle, but I think I may be of some help to dry-fly fishermen, all of whom, as far as I know, would like to catch more trout whether they creel them or release them. For the fact is, I have stumbled onto a far more effective way to take trout on the floating fly. Very likely, others have, too, but since no one has written it up yet as far as I know, I'll make the first cast.

To witness the classic style of American dry-fly fishing that I have become disenchanted with, just drive along any first-rate trout stream once the spring invasion of hatchery trucks and bait-fishers is over. You will soon see at least one man dressed in what looks like the bottom half of a diving suit, waving a long, limber rod. His thick, oily fly line hisses gently as it doubles back on itself, straightens, then loops forward again, darting his small fly out toward a chosen patch of water. You will notice he is casting in an upstream direction so that his fly will float back toward him freely on the current; but this is not nearly as simple as it looks.

The angler has to calculate the effect of current tongues and eddies and cunningly curve or "S" his line onto the water so that the hidden hands in the flow won't pluck his fly off-course from a true, dead-drift float. This unnatural pull would be drag — the dry-fly man's archenemy. He avoids this as the golfer fights looking up or as the skier tries to keep his weight off the inside ski. And it is this ability to achieve a drag-free presentation that separates the true flyfisher from the mere flogger.

After a few seconds of pure float, the angler will snap his line off the water, dry his fly by false-casting it in the air, then send it out to search a new section of the surface. He will repeat this process again and again as he works slowly upstream until he disappears from view or until his rhythm is interrupted by the strike of a trout.

There's an almost ballet-like beauty to this performance and it tends to hypnotize the fisherman, but it doesn't seem to have as telling an effect on the trout. I know because I spent many years acquiring this classical skill, and many more practicing it, and it just doesn't work very well or very often. The reason for this is that most of our natural aquatic insects do *not* float serenely downstream like priceless objects of art. They twitch, flutter, struggle, and skitter before they manage to take off, and our trout seem to know this only too well.

If you watch a trout pool carefully when only a few insects are hatching, you'll see what I mean. Especially on cool or rainy days when takeoffs are difficult, a fly will float down-current a hundred feet or more over the best lies, unmolested, only to be eaten when it makes its first fluttering attempts to get airborne. Yet, only a few moments later, a fly of the same species that starts struggling as soon as it emerges will be taken instantly by a fish that let the previous free-floater pass by. I have seen this happen so regularly that I am convinced this is the rule rather than the exception. The example I just referred to involved mayflies. Caddis flies, the other important order of aquatic insects, are notoriously active when on the water, and it was by trying to imitate them that I finally strayed from the paths of orthodoxy.

Another thing you'll notice while watching such a pool is that virtually all hatching or egg-laying insects will head up-current unless there is a disastrous downstream wind. This tropism is crucial to the perpetuation of the species: So many lumbering nymphs and larvae are washed downstream by floods that the headwaters would soon be depopulated if each generation of winged adults didn't leapfrog back upriver.

Trout are carnivores, and it is motion that most often helps them separate the meat from the chaff that the current brings their way. A bewildering variety of objects, both animal and vegetable, passes over a trout's head all day long during summer. The length of this inventory impresses me every time I hold a piece of cheesecloth in the tongue of a current for a few minutes. Along with the bees, wasps, houseflies, beetles, leaf hoppers, ants, and aquatic insects strained out, I find an equal quantity of small twigs, leaf cuttings, petals, berries, hemlock needles, and assorted debris nearly the same size, color, and shape as the edible insects themselves. Trout can tell the difference, though, without studying entomology and botany. Insects wiggle, hemlock needles don't.

Trout, especially wild trout, make this distinction between food and trash almost unerringly. I have tossed a wide assortment of likely looking objects to feeding trout from a concealed position and had not more than one halfhearted take out of a hundred samples while that same fish rose, from time to time, to a great variety of windfall insects. Those twigs, leaf bits, and small pebbles you find in trout stomachs? Don't let them mislead you. They're almost certainly pieces from the cases of caddis larvae—a favorite trout food that is grubbed off the bottom, abrasive house and all.

It stands to reason, then, that the angler will be more successful if his imitation duplicates not only the appearance of a natural insect, but its behavior pattern as well. A good example might be the case of a fisherman trying to cope with a caddis-fly hatch. This type of aquatic insect is nearly as important to trout as is the hallowed mayfly, though it is skimpily mentioned in most books on fly-fishing and is not closely imitated by any of our most popular flies. In fact, caddis flies are becoming even more impor-

A typical mayfly imitation with upright wings, slim, tapered body, and a tail representing the setae of the Ephemerae.

tant to the flyfisher because they're hardier than mayflies and can stand more of the pollution and deteriorating stream conditions that have plagued us for over a century.

Adult caddis look nothing at all like ninety-nine percent of our dry flies because the latter are patterned after mayflies. Caddis have no tails and fold their opaque wings in an inverted "V," horizontally, covering their bodies. Mayflies, like most of our artificials, have long tails and carry their translucent wings erect, like Marconi-rigged sails, above the body. The differences in the silhouettes of these two orders of insects are enormous. Caddis flies are extremely active both as they hatch out on the surface and when they return to the river later on for mating and egg laying. They twitch, flutter, and zigzag on the water surface in a distinctive manner that the trout find irresistible.

One of the most plentiful of our several hundred species of caddis is a medium-sized, brownish insect known as the shad fly. On some famous rivers like New York State's Beaverkill the shad fly is the most profuse single insect to appear each year, yet most anglers find it a frustrating fly. When this hatch is really on, fish will be rising in the runs and pools all up and down the river, yet most dry-fly men will be drawing blank, or nearly so. For some reason, there just isn't any available imitation that looks anything like this fly, but that's only part of the problem. More important, this insect does *not* float down-current with the statue-like poise of the classic dry fly. In fact, like most caddis, this insect seems to enjoy finding itself on the water as much as the average house cat does, and it protests nearly as vigorously.

Two nearly forgotten fishing techniques duplicated this behavior quite accurately, but, unfortunately, neither is effective with modern tackle. The practice of dapping — bouncing the fly over the surface on a very short line directly below the rod tip — was a telling technique three hundred years ago when fly rods were sixteen to eighteen feet long. With today's seven- to eight-

Left: a fiber-winged "fluttering caddis" with slim, downwinged silhouette. *Right:* a flat-winged stonefly artificial.

footers, dapping doesn't give the angler enough range to be useful except on small, brushed-over brooks. The same is true of dancing a dropper fly which has been tied a few feet up the leader. This second, airborne fly can be zigzagged and trickled over the surface when the rod is held high, but with today's equipment, fifteen to twenty feet is maximum range, and no self-respecting brown trout will allow the angler that close in clear, smooth water. Certainly our shorter rods dictate a whole new approach if the fly is to be manipulated effectively on the surface.

A method of manipulation that I worked out several years ago is surprisingly simple and effective. Since any motion imparted to the dry fly must be in an upstream direction or slower than the current, the way natural flies tend to move, I position myself above and across stream from the fish or its suspected lie. I then cast my caddis imitation three or four feet above the chosen spot, throwing a pronounced curve, bellying my line upstream. Within a second after the fly hits the water—before the leader or line tip can start to sink—I give my rod a short, sharp, upward twitch which sends the fly darting up current an inch or so. Then I feed out slack line and let the fly float, drag-free, for six or eight feet—enough and more to cover the lie of the fish. This "sudden inch" recreates the behavior of a winged caddis closely enough so that it will usually be taken if the presentation is made accurately and if the fly itself is a passing imitation of the caddis that are on the water.

This second "if" posed a problem even more difficult than that presentation one, though. Since the caddis, unlike the mayfly, has no tail, there is nothing to support the heaviest part of the hook which is directly over the bend. The only available caddis patterns with any semblance of realism — and even these are hard to come by in this country—are the English "sedges" which are winged with stiff feather sections laid tent-shaped along the body and finished off with conventional hackle at the head. This type of fly has an excellent silhouette and floats passably—if you fish it dead drift. Twitch it, though, and it sinks tail first.

Hours of tedious trial and error at the fly-tying bench finally produced a fly that seems to solve this problem. I have substituted, for the vulnerable plumage wings, clusters of steely cock's hackle fibers bunched on top and on the sides of the hook shank,

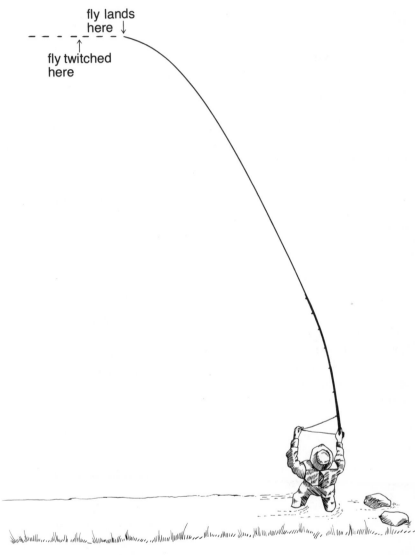

fly lands
here ↓

↑
fly twitched
here

Aerial view of preferred presentation. Cast angled slightly downstream with a curve in the line. Fish sees fly first.

but still lying parallel to the body. The silhouette is very similar to the "sedge" from all angles to my eye and the trout seem to agree. The big blessing of this new fly is that it floats like a ping-pong ball. It should: The entire wing, which is nearly twice as long as the body, is composed of the most water-repellent feathers known and acts as the floatingest tail a fly ever had. I can twitch the devil out of this fly, and, unless the leader sinks and thus tends to pull the fly under, it will skitter buoyantly over the surface even on drizzly days.

Obviously, a fly shaped like this isn't a good match when mayflies are on the water, and when this occurs I go back to the conventionally tied imitations. There have been many attempts to better the basic style of mayfly introduced by Halford more than eighty-five years ago, but I have found them all, including my own innovations, inferior to the original. I do, however, use long-hackled, variant flies quite often—not because they are better imitations, but because they float higher and can stand more manipulation without sinking.

I consider this floatability important because I usually give some motion to my artificial mayflies as well as to the caddis flies. Observation has led me to believe that all but the luckiest mayflies kick and struggle sporadically before they get off the water. I therefore use much the same technique for imitating mayfly behavior as I use when caddis flies are on the water. I make the same across-and-downstream presentation followed by the twitch that I use when caddis are hatching and results are equally rewarding. However, when I'm using the easy-to-drown, conventional dry fly, I ease up on the manipulation. Merely rocking the fly on its hackle tips so that it twinkles in the surface film seems to be realistic enough, and I've found that this mini-manipulation is fully acceptable to the trout during mayfly hatches.

But important as caddis and mayflies are to our fishing and fascinating as it may be to try to match the hatch, the most important and prevalent fishing condition we all have to face today is the non-hatch. For days on end, during the summer months, there will be no hatch worth imitating even in the evening and even on some of our most famous trout streams. We are becoming a nation of prospectors, spending most of our hours trying to pound up non-rising fish. And it is precisely here that the fluttering fly really proves its worth: it can make a feast out of what is usually a near-famine. The moving fly not only spurs indifferent fish to the surface, but it also opens up more hours of the day and more parts of the stream to productive fishing.

Today, the choicest spots on most of our public waters are usually tenanted all day long. You're almost sure to find an angler stationed at the head of a pool where the incoming current slows and fans out and there's likely to be one or two in the pockets and runs above. But the slow part of the pool will probably be unoccupied except for the last few minutes in the evening. This type of water makes up more than half the total yardage on most of our rivers, and it is here that I've found I can enjoy my sport to the utmost without playing an abrasive game of musical chairs with my fellow fishermen.

Let's say that I've rigged up beside the river at three o'clock on a July afternoon. I will now carefully skirt the patient angler lodged at the head of the pool and step into the water a courteous distance below him. This leaves me alone on the body of the pool, a stretch of water one hundred and fifty yards long and a hundred feet wide which, incidentally, probably has not been thrashed for several hours.

Since this pool curves gently to the left, from a downstream-facing point of view, I position myself on the left bank or on the weak side of the current and prepare to prospect the deeper, food-carrying water near the far shore. There are no insects hatching so I tie on one of my new caddis imitations dressed on a #14 hook. It's not that I expect a caddis hatch for hours, if then, but I choose this fly because its down-wing silhouette looks more like the houseflies, wasps, beetles, and stone flies that are the most likely windfalls than does the standard dry-fly silhouette. Then, too, it is the best floating fly in my box and this is pivotal.

I make my first cast twenty degrees downstream from straight across, curving my line so that it bellies upstream, landing the fly on the near edge of the deepish water. Within a second, I raise my rod tip sharply, making the fly lurch upstream an inch or so, then I feed out extra line so that the fly will float directly down-current. I keep my rod point high, to hold more line off the water for a truer float and also to absorb the shock of a strike, for the fish will hit against a tightening line.

Casting upstream to a fish in the classic manner. Line and leader may fall over fish. Downstream drag is a probability.

After six or eight feet of drag-free float, the fly will start to skitter across stream toward me and just as this motion starts a fish will often be goaded into taking. If no rise occurs after the fly has dragged a foot or so, I give a sharp tug on the line with my left hand to drown the fly and then snake it back upstream under the surface so that it won't frighten any nearby fish. My next cast is made eight feet farther across stream and is fished out in exactly the same manner—as is my third cast which is placed eight feet beyond the second. I have now covered the most likely holding water within easy reach with these three presentations so I wade to a position ten feet directly downstream, being careful not to send out advance-warning ripples, and prepare to make my next series of three covering casts. Depending on the size of the water, more or fewer casts may be needed to cover the lies thoroughly and this set of presentations should be repeated at ten-foot intervals all the way down to the tail of the pool or to a point where the water becomes too shallow to be worthwhile.

I have found that this method is not only vastly more productive than classic upstream prospecting, but that it is also far quicker. You can cover the best part of a pool of the size described above in about twenty minutes with this technique and then proceed to the vacant pool below with the assurance that you have covered more fish, and risen far more, than you could have in an hour and a half of conventional fishing.

One of the reasons for this is that a trout will move sideways five, even ten feet for a fluttering fly while a free-floater usually has to pass right over his nose to be effective. Then, too, the twitch pulls trout to the surface from far deeper water. Most flyfishers admit that it's hard to pound up fish with the floating fly in water over three feet deep unless spontaneous surface feeding is going on. Not so with the manipulated fly. It will trigger rises in six feet or more of water time and again — even under the noonday sun.

I'll have to admit, though, that I have drawn some flak from the establishment for angling this way. A couple of years ago, I was fishing behind a very proper older friend who stopped so long to

Casting to the same lie across and downstream. Fly approaches trout before the leader, and any drag is in upstream direction.

rest at a beautiful pool that I decided to pass him and push on upstream.

"Any luck?" I asked as I detoured behind him.

"Not a thing. Just look at that pool, though. It's got to be loaded, but I've been watching it for twenty minutes and I haven't seen so much as a dimple. I've had it. Why don't you show me how with that 'living insect' routine of yours?"

The water and the invitation were too good to pass up. I knotted on a caddis and started in at the top of the pool giving my high-floating fly a tiny twitch soon after it settled to the water.

Twenty minutes later, after I had raised seven trout, hooked five, and landed four good ones, I heard some heavy breathing close behind me.

"Very impressive. That popping bug of yours may well be the greatest invention since the worm."

My friend has since forgiven my fall from grace — somewhat. He will be seen with me in public, now, although he seems to duck me on the stream.

I look at it this way. I may have lost a fishing companion. But I have gained the companionship of a lot more trout. And, come to think of it, when I'm on the stream, that's the company I like best.

2

The Alive-and-Kicking Dry Fly

If the evidence presented in the first chapter and a review of your own experiences have by now convinced you that a dry fly moved slightly and in the proper manner will outfish one that is presented absolutely dead drift, you may still have one lingering doubt. Why have so many seemingly intelligent men fished the standard floating fly drag-free for so long? After all, many leaders in business, science, and the arts (not to mention two of the last seven Presidents of the U.S.) have been dedicated flyfishers. Have they all been duped and deluded?

The answer, I think, lies somewhere between "Yes" and "Probably." And the reason such a thing could happen in this age of enlightenment makes a fascinating, though little-known, story.

Dry-fly fishing may have been developed over many years by many men, but it didn't reach the angling world at large until 1886. In that year, *Floating Flies and How to Dress Them* was published, and anglers haven't recovered from its enormous influence to this day. The author was Frederick M. Halford, an English gentleman, who gave up money-grubbing in all its forms at a relatively early age to devote his life to the nobler ideals of dry-fly fishing for trout.

The streams Halford fished are the most fertile in the world. The Test and Itchen in southern England produce twenty times as much trout food per cubic foot of water as do most famous streams on this side of the Atlantic. Back in Halford's fishing days, before road-washings, insecticides, and other pollutants had begun to take their toll, the hatches of insects, especially of mayflies, on these waters were incredibly profuse.

Under these conditions, a few fish rose fairly steadily all day long, and for several special hours every day when the glut hatches occurred, every fish in the river seemed to be on the take. It was a flyfisher's paradise and too perfect to be spoiled for other club members by some heavy-handed chap who put down the fish by flailing a team of wet flies through these clear waters in the hope of taking an unseen trout.

The accepted drill was quite specific. First a rising trout must be located. Then an accurate imitation of the fly on the water — not just some attractive and buggy-looking artificial — must be cast upstream of the trout and allowed to float, dead drift, over the nose of that particular fish. No attempt must be made to cater to its greed or curiosity. The only proper way to take such fish is to convince them that your counterfeit is, indeed, just another of the duns on which they have been feeding with confidence.

Fishermen on both sides of the Atlantic became fascinated by the science, skill, and delicacy of this new method. Halford became the high priest of a cult that spread the true doctrine with fanatical zeal. Soon the wet fly was considered a secret vice and club members caught using it were asked to resign their expensive rod privileges. The dry fly became a moral issue. After all, dammit, a gentleman didn't shoot grouse on the ground, he didn't cheat at cards, and he most certainly did not fish the wet fly, either!

From what I read, we seem to have shaken off most of our old Victorian hang-ups by this time, but the dry fly is still considered holier than the wet and the Halfordian dogma of dead drift seems to be a vestigial part of this ethical package. The moral origins of this doctrine may be lost in history, as far as most anglers are concerned, but the ritual is still with us.

In all fairness to Halford, though, I must repeat that he was fishing the stately chalkstreams of southern England which team with small mayflies. And, so even so, he included five highly realistic caddis patterns in his final selections of forty-three dry-fly patterns. But can we, who fish rivers that are mostly rain-fed, acid, and where caddis rival the mayflies for top place on the trout's menu, afford to ignore caddis imitations completely?

Rare photograph of Frederick M. Halford (left). "No wading" was his dictum, yet he is the only one wearing hip boots!

For we seem to be doing just that. For example, check the contents of your own dry-fly boxes. How many floating imitations of caddis flies do you carry? Don't count non-descripts or flies like the Adams which are said to duplicate some caddis but which are tied with the characteristic mayfly upwings and tails. I mean true caddis patterns like the English "sedges" with wings tied parallel to their bodies and which show a realistic caddis silhouette. Can you find many—or even any—in your fly boxes?

If you're like most anglers I know or meet—and many of these are advanced flyfishers — you probably don't have a single one. And chances are you can't find any at your favorite tackle shop, either. With the exception of a few terrestrials, nearly all floaters displayed in even the most fully stocked stores are designed to imitate some mayfly or other.

Admittedly, these popular mayfly patterns have proved themselves over and over again—*when there are enough mayflies hatching to start trout feeding regularly and selectively*. But how much of the time do you meet these conditions on the rivers you fish? What do you offer when caddis flies are hatching out in large numbers and trout are feeding on them selectively? What fly do you put on when stone flies are on the water? Or during those all-too-long periods when nothing is hatching and the trout are taking only the occasional, windfall, land-bred insects like bees, wasps, or houseflies? Is the traditional mayfly silhouette the most appealing to trout at times like these?

I think not. And I think this is the reason why the series of flies I have worked out to represent the most common species of caddis flies have proved themselves as excellent prospecting flies, too. Their silhouettes are more accurate representations of most land-bred windfall insects than are the shapes of the standard mayfly patterns.

Straw, ginger, brown, light dun, dark dun, and ginger-and-grizzly mixed have proved the most useful colors, but there are endless variations. Sizes 16 and 14 seem to cover most common caddis hatches, although I always carry some 18s and 12s just in case. Most of the caddis patterns I use have wings, hackle, and body of the same shade because caddis flies tend to be much the same color all over. My stone fly imitations, tied in the same manner, usually show more contrast, as do the naturals.

If you tie your own flies, or have a friend who ties for you, you may be interested in how these new Fluttering Caddis flies are tied. I start out by winding the tying silk back toward the tail, proceeding a little further than is customary, or just a bit around the bend. The reason for this is that most caddis have slightly down-pointing abdomens and because this fly needs more room at the eye-end of the hook. Tie in, at the point, two, at most three, strands of fine herl (pheasant-tail fibers are a good example) and very fine gold wire. Wind the herl up the shank, being careful to keep the body slim and even, to a point just halfway to the eye of the hook and fasten it down. The wire is then wound tightly to the same place with four or five even turns, but in an opposing spiral so that it binds down the herl and protects it.

Next comes the wing, and this must be put on with great care. Take a good spade feather, shoulder hackle, or the stiffest fibers on the neck that you usually reserve for tail materials, even up the points, and twitch off a section about three-fourths of an inch wide. Position this bunch on top of the hook so that from the tying-in point to tips it is about twice as long as the body, and bind it down with one full, firm turn of tying silk. If the fibers lie absolutely flat along the shank, you're in business. If not, take them off and build up the wingbed with thread until it is even with the hard portion of the herl body. When you have wound the body correctly with a suitable, small herl, this is seldom necessary, but these extra turns of silk can remedy any small error.

Once these top fibers are properly set, place two more bunches of the same bulk and length, one on each side of the hook, and tie them in with one turn each. Now half-hitch or weight the tying silk and examine the wing from all angles. When viewed from the rear, it should look like the upper half of a small tube, only slightly larger in diameter at the tail end than it is at the tying-in point. It should also veil the body a bit when viewed from the side. At this point you can still make minor adjustments by pinching and cajoling the fibers where they join the hook. Once you are satisfied with the overall appearance and symmetry, bind down firmly and finally with three or four turns of silk placed in tight sequence toward the head of the fly.

Take a fine, sharp pair of scissors and trim the wingbutts to form a gradual inclined plane, heaviest near the tying silk and coming to a point just back of the eye of the hook. It's a good idea to hold the wings firmly with your left thumb and forefinger right at the tying-in point while performing this delicate process so that the wing is not jostled out of position at this crucial stage. When the taper is absolutely even, take some varnish or cement and work it into the exposed butts to keep the slick hackle fibers from pulling out during the punishment of fishing. When the head becomes tacky, tie in two hackles of the usual size for that hook and wind them on in the conventional manner, being careful to bunch the turns tightly so they don't slide loosely down the inclined plane toward the eye of the hook. Whip finish, varnish the head, and the fly is finished.

Each caddis represents a larger-than-average investment in choice materials and in effort, but it's worth it in the long run. If properly tied, it will float higher and take more punishment than any other dry fly in your box. And, I've found, it will take more fish, too. Even if you're not a tyer, or don't know any, you should be able to give these new patterns a tryout next time you're on the stream, because several tackle companies now offer the caddis patterns in their catalogs.

I know this is not the perfect dry fly for every single situation, although I, myself, now use it the majority of the time. Of course, I still fish standard mayfly imitations when those naturals are on the water—though I often give even these easily sinkable patterns a tiny twitch when a steadily rising fish continues to ignore my artificial. I also know that this new method will never make me into the perfect flyfisherman, either. But with these patterns and this unorthodox presentation, I am now catching several times as many trout from hard-fished waters as I did a few years ago. Try them during a caddis or stone fly hatch or during those all-too-long "non-hatches." I think they'll do the same for you.

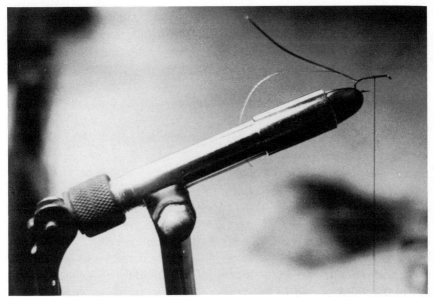

1. Herl and tinsel tied in at the bend. Tying silk returned and half-hitched slightly more than halfway up the hookshank.

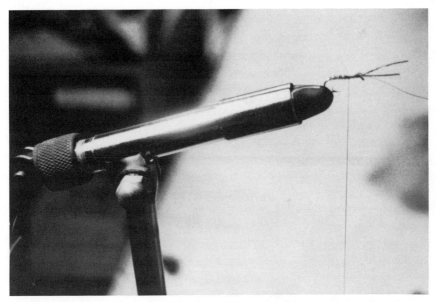

2. Body herl in place and binding wire wound in opposite direction. Keep body slim or wing will flair unnaturally.

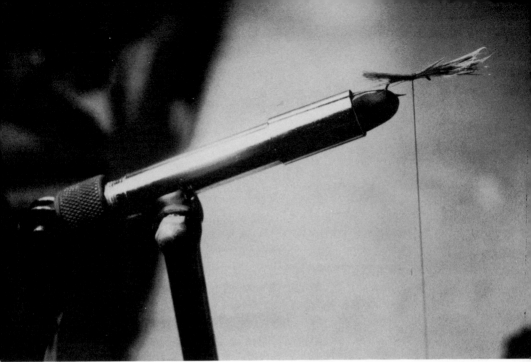

3. Spade-hackle fiber wing tied in. If it flairs, build up bed of tying silk ahead of body and seat it again.

4. Taper wing butts evenly to eye of hook and dose with varnish or cement. Hackle will not lie well on abrupt slope.

5. Two hackles of size appropriate to hook size tied in. Adding more tacky varnish or cement here is good insurance.

Hackle wound in close, even turns. Bunched hackle, small head, and flat wing enveloping body are signs of good work.

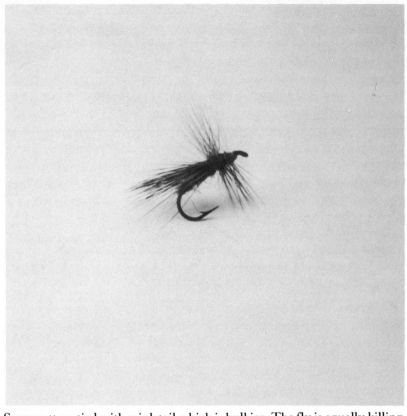

Same pattern tied with mink tail which is bulkier. The fly is equally killing, but less elegant in appearance.

3

The Unsinkable Wet Fly

Most advanced flyfishermen I know seldom fish with wet flies anymore, and the youngest of them don't even carry wet-fly patterns. You don't have to be a research analyst to see that this has all the earmarks of a significant trend and, if it continues, in a few years it will be harder to find a wet fly than a #22 midge hook in a haystack. Today, nearly all sunk-fly fishing is done with nymphs. They've almost completely replaced the small, somber wet flies like the Leadwing Coachman, Hare's-Ear, and Dark Cahill, while the Mickey Finn, Muddler, and Spuddler seem to have shouldered the big, bright wets out of the fly hooks and into the attics where moths can complete their destruction.

This may or may not be a loss to fishermen, but fishing catalogs are certainly poorer because of it. Nothing dressed up a color plate as did the old Scarlet Ibis, Parmachene Belle, Silver Doctor, Jenny Lind, and their peer-group. Even our present-day salmon flies with their plain hair wings seem drab in comparison.

The reason these brilliant wet flies are no longer with us is that the special type of fishing for which they were designed disappeared long before they did. When the brook-trout ponds and lakes of Maine, the Adirondacks, and southern Canada were fished down, these patterns had no further purpose. But in their time and place they were murderous.

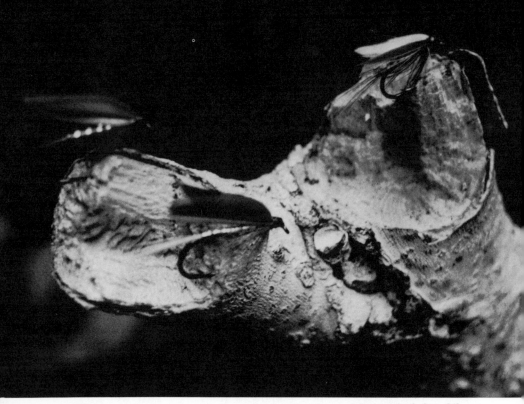

Have you seen any of these in recent years? Montreal (left), Silver Doctor (center), Parmachene Belle (right).

By sheer luck I caught the tail-end of this fishing many years ago in central New Brunswick, and if I hadn't experienced it myself I wouldn't believe the old-time stories. I had been staying at a salmon camp enjoying rotten fishing, and the operator, worried about the possible departure of his paying guests, came up with a delaying tactic. A new area had just been opened up by logging, he told us, and there was now a rough, but passable, road into an almost unfished lake. One logger who said he had fished there swore he'd had a hit on every cast.

We were not a gullible bunch but we were eight hundred miles from home with nothing better to do, so three of us made the trip in an old pickup truck over a road designed to make osteopaths rich. After we had arrived and were able to walk again we found the crude raft the logger had made and drifted out onto the lake. And for once everything we'd been told by an outfitter was absolutely true.

Very soon, the promised hit on every cast became monotonous, so we started experimenting. Two flies? Doubles. Three flies?

Triples. Then the one man who'd stuck with the single fly said excitedly, "Even when I've got a fish on, I'm still getting hits. I'll bet they're striking the leader knots." After he landed the fish he tied a couple of small bare hooks in at the knots of this gut leader and cast out again. He'd guessed right; he landed his first triple.

One thing we all noticed that day was the brighter the fly, the faster the hit and the bigger the trout. One member of the party found a few old Parmachene Belles in his vest and these were the best of all. They accounted for nearly all the big fish—those of a pound or better—while smaller, duller flies caught nothing over ten inches. The reason was simple. The more successful fish, the ones that had grown big, were the fish that won the race to the food, no matter what it looked like, and it paid to advertise your hook to them. Caution and delicate presentation had nothing to do with success on these virgin waters. Here the old bright wet flies on hulking #6 hooks were supreme.

The Muddler Minnow (top) and the Mickey Finn, two attractor flies that have replaced gaudy wets for pounding up fish.

The good old days, when baskets of big trout were expected. Believe it or not, fish once fought each other for the fly.

Though these flashy wet flies had lost their effectiveness on most ponds and lakes long before my day, some of the more subdued patterns from the same generation are still worth carrying. The Black Gnat is a fine imitation of a big housefly or black land beetle. The White Miller can't be equaled when white caddis are hatching out on a Northern lake. The Grizzley King is a useful imitation of many green-bodied caddis flies, and the Montreal duplicates some of the darker species in this order of insects.

When flies like these were arbitrarily discarded along with the Christmas-tree wilderness flies, the baby may have been thrown out with the bathwater. There's a lot about the shape and style of the old wet fly to recommend it—so much that I'm working on a whole series of flies based on this principle.

The emphasis on more accurate imitation, the very movement that brought in the nymph as a replacement for the old wet fly, is responsible for leading me in this direction. The patterns I've come up with so far are different from the old ones, but more in color than in shape. When more anglers and fly-tyers turn their attention to the neglected wet fly I'm sure that even the few classic patterns that have survived the nymphing revolution will be redesigned or replaced.

One of these that is still popular in the East is the wet version of the Quill Gordon, which is carried and used by many who consider themselves exact imitationists. Since many books have told us that this mayfly (*Epeorus pleuralis*) leaves its nymphal shuck on the river floor and ascends through the water to the surface as a winged adult, a wet-fly pattern is the logical choice until, of course, the fish become preoccupied with surface feeding on the fully-formed adults. But which wet fly? The Quill Gordon?

This pattern has yellow wings, a black-and-white striped body, and dun-colored legs. The natural fly is distinctly different, with dark dun wings, creamy-olive body, and dark-brown mottled legs. The old English Greenwell pattern, with a slight alteration in the body, is best imitation I've ever seen or tried. I've fished my version of this fly as part of a two-fly team along with the standard Quill Gordon, altering their positions on the leader regularly, and over the past thirteen springs it has outfished the wet Gordon better than two to one.

The real nymph-maniacs prefer the grey-colored Quill Gordon nymph which tackle suppliers are all too eager to sell you. I wonder why this pattern appears in so many catalogs. The nymph never rises to the surface, as we have noted, and it is one of the last nymphs to be dislodged by high water. It is a fast-water dweller with a short, flattened body and will only be swept away when the rock or boulder it's hiding under gets rolled over by the force of a flood. Long before this occurs the trout will have gorged themselves on the less-secure nymphs washed down to them. I doubt that Quill Gordon nymphs ever lose their grip until the river is so high and muddy that any sort of fly-fishing is impossible. This may be a useful general pattern, but I don't think trout mistake it for the Quill Gordon nymph.

The Quill Gordon, both the artificial and the natural, is an extremely popular and famous fly that has been observed and studied more than most. But how many other mayflies emerge in the same manner and would be better imitated by a wet-fly pattern than by a nymph? And how many caddis flies and stone flies are there that share this underwater emerging behavior? Entomology doesn't provide many answers—aquatic insects haven't been given much attention by scientists lately — but my guess is that this type of emergence is a lot more common than we realize. Remember, the wet fly was not invented in America to catch ravenous and overpopulated brook trout. The silhouette and the style were worked out in England over several centuries to catch sophisticated and finicky brown trout.

There's another part of the life-cycle of aquatic insects that is ignored by the angler who limits himself to dry flies and nymphs exclusively. What happens to flies after they die? The great majority of them fall on the water, of course, which explains why fishing with mayfly-spinner imitations is so effective at dusk. But what about the spent flies—mayflies, caddis flies, and stone flies — that aren't taken in the pool where they fall but get churned underwater in the rapids directly below? Could a dry fly or nymph imitate these soggy, but winged, insects as well as the

The Quill Gordon wet fly (right) and the modified Greenwell, which is a better duplicate of the emerging natural.

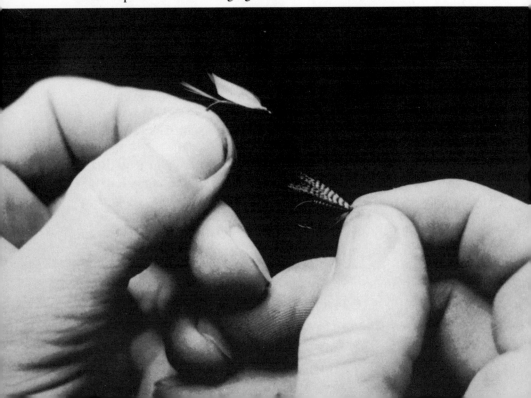

classic wet fly in some pattern or form? I am fully convinced that many early and successful wet flies were winged with pale starling primary feathers to imitate mayfly spinners that had gone down for the third time and had been swept downriver for the waiting fish.

The much-neglected caddis flies may give us even more reasons to reconsider the old wet fly. Some common species seem to spring fully fledged from the water as if they had escaped from their pupal shucks well below the surface. Have they hatched directly out of their cases on the stream-bottom the way the Quill Gordon mayflies do? I'm betting on it. And don't some other species, with their seemingly instantaneous hatch-out on the surface, appear more like winged adults than pupae as they make this hazardous trip? I'm sure this is the case with many common species. And yet all the new patterns of emerging caddis I see in tackle stores and catalogs are slavish imitations of the pupae as they appear when they are hauled dormant from their cases.

Another caddis behavior pattern that recommends a wet-fly imitation is the egg-laying of several species. Did you know that some (we don't know exactly how many) crawl down roots, rocks, twigs or weed stalks to lay their eggs underwater? When these have deposited their eggs and drift down-current, dying, the wet fly has to be the most killing imitation.

It is interesting to note that fishermen who have witnessed this egg-laying technique say that the mature female insect takes a bubble of air underwater with her and that she appears like a moving drop of silver. Modern flyfishermen who wouldn't be caught dead fishing a wet fly sporting a tag or entire body of tinsel have, perhaps, outsmarted themselves.

There's another reason to reevaluate the old tinsel-bodied wet fly. We know that a bubble of gas develops rapidly under the pupal shuck of caddis flies and under the nymphal skin of mayflies just before they emerge. The gas bubble helps them hatch out. How does this make the insect appear to the trout? Is the exact color of a nymph or pupa—examined hours or days before it heads for the surface—what the trout sees during this critical time when the insects are most available as food? Or is there a very different silver or golden flash caused by this gas bubble in emergers that telegraphs to the trout that this is their

The big, bright, brook-trout flies of yesteryear. Tackle catalogs haven't looked the same since trout became scarce.

target of the moment? I am not convinced that modern fly-tying isn't presenting a whole series of death-mask flies to trout. A lot of observation and experimentation is in order here before we completely abandon flies that have served fishermen so well for centuries.

Every year or so now a new series of nymphs is presented to fishermen, and each is highly acclaimed because it appears to our eyes even more faithful to the naturals than the previous attempts. The last group of imitations I saw had the precise number of tails (or setae) the naturals have, and six perfectly formed legs with the correct number of joints in each leg. They were every bit as realistic as the figures in Mme. Tussaud's waxworks. And, like those famous statues, they were also as stiff as boards because their realism had been achieved by stiffening the appendages of the flies with lacquer.

Flies like these deserve to be carefully mounted and exhibited, but it would be almost sacrilegious to fish with them. It might also be a waste of time. A few years ago there were many nymphs made of molded plastic that looked as if they could crawl out of their fly-box compartments, and yet they were indifferent fish-takers and have nearly disappeared from the market. The shortcoming was that they, and many of the newer patterns formed with lacquered feathers, were designed from models that were the preserved corpses of nymphs. Have you ever watched a living mayfly nymph or stone fly larva underwater? The gills appear enormous, are fluttering constantly, and are very often quite different in color from the body of the insect.

There's a lot of evidence that the motion of these gills and the scampering movement of the legs identify these nymphs as living food to the trout, and that the precise color and size, though important, are secondary. Any stiff, lacquered imitation loses this seductive quality of movement and much of the natural insect's translucence as well. I admire these new photographically realistic nymphs as art forms, but they leave me lukewarm as lures for trout.

Perhaps the most compelling case of all for the old wet fly is that it moved and breathed with every subtle change in current. Wet flies, as we have noted, were probably designed to imitate many life-phases of many types of insects, yet they can perform splendidly as imitations of mayfly nymphs when specifically tied for this purpose. The wet versions of the Light Cahill and March Brown, for example, with their darker, striped topsides, can be deadly imitations when the corresponding nymphs are hatching out. The secret here is to tie the wings in low and on the sides, as you would with a strip-wing salmon fly, so that they hug the top half of the body. Their silhouette is then sleek and nymphlike, yet there's still an extra "aliveness" to the play in the wing-fibers that the standard nymph-dressing can't equal.

I have a whole series of wet flies like these—different from the ones duplicating emerging or drowned flies — and I have more confidence in them than I have in the popular nymph-dressings of the same insects. I'll admit I haven't tested these against the standard nymphs, two on a leader, the way I have the wet Quill Gordon, so I can't quote any catch figures. However, everything I've learned about trout and trout-fly tying, as well as my results, convince me that I'm on to a more productive style of fly.

To increase the breathing, moving characteristics of these patterns, I pluck out a lot of body dubbing with a needle or substitute ostrich herl dyed to an exact color for the body material. This increases the fly's similarity to a living nymph with its fluttering gills, and I'm sure this adaptation will increase the effectiveness of most nymph patterns, too.

I came upon this trick, which is certainly not original, after many years of learning the hard way. I didn't jump to this conclusion easily after hearing all those stories about the chewed-up, tattered fly outfishing all others, although it is now one of the few pieces of fishing folklore I firmly believe. No, I had to be taught this lesson, piece by piece, by a kindly but self-serving expert.

Early in my fly-fishing career and before I tied my own flies, I often fished with an elderly gentleman who appeared to be uncommonly generous. He would press on me all sorts of wet-fly and nymph patterns during a day's fishing, and since good flies cost the princely price of a quarter apiece in those days, I looked upon him as a walking gold mine. However, at the end of each day's efforts he questioned me about the performance of each of the donated flies, and graciously accepted the slightly used artificials back into his own box. With my usual hawkeyed hindsight, I'm now convinced that the old bandit wasn't the least bit interested in my researches; he knew exactly what he was doing. He was using me to "warm up" his flies for him, to get them into shaggy, fish-catching shape while he used the ones that were already in vintage condition. It turned out to be the classic case of one hand washing the other. My weekly allowance was minute and his fly supply was almost infinite.

Imitation of some sort or other is probably the key to success with today's hard-pounded trout. But what sort of imitation? You can imitate an insect's overall behavior pattern, for instance. You can also imitate the small motions of its gills, tails, legs, and antennae. Or you can imitate its color, shape, and appendages down to the minutest detail. I doubt, however, that any single nymph dressing can excel at all three types of duplication. You have to compromise somewhere and, with nymphs, I prefer to skimp on exact anatomical details. I feel my more alive patterns perform at least as well as the more static, more photographic,

Wet fly imitating the March Brown nymph or emerger. Notice how mallard-flank wing hugs ostrich-herl body.

dressings when matching a specific emerging nymph, and that when I use them for random prospecting they are far superior.

The wet flies I use to represent winged emergers, drowned adults, and egg-layers seem to be without any major shortcomings. Wings and legs are responsive and mobile without sacrifice of true-to-life detail. I can't fault them in accuracy, theory, or performance.

I think the easiest and most convincing type of wet-fly fishing, if you want to take it up or try it again, can be experienced at the end of a summer evening. Until the light gets too dim to see your fly on the water, fish the dry-spinner imitation of the spent mayfly you've seen fall to the water, and fish it dead drift. Then, for the last fly of the day, tie on a standard wet fly of the same size and color. Go downstream a short distance to the head of the pool below where the current begins to lose its chop, and cast your fly straight across stream, letting it swim till it comes to a stop directly below you. Repeat at one-step intervals until the water gets too slow to pull your fly through the arc in a satisfactory manner.

Feel your way carefully downstream with your feet, but be sure to feel your line and rod with equal sensitivity. You should get some thumping strikes and — if you don't strike back too quickly as I usually do—some exciting fish. If you're like me, you'll probably find that the night is absolutely black before you decide it's time to stop.

Even the most fastidious flyfisher should feel happy after this type of angling, for he has been an exact imitationist the entire time. This is not chuck-and-chance-it with a nondescript. He has been presenting the closest possible imitation of the fly of the moment to the fish in exactly the same manner in which the naturals are coming to them. Most important of all, at a time of day when he is likely to be bone-tired, the angler has not had to strain his eyes, strike on hunches, or worry about whether or not his fly is still floating.

If this experiment in wet-fly fishing convinces you there's something here, perhaps you'll tie and try the wet fly on other occasions, too. Not as a mere blob of food, but as an imitation of a specific life-stage of an identified insect. If you keep an open mind and compare results with fishing companions, I think you'll find the drill exciting and rewarding. You won't be exploring a new frontier, but you will be adding a third dimension to your dry-fly/nymph style of trout fishing, and, when you start observing flies and fly behavior for yourself without relying on some other man's word, you'll find a whole new and productive world of fishing.

Every year sunk-fly men seem to add more weight to their flies, leaders, or lines to make sure their nymphs bump along the very bottom of the stream. No doubt this has made fly-fishing more effective—especially when the trout aren't feeding. But it has also made casting and fishing less pleasant. So much so that many anglers will spin or bait-fish rather than torture their rods and their arms in this manner.

The wet-fly fishing I'm practicing and proposing takes a middle ground and covers the middle depth of the water. Here you don't need sashweights or heavy lead-core lines because emergers, egg-layers, and drowned flies don't hug the bottom the way nymphs do. They're not far under the surface, and you can present their counterfeits realistically with regular tackle and a floating line. Surprisingly often, this is exactly what the trout ordered.

It seems that fly-fishing becomes more complicated and technical every year, and perhaps this is necessary to achieve best results under demanding circumstances. But shouldn't fly-fishing be a joy as well as a challenge? Men in less harried times certainly thought so. They fished the wet fly with grace and pleasure, not feeling that every fish in the stream had to be yanked out of it. The surprising thought is that they just may have been using the most effective imitation of all.

4

Give Summer Trout a Moveable Feast

The average dry-fly fisherman is about as well equipped to fool summer trout as a golfer would be to win the Masters with a bag full of putters. For in any sport you're handicapped when you limit yourself to just one aspect of the game.

All those patterns, sizes, and colors you see in a fly box don't mean real variety to a trout. Most of the flies will be the same shape. The reason for this is that over ninety-nine percent of the dry flies sold today — from minute midges to galumphing #8s — have an identical silhouette. Their sweeping tails, slim bodies and upright wings show they're an imitation of some type of mayfly and, unfortunately, mayflies are only an occasional snack for summer trout.

Most of our dry-fly patterns have been handed down to us from happier days on insect-rich streams where mayflies were, indeed, the major source of insect food. Our most popular dries are direct descendants of mayfly imitations worked out by Frederick Halford on England's prolific chalkstreams nearly a century ago. We still slavishly cast these imitations to our trout, despite the fact that entomologists — and the proof-positive stomach contents of our trout — tell us that trout in America today make far more meals on the three other orders of insects that hatch off the water and on random, land-bred insects than they do on Halford's hallowed mayflies. In light of this, casting a repertoire consisting of artificial mayflies only is about as realistic as Marie Antoinette's advice for the starving peasants: "Let them eat cake."

Similarly, the dead-drift, upstream presentation preached by Halford is a relic from the good old days, too. An accurate imitation of a natural fly fished in a free-floating manner may still work—and work well—when trout are rising regularly to a particular species of fly. But what about all those hours when trout aren't actively feeding? Will a totally unexpected fly with some fifty extra legs, too many tails, and a great hook hanging down below it seem real enough to pull a wary trout up off the bottom? Or will he class it with the twigs, berries, hemlock needles, and leaf cuttings that also drift over his lie all day long? The latter is usually the case as most of us know from sad experience. Under these conditions, your imitation needs something extra going for it if you are to convince the trout that your counterfeit is, indeed, alive.

To catch a loafing trout's attention and to gain his confidence, your dry fly should move—and move as a living insect does. This means a small movement, not a great plowing wake. And it should move in an *upstream* direction. For all stream-bred flies, whether hatching out or returning for egg-laying, move in an up-current direction.

The reason the moving dry fly has been damned for decades is not that natural flies don't move, but that when the fisherman cast his fly up-current—as doctrine dictated—any motion except for a free drift was either downstream, across-stream, or both . . . behavior patterns so unrealistic and alarming that they send all but the most calloused trout scurrying for cover.

If, on the other hand, you break with tradition and cast your fly in an across-and-downstream direction, when you give it a tiny twitch it will lurch upstream. Then let it float free again as long as it will. That small motion is enough to catch the trout's attention and tell him that your offering is, indeed, alive and edible. Gently does it, though. The game is like calling ducks. Overdo it and you defeat your own ends.

This slightly moved dry fly is the only way I've ever been able to raise trout consistently when they're slightly lethargic during the summer months and there are no big fly hatches to keep them feeding regularly on the surface. This method will even raise good fish out of a deep slow water at midday when only mad dogs and Englishmen would think of being astream.

There's just one problem with this seemingly unorthodox system. You probably haven't a fly in your box that will keep floating—and floating high—after you've given it that tantalizing twitch. Then, too, the mayfly silhouette—even if this type of fly occasionally remained afloat—doesn't look like most midsummer insects. It has long tails, is basically translucent, and has upright wings. The other important insects that emerge from the water—caddis flies, stone flies, true flies, and nearly all insects that are blown onto the water from the neighboring land—have no tails or very small ones, wings that lie along the top or sides of the body and are basically opaque.

Cut open the next trout you catch on a midsummer afternoon (if you can take one on a standard fly) and examine the stomach contents carefully. I'm sure that what you'll find there would make Halford whirl in his grave like a #10 fanwing cast on a gossamer 8X tippet. Ants, wasps, bees, crane flies, beetles, and houseflies will form the bulk and, if there are any aquatic insects in the mix, there will probably be as many caddis flies and stone flies as there are mayflies. If you'll take a trout stomach's word for what he's been eating, you'll have to ask yourself the agonizing question: "What do I match when there's no hatch?"

And this is a question you'll have to answer for a greater part of the day over a longer portion of the season in the years ahead. For good hatches of mayflies are disappearing on most of our waters. They are already a great rarity on most northeastern waters after June 1, and really profuse early-season hatches are becoming infrequent enough to be talked about again and again as major events.

Caddis hatches, on the other hand, seem to be as heavy as ever and stone flies, the third most important order of aquatic insects, seem to be holding their own, too. Apparently, both of these types of insects are tougher and more tolerant of the flooding, heating, and polluting that progress brings to our running waters.

Yet perhaps the most important part of the trout's diet during mid and late summer is made up of the wide variety of land-bred insects that fall onto the water. Grasshoppers and beetles have long been recognized as trout delicacies, and good imitations are available at many tackle stores. But what about the other windfalls that trout feed on during hot weather?

The observant fishermen in Pennsylvania's limestone country have come up with ingenious imitations of the leaf-hoppers, Japanese beetles, and tiny ants that fall onto their waters. But little attention has been paid to the corresponding insects that tumble into woodland streams at this time of year. Terrestrial insects are equally important to mountain trout as they are to fish inhabiting meadow streams flowing through rich agricultural areas, but they are a very different looking collection.

In an attempt to fill this important, though empty, corner of our fly boxes, I have experimented with a series of prototypes that cover most of the insects I find on mountain streams and inside trout during midsummer. You should certainly enlarge on and vary this selection by copying insect types you find most frequently in your area. All these flies, despite their apparent differences in size, shape, and color, have one characteristic in common. They are the most buoyant artificials I have ever fished with. They will ride high and cocky on the surface even after they have been twitched smartly.

These imitations are no more difficult to tie than standard patterns, but there are a few tricks that may make your first attempts easier. This series of flies, for tying purposes, can be separated into three broad types that are different in small, though important ways.

The tying of caddis imitations was treated earlier in Chapter 2. Stone fly imitations are made in much the same way except for slight variations in both the body and the wing. Stone fly bodies should be more succulent, should be colored yellow, brown, or an alternating pattern of the two. Ostrich herl is a good choice here since it gives a chunky appearance without adding much real bulk. This wing, too, should be twice the body length and placed on top of the hook only instead of on top and along the sides. Use light grey or pale dun hackle since these are the usual stone fly wing colors. Hackle at the head should be the same size as you would use for the caddis and wound on in the same

A dry stone-fly artificial on long-shank hook with ostrich-herl body. Hackle-fiber wing hugs top of body.

Top view of dry crane-fly imitation. Outrigger wings of dun-hackle fibers recreate flair of natural's wings.

A flying black-ant pattern seen from above. Ant wings also flair to the side away from distinctive body silhouette.

Side view of floating bumblebee. Body is formed of alternating black and yellow ostrich herl. Outrigger wings on side.

manner, but choose a shade that matches the body rather than the wing color. The above suggestions cover the great majority of stone flies you'll see on mountain streams, but by all means imitate any other color combinations you see regularly on the streams you fish.

Crane flies, houseflies, wasps, bees, and flying ants are the easiest of all to tie. Start with a good, meaty body, colored to match the species in question. You won't have to stint here because you'll want the wings to flair on these flies. Here again use pale dun or grizzly hackle fibers, keeping them the same length as before, but positioning them on the sides of the hook shank only. The finished wings should flair out to the sides at an angle of about thirty degrees the way a bee's or housefly's wings do. These outriggers of steely hackle will not only make your fly ride high but will help it sit squarely, hook down, every time you cast it. Finish these flies as you did the stone fly imitations, with two conventional hackles suggesting body color rather than wing color.

These summer flies will float twice as well as standard mayfly imitations if you tie them with the same quality of hackle. The only trouble is that you'll be using a lot more long-fibered hackle which is often hard to get in first-rate quality. Substitute hair whenever you can get good water-repellant guard-hairs of the right color. Mink tail is excellent and is produced by breeders in a wide variety of shades. Beaver gives a good dark brown. Woodchuck tail — even though the animal isn't aquatic — sheds water beautifully. So does moose mane. Be careful with deer tail, though. Some portions are useful, but most of it is hollow and will flair badly when tied to the hook.

Admittedly, these patterns are not exact imitations of the flies you'll find in midsummer trout. But they are very appealing *impressions* of these windfall insects, and fish aren't highly selective at this time of year because they don't often see large enough quantities of the same insect to get psychologically imprinted with an exact size, shape, and color. The trick is to give them the *sort* of fly they've been taking and to present it as a struggling, but sitting, duck.

On some afternoons one fly will be preferred; on others a different one will pull more trout to the surface. Experiment. But be guided in your first choice by what you see in the air and on the water. Crane flies often hover and dance over the surface, and an imitation can be deadly when you see a few yo-yoing over a pool. Always be on the alert for a flight of ants—especially when the weather is hot and sunny.

You may wonder why I tie my flying-ant imitations in this manner since it is well known that these insects usually ride flush in the surface film, rather than high and dry like stream-bred insects. The answer is that, when flying ants fall on the water during midsummer afternoons, they are liable to be so numerous that your artificial stands a fractional chance of being taken unless it advertises itself as a newcomer by its activity. A standard ant can't take the twitch and remain floating while this pattern can. I've found that the twitched imitation will outfish the low-riding, dead-drift one by a wide margin — especially when there are a dozen or more ants per square foot of water.

Above all, when you're prospecting with these flies on a midsummer morning or afternoon, spray or anoint your fly liberally and change it at the first hint of sogginess. In this type of fishing a half-drowned fly is as much use as wet matches.

Why do I continue to fish the dry fly during the dog days—and hours—when nothing seems to be rising? Why don't I turn to the upstream, dead-drift nymph that so many authors recommend for these conditions? There are three reasons, and any single one of them would be enough to keep me fishing on the surface.

First, upstream nymphing is the most demanding and least diverting kind of trout fishing I've ever tried. It takes far more judgment and concentration to fish an unseen nymph up-current without any drag than it does to fish the dry fly in this manner. There's no visible fly to help you regulate your rate of retrieve or to tell you when to strike, either. I find this technique cruel and unusual punishment unless the fish are taking readily. A half-hour without a hit is the outside limit of my attention span.

Second, I think it's harder to deceive a trout with a nymph than it is with a dry fly. A floating fly has to be glimpsed through the distorting prisms that hackle fibers set up in the surface tension giving the trout a blurred view. A nymph, on the other hand, is seen directly through the clear water and any imperfections stand out sharply—probably the reason why wet flies and nymphs work best only in fast or turbulent currents.

But the third, and main, reason that the dry fly, properly fished, will beat the sunk fly under low water conditions is that the surface carries most of the insect food at this time of year. The stream-bed may be teeming with nymphs, but they hide under rocks during the day and crawl out only at dusk or after dark. Summertime aquatic insects rarely swim up to emerge till late evening and even then they may be pitifully few in number. The main food supply most of the day is made up of insects that have flown or tumbled onto the surface and these, trapped in the rubbery surface film, are carried downstream on top of the water. Sample the drift food in a stream at this time of year with a cheesecloth net and you'll find that the middle and lower layers of the current yield almost no food at all.

For all of these reasons, then, you can presume that daytime feeding fish are expecting their food on the surface. This is fortunate for the angler, for here his fly stands the best chance of both catching the fish's attention and preventing him from getting too close a look at the imitation.

This type of floating fly fished with motion not only helps you catch more trout, but it lets you catch them out of more parts of the stream or river. With this technique in hand, you won't have to compete with other anglers at the heads of pools or along the few fast runs. A fly twitched slightly on the surface will raise trout all day long on the much-neglected pools and long flats where the dead-drift nymph or dry fly would seem very dead, indeed.

Equally important, this method will help you catch fish during more of the daylight hours. You will no longer have to pin all your hopes on that last-minute flurry of feeding as darkness ends the summer day. If you have a several-hour round-trip drive to your favorite stream — as most of us do — this benefit alone is enough to make this technique worth cultivating.

I hold no brief for quoting scripture loosely just to prove your case, but I can't resist pointing out that the Old Testament Book of Proverbs advises "Go to the ant, thou sluggard . . ." I think all flyfishermen will agree that before editing and translating the line must have read, "Go to the ant, wasp, bee, beetle, crane fly, housefly," and so on. After all, the Holy Land is warm-weather territory. And from where else would you expect such good advice on how to catch fish when the rivers are low and sluggardly?

5

Izaak Who?

We all know that fame is a fickle thing at best, yet when it comes to angling laurels we have the crowning irony. Not one person in a hundred has ever heard of Frederick Halford or Theodore Gordon—flyfishermen whose pioneering changed the way millions of people fish today—while every man, woman, and child seems to know the name of that unrepentant baitslinger and wormfisherman, Izaak Walton.

It's not that I'm judging the man on the basis of what he put on his hook. I'm no archpurist and I've wet a worm or two, or worse, in my day. The reason I find Walton's immortality a mockery is the fact that the man was a plagiarist.

Now don't start reaching for your well-thumbed copies of Krafft-Ebing or Havelock Ellis because I'm not accusing Walton of some unmentionable and degenerate deviation. A plagiarist, as any Ph.D. in English literature well knows, is simply a literary thief, and on this count Walton was as guilty as sin.

The literary critics and English professors of the world, to whom Walton had always been a darling, were badly shaken up on the morning of December 17, 1956. On that day, a front-page article in no less than The New York *Times* headlined, "Did Walton Hook 'Angler' From Older Book?" exposed the original, and long-lost, source from which much of Walton's classic had been, shall we say, borrowed.

This news item described a book called *The Arte of Angling*, printed in London in 1577, that had recently been found in the attic of an old English country home. It consisted of a dialogue between Viator and Piscator, the same two characters we find in Walton's book. The general narrative line and structure of the two books were surprisingly similar, the experts noted, and several passages were almost word for word the same. Coincidence? Two great minds working alike? Little chance of that, said the learned men who were analyzing the new find. *The Arte* had been published eighty years before Walton's book, or well before Izaak had been born.

This exposé and its implications did not go unchallenged. The very next day a short item on the Walton affair appeared in the middle of the *Times* with a defense of Walton by D. E. Rhodes, a British expert on early fishing classics. "It seems to me unjust," said this authority, "to accuse Izaak Walton of plagiarism, because plagiarism did not exist in the seventeenth century. All authors in that and earlier ages read what they liked and used what they liked without acknowledgment." True, perhaps, but I am not swayed. Monarchs, in those days, frequently and quite legally chopped off the heads of those who disagreed with them, but the fact that this was no crime does not convince me that head-chopping-off is a blameless form of recreation. (Furthermore, as we shall see in a moment, one of Walton's own contemporaries considered word-larceny a vulgar enough offense to be labeled a "common calamity," and he forthwith accused Walton of "Plagiary.")

A few smaller stories and mentions appeared in the press over the next month or so, and then the whole issue became history. Walton's reputation remained untarnished.

Why wasn't Walton discredited and defrocked by the literary pundits? It wasn't as if some new Dead Sea Scroll had been found showing that St. Peter had actually been in the wholesale fish business and had never caught a fish in his life. St. Peter is a towering figure in both history and religion, and fishermen are justly proud that their patron saint is one of the most important of all.

But Walton . . . who sanctified him? He is of very little interest to contemporary fishermen and owes most of his fame to the fact that his book is required reading in many English literature courses. Were the implications of this revelation too uncomfortable to the academic establishment of Walton-worshippers? Was Walton too small a fish in the literary swim to merit a major Shakespeare-Bacon controversy? Was the word "Walton" too indispensable to journalists as a synonym after they had used up "fisherman" and "angler"? Did the Izaak Walton League exert its influence to clamp a lid on the story? Nobody has yet come up with an explanation.

Equally hard to understand is the fact that the scholars were taken by surprise when this new evidence emerged. Actually, Walton had been caught out very early in the game. His contemporary, Richard Frank, whose *Northern Memoirs* came out in 1658, just five years after the first printing of *The Compleat Angler*, called out "foul" loud and clear: "He stuffs his Book with Morals from Dubravius and others, not giving us one Precedent of his own practical Experiments, except otherwise where he prefers the Trencher before the Troling-rod; who lays the stress of his Arguments upon other Men's Observations, wherewith he stuffs his indigested *Octavo*; so brings himself under the Angler's Censure, and the common Calamity of a Plagiary, to be pitied (poor Man) for his loss of time, in scribbling and transcribing other Men's Notions."

Walton may or may not have been a great stylist, but Frank could wield words with the best of them. He winds up the above indictment of Walton and his kind with ringing words: "These be the drones that rob the hive yet flatter the bees they bring them honey." Didn't anyone read, or listen to, Frank?

Elsewhere in *Northern Memoirs* Frank describes a face-to-face argument he once had with Izaak, and we get more clues to Walton's original sources. Walton took the position that pickerel were generated from pickerel weed while Frank claimed that they were born from eggs laid by their parents, like every other fish. Walton cited his authorities for this point — Gesner, Dubravius (there's that man again), and Androvanus—and, when pressed by Frank, refused to discuss the matter further and walked off in a huff.

We have always known that Walton was a rotten speller, but this incident reveals that he was also woefully misinformed about the habits of fish — even for his own time. Again we find him borrowing from outdated authorities. One of them, Dubravius, was mentioned specifically in Frank's earlier accusation of outright theft, but had Walton also cribbed from the other two to fill his book? And is the author of *The Arte of Angling* yet another source, unknown to Frank, that Walton may have dipped into? We may never know. The first three pages — including the title page — of that recently discovered work were missing and there isn't another copy anywhere.

One of the commonest tributes paid to Walton's book is the serenity and tranquility of the work even though it was written during Britain's bitter Civil War. This is often cited as proof of the beauty of Walton's soul. I hope we don't hear that argument anymore. It appears certain that the original had been conceived back in the rollicking days of good Queen Bess.

As a matter of fact, *The Compleat Angler* has never been very popular reading with fishermen — at least not Walton's portion of it. Walton was more concerned with how to prepare baits, cook fish, and watch milkmaids than he was with fly-fishing. The raising and care of maggots and the kneeding of exotic paste-baits to entice overgrown, vegetarian minnows haven't fascinated anglers for many years. Most of the passages quoted by fishing authors are from Part II, written for later editions by Charles Cotton. This prompted the late Eric Taverner, one of the finest fishing writers of our century, to say, "Walton without Cotton is like good manners without meat." A little-known fact is that the fly-fishing sections of the earlier editions were contributed by an expert cook named Thomas Barker who was also a fine fishing writer in his own right.

Walton has not always received universal acclaim. Several non-fishing writers of note have taken issue with Walton on other grounds. Leigh Hunt labeled him a "worm-sticker" and went on to find fault with his face as well. "It is hard, angular, and of no expression. It seems to have been 'subdued to what it worked in'; to have become native to the watery element. One might have said to Walton, 'Oh, flesh, how art thou fishified!' He looks like a pike dressed in broadcloth instead of butter."

Lord Byron was even less generous, calling him a "sentimental savage whom it is the mode to quote (amongst novelists) to show

Izaak Walton lived to a ripe old age—as this portrait
by Jacob Huysman proves. Did his conscience ever
bother him?

their sympathy for innocent sports and old songs, who teaches
how to sew up frogs and break their legs by way of
experiment. . . ." Byron goes on to cap his condemnation with a
bit of doggerel:

> The quaint, old, cruel coxcomb, in his gullet
> should have a hook, and a small trout to pull it.

While it is interesting to note that writers were quoting Walton
over 150 years ago to show how with-it they were in an outdoorsy
way, the influence of Walton has had another, more pernicious

Charles Cotton by Sir Peter Lely. Without Cotton's contributions, *The Compleat Angler* would never have been compleat.

effect: It has ruined more fishing writing than any other single cause. The entire time-honored "cutesy-poo" school of outdoor writing is directly descended from *The Compleat Angler*.

Ever since that book was first acclaimed as a classic because of its scope and style, other fishing writers have tried to follow in the great man's footsteps. They have wanted it understood that they, too, were beautiful, sensitive people who had discovered deeper truths through fishing and other pastoral pursuits.

This type of prose is the high-wire act of the writing business. You have no facts, no characters, no suspense, no narrative to sustain your writing. You're in the wispy world of parallels, metaphors, and other conceits. One forced phrase, one false step and your entire piece comes tumbling down in front of an audience that has been secretly hoping for just such a catastrophe.

Very, very few writers can bring this stunt off. Thoreau was a master at it. Several excellent nature writers can do it now and then. Fishing authors, in general, have racked up a miserable record, and, out of fairness to themselves and their readers, should keep their feet planted firmly on more familiar ground.

What, I'd like to know, is wrong with a lean, taut narrative, telling what a fishing incident was really like and making the reader feel he had been there? There are enough examples of this scattered through the pages of fishing literature to fill many bookshelves. Negley Farson's *Going Fishing* is packed with such writing from cover to cover, yet it seems to have escaped the attention of most self-appointed critics of fishing writing.

And what is wrong with a clear, crisp description of some tactic or technique that helps catch more fish? Does this, too, have to be embroidered with musings about the freckled cowslip, the jaunty jay or the majestic hemlock? Can't we enjoy our annual Maytime without moral uplift? There may be, as I've noted, a whole library of good paragraphs, pages, and even, occasionally, entire books on fishing, but there is also enough rot and rubbish by pretentious writers to fill fifty big stores devoted to remainders.

Two highly esteemed gentlemen come to mind here, and since both are dead there's little chance of hurting their feelings by citing them as examples. Henry Van Dyke and Bliss Perry were both ardent anglers and men of literary bent. Van Dyke, in particular, was widely acclaimed in his day and still has many admirers. Have you read any books by him lately? Or by Perry? I have, and I don't think I can stomach another fulsome phrase or mealymouthed moral for years to come. Both gentlemen would have you believe that fishing is an exercise in character development that would make the playing fields of Eton seem as self-indulgent as side-street stickball.

The spiritual descendants of these men and of Walton are with us today, of course. It wouldn't be fair to mention any names, for I have probably been guilty, myself, of the "Waltonian fallacy" no matter how hard I've fought to avoid it. Walton's influence is almost as strong and all-pervasive as original sin.

That just about winds up the case against Walton and, now that I've finished, a disturbing thought occurs to me: Perhaps I'm giving blame where blame isn't due. I may have been sniffing a cold trail while hounding the gentle Izaak. Perhaps he was a fine man, good friend, and great fisherman after all. Very possibly the real culprit lived many years earlier than the old plagiarist, whose only crime was pilfering an out-of-print book called *The Arte of Angling*—in which case the man I should be taking to task is that familiar and famous author, "Anon."

6

Go Low and Slow for Big Salmon

Every month I see articles telling how to catch titanic trout, buster bronzebacks, colossal crappies, whopper walleyes, and the like. Yet I've never seen a piece on how to catch king-sized specimens of the king of fishes. Have you? Did you ever read anything about how to catch big Atlantic salmon?

Thirty years ago this topic might have been considered academic, for before World War II salmon were mainly the quarry of a privileged few. No longer. In 1973 an estimated 200,000 Americans (and nobody knows how many Canadians) fished for *Salmo salar*, and the numbers are increasing every year.

Despite its growing popularity, though, salmon fishing is rarely free, seldom cheap, often damnably expensive. Returning from a big-game, big-expense expedition like this with nothing over four or five pounds to show for your time, travel and camp fees can be disappointing, to say the least. Yet with salmon the rules are simpler and the odds more in your favor when angling selectively for big fish than in any other kind of freshwater fishing I know of.

By big salmon I don't necessarily mean thirty- to fifty-pounders. I know guides who have fished part of almost every day of the open season for years and have yet to land a salmon of this super-trophy size. But there are plenty of salmon in the ten- to twenty-five-pound class in every salmon river worthy of the name, and these are a whole different class of fish compared to the adolescent salmon of three to five pounds, called grilse, which make up the bulk of the catches on most popular rivers.

There are two reasons why most fish taken fall into this latter and less-than-heroic category. First, the more accessible rivers happen to have a high proportion of grilse in their run of fish. Why this is so, why a very few rivers contain mainly big fish while the others run to mostly small ones is hard to explain. One theory is that on some rivers the eight-inch young of the salmon, called smolts, which leave fresh water for the richer pastures of the ocean, may find their traditional feeding grounds nearby and tend to come back to their parent river in little more than a year, while fish from other river systems may travel so far that they don't return till after two or even three years of sea-feeding. Another theory suggests that, since all salmon return to the river of their birth for spawning, subspecies with different habits have been built up over the years. Whatever the reason, catches on some of the more popular rivers such as New Brunswick's Miramichi often run from three to five grilse for every mature salmon, while on others a fish of under ten pounds is a rarity.

The other reason the catch ratio often runs heavily to the grilse side is that grilse take a fly much more readily than older, larger salmon. This statement may baffle anglers who have heard that neither salmon nor grilse take food after their return to fresh water. The accepted explanation for this is that re-entry into fresh water awakens the insect-feeding reflexes these fish lived by during their early, trout-like life in the river. The longer the fish has been away at sea, this theory claims, the weaker this instinct will be when the fish returns.

Results in terms of catches certainly support this hypothesis. One year when the take on a New Brunswick river was running five grilse for every mature salmon, I went down to a bridge just above the head of tide to watch a run of fish moving up into the low, clear water. I was surprised to discover that the grilse/salmon ratio was about fifty-fifty. There were plenty of salmon coming into the river, including some very big ones, but they just weren't taking nearly as well as the grilse.

Similarly, there's a river in Newfoundland I have fished several times where camp records show that ten to twelve times as many grilse as salmon are caught year after year. I accepted this as a true sampling of the river population until one day when we lunched at the base of a falls that was impassable at that height of water. Here fish were piling up in large numbers and every few seconds a fish would make a futile leap for the lip above. From the sample we counted in over an hour, it appeared that here, too, the salmon were almost as numerous as the grilse, even though our ice house held ten times as many grilse.

Now don't jump to the conclusion that I am some sort of salmon snob. Grilse are marvelous fish. They would magnify and glorify any trout river in the world, bar none. They jump more often, put up a brighter, brisker fight than their more stately seniors, and often stage almost as long a fight. But, and this is a terribly important "but," salmon fishing brings out the big-game instinct in all of us. You don't go on safari in Africa to shoot 60-pound Thompson's gazelles. Nor do you invest all the time and money a good salmon trip takes to catch three- to five-pound grilse exclusively.

And, when it comes to grilse, that's about the size of it. There's an unwritten rule at most salmon camps that grilse are never weighed. They are "estimated" at five or six pounds by a tactful guide or camp operator, and this makes the angler happy. I have broken this gentleman's agreement on the sly often enough to know better. Having weighed and measured well over one hundred grilse from several rivers, I can cite the following figures with confidence: Grilse average twenty-two inches long and weigh a shade under four pounds. Some rivers in Britain have records of eleven-pound grilse (scale readings proved they had spent less than two years at sea) but the largest I have ever seen weighed five and a half pounds, while the smallest was a runt of eighteen inches and two pounds and a quarter. However, even these modest extremes are rare, in my experience. Nine grilse out of ten seem to fall within a fraction of the average.

At this point it would be encouraging if I could reveal the names of several undiscovered or neglected rivers where huge salmon pass upstream all day long unmolested by anglers. But I'm

afraid this can't be a fish-and-tell gambit. The few rivers where salmon average very large have been known, cherished, and bought up long before you and I were born.

For example, there are rivers in Norway where "ordinary" salmon will scale well over twenty pounds and where fish of over fifty pounds are killed each season. The rod fees there may run over $3,000 a week plus your transportation and other expenses. And, even if you have this kind of spending-money, you may have to stand in line for years to reserve a decent beat during a traditionally productive week in the short season.

In Canada, too, big-fish rivers like the Restigouche, Matapedia, Moise, and Grand Cascapedia have been mainly privately owned or controlled since before the turn of the century. On one of these rivers an acquaintance of mine once killed three salmon of over thirty-five pounds apiece in a single morning. However, the initiation fee to the club that controls this water, in case they invite you to join, is reported to be some $50,000 and dues $5,000 a year. After that you can pay for your two guides, food, accommodations, and tips with your leftover change. On the brighter side, though, if you're now feeling, as I am, like the kid with his nose pressed to the outside of the candy-store window, another acquaintance of mine once fished an equally rarified stretch of Canadian river for three full weeks and killed only two very mediocre fish!

If someone has been kind enough to leave you several miles of big-fish river complete with lodge or a vault full of blue-chip securities to buy your way in, read no further. You should catch plenty of big salmon without any advice from the cheap seats. If, on the other hand, you have to work for a living you can still catch some sizable salmon. Only in this case, more depends on *what* than *whom* you know.

The first thing you have to know is that most of the things you've learned about freshwater fishing don't hold true on a salmon river. Pay no attention, for example, to the old saying, "Big lure, big fish." It just doesn't work out that way in this type

At Left: Four mature salmon running from nine to twelve pounds. It would take at least ten grilse to weigh as much.

of fishing. A fly of one particular size will trigger the old, freshwater feeding instinct while, under the very same circumstances, one size smaller or larger may not. I have seen large salmon taken on a small #10 fly from the same pool where other anglers were simultaneously hooking only grilse with flies almost twice as large.

Admittedly, there is no exact rule regarding size of salmon fly, and this is one of the great mysteries — and charms — of salmon fishing. I have had to use flies two to three inches long (5/0s) to get the salmon's attention in the cold water of early spring in Spain. Even in the warm water of midsummer, you'll often have to use quite large flies to get results in the fifteen-foot or deeper pools on some very large rivers. However, it takes a big fly to interest the grilse, too, in this deep water and fly-size has apparently no influence on fish size.

A friend of mine who was new to salmon fishing once gave me a vivid example of this fact. We were fishing a very grilsey river in Labrador and my friend decided to concentrate on catching a truly big fish. He tied on a four-inch white bucktail he'd used for bluefish in salt water and fished it religiously all day. He took three grilse, by far the lowest score in camp. The rest of us had more fish and at least one good salmon apiece. Apparently, when there are that many fish in the river, you can find a few that will take anything, but most of them preferred the more modest #8s the rest of us were using.

Experienced trout fishermen will probably play a different hunch when trying to catch a trophy salmon. Since most big brown trout are caught at dusk or even after dark, they'll make their maximum effort after supper every evening.

The fact is, though, that salmon seldom take after dark. Perhaps the fly isn't visible enough in that weak light to activate the fish's nearly forgotten freshwater feeding instinct. Anyway, if there's even reasonable traveling water in a river, salmon will tend to continue their trip upriver at dusk and your chances of hitting a traveling fish on the nose with your fly are so slim that you might just as well forget night fishing altogether.

The trick of catching larger salmon is not, then, so much a matter of what you fish or when. It's *where* and *how* that will make the real difference. And of the two, *where* is perhaps the more important.

One of the least publicized facts about salmon is that they like, or will tolerate, slower water than grilse. Since these conditions usually occur farther downpool from the rapids at the head of it, salmon will usually be found in deeper water, too.

One famous pool on the Miramichi that I have fished for over twenty years is a textbook example of this. One side of this pool which is public water will host from fifteen to thirty fishermen all day long during the peak of the season. The fishing starts just below the shallow bar and by custom the anglers take a step down-current after each cast so that others can fish down the pool in turn. Some 150 yards downriver, where the current has slowed considerably, lies the traditional stepping-out point. This is marked by a jerry-built stone fireplace where fishermen warm up after their long immersion or boil a kettle of tea while waiting their turn at the head of the line.

The foreground angler is fishing the grilsey chop at the head of the pool. Distant angler is down into salmon water.

Over ninety percent of the fish I have seen taken in this conga line over the years have been grilse. The stretch is justly famous as one of the most productive on the entire river, but it produces very few salmon from either the public or the private side.

The price I willingly pay for fishing this choice water is the hour or more it takes me to work my way down-traffic to the fireplace. Below this, I have the rest of the pool—or "dead-water," as it is locally called—all to myself. Fortunately, this lower stretch lies around a slight bend and just out of sight of the anglers above.

I say "fortunately" because in the next two hundred yards I have caught more salmon and a higher percentage of salmon (including a twenty-pounder—my largest ever on the Miramichi) than on any other part of this river. The surprising thing is that, although I've told many friends about the productivity of the slow-water portion of this and other pools, I have had no company. I always seem to end up down there solo with a guide so disgusted that he soon goes to sleep. He does, that is, until I hook into a good salmon—which I do with pleasing regularity.

To go to the opposite extreme, which this same pool also illustrates, there's a small pocket just above the bar at the head of the pool. This slight indentation in the bottom can't be seen from the shore, yet it always seems to hold one and sometimes two grilse that have passed over the bar but not yet run the shallow rapids to the pool above. A guide I know often heads for this spot when the fishing gets slow and almost always hooks a fish there— much to the chagrin of the line of fishermen who have started in some hundred feet below. However, I have never, repeat *never*, seen a salmon hooked in that lie. It is apparently a grilse lie pure and simple—too fast and shallow to hold a big fish.

For some reason, guides—and they are mandatory for nonresident fishermen on salmon rivers throughout Canada—seem to favor grilsey water. This may be because the action is usually faster here and guides understandably like big tips from satisfied customers. However, and this surprises me, I find guides fishing these same grilsey lies on their days off when they're trying to pick up a fish for their own supper. Far be it from me to argue with a man who was born and raised on a river, but my advice to you is to fish a hundred or more yards down into the slower part of any pool—no matter how much your guide may grumble.

How you fish, even if you're casting over known big-salmon lies, can also affect the size of fish you take. Salmon are not only harder to rise to a fly, but they are also less likely to take a fly that is moving rapidly. I have seen many grilse rush at a fly that was whipping past them (and usually miss it), but I can't recall ever seeing a full-grown salmon behave in this manner.

The few times I have witnessed a salmon's rise to the fly from start to finish have borne out this theory. Salmon take as if they were in a trance (which seems to confirm the triggered-reflex theory) and without a trace of either greed or anger.

I was never more impressed by the robot-like quality of this rise than one noon when I was crossing a bridge to get back to my car. A guide was fishing by himself below me and I stopped to watch for a few moments since I had never seen an angler try this slow, deep water before.

When the unknown angler reached the bridge abutment below me, a salmon of ten to twelve pounds appeared below and behind his fly and then turned down and away again. I was so surprised by this sudden appearance that I said nothing, but put on my Polaroids to see if I could spot the salmon in his lie on the bottom. I couldn't make out the fish in that deep water, but then the angler, blocked from further downstream travel by the bridge, made another perfunctory cast from the same place. And this time I saw it all happen.

As the fly started to swing in toward the bank a shadowy form appeared about five feet away, rising slowly up through the water and quartering the current toward a point where it would surely intercept the fly. But again the fish stopped just short and drifted back down to his lie at exactly the same speed and on precisely the same course that he had taken on his exploratory trip toward the fly. The unhurried behavior and the precision of the course gave the impression that the salmon was some large, mechanical bathtub toy rather than a wild, living creature.

This time I yelled to the angler below who hadn't noticed me. I told him a salmon had come to his fly twice and he shot out another cast with renewed interest. Apparently, since the fish

hadn't broken the surface either time, the fisherman had no idea
he'd interested a good fish. I've since felt that this must happen to
all of us more times than we imagine.

Even though the fisherman changed patterns twice, the results
were the same: a near take or a last-minute refusal — whichever
way you want to describe it. I thought the fly might be passing
the fish's lie at too great a speed and suggested to the angler that
he wade out deeper to try and get a slower swing over the fish.
Out he went, but the deep water kept him right by the bank. I'm
virtually certain that if he could have cast from ten feet farther out
in the current, reduced the angle of his presentation and slowed
down his fly, he would have taken that fish, but without a boat
such a presentation was impossible.

The moral here is that, when in doubt, you should slow down
the speed of travel of your wet fly. Many times I have heard
salmon anglers claim that the best lies seem to be close to the bank
they're fishing or that the most killing part of any presentation
occurs during the last part of the swing when the fly is straightening out below them. I'm convinced, though, that the reason why
so many fish are risen in the last moments of the presentation is
that during the first part of it—the part that may well be covering
the most productive big-fish lies — the fly is whipping over the
fish at a speed too great to interest them at all.

To see why this is true, imagine a pool or run with a current
speed that is the same from bank to bank. If you cast your line
across this at the traditional 45-degree angle downstream with a
perfectly straight line, you won't be fishing your fly effectively
during the first half or more of your presentation. That portion of
your line that enters the water nearest your rod-tip will, in a very
few seconds, have traveled to a point directly downstream and
will start playing crack-the-whip with your leader and fly which
are still far across stream. The fly will only begin to fish properly
when it is about ten degrees to one side of a straight downstream
position.

The ways to defeat this disastrous effect are to cast downstream
at a sharper angle when fishing fast water, mending the line near
you in an upstream direction shortly after it enters the water or by
casting an upstream curve in your line and then mending upstream as necessary. There's a nicety of judgment needed in

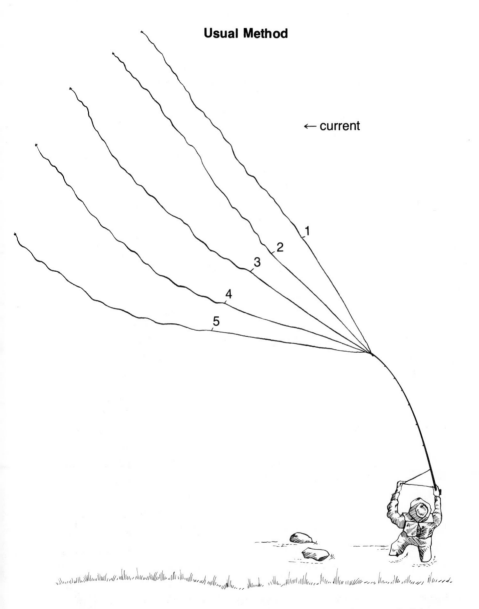

Usual Method

← current

1
2
3
4
5

When cast across and downstream the fly soon speeds up and fishes at proper speed only when just below angler's rod.

wet-fly presentations and, since the currents in every pool are different, there can be no pat answer. However, it is this ability to control the speed of travel of the fly that separates the expert from the chuck-and-chancer.

Presenting your fly *lower* in the water can sometimes be as important as fishing it *slower*. Big salmon are not only more reluctant to rise at all, but they are often less likely to rise all the way to the surface. I can't help wondering whether or not the angler by that bridge abutment wouldn't have taken that salmon if his fly had been riding a foot or so deeper in the current. After all, that would have reached the height from the river bottom to which that particular fish seemed willing to rise.

Fishing your fly deeper is axiomatic early in the morning or on raw days when the air is cooler than the water. Both salmon and grilse are notoriously shy about poking their noses out of a warmish river into cold air. When fishing your fly deep on a sinking line (weighted flies are forbidden by law) you may miss the thrill of seeing a classic head-and-tail rise to your fly, but that's not nearly as disappointing as no rise at all.

I have been presenting my fly lower and slower and casting it into deeper, slower water for twelve or fifteen years now. Every fish I hook isn't a huge salmon, but the *average* weight of fish I am now taking from grilsey rivers has nearly doubled with this change in tactics.

On one recent trip to the Miramichi when there was only a small run of fish my diary shows the following results. Our party of four took 27 fish that week and probably because I fished longer and harder than the others I accounted for nine of these. But seven of my nine were mature salmon while there were only two salmon in the other 18. As it turned out, my nine weighed slightly more than all the other fish put together.

The results of this and many other trips have been so rewarding that I recently described my theory and tactics to Charlie DeFeo. Charlie, I should explain, is one of the all-time great salmon-fly tyers and salmon fishermen. He has probably fished Canadian rivers for more days and over more years than any other living American. His opinions on salmon have nearly the weight of Supreme Court decisions.

Correct Method

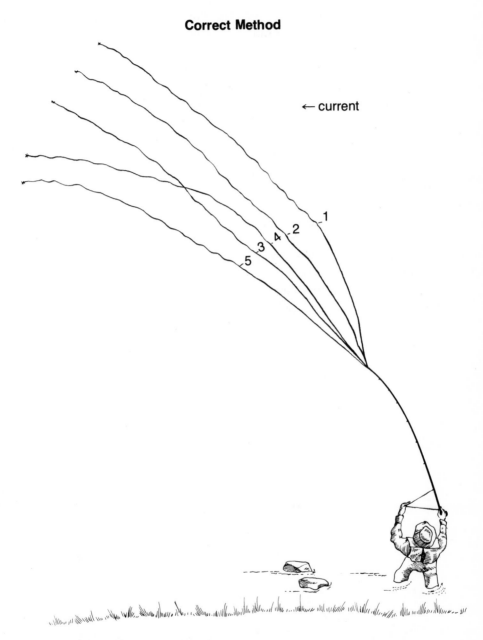

← current

By casting a curved line and then mending it upstream, as necessary, you can make fly travel at "taking" speed.

"The way you describe it," Charlie said, "reminds me of something Ira Gruber once said."

Ira Gruber, who died about ten years ago, may well have been the most expert and important salmon fisherman America has ever produced. He retired at an early age and devoted every summer until his death to fishing and understanding the Miramichi River. There he pioneered and developed many of the most popular flies used throughout Canada to this day. Over the years, he caught so many salmon that, once he'd hooked a fish properly, he's pass the rod over to his guide, pick up another one and continue his research on flies and presentations. Any man who managed to get that bored with playing salmon deserves to be a legend.

"I remember," Charlie continued, "back in the thirties Gruber once said to me that if half the fishermen made their flies swing slower and fished them down deeper there'd be darned few big salmon left in this river."

In times of scarcities like these, I'd hate to see that happen. I don't think it ever will with our new, lower bag limits. But, if lower and slower were the great Ira Gruber's secret formulas for catching big salmon, I know I've been on the right track for years.

7

Long Live
the Long Rod

I wish I had a day off to go fishing for every time I've heard a
flyfisherman say something like ". . . they were mostly small fish,
but since I was using that little six-foot rod of mine, I really had a
ball."

My instantaneous reaction to such statements is, sure he did—if
"ball" is short for balderdash.

· For I'm convinced that the most overrated thing in America
today (with the possible exception of home movies) is the short fly-
rod. It is the least effective, least comfortable, least "sporting"
fly-fishing tool ever invented for fishing running water. I know
it's risky to knock another man's woman, dog, or favorite rod, but
look at the evidence.

At first glance it may seen that the choice between a short rod
and a long one for stream fishing is simply a matter of whim.
After all, a fairly skilled caster can lay out sixty, seventy, or more
feet of line with a tiny rod—more than enough distance for most
trout-stream situations.

However, staying away from, and out of sight of, the fish is
only a small, easy part of the game. It is the ability to present the
right fly in a way that deceives the trout and the knack of hooking

those you've fooled that separate the fishermen from the casters. And here, the short rod short-changes you in any number of ways.

A stubby rod leaves far too much line on the water while you're fishing out the average cast, and every extra foot of this is a crippling disadvantage, whether you're presenting a dry fly, wet fly, nymph, streamer, or (forgive me, Federation of Fly Fishers) live bait.

Suppose, for example, you're casting to a fish thirty feet away. With a six-foot rod, tip held high, you'll probably still leave eighteen feet of line and leader on the water when you make your presentation. A bit more when fishing upstream, a bit less when working downstream. On the other hand, with a ten-foot rod, casting under the same conditions, only about ten feet of terminal tackle—perhaps just your leader—would be lying on the surface. You judge which presentation is most likely to give you a badly dragging dry fly or a sunk fly that's traveling unnaturally and out of control.

Admittedly, the amount of line on the water isn't a critical factor when you're fishing a still-water pond or lake. But remember, my complaint about short rods was made about running-water fishing. And on streams with braiding currents, tongues of fast water, and unpredictable eddies, the more line you have on the water the more you're inviting an unappetizing presentation of your fly.

It is also much easier to hook a fish when most of your line is off the water. You're in more intimate touch with your fly and you don't have to guess at how hard to tug to straighten out the esses in your line, overcome the friction of water, and then set the hook delicately. Over ninety percent of the trout broken off are lost at the strike. Examine the circumstances the next time you leave your fly in a fish. I think you'll agree that the problem nearly always is too much line on the water when the take occurs.

It took me years to learn these simple fly-fishing facts of life. The truth started to sink in only about a dozen years ago when I was fishing in the mountains of southern France. I was using a snappy, eight-foot rod (certainly a sensible length by eastern U.S. standards), but I wasn't catching many fish and almost no really

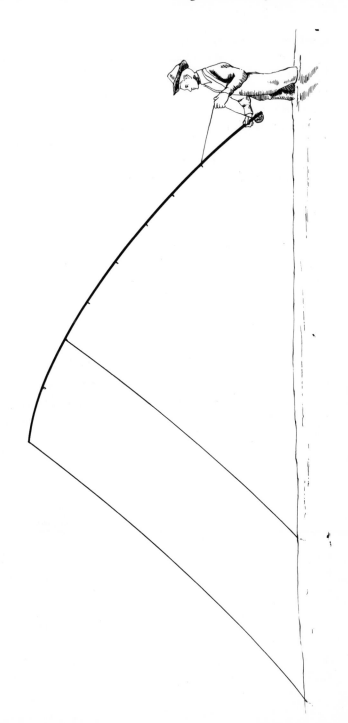

A long rod keeps more line off surface—meaning less drag with dry fly and better control of speed with wet fly.

good ones. This was slow, clear, limestone water, heavily fished by vacationers and constantly harvested by a troup of professional fishermen who supplied the local hotels. Any fish that had run this gauntlet and grown to decent size was as carefully trained as a moonshot astronaut.

The professionals finally showed me their secret—though they looked on it more as common sense than as an ingenious technique. They'd learned that, in this clear, slick water, they couldn't approach these fish from upstream. Yet neither could they give the trout a look at their leader. So they cast upstream to a rising or observed fish, but with a variation of the conventional method. They'd drop their fly—usually a sparsely dressed wet pattern on a light hook — just downstream of the trout's tail so the leader wouldn't pass over his head. When the tiny ripples from the fly's entry passed over the trout's nose, he would usually turn around to see what sort of insect had fallen into the water behind him. If the stunt was pulled off perfectly, all the trout could see now was the artificial sinking slowly down-current. No leader showed at all because it would be pointing directly away, behind the fly.

Any line splash or drag meant instant failure, and I began to see why these experts, who supported their families with their catches all summer, used long rods—ten to ten and one-half feet long, in fact. "With a rod of three meters you are just beginning to fish," they told me. Three meters — that's nine feet, ten inches. Their long rods let them cover a fish from a safe distance with only part of the leader entering the water. I finally learned how to execute this presentation with occasional success after days of practice, but my eight-foot rod, even though it could throw seventy to eighty feet of line with ease, was a big handicap here.

Fishermen I saw in the Pyrenees on the Spanish border had taken this theory one step further. They used rods twelve to fourteen feet long on the tumbling mountain streams and these kept so much line off the water that there wasn't even a word for "drag" in their local *patois*. They would simply swing their fly (or more often maggot) directly up-current and let it drift back naturally, keeping in touch by raising the rod-tip. They neither added nor took in line, but they took in trout with such regularity that a really devout conservationist wouldn't even mention this method.

The implications of all this are enormous to the dry-fly man with his almost paranoid fear of drag. The perfect presentation of his fly has to be one dapped on the surface with no leader at all touching the water. This is as true whether the offering is to be made dead drift with the natural flow of the current or whether the fly is to be bounced on the surface like a hovering or egg-laying insect.

I proved this to my satisfaction several years ago after a neighbor of mine had been given an ancient and enormous English fly rod. This awesome wand was a full twenty feet long, was made of a solid wood called greenheart, and must have weighed over three pounds. However, this 36-ounce beauty had a light, flexible tip—

A professional French fisherman with a twelve-foot rod fishing upstream without taking in or letting out line.

it was built when single strands of horsehair were used as leader-tippets—and I decided to try out a hunch with it.

I found some pretext to borrow this rod for a couple of hours and, after I'd rigged it up with a light line and fine leader, I headed for a nearby river. Once I got the hang of it, I could dap a fly on the surface thirty to 35 feet away and make it dance and hop there with no leader at all touching the water. Smart, overfished trout nearly herneated themselves to grab my fly. If I'd continued to use that rod the State Conservation Department would have named me Public Enemy No. 1. However, my friend soon retired the rod to his collector's case and perhaps that was just as well. After two hours with that wagon-tongue, I felt as if I'd slipped every disc in my back. I guess they don't build men the way they used to, either.

Until a hundred years ago most trout rods were twelve feet long. Two centuries before that they ran up to a healthy eighteen.

Going to the opposite extreme, you can cast and catch fish with no rod at all. This would give you a rod some twenty feet shorter than the old English muscle-builder I just described. I have never seen anyone over five years old fishing a trout stream with a handline, which would have to be the worst possible tackle for trouting. However, the reason is not that you couldn't cover the water or land the fish.

The late Ellis Newman could take the reel off the rod and with his bare right hand work out all ninety feet of a double-taper and keep it in the air, false-casting. Perhaps you could, too, if you practiced long enough. But would you catch as many trout that way?

Similarly, Lee Wulff once hand-cast to a nearby salmon and played that full-grown fish to the beach with just the reel in his hand. No rod at all. Again, you might do that, too, with practice. You might be able to dine out on this feat for weeks if you could tell the epic story with enough suspense and gusto. But I don't think you'd want to make a habit of fishing like that.

So you see, a fly-rod isn't a necessity. It's merely a convenience and a comfort.

How can I say "comfort" after that twenty-footer nearly put me in bed under traction? And doesn't a long rod have to punish the angler more than a short one? Well, yes and no.

In the first place, sheer lightness in a rod doesn't necessarily mean less effort. The difference between a five-ounce rod and a longer two-ounce model in ratio to the angler's total weight on the scales is about the same as drinking half a tumbler of water or going thirsty. So rest assured that the longer, slightly heavier rod won't weigh you down.

I have fished with many superb casters who said they revelled in the lightness of their short rods. But how they huffed and puffed and sweated. They were using both arms, both shoulders, and their back to make those long casts with their toy tackle. Double-hauling may be the ultimate technique for tournament casting, but it's about as placid a way to enjoy a summer evening as alligator wrestling.

The point is, ask not what you can do for the rod, but rather what the rod can do for you. With a long rod, a small movement of the arm or wrist will take any reasonable length of line off the water for the back-cast because there really isn't that much line clutched by surface tension. The line then goes back over your head, straightens out, and bends the rod backwards. Now a minimal effort forward with forearm, wrist, or both, and the rod snaps back, propelling the line forward again. What could be easier than that? The rod has done most of the work for you. Your hand has moved a foot or so with very little exertion instead of moving three feet or so and bringing shoulder and back muscles into play, as well.

My experiences in France were not the only reason my rods became longer about a dozen years ago. At approximately that time, I read an article in an outdoor magazine extolling the joys of minirod fishing. The author honestly admitted that he did, at first, have trouble avoiding drag with his shorter rod, but that he had solved this problem by holding the rod high above his head as he fished out every cast. Thus his six-footer, he claimed, was every bit as effective as an eight- or eight-and-a-half-footer and (get this) because his rod weighed only 1¾ ounces, it was far less fatiguing to fish with. Anyone who subscribes to that theory should now hold his right arm fully extended over his head for two or three minutes and tell me how it feels. I can't recall seeing any more articles from this man and I can only assume that acute bursitis has prevented him from taking pencil in hand ever since.

If a twenty-footer can break your back and a six-footer gives you too much drag and too much work, what length should an efficient and comfortable fly rod be? A lot depends on your physical makeup and your style of fishing. If, on the one hand, you're a continuous and compulsive false-caster who likes to fish pocket water upstream where the effective float is a foot or less, any rod over eight feet might put your arm in a sling. If, on the other hand, your style is more deliberate and you spend most of your time on slower water where you may make fewer than ten casts per minute instead of nearly a hundred, you could probably handle a ten-footer with ease for a whole day's fishing.

And don't be misled by the "bush-rod" addicts. They argue that you get hung up too often fishing small, overgrown streams if you use anything longer than a five-footer. But the fact is, you'll get hung up a lot with a very short rod, too, because any form of true casting here will put your fly and leader in the branches. A long line presentation is seldom an effective way to fish a string of small pot-holes, anyway. Drag is instantaneous and disastrous with a lot of line out on this type of water. Here, you're far better off with the long rod, flipping or swinging your fly to the chosen spot while you make the extra effort to conceal yourself.

Use as long a rod as you comfortably can. I have been fishing with an 8½-foot bamboo that weighs 4½ ounces for the past several years. I am now going through a trial-marriage with a 9½-foot glass rod that weighs about the same. This liaison has been so enjoyable that I'm now searching for a ten-footer with the same qualities.

On salmon rivers where I make only four or five casts per minute, my favorite wet-fly rod is a 10½-footer that works beautifully with a medium-weight #6 line. But I'll admit that I have to drop back to an 8½-foot stick for dry-fly fishing. I just can't false-cast that often with the long rod—although that

The author fishing across stream with a favorite 9½-footer. High rod-tip keeps even more line off water.

10½-footer is the most effortless wet-fly rod I've ever hefted. And let me repeat: I find all these rods, both trout and salmon models, comfortable for a full day's fishing.

In case you're interested, the man who wields these monster rods bears no resemblance to King Kong. I don't tip the scales at 140 pounds with chest waders, spare reels, and enough assorted fly boxes to drown me if I fell into deep water.

I'll have to admit, though, there's one disadvantage to long fly rods — and it's a beauty. When you've finally hooked a fish, the long rod makes the fish grow stronger. For that extra length gives the fish greater leverage against your hand.

But isn't this precisely what the short-rod people are espousing? That fish are now smaller and tamer so we must use tackle that magnifies the quarry? Yet aren't they actually doing just the opposite?

There are only two basic ways to measure a rod's ability to glorify the struggles of a fish. One is the weight or force it takes to bend the rod properly. This factor is usually printed on the rod just in front of the cork grip in terms of the weight of line it takes to bring out its action. I've seen a lot of 6-foot rods that call for a #6 or #7 line to make them work properly. This means that it takes between 160 and 185 grains (437½ grains equal one ounce) of moving line to flex the rod adequately. My 9½-footer, on the other hand, needs only a #4, or 120 grains, to flex the rod to its optimum. Draw your own conclusions.

But there's yet another factor that makes one rod more sporting than another for playing a fish. That's the leverage against your hand. With a fly rod—which must be considered a simple lever once a fish is hooked — the fulcrum is where the hand holds the rod. You don't need an M.I.T. degree to see that the mechanical advantage is approximately fifty percent greater in favor of the fish and against the sportsman with a nine-foot rod than it is with a six-footer.

Despite this elementary fact, I am often accused of derricking small fish out of the water with a whacking great salmon rod. Fault my reasoning if you can: I'm convinced the shoe is on the other foot. I maintain that short-rodders are not only selling themselves short on presentation and overexercising themselves needlessly, but grinding down small fish with mechanically superior weapons, as well.

If you have followed my argument carefully so far and, I hope, found it airtight, you're probably asking, "How can so many of nature's noblemen have been taken in by this cruel hoax?" The answer is a believe-it-or-notter that would have Ripley sitting on the edge of his chair.

In the beginning, all rods were long. They were used to swing some lure out to the unsuspecting fish and to haul the catch back to shore again. They were very much like our present-day cane poles and probably just about as long.

Rods were still very long in the seventeenth century. Izaak Walton recommends a snappy eighteen-foot, two-handed model as the best choice in his day. He and Charles Cotton dapped, dibbled, and dangled their flies (and worms and maggots) on the water with these mighty poles with killing effect on the trout — and probably on their backs, too.

A nine-foot rod gives the fish a fifty percent greater mechanical advantage *against* the angler than a six-footer does.

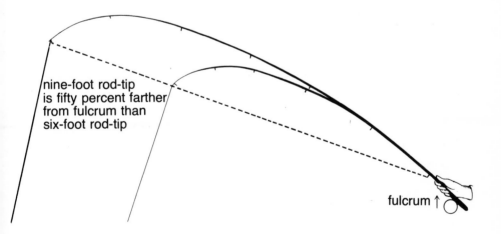

nine-foot rod-tip is fifty percent farther from fulcrum than six-foot rod-tip

fulcrum ↑

In the following century the scientific progress of the industrial revolution reached the angling world. Fishing reels appeared on the market and soon became popular because they allowed fishermen to lengthen or shorten line easily and to play larger fish more effectively. But the rods themselves remained long.

One hundred years after that, in the not-too-distant 1800s, rods still averaged a sensible twelve feet until dressed silk fly lines and split bamboo were introduced just after the midpoint of the century. This made true fly-casting, as we now know it, possible for the average angler and, as this novel technique became popular, rods grew shorter and lighter. After all, why should the angler stand there waving half a tree over the water when he could cast to the far bank and beyond with a zippy little ten-footer?

But along with these advances came another type of progress: overpopulation, overfishing, and pollution. Trout became fewer and farther between. Fishing could no longer be the simple culling of nature's bounty as it had been in Walton's day. It needed a mystique, a philosophy, a *raison d'être*. This, Frederick M. Halford and other British Victorians readily provided, and their code soon spread across the Atlantic in a slightly modified form. If the sheer joy of catching fish was no longer a sure thing, at least there was the joy of casting. A day astream, the play of the sweet bamboo, the lovely hiss of the line, the fly cocked perkily on the sparkling riffle—who cares for a full creel with all this? You've read it all a hundred times in a hundred different forms. (I've even seen true believers act annoyed when an occasional hooked fish interrupted the rhythm of this ritual!) Under this type of credo, it's easy to see how rods were miniaturized into today's six-foot toys.

All the while, of course, anglers still secretly wanted to catch fish—and I suppose you do, too. But our artificial Victorian code insists that this be done only by improving your casting or presentation or by tinkering up a bit better imitation of, say, the female Iron Blue Dun. Reverting to aboriginal tackle and the more varied presentations it puts at your fingertips is unthinkable.

Well, I for one think it *is* thinkable. And, if you really want to catch more trout and enjoy more sport doing it, perhaps you should think about it, too. Going back to eighteen-foot poles might be a bit much. But do try a new nine or ten-footer. If a ribbon-clerk like me can swing one all day long, you'll be able to handle one like a conductor's baton.

Can't I, after all this, find at least one kind thing to say about our new short fly rods? Well, yes, perhaps this. I am reminded of the country sage's defense of bad breath. "It's mighty unpleasant, but it sure beats no breath at all."

So I guess short fly rods beat handlines—or no rods at all. But not by very much.

8

The Backyard Angler

Every time I am introduced to somebody as "a fisherman" the conversation seems to start out like this.

"So you like fishing, eh? Then you probably know my friend Marmaduke—we call him Duke—Thornberry."

"Well, no. That name doesn't ring a bell. Does he fish around here often?"

"Oh no. Duke's a *real* fisherman. Spends two or three weeks every summer up near the Arctic Circle. You ought to see the fish *he* brings back. Yeah, Duke is some kind of fisherman, all right."

Sure he is, and it's not too hard to figure out what kind. Nine will get you ten that Duke is a very mediocre fisherman, indeed, if that's where he's done all his fishing.

For, wonderful as wilderness waters may be, as schools for fishermen they're about as useful as shooting galleries are for hunters. Hauling in unsophisticated fish, cast after cast, may build ego and even muscles, but it certainly doesn't build skill. In fact, I've found it can get so monotonous that I don't see how old Duke can stand it for three whole weeks unless he has several packs of cards and cases of whiskey along.

I'll admit the man is probably an accomplished caster by now and he should be able to play a fish in his sleep. But if he's done all his fishing in the true wilderness, chances are he doesn't know who have brought us the major forward leaps are remembered as the truly great ones and all have been basically stay-at-homes.

The reason for this, I think, is that one man can do only so much in his fishing lifetime. Apparently it takes many years of painstaking observation before the intuitive leap to discovery takes place, and then many more years of trial and error to refine the idea into a usable practice. When there are too many variables in place, conditions, and happenings this flash of understanding rarely occurs.

Then, too, the man fishing exotic, remote places is seldom really challenged. If one fish proves stubborn, there are many more willing — and perhaps bigger — ones waiting for the next cast. Truly rotten fishing is tedious, of course. But demanding fishing makes the great anglers. Gordon was one of the first writers to emphasize this point. Over and over again in his letters he told how he turned down offers of easy fishing on heavily stocked waters because he learned nothing there and found it uninteresting.

Classic wet and dry flies sit harmoniously side by side on a fly-tyer's table. This could never happen in Halford's day!

G.E.M. Skues may look stodgy and proper enough to us, but he was an anti-establishment free-thinker to Edwardians.

When you're continually fishing new and different waters — even if they're not overstocked and too easy — the chances are against your learning anything new and important from them. Here you're usually under the care of a sponsoring host or an expert guide—either of whom knows the lies and the habits of the fish so well that you're spared the enlightening agony of finding out what it has taken them several years of trial and error to discover. Only the most introspective and analytical angler begins to question and research when he is placed in the prime places at the best time with a taking fly and is catching fish at a satisfactory rate.

This is one of the few things I find displeasing about Atlantic salmon fishing. You are usually accompanied by a guide, and in Canada you must be by law. This local expert takes you to a pool, tells you what fly to put on, where to start in, and how to angle your cast. If you're on new water, this service can be invaluable. But do you need—or want—this day after day? Once you've been shown the most likely holding spots, it's a lot more fun (and often more productive) to experiment with other types of flies and techniques. For example, I caught all my salmon last September on the dry fly though I fished it only ten percent of the time because the guide had told me it just wouldn't work at that time of year.

The art of reeling in a fish — no matter how hard it may struggle — is the least absorbing part of the game. Men I know who specialize in tarpon, bonefish, or salmon always tell me that what attracts them is the peerless fighting quality of the quarry, but I don't completely believe them. That may be part of the excitement, but their main involvement lies in making the fish strike under all—especially difficult—conditions. The subsequent battle is merely the frosting on the cake.

No, the reeling in and netting of a fish may be the finale of any fishing episode, but it's certainly not the climax. It's when you've induced the fish to hit and felt you've hooked him solidly that the main satisfaction occurs. People who merely harvest fish— something most of us only dream about—seldom enjoy fishing. I knew many New England coastal fishermen in my youth who spent all day under treacherous conditions hauling in nets and trot lines from the sea. Not a one of them would go fishing with me with rod and line. They seemed to think that taking a few fish, the hard way, on rod and reel was merely a busman's holiday.

Similarly, the best salmon guide I have ever met couldn't understand why we "sports" from America would put in the long hours under awful conditions to take fish which we usually released. He was caretaker of a small camp on a desolate northern river, and he knew every lie as well as a tongue knows a sore tooth. I saw him fish for himself a few times and it was a sobering experience. He would step out on a rock in front of camp, cast expertly to a known lie, hook, land his fish, and be back to his cabin in fifteen minutes. But you could see that it was just another daily duty to him like splitting kindling, lugging in spring water, or opening a can of beans. He was in no way interested or challenged. Since even some of the more persistent visitors to this river could hook up to fifty salmon and grilse a day during the times when the salmon were running well, the whole drill was a bore and a chore to him.

Of course, everyone wants to fish new and better waters from time to time for a change of pace or scene, even if he doesn't have a pet theory to try out under other conditions. And everyone deserves the exhilaration of catching too many fish once in a while after the usual weeks or months of catching too few. But enough is enough, and sometimes overkill is worse than underkill. I remember once fishing for bonefish with a very young and inexperienced angler when the water was too cold and the fish few and choosey. After two days with one fish between us I decided he might quit fishing forever if things didn't pick up. That afternoon we hired a guide who took us to a small channel hole that was paved with bottom fish. We took fish on nearly every cast—mostly grunts, porgies, yellowtails, and triggerfish that fought very well for their size—until we had a glass-bottomed bucket filled with these panfish. After about an hour my young companion either got his belly full or got the idea. He turned to me and said, "The tide seems to be coming in again now. Do you think there might be a few bonefish up on the flats?"

For every fisherman who thinks difficult fishing is bad fishing there seems to be two who think that their nearby waters are poor simply because they are nearby. Familiarity can breed too much contempt. I know a fisherman who averages several trout each fishing day that run from one to three-and-a-half pounds. Remember, that's his *average*. On good days he often takes ten or more such fish. All are taken on the dry fly from a public river that's within a three-hour drive of New York City. His secret? He lives nearby, fishes almost every day of the open season, and has done so for years. He knows the lies, the flies, which stretches produce best at different times of day and under different conditions and, perhaps most important of all, how to duck the crowds. It sounds incredible, but I've fished with the man and he really does that well.

So don't eat your heart out when you're doing your armchair fishing next winter and reading tales of monster fish being piled up like cordwood. Fishing on your own familiar, home waters can be not only productive—it can be even more rewarding than some safari to the land of the Leviathans. All that's gold does not necessarily glitter.

Think of it this way: Aren't you always more comfortable and content in your familiar bed in your own home than you are in someone's guest room or in a hotel? No matter how luxurious your strange new quarters may be? Almost everyone is.

A stream, river, or lake is like that, too. It's not just that you may be familiar with the shoals and hazards of a stillwater or the slippery ledge-rocks and deceptive drop-offs in a river. You also know approximately how many fish, and what sizes, to expect from past experiences or observations, and you can concentrate on catching some of them. On unfamiliar waters, however, if you don't see or take a fish in the first hour or so you can easily become convinced the place is fishless and thus lose heart.

Most important of all, memories of past occurrences — of fish caught or merely seen — in that exact place add excitement and anticipation to every cast. Few of us fish to revive old memories, but they do come back whether we wish it or not when we revisit familiar territory and they add richness to the day. Hemingway's famous story, "Big Two-Hearted River," shows he felt this way, too.

The best day's bass fishing I ever experienced was far from the most enjoyable one. A friend and I had portaged a canoe into a small Canadian lake that hadn't been fished in years. We caught only a few small fish during the first two hours and were thinking of turning back when we hit the jackpot.

We had pulled the canoe up onto an undercut rock ledge to eat lunch when I spotted a bass drifting out from under this hidden lie. I called to my companion and quickly we both started casting. His aim was better than mine and he hooked the fish, but I wasn't disappointed for long. A huge school of smallmouths poured out into the open, fighting to get the minnows the hooked fish was choking up as he fought.

I've never seen anything like it before or since. One of us played a hooked fish to keep the school nearby while the other picked out a postgraduate and cast to it. If a freshman of under two pounds came near the fly the cast was made again. I kept count of the fish landed—not just hooked—for a while, but gave up after we passed seventy-five. We must have caught and released nearly fifty smallmouths apiece—each more than 2½ pounds—in less than two hours. We kept two of over five pounds and then called it a day even though the bass were still hitting on every cast.

A few weeks later that same season I made a weekend visit to the lake in central New England where I had spent all my childhood summers. During those carefree years I had canoed, fished, lived on that lake from sun-up to dark, and I knew every inch of shoreline, every sunken boulder, ledge, or drop-off as I will never know any other body of water no matter how long I live. Even during my childhood there had been too many motor-boats, too many fishermen, and not too many fish here. The man who ran the boat livery said it had been getting even worse for several years. How right he was.

I worked like a bird dog all day long finding every favorite spot and using every secret stratagem I'd worked out as a boy, and I didn't give up till dark. My twelve hours' rowing and casting had netted me two bass well below bragging size — one just over a pound and the other not quite two. I'll admit I was pleased with the expression on the boat-renter's face when I held up what were apparently the first two bass brought back that week, but that was far from the best part of the day.

I hadn't fished that lake for over a decade, yet I had been able to locate every special fishing place unerringly. Each underwater rock, ledge, shoal, or weedbed was just where I'd left it and hadn't withered or wrinkled a bit with age. When I made a cast after a cautious approach, big fish seen or caught here years before seemed to be following my fly or rising up under my bass-bug. That day was a full program of instant-replays, and I was so absorbed that the great bass bonanza that I'd lucked into a few weeks earlier never crossed my mind.

I'm quite sure I didn't draw any morals or precepts from that day's mediocre fishing at the time, but it appears that as an older dog now I still haven't learned any newer tricks. For the past fourteen years I have trout-fished on my home river for fifty to sixty days each season. On those few days when I wrench myself away to fish what may be a far more productive river I feel a keen sense of loss.

Late last July I went up salmon fishing in Canada to try out some experimental flies I had great hopes for. Admittedly this is the period of summer doldrums on Catskill rivers, but I felt I would be missing something important. There is a late-evening hatch of two small mayflies and one caddis at that time of year, and I had yet to work out a decent imitation of any of them. I came back from an interesting and fairly productive trip with a nagging sense of guilt. I knew that while I'd been indulging myself in salmon I'd lost a full year as far as solving a difficult but intriguing trout-fishing problem was concerned.

Though I may be a slave to this river, it is *voluntary* servitude and I wouldn't have it any other way. I watch the big fish spawn in November. I check the shallow eddies along the shoreline to get an idea of how early and how many eggs have hatched out in March and April. I read scale samples during the open season to determine growth rates. I study stomach contents. I tag fish to learn more about their seasonal movements. I put on mask and snorkel on warm days to try to understand why some lies hold several good fish while others, that seem as good to me, hold none. And I give the river a thorough physical after each flood or high water to see why pools, pockets, and cut-banks change the way they do and to predict where the best lies will occur next season.

Then there are all the insects to observe and imitate. Which species do the trout like best and which do they take half-heartedly? Is it possible to tell from the rise-form which insect is being taken? Which types are decimated by higher than usual spring floods and which are so hardy they contribute full hatches in bad years as well as in good? I spend as much of my time digging into questions like these as I do in testing my observations and theories in the delightful act of fishing.

Because of this I may now fish less than I used to, but I feel that I'm learning something and I enjoy each fishing hour that much more. Several mystery stories are unfolding simultaneously and the one titled, *Will I or won't I hook that eighteen-inch brown that lives under the willow root tonight?* is not always the most absorbing one.

I don't consider myself a fish-farmer in any sense of the word, and yet this familiar portion of the river is in many ways like a garden to me. Its seasonal changes and the progress of its crop of trout have the same fascination for me that the growth of a flower bed or vegetable plot does for the enthusiastic gardener.

And, as any gardener can tell you, no one else's garden is half as interesting as your own — no matter how lush or weed-free theirs may be. The French poet-philosopher Voltaire summed it up perfectly when he gave his famous formula for happiness: "Cultivate your own garden."

Some may interpret this as a sly hint to worm-fishers as to the best place for digging bait. However, I like to think it was the best and soundest advice ever given to us flyfishers, too.

9

Spare the Rod and Spoil the Trip

Hundreds of thousands of American fishermen probably visit Europe each year but never think of bringing their rods and reels. More than forty million Americans cast a fly, hurl a plug, or dunk a worm at home each summer, yet I can't recall ever meeting another American fishing on the mainland of Europe. Perhaps the reason American anglers don't think of Europe (with the exception of the British Isles and maybe bits of Scandinavia) as fishing country is that it seems too civilized. This continent is known as museum-touring, cathedral-watching territory, and since there aren't any swarms of black flies, grunting Indians, or camp-raiding black bears, how can there be any fish?

Well, don't let the fact that your wife may be with you or that you're bathing and shaving regularly make you feel that fishing is gauche. You can find superb trout fishing without tears and tribulations here, and the fact that you dress and smell a little better, as you probably will on a continental tour, won't bother the trout a bit. By all means take some tackle with you next time you sacrifice some vacation to take your wife to Europe. And keep your eyes and ears open. You just might have the fishing trip of your life.

The surprising truth is that continental fishing runs from good to superb, despite the density of the human population. For centuries, good fisheries have been cherished and preserved—not democratically, perhaps, but preserved. Nearly all the productive lakes and streams are either privately owned or controlled by the State or an association. And yet, you can gain access to most of these waters by simply asking the right questions or by paying a modest fee.

When I first wangled several months' vacation and decided to fish my way through Europe, I had become accustomed to impersonal treatment in the great cities. I wasn't prepared for the reception I got from rural residents of the same countries. For example, I found Frenchman after Frenchman listening to me with courtesy, even with empathy, as I talked about fishing. The only explanation I can give for this is that there's a freemasonry among fishermen. When I appear with a rod instead of a *Guide Michelin* in my hands, I am treated as a fellow fisherman and not as "the American tourist."

A striking example of this hands-across-the-river understanding occurred early one trip while I was fishing the salmon rivers of

Casting my way down a salmon pool on the heroic Rio Narcea in Austrias, Spain, on a bluebird April afternoon.

northern Spain. My wife and I had put up at a small *fonda*
upriver, near the fishing spots. The other guests were Europeans
of a type we hadn't met on previous trips and haven't met since
without persuasive letters of introduction. They were a young
Spanish marquis, his cousin, son of some duke, and a chateau-
owning Frenchman.

We soon found ourselves chatting together about the day's
fishing, since all meals at this simple inn were set at a communal
table. After dinner, the talk became more intimate and the
marquis, quite suddenly, insisted on boosting me to an honorary
peerage.

"Oh, I know there are no titles in America," he said, with the
authority of a young man who had spent a year at an American
college. "Things are very democratic. But, after all, a man who
fishes for salmon . . ." He shrugged his shoulders and I began to
sense the great cachet Europeans attach to salmon fishing. I was
toying with the idea of accepting only a temporary knighthood—
just to avoid an argument, mind you—when my wife, a devout
commoner, vetoed the idea. The next evening these aristocrats
explained in detail how they avoided paying income taxes—for a
European, an intimate act of disclosure that rivals the sharing of a
toothbrush.

I cannot promise that fishing is a surefire method for social
climbing. Most of our fishing encounters have been far less lofty
—though not necessarily less rewarding.

Trout fishing in Austria won't make you feel like a member of
the nobility, but it will make you feel like a minor celebrity at
times. Townspeople walking back from the day's haying wave and
call out "Petri Heil," thus summoning for you the support of the
fisherman's saint. And I remember supper, back at the fishing
inn, with its ritual serving of the trout — which had been kept
alive in a springhouse across the courtyard. Austrians would no
more eat an hour-dead trout than a Down-Easter would cook a
dead lobster. And the foreign fisherman quickly adjusts to the
idea of keeping his catch alive for the springhouse. A waitress
once asked how I would like my trout prepared and then dashed
out with a huge brass key to unlock the springhouse and deliver
the fish, still wriggling, into the hands of the cook. There is a

Live trout being poured from the barrel-like *Lagl* into a spring-water *Kälterer*. Austrians insist on fresh-killed trout.

reverence for trout in this countryside, and just a touch of it is also bestowed on the captor.

Our stay in the Cévennes Mountains of south-central France was the most enjoyable of all. People went out of their way to point out the choicest holding water, even the lies of legendary monsters. A few of our neighbors here were professional market fishermen who supported their families all summer with the trout they caught from these hard-fished public waters; yet, after a proper interval, they shared with me some of their secret fishing methods. One of these was especially ingenious.

Once the sun hit these clear waters, the sensible fish would tuck themselves under the overhanging willows near the banks. If you then approached them from upstream, or the direction they faced, they would spot you and sink out of sight before you could get within casting range. A midstream attack was out of the question because the channel was too deep for wading. And, when you tried to cast your dry fly above their noses from below, your line or leader fell to the water over their heads and they scattered in terror. These were frequently harassed, sophisticated fish. The solution the native fishermen offered was to deliver a small wet fly with a distinct "plop" to a point just behind the fish's tail. This slight noise and the spreading ripples caused by the entry would tease the trout into turning around to investigate, hoping an ant or beetle had fallen out of the foliage. The rest was a foregone conclusion.

One of the joys of our visit here was watching the children go after tiny fish called gudgeon. The kids cut their own rods on the spot every day—slim two-foot pieces of peeled willow. To such a rod they knotted a similar length of light monofilament, and at the extreme end of the line a small split shot, a miniature hook, and bait.

Their strategy was to lie down on a cutbank or large rock with just the head and right arm sticking over the edge. From this vantage point, the kids could see several of the small fish lying inert and almost perfectly camouflaged on the sand and pebbles. They then lowered their baited hook to the bottom, inched it up

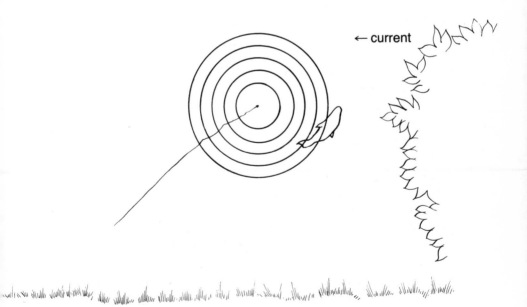

Casting the wet fly behind the trout in the French manner. Gallic anglers know better than to cast above these fish.

to a fish's chin and, when it finally opened its mouth and took the bait, jerked this tiny fish up onto the bank.

Caught up in the enthusiasm of the mini-fishing, we gave it a go. It was certainly a far cry from past heroics on the salmon rivers. And yet, one had to exercise great skill and patience. There was a hidden reward to this child's play. The four-inch, dark-meated gudgeons turned out to be the only freshwater fish I've ever eaten that were even tastier than pink-fleshed, wild trout.

The finest trout fishing I have ever enjoyed anywhere, any-time, was on the Traun River in Austria, just below Gmunden at Marienbrucke. This choice water was controlled by the State, yet the license fee then was only two to three dollars a day. To give you an idea of the quality of this fishery, all trout under sixteen inches had to be returned according to the regulations. It was fly-fishing only—no bait, no spinning—yet most of the fish which rose were well over the minimum.

Unfortunately, the lower Traun has since been ruined by the erection of a dam, but there are other rivers in Austria and Yugoslavia that could rival this fishery. I have also enjoyed excellent trout fishing in Luxembourgh, Germany, and even in the crowded regions of France.

Don't be put off by those stories of $3,000-a-week rod fees on the famous rivers of Scotland and Norway—even though out-landish fees are charged in some areas. Some of the most productive fishing I ever had on the Continent was absolutely free simply because I was staying at the inn that controlled the water. I have never been charged as much a $5 a day for trout fishing. Two dollars per rod-day might be a fair average. I'll admit, though, that my salmon fishing in Spain was almost the price of an all-day lift ticket at an expensive ski resort. Accommodations, on the other hand, were so much cheaper that my two-week stay cost a good deal less than a fortnight's skiing in the Rockies.

How will a wife feel about a trip like this? I wouldn't try to tell you how to sell this bill of goods, but the facts are in your favor. Continental fishing is a far cry from the black-fly-and-bear-infested barrens of northern Canada. You are rarely more than a half-hour's drive from an excellent restaurant or interesting his-toric site. If the weather's rotten or the river is muddy, you can always go on an enjoyable day's excursion. When we were rained out in southern France, we'd spend the day in the cathedral town of Albi or at the Roquefort Caves, both of which were within an easy hour's drive. In Spain we'd visit the Altamira Caves or explore the picturesque coves and fishing towns of the north coast. At Gmunden, we'd drive into Salzburg, barely an hour away.

Even on perfect days, nobody flogs the water all day long. Dawn patrols are unheard of. Breakfast is leisurely and fishing usually starts at about ten. Afternoons are spent hiking, napping, birding, reading or doing whatever you like. You take the cream of the sport — a few hours in the morning and the best of the evening—and that's usually enough to satisfy anyone.

Nearly half the Europeans I met on these waters were accompanied by their wives. Very few of the women ever fished, but most had been going on these trips with their husbands for years and they seemed to enjoy their holiday as much as the men did.

Food and accommodations at European fishing inns are up to

An Austrian lady angler properly equipped with knee boots, wool skirt, and a sensible ten-foot fly rod.

the best the region affords and that is usually very good indeed. Life is, admittedly, a bit simpler than at the large Continental resort hotels. You won't find roulette, dancing or floor shows. On the other hand, there are no all-night, whiskey-drinking poker games, either.

Even the most primitive regions can come up with some surprising amenities. At that small *fonda* in northern Spain, I was assigned a *ganchero*, or guide, called "Chamberlain" — a name he had earned because he always carried an umbrella to protect his fisherman in case of rain.

Despite the single-minded purpose of my fishing trip, I was never very far from the world of art and architecture. One evening on a river in southern France, for example, I took a shortcut home through the woods and stumbled onto a superb, thirteenth-century chapel. I was surprised when I couldn't find any mention of it in the guidebooks covering the region. Later, the townspeople, who took its presence for granted, told me it was the only building left in the valley where their town used to be. More than 600 years ago everyone had moved up onto the cone-shaped hill nearby for protection during a long, and now almost forgotten, war.

Unlikely as it seems, my wife and I may be the only Americans who have ever seen that small church. Come to think of it, if I'd been off looking at cathedrals instead of fishing, I never would have found it at all.

Idyllic surroundings on the Mur in Austria. Dramatic scenery, quaint buildings, and no other fishermen.

10

The World's Best Trout Fishing

When you daydream about trout fishing in the perfect place, where do you find yourself? In the Canadian subarctic with its big, beautiful brookies? At Lake Taupo, New Zealand, with its huge rainbows? Southern Chile with its oversized browns? The stately chalkstreams of England with their legendary, free-rising trout?

All of these places rate high on my list, but none reaches the very top. The brook trout of northern Canada are either impossible or too easy to catch, and I really don't enjoy playing blood-bank to clouds of black flies. Taupo rainbows are big and lively, but lakes have always been my second-choice location for trout fishing. Trout down near the tip of South America may average bigger than anywhere else in the world, and it's thrilling fishing if driving a large streamer into gale winds is your favorite exercise. And the water-meadows of Hampshire, for all their beauty and history, offer fishing that's a bit too picky for my taste, and besides, most of the fish you catch there today have been stocked.

No, I'd take Austria's River Traun, the stretch just below Gmunden, that I fished for part of two seasons fifteen years ago, over any other trout fishing I've seen or even heard about. Here was a pleasant, nearly bug-free climate, the most perfect fishing inn I've ever seen, the widest variety of fishing conditions on a single river, sport difficult enough to leave you with a sense of accomplishment yet not so demanding as to be frustrating, and a marvelous head of fish—including some enormous ones if trophy-hunting was on your agenda.

Don't pack your rods and waders, though. The Traun fishery was ruined about six years ago and all that's left is the memory. But it was good enough for a lifetime of those in the good old days.

Why reminisce about what no longer exists? Not simply for the taste of nostalgia, though there is that, admittedly. In part, I want to write about its delights for the same reason authors write about so many departed joys—to share them. But there is a more important motive, for I think there are lessons to be learned from the Traun. I would like American anglers to know just how good a river can be, and I would like them to know that it is not beyond possibility for us to establish and maintain our own Traun somewhere, someday. I indulge the hope that the question is not whether it can be done but how it can be done.

The first time I ever heard of this river was while talking fishing with an English diplomat at a party in Germany. After swapping several fish stories, he told me he thought the Traun at Marienbrucke offered the finest fishing on the Continent, very probably the best in all Europe. Somehow his description rang true and I jotted down the details for future reference. A few months later, when I had some spare time, I drove down through Austria to Gmunden with a trunkful of tackle and gear. I found the Marienbrucke Inn easily from his directions, parked my car, and prepared to enjoy a week's superb trout fishing.

Life was not to be that simple, though—not in Austria during the high season. I was told politely but firmly that the inn was full. When would they have a vacancy? Perhaps not for the rest of the summer. Most of their customers, I was told, were regulars who booked almost a year in advance. No wonder the fishing was excellent, I thought. You couldn't even get near it.

I was shaken, but couldn't believe things were as impossible as all that. I would spend the day sightseeing in the area, I said, and would return later in the day to see if something had opened up. I even went so far as to mention the diplomat's name to show I had some sort of credentials. There was a look of honest pity on the good innkeeper's face, and as I drove away I was not nearly as confident as my manner had indicated.

After a lovely lunch at the head of the Traun-see, the lake that stretched above Gmunden, I spent the afternoon gawking at the scenery of the Salzkammergut — grandeur that was temporarily wasted on a fidgety fisherman — and drove back to Marienbrucke trying to convince myself that something good was about to happen. The innkeeper's wife met me before I reached the door. I was incredibly lucky, she told me. They had just that minute received a cancellation by phone. A serious illness. She would send a boy out to my car to help me in with my gear.

I thought they were simply playing hard to get and congratulated myself on going along with their ploy. I was mistaken, however, as I soon learned by talking with other guests. You did, indeed, need to book far in advance and I had just won a thousand-to-one long shot.

The inn was perfect, and many North American fishing camps have much to learn from the comforts it provided: a room with racks for rods, nets, etc., and just inside that, a warming room for wet waders and outside gear. These first two rooms inside the door were for fishermen and fishing gear; after that, gracious living took over. Most bedrooms had a small balcony, comfortable beds, and pleasing decorations. Meals were excellent, sometimes even superb, offering a reasonable choice of home-cooked dishes

The beautiful Marienbrucke Inn viewed from across the still-water where monsters smash your tackle at dusk.

that were planned around a fisherman's hours, rather than vice versa. Breakfast was particularly large and enjoyable, and there was no noticeable rush for choice water. A 9:30 start was early enough even in midsummer, and desperate dawn patrols were unheard of. With these amenities you could convince even your wife that fishing and fishing camps can, indeed, be couth.

The fishing itself was usually so good you didn't have to overdo it, and there was an almost infinite variety of fish and fishing in the ten miles of water this fishery controlled. The size limits, which were strictly adhered to, give you some idea of the quality of this water. Grayling, which were considered only a cut above trash fish, could be taken at twelve inches. Brown trout had to be sixteen inches. And *Lachsforelle* (which translates into salmon-trout) had to be twenty inches. Such limits may seem like the rules set for "one-trophy-fish-only" stretches of some Eastern U.S. rivers, but the surprising fact was that on the Traun some eighty to ninety percent of the fish you took—even on the dry fly —were over these lofty limits. The fish themselves were in beautiful condition and absolutely wild. There was no record of the river ever having been stocked. A very few coarse fish shared this river with the trout: some *Ettel* (a large European chub) and a few *Hecht*, or pike. The chub seemed to serve no purpose and were few in number, but the occasional large pike probably kept the trout on their toes, weeded out weaklings, and thinned the younger generation so that the survivors had more to eat.

This portion of the Traun was the outflow of a ten-mile-long, glacial-groove lake and, unlike most lake-fed trout fisheries in the U.S., the water entering the lower part of the river came off the top of the lake rather than from some deep, cold subsurface pipe. Apparently, the lake was cool enough, due to glacial melting into feeder streams from the high surrounding mountains, so that the plankton-rich surface water was below the upper limit which trout will tolerate. If you've ever seen the breathtaking Salzkammergut, either in person or in pictures, you'll see why this may be a nearly unique situation.

Both the insect hatches and the trout were far larger than they were in the only slightly smaller inflow river ten miles up the lake. Were the windfall insects and the surface plankton responsible for this increase in fertility or did the treated sewage effluent from the small city of Gmunden (which straddled the outlet from the lake to the river) play its part, too? I never ran a test on a water sample to find out, but one thing or another certainly agreed with the lower Traun trout.

The water below Gmunden was more like a salmon river than a trout stream in size. It averaged only one hundred to one hundred and fifty feet wide, but the banks were so firm in most places that it had dug itself down into the deep, big-rocked layer of its bed. I never found a place I could cross it — even in August dead-low water — with chest waders. The river had variety to surpass its size; every mile contained a full choice of every type of trout habitat imaginable. There were long, deep still-waters, dams, plunge-pools, runs, rapids, classic pools, pocket-water, and flats repeated again and again with foot or car bridges every mile or so to let you cross over.

If I could have one more day on this water, as it once was, I would fish it as I never did when it seemed sure to be there forever. I would disregard the European convention and spend a full fourteen hours flogging the stream as if there were no tomorrow—which turned out to be the case. This daydream day, however, is not so much of a dream as it may appear. I am scrupulous in my fantasies, and every part of the day we are about to spend fishing this river of memory occurred at least once to me on actual fishing days.

In the first place, I would not lie abed and then enjoy a leisurely breakfast as I once did because I have to pack everything into this one day. I'd ask for a seven-o'clock breakfast which would be served to me with raised eyebrows but with politeness. Admittedly, this is not a desperate hour of the day for an American trout fisherman in mid-summer, but on the Traun it would have caused discussion. Was I an eccentric or merely an insomniac? No matter. I would be on the water two hours ahead of any other angler and the weir pool, less than a hundred yards from the inn door, would be mine exclusively until I hooked or landed the most eager fish, at least.

This pool started with a roaring, narrow chute of water, concentrated enough to run the full 150-foot length of the short pool with slack water and return eddies on both sides. For this heroic water I put on a light salmon leader tapered to OX, or about eight-pound test, decorated with a large #4 Grey Ghost streamer. I cast this quartering into the choppy current and when it has swung into the slower water retrieve it with short twitches. These trout have never seen an American streamer fly before (Europeans use large, fancy Scotch salmon flies for this type of angling) and the sleek, sinuous profile of this famous smelt imitation is more than these fish can resist. Every few casts I get a bruising strike. Hooked fish play hard and deep, threatening to run out of the pool, and it is only when they are quite tired that they can be urged into the quieter water and played back up toward the dam I am standing on. Unfortunately, a small tree, the relic of a spring flood, is wedged up under the apron and the tiring fish head for this sanctuary with their last ounce of strength. I can control fish up to three pounds or so easily, but some dreadnaughts cruise relentlessly into this snag and I have to break them off by hand, wondering if that might have been the fish to beat the local record of a shade over seventeen pounds.

One morning I hooked seven fish here and lost them all at the last minute. The *Fischmeister*, Hans Gebetsreither, was watching this performance from a window in the kitchen where he was enjoying his morning cup of coffee, and he marched down to the dam to see what was going on. He tested my leader and gave a grudging grunt as the tough monofilament nearly cut his hand and then swished my stiff eight-foot rod, which had killed several salmon in Canada, and shook his head in disgust. "When you are with a salmon fly-fishing you should also a salmon-rod be using," he said, or words to that effect. My German is a low-grade pidgin at best, but Hans's guttural grumbling was easy to translate: "Stop butchering my lovely fish with that Mickey-Mouse rod. Instantly." I skulked downriver to more open, snag-free water.

The fish I had been hooking—and mostly losing—here were mainly *Forelle* or brown trout, but some were the green-backed, silver-sided *Seeforelle* (lake trout) and once in a while a leaping *Lachsforelle* (salmon trout). The *Seeforelle* were flashier fighters than the regular, yellow-bellied browns, but were probably relatives that had recently drifted down from the lake above where they had been enjoying a different diet and habitat. *Lachsforelle*, however, puzzle me to this day. The Europeans who fished here said they were a true landlocked salmon, and their love of fast water and habit of leaping when hooked made a strong case for this parentage. On the other hand, no salmon of any kind are native to the Danube watershed, of which the Traun is a part, and the black spots on the backs and sides of these silvery fish were too large for salmon. Whatever their exact ancestry, they certainly fought like landlocks every inch of the way.

By now it is 9:30. I am running out of streamer flies and ready-taking fish so I head for the stretch of pocket-water below the tail of the weir pool. It is still too early for hatching flies and rising trout, so I change to a #10 wet fly, say a gold-ribbed Hare's Ear, and fine my leader down to 3X. I have had a lot of exercise above and decide to fish in the lazy man's manner for a while, letting the fly swing down-current on a quartering line and taking a step downriver after each presentation.

Every ten casts or so there is either a thump on the rod or a yowl from the reel, or both, and a fish runs down-current. Wading is slow and treacherous in this stretch, and I lose most of the fish trying to bring them back up-current. These are browns in the one-to-three-pound category, but they fight like full-grown grilse in this fast water.

I am through the pockets and into the flat below by 10:30 and I have been noticing rising fish working below me in the slow, deep water. Now I have to go back to work again, and I follow the path to the foot of this flat, add a 4X tippet, and rummage through my box for a likely imitation of the dark dun I have seen hatching. A #12 Quill Gordon doesn't seduce many fish so I change to a #14 Red Quill and the fishing picks up. These are chalkstream conditions; weedy bottom, slow, deep water that calls for snail-like wading and delicate presentation. These trout are all browns, mostly near the 16-inch limit with a few larger ones thrown in for excitement, but this is the Lilliputian fishing of the day. It is as rewarding as it is demanding, though, and an hour of fishing of this quality on the Battenkill or Beaverkill back home would make a "remember the time when . . ." story to be told and retold.

Just before noon I head up to the weir again, cross over to the left side of the current on the small catwalk, walk out on the bar

A three-pound *Lachsforelle*, the mystery fish of the Traun. At twenty-one inches, it was just barely a keeper.

formed below the plunge-pool, and face up-current. On this side of the main spillway current there are more than a dozen small rivulets formed by leaks in the weir-boards that bubble into minipools just below the dam-apron. The air temperature is nearly eighty degrees by now and there's a blazing sun overhead so I don't expect to see fish rising. I must pound them up with a variant. I put on a ginger-and-grizzley that's as big as a silver dollar and start prospecting the tail end of the poollet on the extreme right, extending each new cast up closer to the bubbles at the head.

The drag here is tricky and in some trickles I do nothing, but I raise a couple of fish in some of the bigger ones. In all, I raise eight fish, hook six, and land four from fourteen to eighteen inches — all browns. This is a modest showing. I once took ten from these same runnels in forty-five minutes before going in to lunch.

The midday meal is served with choice of beer or wine and is topped off with fresh fruit or berries and a selection of the world's great cheeses. It is perfect weather for a midday nap. There are also several afternoon performances of operas, concerts, and plays in Salzburg, one of the world's few great small cities, only fifty minutes away. But this is to be an all-fishing day, a maximum effort.

I get my tackle into the car and drive four or five miles downstream to a long, sandy-bottomed flat below an old mill. There are very few trout here but there are schools of grayling, pale grey shadows fanning the sand with their pectoral fins waiting for food to pass overhead. They are only partly competitive with trout; they live in different water and eat midges and small insects that the trout usually consider beneath their dignity. I go down to a 5X leader with a #18 black nymph and slowly prospect down-current. I miss my first hit—these fish shoot straight up from the bottom and are back down in a wink—and decide to stay put, for these are usually school fish. I get no more hits on the nymph so I wade thirty feet downstream and spot the school not twenty feet away when one of them rises. Grayling are much less shy than trout and will rise to your fly even when they can see you clearly, but they are choosy feeders and hard to hook. I put on a dark #18 dry fly and that's just what they've been waiting for. I get hit after hit, hooking every other fish that rises, till the school finally catches on and moves away. They were

A lovely flat, down-river from the inn, where grayling up to three pounds rose steadily under the afternoon sun.

typically all of a size, 12 to 13 inches in this group, and put up a reasonable fight although not as long and strong-hearted as a trout's. They are beautiful fish in the hand, though, sweet-smelling with a few black specks on their silverish sides, lavender backs and long, soft dorsal fins that try to convince you these are freshwater sailfish.

I run through two more schools on my way down the pool before I spot a large solitary fish lying between two patches of weed. It could be just a chub, yet it might be the grayling I'm hoping for. I cover him with the small dry fly and up he comes with the flash of purple that says grayling. The first two minutes of fight are vigorous enough, and then he comes in like an old shoe and I am disappointed with his lack of stamina. This is only July, though, and the big spring spawners aren't back into fighting shape yet, I have been told. In October they are something else and Charles Ritz rates them better than trout in their own proper season. Anyway, this fish is just a hair under twenty inches and the best one I have taken to date.

It's five o'clock and early dinner will be available in an hour, so I decide to finish off the afternoon with a few trout. With no shadows falling across the river yet, my only chance seems the plunge-pool below the old mill just above the grayling flat. I prospect the bubbly edge of the fast water here with the big variant again, raising six and landing three in the next half-hour. The shadows finally start to creep towards me from the far bank and I have to make a difficult decision: Should I continue fishing or head back for an early supper and enjoy more of the late-evening fishing? I hate to leave, but I know my chances for really large fish are better once the sun is down. I head for my car to make the short run back to the inn.

By 7:30, somewhat rested and refreshed by an *apéritif* and a cold supper, I walk up the formal promenade path that lines this portion of the bank to the very head of the river, nearly half a mile up-current where the water pours out of the lake through sturdy gates. It's a pleasant walk in the cool of the evening, and since I won't need waders the stroll can be made in the comfort of sneakers and slacks. Couples sitting on the benches murmur "Petri Heil," giving me the best wishes of our patron saint. The proper reply, I have learned, is "Petri dank."

To go fishing again after all the trout and grayling I have raised, hooked, and either lost or caught seems gluttonous, but this is to be a day remembered for a lifetime and it would be unthinkable to miss the *crescendo* of large fish and frenzied rising that will occur as darkness settles. First, though, I will warm up on medium-sized fish, cast to in a leisurely manner.

The narrow rush of water into the wide riverbed here causes curling counter-eddies on both edges where unseen fish rise like small minnows, poking their noses up into patches of foam for trapped insects. I have fished here only once before and on that occasion Hans, the *Fischmeister*, rigged me with two medium-sized wet flies which he told me to cast straight across the counter-current to float dead drift, and then to dance the dropper for a second or two before retrieving once drag had set in. Since I am standing three or four feet above river level this latter maneuver is easy to execute—even though it's nearly impossible when you're waist-deep in the water.

This is easy fishing from an eagle's vantage point, and I begin to wonder whether or not a spent-wing dry fly will work better when the rod is wrenched downward sharply and then flies back up. My point fly is gone and it's all my fault, but I was using a 2X leader and had felt that such a hefty tippet was plenty of insurance. Not with these fish, though. The ones I hooked or saw last time ranged from two to six pounds and they darted back to their lies desperately when hooked in this slow water.

I re-rig and pay more attention to my work. In several minutes I am into another and give line quickly enough this time. When I have the fish under control just below my feet, I realize I've made another mistake. Without a guide or long-handled net, how can I get this three-pound *Seeforelle* up a sheer masonry wall more than three feet high? I try to handline the trout up to the rail, but he wakes up and kicks off halfway to the top. I continue fishing, luckily landing one slightly smaller fish and being wound around underwater pilings by two far bigger fish that took control from the start.

My watch tells me I have ten minutes to cross over and meet Tony, the assistant *Fischmeister*, nearly a quarter of a mile downstream, for the last pitch of the day — awesome fishing for huge trout that go bump in the night. I reel in and "Petri dank" my way downriver to an old pier that juts out a dozen feet or more into the slowed river.

Tony is there rigging up new leaders, sturdier ones of about 1X with #14 dry caddis imitations on the point and on the dropper. He knots one onto my line and keeps two spares handy. After a break you can't risk a light on this water to tie on new flies, but whole rigged leaders can be attached by feel.

It's 8:30 and I sit there with my feet dangling just above the water, resting up for the grand finale. This will be the slowest fishing of the day. I will get only two or three hits in the coming hour of painstaking casting and feeling my flies gliding over the water, but this will be my chance for the biggest dry-fly trout of a lifetime. It isn't pleasant fishing, though, or even very interesting. It is simply trout fishing on a scale that I may never see again.

When it is finally too dark to tie on a fly, something brushes my face and then I feel a tickle in my hair. It's starting. I look up at the sky directly overhead and see a few, then several and, finally, many tiny forms hurrying with batlike, erratic flight through the

An Austrian *Fischmeister* with leather knickers, national hat, and a bring-'em-back-alive *Lagl* heavy with fish and water.

air. The caddis are up and a glance across the leadlike surface of the pool shows me that the trout are, too. Small dimples appear everywhere as if someone had scattered a handful of birdshot across the water. I am not fooled by the dainty, dace-like quality of the rise-forms, though, for I have been here before at this time of day — or is it night? These are usually huge fish up from the fifteen-to-twenty-foot depths for their only outing of the day.

I screw down the drag on my oversized trout reel as fast as it will go and start stripping line from the spool. There's no need to cast far. There are enough fish rising within twenty to thirty feet of me to fill a barrel. I shoot my team of dry flies twenty-five feet straight across the stream and strain my eyes to follow their progress on the surface. They move so slowly that when they start to drag they leave no wake, but merely cruise in toward the shore below me. Each cast takes a minute or two — it seems like much more — to fish out and then I repeat the procedure. These fish are old and wise and make very few mistakes even in pitch-darkness.

In a few minutes I am casting like an automaton, my arm making the prescribed motions every minute or so, but my mind is elsewhere. Tony is waiting patiently, standing at my left shoulder, uttering occasional phrases of encouragement, but my German is too weak for any sustained conversation. When my mind has finally drifted several thousand miles away, my line slowly grows tight, as if it has caught a snag, and I give the rod a twitch to free it by reflex action. Damn! There aren't any snags out there. I have just pulled the fly out of the mouth of the evening's first unwise fish. I reel in, Tony patiently feels the flies to be sure all is still in order, and I start casting again.

Fifteen minutes later I am napping so deeply that a fish is on before my tired reflexes can betray me. I raise my rod-tip and apply all the pressure I dare, but without result. The reel gives up line with short, grudging grunts, and if I didn't know better I would be certain I had hooked into a rowboat passing by in the dark. A short while after I feel the line-to-backing splice slip through my fingers, the procession comes to a halt, but I still feel the slow, steady throb of the fish's tail telegraphed up the line. Then, after a minute or so, all I can sense is the steady pull of the current.

I hand the rod to Tony. He plucks the tight line like a bass-fiddle string, pulls hard from several angles and then I hear him reeling in. Miraculously, he ties on another fully rigged leader and the rod is back in my hands again. I glance at the radium dial of my wristwatch and see that it's 9:45—only a quarter-hour of legal fishing time left.

Again I cast out into the nothingness and stand there listening to the soft sound of fish sucking in flies. I am determined to concentrate and not spoil my last chance of the day. I have no notion of where my flies are. Am I waiting too long between casts, or not long enough to fish the presentation out? No matter, really. Each swing must pass over a dozen fish or more and I must wait for the law of averages to catch up with some trout.

It does, just before quitting time. This fish starts off more rapidly at first, then stops and shakes his head for a while and continues on majestically again. This time I'm in touch for a full five minutes and then the line comes back to me. At least I wasn't wound around a snag by this fish. The flashlight shows a straightened hook on the dropper fly. The first time I had been too gentle and on the second try I had been too heavy-handed. Or were these fish meant to remain uncaught? Tony says they land one occasionally, but that the chances are better slightly upriver and near the opposite shore. There are fewer boulders and snags there, and it can be fished from an anchored boat. Perhaps I would like to try there tomorrow evening? I agree to the plan even though I know tomorrow will never come. We have a cold beer together back at the inn, then I bid him a drowsy goodnight. I am bone-weary and half asleep.

How many fish have I hooked this day? I try to tally up the number of rises, fish hooked, and fish landed. I was into at least fifty, probably nearer to a hundred including the grayling. I landed less than half of them, though, and very few of the big ones. Too tired to make an exact accounting, I head upstairs to bed. I feel sure, though, that I have had a larger poundage of fish on my line during this one day than I might hook into during an entire season back home on northeastern waters.

Admittedly, this was a daydream day — a composite patched together from the best parts of other days I had enjoyed on the lower Traun. Even so, such a day had been a possibility. How could fishing be so good? This was no mountain wilderness. The Traun valley had been settled, farmed, lived in for a dozen centuries or more and it had even played host to a certain amount of industrial development. For example, the weir across from the inn backed up water for both a local brewery and a small textile mill and yet the water was returned to the river in "troutable"—if not quite potable—condition.

This land had become populated gradually and lovingly. There had been no sudden housing developments or rush of industrial exploitation in this area. As the population grew, safeguards on water usage and sewage treatment had been written and enforced *before* any damage could be done.

That the river was pure enough for trout was due to one type of planning, but that doesn't explain the size and the number of trout. This was the result of a fishery-management policy that ensured good fishing for native species without any necessity for stocking. In fact, it is hard to imagine that the fishing here had possibly been any better a hundred, five hundred, or even a thousand years ago. The harvest was in perfect balance with production.

The size limits I mentioned earlier had a little to do with this, but several other rules, written and unwritten, safeguarded this fishery. First, and perhaps most important, was a limit on the number of fishing permits issued per day. These cost about $3 per day or $12 for a full week back in 1960 — a modest sum, but enough to keep all but serious anglers off the water in those days. More important, the limited number of permits kept the water from being overfished and the fish from being harassed to the point where they'd hide during the day and rise only at dusk. I am convinced that the brown trout's reputation for being a night-feeder is due to his being stepped on by an army of anglers during daylight hours on our most popular public rivers and that fish would feed far more steadily during daylight hours if there were less traffic.

Second, anglers here paid for every fish they kept. The price was about three-quarters of the open market price for trout (wild fish *can* be sold in most parts of Europe) so that few fish were kept for bragging purposes. If you wanted a fish for a meal you kept

Looking down-river from the dam beside the inn. This section of the river alone could have kept an angler happy for life.

one, and the smallest keeping-size trout here (16 inches) made a hearty meal.

Lastly, anglers didn't carry off crates of iced fish with them when their time was up. Whether this was an aspect of the law or merely a tradition I never found out. Countless fisheries in Canada have been skimmed down to mediocrity by anglers who insisted on taking coolers and crates of iced fish back home with them. Anglers on the Traun might take a fish or two with them if they were within a day's trip of home, but there was no wholesale haulage, and I'm sure any guest who tried this—even though the catch was legally paid for — would subsequently find the inn booked solid no matter how far ahead he called in his reservation.

When a dam was built downriver from the Marienbrucke fishery several years ago, it backed up the water and flooded this stretch, destroying a showcase fishery for all the world to wonder at and imitate. The power dam may have been an economic necessity for the region, but the world is the poorer for it. And dams are like taxes: They never disappear, they only increase.

Perhaps we can never have a Traun-like fishery in this country. The rich though cool lake water that fed it might be hard to duplicate, but we might get three-quarters of the way there by following some easy examples. We could make sure the water used by local industry is returned to a river with trout-tolerable quality. We could raise our size-limits. And we could limit the number of fish taken. And just possibly, a few enlightened years from now, we could limit traffic on a few showcase stretches by issuing permits in a limited number on a lottery basis so that anglers who really cared might see free-rising trout all day long for at least a few days each season. I don't know how state conservation departments would react to this last suggestion. But I do know a lot of fishermen who would stand in line a long time for the chance to fish quality water like that, and I am one of them.

11

The Ultimate Fly Rod

Men are emotional about fly rods. Trout rods in particular, yet perhaps even about the hefty rods used in salt water for bonefish and tarpon, or about freshwater rods used for bass bugging and streamer fishing. Men may love a salmon rod. But light, split-cane fly rods are objects of reverence. A Payne, Halstead, Gillum, Garrison, Leonard, Orvis, Winston, Young, Thomas, or an Edwards trout rod may well be the most cherished piece of equipment used in any sport.

The only serious rival is the wing shooter's fine double shotgun. In fact, fly rod and shotgun have much in common. Both are used in the beauty of the wild outdoors. And both become intimate extensions of the body in motion. In some respects, though, the fly rod is the more intimate companion. It seems to be alive. It bends and moves in response to the angler's touch. The rod is a more constant friend, too. Fishing seasons are longer than shooting seasons, and, while a bird shooter may fire several times in a day afield, the trouter will number his casts in the thousands.

Add to this the fact that a day on his favorite stream is a semireligious experience for the dedicated angler. The trout stream is set apart from other scenes of sport — by hemlock and rhododendron, willow and warbler, the play of sunlight on a riffle. Many fine authors have tried to capture this magic, but it beggars description. A great naturalist once described a stream as "the artery of the forest." It is that and more. It is also the life blood of the trouter.

In this setting and in this spirit, a rod becomes far more than just a tool for casting. And, fortunately, this bond between rod and man is an especially happy one. The experienced angler seldom blames his rod. In fact, he is all too liable to consider it perfection.

This happiness with things as they are can be observed in almost any fine tackle store. There are seldom requests for unconventional rod actions or special embellishments. If you examine a sampling of rods by the finest makers, you will see that they are almost uniformly modest in appearance. The brown cane glows warmly through the clear varnish. The reel seat is a harmonious cedar or walnut. Windings will usually be a neutral tan. This is the quiet beauty of the partridge, not the gaudy beauty of the cock pheasant.

And yet, despite the generic description above, each maker subtly signs his own work. Custom-made reel fittings differ from one another. The shape of the cork grip often indicates the maker. And then there's the cane itself. Most Leonards are quite light-colored. So are Garrisons and Gillums. Paynes are medium-brown. Halsteads and Orvises are quite dark brown.

Any of these fine rods is fairly expensive. One may cost from $200 to perhaps slightly more than $350. But it is definitely not a rich man's plaything, or a status symbol. A great many of these rods are in the hands of people of very modest means. I once saw a farmer fishing with a Gillum in the stream that ran behind his barn. When I admired the rod he looked a bit sheepish and admitted, "I've always wanted one of these, and then I made a bit of extra money trapping last winter. But my wife sure doesn't know how much I paid for it." You can be sure that many lunches have been skimped or skipped in order to pay for a dream rod.

Is a $250 bamboo rod ten times as good as a $25 glass rod? There's no pat answer. It all depends on your sense of values.

The recently deceased Everett Garrison, one of the very finest custom makers, defended his art with some science. "A glass rod doesn't throw the smooth curve of line that a fine bamboo does. Stop-motion photography proves this." All well and good, but why do most tournament distance casters now use glass? "It's a very powerful material, all right," Garrison admitted. "But they haven't got the tapers worked out yet. Perhaps some day."

There's more to it than that. There's a "sweet feel" to a great bamboo rod that just can't be duplicated. When you're casting thousands of times a day, this advantage may be worth a lot in pure enjoyment—even if it won't catch more fish. A bamboo rod should last the average fisherman at least twenty years. That comes to $12.50 per year. When you look at it that way, a great rod isn't an extravagance.

There's a joker in that twenty-year life expectancy, though. It's only a median figure. A rod may last a man a lifetime if he fishes only several times a year. On the other hand, the screen door has ended the life of many a rod before it delivered its first cast. Each year hundreds of fine rods are crushed underfoot, splintered against tree trunks, or chopped off by car doors. Surprisingly, rod breakage while actually playing a trout is one of the rarest forms of disaster.

Perhaps it isn't fair to measure a rod's life in terms of years. Barring accidents, it should be measured in numbers of casts. For each time a bamboo rod flexes, it dies a little. It may take years to notice a change in power and action, for an angler unwittingly suits his casting style to the rod in hand. But fatigue is inexorable. The finest, steeliest dry-fly rod I ever owned — or ever handled for that matter — was an eight-foot Halstead. I still own it and cherish it, but I seldom fish with it. After some seven hundred and fifty days of dogged dry-fly fishing, it's a slow, lazy parody of its former self.

All great rods don't die; some escape both catastrophe and senility. But they survive in collections, like pinned insects, as a matter of record. In one notable collection is a priceless "gold" rod. Its history belongs to a brasher era, when the president of a kerosene company (which grew into Standard Oil) refused to be outdone by royalty. When this captain of industry heard that Queen Victoria had a rod with all-gold fittings, he decided to match her. He commissioned America's top rodmaker to make him a rod with all-gold ferrules and reel seat — then had all the metal intricately engraved by the finest gun engraver of the day!

In the same collection is a more modest, yet more historic rod.

It was the favorite of Theodore Gordon, who, before his death in 1915, pioneered and established dry-fly fishing in America. The many excellent rods of the great Edward R. Hewitt seemed to have escaped the collectors, even though Hewitt died less than two decades ago. His grandchildren don't know where they all went. Have they fallen unceremoniously into the hands of the great-grandchildren? I hate to think that these rods might be suffering the same fate as my grandfather's ten-foot Thomas. I well remember using it with a quarter-ounce sinker, fishing for flounders off Cape Ann, Massachusetts, when I was a larcenous and untutored eight-year-old.

Sadly, great rods are being ruined or retired faster than they are being built. Demand for the very finest easily exceeds supply in our affluent society.

One hundred years ago, production was also negligible. The ardent angler made his own rods and perhaps a few extras for his friends; these rods of ash, lancewood, or greenheart, while finely finished and ferruled, were relatively simple in construction. Rod guides were often simple unbraced rings which flopped as the line struggled through. Samuel Phillippe changed all this.

The art of lamination had been used in older bows; in the early nineteenth century, English rod tips of three-part design were used, and some glued work must have appeared then. Phillippe was an Easton, Pennsylvania, gunsmith who fished. He made violins as well. With the skill of a minor Stradivarius, he revolutionized the trout rod.

What was probably the first entire split-cane rod appeared in America in 1848—Phillippe's "rent and glued-up cane" rod, as it was called then. He wisely chose the six-part, hexagonal cross-section, which offers a flat, glued plane for flexion. Nine-, eight-, five-, and four-segment rods would be tried and discarded.

Phillippe's son, Solon, and later Charles Murphy, learned from the master. In 1870, the great self-taught builder Hiram L. Leonard began varnishing wonderful rods in Bangor, Maine. Thomas, Edwards, and the elder Edward Payne, whose son James became the finest rodbuilder who has ever touched a plane, learned at Leonard's bench.

George Parker Holden, a hobbyist and writer on rods many

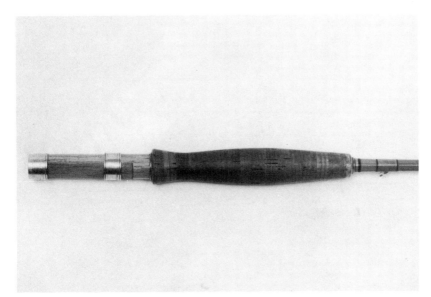

Close-up of typical Leonard trout-rod hardware. Grip shape is not standard, but light-colored reel seat and slip ring are.

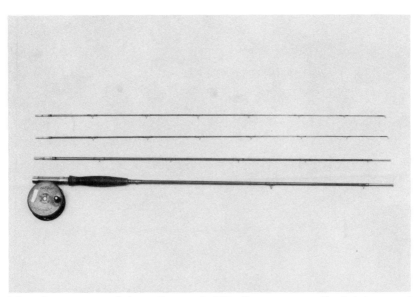

Nine-foot trout rod from Leonard. Windings are usually brighter and bamboo tone lighter than somber, monotone Paynes.

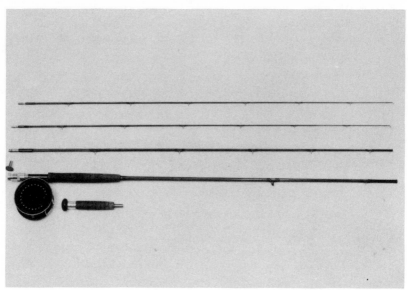

Ten-and-a-half-foot single-handed salmon rod by Jim Payne. Small butt-plug pulls out, extension is inserted for playing fish.

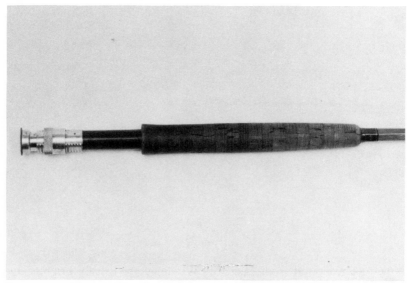

Distinctive Payne cork grip and hardware. Notice that the screwlocking mechanism is at rear, keeping reel near grip.

years ago, made his own, and trained Everett Garrison, an architect, to build by fits and starts for the custom trade.

But one day several years ago, Jim Payne told a friend, "I'm leaving the shop, I don't know when I'll be back." He died a month later. The announcement of his death in the New York papers precipitated a run on Abercrombie & Fitch's stock of used Payne rods — his output had been low for years. Paynes have doubled in price; the big salmon rods, which he stopped making about twenty years ago, are worth $750, prime condition, against $150. Younger hands struggle to keep the Payne shop going. Pinkey Gillum, Payne's fine apprentice, who built rods independently for years, had been dead for nearly a decade when Jim Payne left the shop for the last time. Nat Uslan, who also learned from Payne, retired a few years ago. Edwards, Thomas, and Garrison have all died. The masters are not being replaced.

The Charles Orvis Company in Manchester, Vermont, must be credited with offering the contemporary angler a fine rod on the retail rack. Their 2,500 pieces a year, along with the production of Young of Detroit, Winston of San Francisco, and Leonard of Orange County, New York, barely touch present demand, despite the inroads of glass. Very little that is wonderful is coming out of England or France, and the Japanese seem to have failed as rodmakers.

What makes one rod great, another mediocre? Materials and workmanship. The trout rod is pared to an irreducible minimum, a trend that began when the dry-fly method reached fad proportions under Theodore Gordon's tutelage in the early 1900s. False casting, short float, and recasting made the old ten-foot rods instruments of torture after an hour or so of fishing. Builders competed for lightness by sixteenths of an ounce. While the salmon rod remained a symphony, the dry-fly rod became a quartet. The slightest flaw in taper or action is quickly transmitted to the hand. The real devotee pursues his jewel-sided quarry with bamboo; glass is rare in the top trout clubs.

Bamboo, the muscle and sinew of the rod, is a large grass of which there are many species, sizes, and qualities. The first rods —perhaps Phillippe's original rods—were built of Calcutta bamboo. Today this is porch-furniture bamboo, not rod material.

Modern rods are built of what is called Tonkin bamboo, said to be found only in a small area in southern China. One legend has it that only those stalks that grow on the hilltops are first rate, because they have been strengthened by resisting the wind. Another story is that this bamboo has ceased to exist in a wild state and is a cultivated crop. Most likely, there are several species of bamboo that have the desired strength and straightness for rod building.

A store of well-aged and dried canes of this type is the rodmaker's bank account. They are eight feet long, three inches in diameter, and may have cost only $2 apiece. They are the first key to quality, as is the stock of hackle necks or a particular strain of live roosters to a fly-tyer.

But even a plentiful supply of the best cane is no assurance of perfect materials, for individual canes must be specifically selected for special tasks. Here a knowledge of the microscopic construction of bamboo and how it works is essential. A cross-section of a piece of bamboo reveals small, powerful fibers that run the length of the section of cane and are embedded in a relatively neutral, but binding, matrix. A closer examination of this cross-section reveals that these fibers are very close together on the outside of the cane, or nearest the exterior enamel, and that they become less and less dense as you approach the pithier interior.

A rodmaker examines this cross-section very carefully as he selects a cane for a particular purpose. If he is going to build a seven-and-a-half-foot dry-fly rod, he looks for a cane with a dense cluster of fibers on the outside edge. He may have to examine and discard several canes to find this type. On the other hand, he may find one with an exceptionally dense power structure running well into the interior. This is a special prize, but not for the seven-and-a-half-foot trout rod. This cane he marks and puts away for use in a larger, more powerful salmon rod.

Only when a suitable cane has been selected from an already highly-selected batch of bamboo can the work proper commence. This consists of turning a single piece of cane into a fly rod of several sections, each of which is made up of six separate but absolutely equal slices of bamboo. While this fact of hexagonal structure is widely known, it is also often the sum total of an angler's knowledge about bamboo rods — even among men who own several of the finest. Yet, this is about the same as a sports-car driver knowing only that cars have four wheels!

Actually, the hand-making of a fine rod is part art, part craftsmanship, and it is a lengthy and painstaking process. Here are some of the major steps involved in the order that some, but not all, rodmakers follow.

First, the selected cane is split in half and the partitions inside each node are cut out with a gouge. If the rod is to be the popular seven-and-a-half-footer, in two pieces and with an extra tip, one half is split into six equal sections and put aside for the butt section. The other half is split into twelve pieces for the two tips. The pieces forming each section are cut and arranged with nodes staggered so that no two fall opposite each other. Pieces are numbered so they can be reassembled in the same sequence.

Each piece is then placed in a V former, and the two split sides planed to an angle. The nodes, which protrude slightly on the enamel side, are then filed approximately flush, and now the eighteen strips are ready for straightening. If the bamboo had been sawed into strips — as is the case with many high-quality rods made by larger concerns — this step would not be necessary. But Tonkin cane grows straight once in a blue moon; normally, split-cane sections veer off a few degrees at each node, and it is at these awkward natural joints that the rodmaker sets to work.

Fortunately, bamboo has very plastic qualities when heated to a certain, rather high temperature. By holding the node over a small lamp and turning it carefully to prevent burning or charring, bamboo may be straightened by applying moderate pressure, and the strip will hold its shape after it has cooled.

The straightened strips are then heat-treated to give them the extra steely quality that even well-seasoned cane does not possess. It would be easier to do this baking after they had been planed to size, but the process causes some shrinkage that might make the final rod thinner than planned. It is best to heat-treat before planing even though the extra hardness will make the planing a bit more difficult.

Hours of this delicate work make all the pieces of each section alike to within one-thousandth of an inch. The strip is placed into a V form which has caliper adjustments every several inches; all pieces comprising that section are cut flush to the form. Only two sides of the strip may be worked on. A cut off one side. Turn the strip. A cut off the other. Near the end of this process, the enamel, which has no power, is removed with one clean stroke. No further planing on the rind side is permissible on a fine rod.

From the artisan's point of view, the rod is now done; its final action and feel have been fully imprinted into the bamboo. Of course, there are many hours of work left: glueing and pressure-winding the strips, trueing them up, seating of the ferrules, fitting the grip and reel seat, winding and fixing the guides, and three coats of varnish. But though it must be meticulously done, all this is journeyman's work.

A top rodmaker says it takes him a minimum of twenty-five hours to make a rod. Working hours—not counting the hours and days he must wait for glue or varnish to set. I think he's underestimating his labor considerably.

When you consider that the top custom-made trout rods sold for as little as $100 only ten years ago, the economics of fine rodmaking seem incredible. Without figuring in the rent, the materials, or the tools, the finest craftsmen in the field were probably making less than $4 an hour!

But these are proud and devoted men. You stand in line for a rod. Often you have to wheedle and cajole. I know one board chairman of a huge company who waited a year and a half for his nine-foot salmon rod. Finally he called the rodmaker and approached the matter with tact. He was told, "I haven't had time to start it yet. I'll call you when it's ready."

Another builder, troubled by telephone interruptions, calmly ripped the old-fashioned receiver off the wall and went on about his business.

It was a fine, monastic life, at $4 an hour.

The trade cannot possibly survive; but the rods, and the tradition, do.

12

Dream Tackle

Although I may be too old to believe in the Tooth Fairy, I am not yet so calloused by the years that I can't enjoy my own grown-up gift fantasies. One of my favorite daydreams starts with an imaginary rich relative telling me to pick out for myself the two finest fly-fishing outfits I can find — regardless of cost. Sensibly enough, one is to be for trout fishing and the other, a bit heftier, for Atlantic salmon and the like. There is only one condition: this must be tackle I will fish with regularly, not museum or elaborate presentation pieces that might be resold for a mint.

Outside of that there are no strings attached and no obligations. This is important. Since I can't pay for this gear and I can't profit by reselling it, I won't be snatching the bread from the hungry mouths of my children. I can even assemble the rods and swish them fondly through the air right in front of my wife without the tiniest twinge of guilt. The advantages of this particular wish-fulfillment game are enormous and it beats counting sheep when you're tossing and turning in bed.

Have you got the rules straight now? Then put your money away and let's go shopping.

We'll look at rods first. Reels are not nearly as important and should be matched to the particular rod chosen, anyway. Lines, too, must fit the rod and with the new AFTM numbering system and the many excellent floaters and sinkers now on the market, this will be the easiest part of the game.

Since money is no object, I will look at bamboo rods only. This is not snobbery or affectation. I know that good fiberglass and graphite rods will cast farther per ounce of rod, and when I'm occasionally granted a third outfit for saltwater work one of these easily comes in first. But for ninety-nine percent of all freshwater fly-fishing, sheer distance is not the first consideration. Synthetic fiber rods are also more durable and virtually maintenance-free but these qualities don't turn my stubborn head, either. I don't mind the extra task of wiping bamboo dry and caring for it after fishing any more than I feel put upon when I clean and oil-wipe a fine shotgun. Come to think of it, I rather enjoy the ritual.

No, the reason why I will choose split-cane rods for both outfits is that they are not only lovelier to look at, but they are sweeter in the hand than any others and they seem to present a fly more delicately. Why this is so I cannot explain or prove. Perhaps it's because they are solid instead of hollow. Perhaps it's because split cane is a living, organic material. (After all, fine leather feels better than vinyl, rubbed wood better than plastic.) Or it may be that the finest bamboo rods have been tapered and tailored with an artistry that mass-produced synthetics can never capture. If you've ever fished with a great split-cane rod you'll know what I mean, and perhaps you can explain the difference to yourself.

My choice of length for a trout rod will surprise you only if you haven't read Chapter 7. I will want something between eight and nine feet. Shorter rods may be interesting conversation pieces and even quite adequate for specialized situations, but I'd never choose one for all-around trout fishing. A rod of that length would make me work too hard to cover the river and, more important, it would leave more line on the water, causing drag to set in much sooner after each presentation. I know from experience that ultra-short rods are more tiring, despite their lighter weight, and that they are inferior trout-catching tools.

On the other hand, a rod of over nine feet might seem superior for all the above reasons, but such is seldom the case. Really long single-handed rods can be tiring for the rapid-fire casting that's often necessary in trout fishing, and a bamboo rod that works best with a #5-weight line starts to lose its decisive, crisp action after a certain critical length. I have handled many delightful 8½-foot trout rods, and I'm pretty sure I can find exactly what I want in this length.

For salmon fishing I will want a longer, stronger rod, and since I won't be casting or false-casting nearly as frequently I'm sure I can handle one all day that measures from 9½ to 10½ feet. The longer rod will give me slightly better control of the speed of my fly when wet-fly fishing, and since I will only be making a cast every thirty seconds or so my arm won't complain. Another advantage of this longer rod over the now-popular eight-foot salmon stick is that it casts farther with less effort and will let me pull more line off the water for the back-cast without stripping in so many coils of line before the lift-off. While it can be argued that the short rod can cast just as far with the double-haul, casting is not the same as catching. You will spend much more time false-casting (and checking for leader knots!) and stripping in line for the lift-off than I will with my longer rod. My fly will be fishing the water and not flying through the air many more minutes each hour than yours will, and with the better line control and mending capabilities of the longer rod my fly will be traveling at the proper speed during more of each presentation, too.

There's only one drawback to my 10½-footer. When I change to a dry fly to cover a rolling fish I haven't been able to raise with a conventional wet, I will have to admit I have too much rod for this tactic. The frequent false-casting to dry the fly and the staccato presentations weary my arm in a few minutes. I can fish a 9½-footer with comfort this way, but it's not my ideal wet-fly rod. The great Edward R. Hewitt always used a 10½-footer for dry-fly, but he was made of sterner stuff than I am. How do I solve this wet-dry conflict? Compromise. A ten-footer gives excellent control for wet-fly fishing — which I find is about eighty to ninety percent of the fishing — and is also feasible for dry-fly work if I pace myself.

This ten-footer will have a lot of backbone, and I'm sure the maker would suggest an AFTM #9 or heavier for it, but I will match it with a selection of #7s and #8s. The reason for this is that I will be pulling forty feet or more of line off the water with its superior length and will false-cast fifty, sixty feet or more line in the air when wet-fly fishing. Since rodmakers estimate only thirty feet of line out beyond the tip in their calculations, my rod will be fully loaded with these lighter lines.

I have now decided on the lengths and strengths of my two ideal bamboo rods and that leaves only the brand or maker up for grabs. This is a ticklish situation since bamboo rods are as much individuals as people are, and no two, even of the same measurements by the same maker, are alike. Though several companies and makers are turning out excellent rods to this day, most of the superb ones I've handled came from a slightly earlier era. I'll probably choose a rod that was varnished during the golden age of American rodmaking—the '20s through the '50s.

Does this mean that with the whole world of rods to choose from, I'll end up with some second-hand stick? Well, yes, but let's not put it that way. If Cadillac can call a used car "previously owned," I can label my rods "previously cherished." Or look at it this way. Yehudi Menuhin and Jascha Heifetz aren't performing with brand-new fiddles, either. The violins they play are over two hundred years old and may have had dozens of previous owners.

Among rods of the great makers that I have seen and hefted, the ones by Jim Payne seem to have the edge on the average, and I think most fine-rod fanciers agree. Not only are they most beautiful to behold but their actions and feel are nearly always ultra-pleasing. An awkward or "sour" Payne is so scarce as to be a collector's item.

However, this is tackle for fishing, not for bragging, and I may end up with a Garrison, Gillum, Halstead, or even a rod by some lesser-known custom rodmaker. In fact, there's always the possibility that I'll be persuaded by a particularly choice rod by Thomas, Leonard, Orvis or one of the other excellent production companies past or present. But the percentages say I will end up with two Paynes that have had a lot of care and little fishing wear and tear, just as a concert violinist would probably choose a Stradivarius if he could take his pick from all the violins in the world.

We're coming down the home stretch now, with only reels to go, and again I find that we have just passed the pinnacle of design and workmanship. This is partly due to the confiscatory costs of hand-machining and partly to the current craze for ultra-lightness.

For a trout reel I can choose almost any model I want because I need one with some weight to counterbalance my 8½-foot rod. The Hardy Perfect reel, discontinued about ten years ago, will be my first choice. It is more reliable and can withstand more punishment than the lighter-frame reels being turned out today, and I know it will last me a lifetime and then some. I have seen fifty-year-old Perfects that have been used steadily and heavily and are even smoother than the late-production models. One with a 3⅝-inch diameter seems to balance best with my chosen rod and I know that, like a fine vintage wine, it will only get better in the next ten or twenty years.

Weight will not be an important consideration in choosing a salmon reel, either. In fact, one too light might tire my hand and cramp my fingers. I can think of four reels that are perfect for my ten-foot rod: the old Hardy Cascapedia, the Vom Hofe, the Zwarg, and the Walker. They all look alike, seem to be built on the same principles, and all are finely machined. Unfortunately, only the Walker is built today, so I might as well take one of their new ones. The size 2/0 balances my rod best and I prefer the model with a gearing advantage to take in line more rapidly.

Two Payne salmon rods: a rare twelve-foot, two-hander with a Vom Hofe reel (top) and a single-hander with Hardy Perfect.

Lines, as I've said, are easy to choose. I will need floaters, sinkers, and sinking-tip styles in size #5 for trout and size #7 (plus a few #8s for very windy days) for my salmon rod. I have no strong preference for any one brand among the top-quality plastic-line manufacturers. The good ones seem much alike to me. I will, however, also want a few silk lines that I can grease up for high floating and easy pick-up, and these are still being made in England.

And that's about it. I have now assembled the two finest fly-fishing outfits money can buy (or so I feel) and the good news is that money can, indeed, buy them. The rods and reels (minus the unspecified number of lines) could be picked up with a little hunting for about $1,000, and an astute or patient buyer might shave $100 or even more off this. Not a sumptuous sum really, when you consider that used private planes, sports cars, and fine shotguns come in at several times this much. This may be dream tackle, but it's a dream that's not so impossible if you can squirrel away a bit of cash after taxes.

So here we are now, back to the dream-game where this all started. It's an enjoyable game, as I've said, and there's even an ace-in-the-hole blessing to it. If, after shopping, comparing, buying, possessing, polishing, and assembling these outfits you still can't manage to get to sleep, be of good cheer. You can now start fishing the choicest sections of your favorite rivers and streams with this dream tackle, and if this secondary gambit doesn't lull you into slumber, so be it. Can you think of a more enjoyable way to spend a whole night of insomnia?

13

The Deadliest Lure

There is a popular notion that flyfishermen are people who nobly impose an artificial handicap on themselves to make the catching of fish more difficult. But it just isn't so. Fly-fishing may be noble in its ideals; it is also devastatingly effective. In an appropriate form and properly fished, flies offer sport that cannot be duplicated by the wood or metal or plastic gadgetry of other lures.

Consider the evidence. For trout, the case is easy to build. Flies were originated to kill trout. The fragile aquatic insects which are the staple trout diet break up when skewered on a hook. Something more durable had to be created—and created it was, some two thousand years ago according to surviving records, and perhaps artificial flies were no novelty even then. The worm and the minnow may have their innings under certain conditions, but the fly is the most consistent trout killer and has been for centuries.

No less an authority than Edward R. Hewitt stated that the skillful nymph fisherman was the only man who could clean a stream of sophisticated brown trout by legal angling. And the nymph, though a fairly recent refinement, is very much a fly and in the classic tradition of close imitation.

Further proof is provided by the fact that professional fishermen use flies, perhaps not exclusively but very regularly. In

France, anglers who make a living by supplying restaurants with wild trout taken from heavily fished public streams use flies most of the time. In high water or when they're after a specific large fish, they may turn to the spun minnow, but they earn their daily French bread during most of the season with the fly. And I might add that the best of them may be the finest trout fishermen in the world.

The same is true in Spain. Men who fish the few public salmon rivers in the north use flies regularly when the water is neither too roily nor too deep. And when you consider that the average Spanish salmon can be sold for as much as a laborer earns in two months of hard work, you can be sure that the fly is no affectation there.

Trout and salmon may be the traditional victims of the fly, but all game fish, except perhaps those which live in unreachable depths, are highly susceptible to fur and feathers. Spinners, plugs, and naturals are not so universally effective, regardless of what their adherents may claim. New York State employs an expert fisherman to check populations of lakes, ponds, and streams and to catch fish for scale samples. His quarry are mainly smallmouth and largemouth bass, yet he uses a fly rod exclusively and claims that an orange streamer is his most effective lure.

Even commercial tuna fishermen in the Pacific use flies. For on the end of those two- and three-pole rigs with which they yank tuna into the boat there is a special quick-release hook covered with white feathers. And large white-feathered jigs have been used for decades by sport fishermen and commercial trollers.

Of course, the flies just described wouldn't be recognized as such under a New England covered bridge. Are, then, these large minnow and squid imitations really flies? In one sense yes, and in another no. The Spanish say no. They make a clear distinction that is surprising for a country not noted for its sport fishing. There, a fly that imitates an insect is properly called a *mosca*, while a streamer or salmon fly is a *pluma*. I think they are right in calling one the fly and the other the feathers, but our own language has no such nicety.

However, the English definition has its merits, too. Both the dainty insect imitation and the large feather squid owe their effectiveness to the same qualities — qualities that separate them

Modern minnow-imitating and attractor flies shown against a catalogue page picturing those of our grandfathers' era.

from the live bait, spinners, or solid wobbling plugs. First and foremost of these is the action of feather, fur, and hair. They breathe, wiggle, and kick in a unique manner when drawn through the water. And perhaps equally important, all these materials are translucent in the water, as are insects, minnows, elvers, or squid that they counterfeit.

In the beginning, of course, was the wet trout fly. In fact, until about a hundred years ago it was *the* fly. The great blossoming into many styles for many types of fishing is a rather recent development, and testifies to the high quality of the materials that flies are made of.

The artificial nymph, for instance, is merely a refinement of the basic wet fly, and it came out of England at the turn of the century. Probably the great Frederick Halford of dry-fly fame was indirectly responsible for its development, although he was to fight till his dying day against the use of nymphs. It was Halford who established the doctrine of exact mimicry in dry-fly fishing. So successful was he in implanting this ideal that wet-fly fishermen took to more exact imitation of the underwater, or nymphal, forms of aquatic insects. Under the leadership of G.E.M. Skues, the nymph fishermen fought the Halfordians for over a quarter of a century. While neither side ever won a clear-cut victory, the literature that resulted is some of the most spirited in the entire angling library. Since the turn of the century, the nymph has appeared in a wide variety of patterns. It is not only a recent invention but an extremely important one, for Hewitt was right in his estimate of its efficiency on wary fish such as the brown trout.

The streamer fly and its cousin the bucktail are purely American in origin. One story has it that a man was fishing with a large wet fly when the throat hackle broke, unwound, and streamed out behind the fly. This accidental lure was an immediate success and an idea was born. After all, big trout and landlocked salmon feed heavily on minnows, and a hackle feather of suitable color, undulating along the hook-shank, makes a very likely imitation, as we now know. However, the story is considered apocryphal. Officially, the streamer is credited to Maine fly-tyer Herb Welsh, and the date is recorded as 1901.

The bass fly was also developed in this country. In its older, purer forms, it is basically a huge trout-type wet fly, usually in one of the brighter patterns and dressed as fully as possible to make it a chunky mouthful. You don't see this type of fly around much any more, though. The big streamer fly has largely replaced it. And the exciting surface lures of clipped deer hair are becoming more popular each season. They mimic such delicacies of the bass menu as frogs, dragonflies, crayfish, and even mice. If hair-and-feather minnows and squid are to be considered flies, then these hair-bodied counterfeits would also seem to fit the category. And they do catch fish with gratifying regularity.

But unquestionably the most important fly development in recorded history is the dry fly. Here, too, there has been progress in recent years but, surprisingly, not because of any great advances in the science of entomology. Ronalds' *The Fly-fisher's Entomology* was published in England in 1836 and is still widely quoted. While it may be a taxonomist's horror (it avoids Latin names, preferring terms like Pale Watery Dun), it speaks the angler's language. In America we have no such single standard work. There have been valiant attempts like Ernest Schwiebert's *Matching the Hatch* and Art Flick's *Streamside Guide to Naturals and Their Imitations.* Schwiebert dealt with the entire United States, while Flick limited himself to New York's Catskills. Both books are often very useful. Yet I know a stream ecologically similar to Flick's Scoharie, and not forty miles from it, where half of the important insects bear no resemblance to Flick's favored dozen. Apparently, America is too huge, too rich, and too diverse a habitat for any one man to entomologize. This may be an argument in favor of the slight leaning toward impressionism discernible in many modern American flies.

There has also been a trend toward drabness, simply because drab flies seem to work well on our streams. No longer are flies designed primarily for brook trout in ponds, as they once were, because the ecological picture has changed. The colorful artificials which were used for that purpose evolved into bass flies.

Finally, there has been a trend toward chunky, less delicate dry flies on both sides of the Atlantic, and this has a simple explanation. Trout streams in most well-populated countries have a higher percentage of newly stocked fish each year. These trout must remember the hatchery mouthful better than the mayfly. They simply go for something which looks like an insect and is fat enough to rivet their attention. The highly selective wild brown trout of Halford's day are now hard to find, and today's flies reflect this change in conditions.

Furthermore, many more fish are considered game species now than in the late nineteenth century, and many more sportsmen have learned to use the fly rod. This has resulted in an incredible proliferation of both classic patterns and relatively new ones. Even if a fisherman finds himself on strange water with nothing to match the hatch precisely, he can switch from fly to fly until he finds a good one, or he can shop for local patterns. Being inexpensive, flies encourage experimentation.

Of course, certain of the oldest classic patterns are still with us in pretty much their original form — dries like the famous Blue Dun, wets like the Wickham's Fancy, Coachman, Leadwing Coachman, and Royal Coachman. They are far too effective to be forsaken. But excellence has not hindered experimentation. For instance, it was discovered quite early that some dry flies could be tied as wet patterns to imitate drowned insects. Hence, we have both wet and dry versions of the great Quill Gordon, Light Cahill, Greenwell's Glory, Gold-Ribbed Hare's Ear, plus many newer patterns.

Through experimentation by anglers and professional fly-tyers, the list is constantly lengthened. Among the relatively new and vastly popular wets are the Fledermaus, the Muddler Minnow streamers, and the woven-hair-bodied nymphs which are now being used extensively in the Rockies. And recent years have brought fame to such dry patterns as the Rat-Faced MacDougal, Gray Wulff (and other Wulff variations), Jassid, Irresistible, and a whole batch of small midges and terrestrial insects, such as beetles and ants. These little terrestrials, which originated with the "Pennsylvania school" of fly-tyers, have provided still further possibilities for dry-fly experimentation.

The name of the actual inventor of dry flies has been lost—if, indeed, one person was the inventor. Late in the nineteenth century a number of factors made the development of the dry fly almost inevitable. One was the introduction of the split-cane fly rod. Here was an instrument that could not only reach out to shy fish in clear, low water, but could also flick the droplets off a fly and dry it on the false cast. Then came the vacuum-dressed silk

A present-day fly collection showing the wide range of sunk flies: nymphs, emergers, wet flies, streamers and lures.

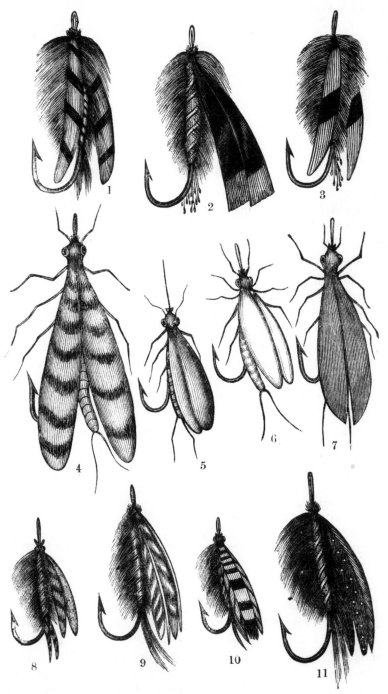

"Exact imitation" is hardly a new idea, as these artificial stone flies and caddis flies from the last century prove.

line that brought out the potential of the bamboo as the older braided horsehair and linen lines never could. And perhaps most important of all was Henry Sinclair Hall's perfection of the mass-produced, eyed trout hook. Before it appeared on the market in 1879, trout hooks were "blind." Their tapered shanks were whipped to a piece of gut or to a single strand of horsehair. Changing a sodden fly for a fresh one under those circumstances meant changing the leader, or at least part of it. Without the eyed hook, dry-fly fishing would have been too tedious to become popular. And it was with the rising popularity of the dry fly late in the last half of the nineteenth century that the hackle feather became the rightful center of fly-tying attention. For a dry fly must float on its hackle tips, and most of its effectiveness depends on hackle quality and color.

Halford and his crew of dry-fly zealots had little difficulty obtaining their feathers. Since their numbers were small, their demands were not large. As a matter of doctrine, they cast only to rising fish; this meant that even mediocre hackle could be used, because the fly had long periods of inactivity in which to dry off. Lastly, cock fighting had been abolished as recently as 1849, and many a stiff-hackled cock still strutted the British barnyards.

The dry fly was launched in America in 1885, when Halford sent a set of his dry flies to Theodore Gordon in New York State. Gordon was an inventive and observant sportsman. He realized that Halford's flies imitated British insects and that insects on this side of the Atlantic were quite different. He originated many impressionistic imitations of the naturals he found on his own favorite streams—the Quill Gordon being perhaps the most famous of his patterns. His flies seem a bit large-winged to us today, and the style of winging has changed slightly, but the present-day master tyers of the Catskills carry on his basic tradition.

The first American book on dry-fly fishing didn't appear until some twenty years after Gordon began his experiments, and by the time the dry fly became really popular here, a bit after World War I, the materials situation was becoming acute. First, American demands on hackle were far more severe than Britain's. Our streams are more turbulent than Halford's stately chalkstreams. Only the very stiffest hackle would do. Then, too, our insects are larger, and a bigger, heavier hook has to be supported. And, finally, casting only to the rise doesn't work well here. An angler must prospect likely water in our mountain streams, rise or no rise. So the fly must float, cast after cast, with only a false cast or two to dry it.

Even today, there is no synthetic dry-fly hackle on the market, nor any miracle chemical that can transform soft hackle into needle-sharp barbs. Superb hackle can float a fly unaided, but the pioneer dry-fly anglers in England often resorted to coating the hackle with paraffin solutions. Theodore Gordon frequently used kerosene. Until a few years ago, standard fly-line dressing was dissolved in gasoline or the less flammable carbon tet. Now we have the superior silicone preparations, which represent another advance in fly-fishing, but this is not to say the problem has been solved. Poor hackle still floats poorly.

By the time the dry fly gained wide acceptance in America, the source of hackle supply was diminishing. Not only had cock fighting long been outlawed here, but the agricultural revolution had transformed chicken-raising into a mass-production industry, to the detriment of the hackle supply. Birds were now bred for fast growth and plump breasts, or for greater egg production. Certainly not for first-class hackles. And to top it all off, most cockerels were killed for fryers when only months old.

To see the full implications of this fly-tyer's nightmare, you must understand a few facts about the nature of the bird that bears the indispensable hackle. All of our current breeds of chickens are descendants of a wild bird from India called the Bankiva fowl. The males of the species are extremely polygamous and, hence, highly combative. While the females have unimposing neck feathers, the males have long, stiff, glossy hackles, which protect the vulnerable neck and throat area from the leg spurs and beaks of rivals. Since the bird that survives the fight gets the hens and begets the chicks, birds with the stiffest neck feathers prospered. The process of natural selection toward stiff neck feathers was started in the wild and continued until cock fighting was outlawed. Then the purveyors of eggs and white meat stepped in, and the tyer had to scout the ever-decreasing subsistence farms for a source of supply.

How then, you may ask, is the current army of several million flyfishermen supplied? The answer is, poorly — except for the anglers who deal with top custom tyers. General stores, hardware stores, and even sports shops have to take what they can get.

Most of the hackle is soft, and half of it has been dyed — a process that further reduces the quality of already indifferent hackle. The necks are bought in bulk from importers who buy them by the hundreds of thousands in India. Most of these necks are ginger, red, or white—useful colors, but not the full spectrum a tyer would like. A few of the necks are first-rate, and you're fortunate if you can pick and choose from a boxful. But commercial houses can't afford such sorting and discarding. Surprisingly, top-notch flies can still be obtained if you know the right professional tyer. There are a few of these men left, yet very few young tyers are coming up. The reason is that there's no money in producing quality flies.

A tyer must raise most of his own roosters. True, some necks in the more common colors can be picked up from a friendly importer, but none is likely to be found in the all-important shades called natural duns. These are a slaty blue-grey color, and fly-tyers have made their reputations on their dun hackles. To get such hackles, birds must be bred, crossbred, pampered, and plucked, and the price of doing this is almost confiscatory. Yet nearly half of the most popular dry flies call for this shade, and a dyed feather always shows a bogus blue or purplish tinge when held up to the light—which is precisely how a trout sees it.

To get the natural duns, you have to raise a lot of birds. About fifty percent of the eggs hatched will produce cocks, but only a few of them will have top-quality hackle. Then, too, the blue-dun color is recessive. No matter how you breed, you'll end up with lots of badger (white with black center), black, and white hackles. Only a small percentage will be true duns.

Since I myself have raised birds for hackles, I can readily understand the economic plight of the professional tyer. It cost me $10 a year per rooster just for the special small-grain feed that hackle-producing birds are supposed to have. It takes two years for birds to reach full maturity, so a bird has eaten $20 worth of feed before he starts producing.

With luck, a bird should produce excellent hackle for several years. A prize rooster is seldom killed; he is plucked with tender, loving care three or four times a year.

Curiously, despite the costs and risks of trying to raise excellent hackle, flies tied with these superior materials by the finest artists of the day cost only pennies more than run-of-the-mill shop-tied flies. I once asked Walt Dette, the master fly-tyer of Roscoe, New York, why this should be so. "It's all the traffic will bear," he explained. "After all, trout flies are expendable. The average guy leaves several of them in trees during a day's fishing. Who'd pay a buck for a fly?"

There is only one factor that sweetens the pot for independent, custom tyers. There's no middleman. The feathers go straight from rooster to fisherman, and fly-tyer takes all. Even so, most fly-tyers drive old cars. And the finest craftsman that I ever knew gave it all up to work in a barbershop a few years back. Once a man has paid for the hooks, thread, wax, and other purchasable materials — not to mention costs of rooster-raising — he can't tie much more than $8 or $10 worth of flies in an hour. If machines

Wild jungle fowl rooster and subservient mate as seen in Asia. This strain is disappearing—and so is our best hackle.

were available, the economic picture might be brighter. But every fly must be tied from start to finish by hand.

What, then, keeps the few remaining perfectionists in the business? Pride, certainly. The good life, probably, too. Tyers live near good fishing and shooting. But there seems to be more to it than that. They are celebrities in the eyes of dedicated fishermen. Their advice is sought by presidents and board chairmen. You stand in line to get their flies and you don't dare annoy them even if your order doesn't arrive by opening day.

Since the basic materials of most flies have always come from the barnyard, it's natural that there's a touch of barnyard earthiness in some of the flies themselves. One all-time favorite is named the Cow Dung because it imitates a green-bodied fly that is usually found on meadow muffins. Another classic is the Tup's Indispensable, invented by R. S. Austin of Tiverton in Devon. The exact dressing of this killing fly was a closely kept secret for years. Sound business was one reason. Victorian prudery another. For how would you explain to a nineteenth-century gentlewoman that the beautifully translucent yellow body was dubbed with urine-stained hair taken from the indispensable portion of a ram, or tup?

The famous Hendrickson dry fly originated by Roy Steenrod, an early pupil of Theodore Gordon's, has a similar origin. The body is dubbed with fur from the crotch of a red fox vixen, which has a permanent pink stain.

Those are some of the more esoteric materials—including a few of the most expensive ones. Feathers, and particularly hackles, are still pivotal to fly-tying and to fly-fishing, but long evenings at the tying vice produce a lot of experimentation. In streamer flies, maribou stork feathers with their octopus-like action are rivaling bucktail and saddle hackles. Silk floss and similar body materials have always had their place, but newer materials are now finding other uses. For instance, tarnish-proof strips of Mylar tinsel are showing up more and more in the wings of these flies.

Bucktail flies obviously get their name from the deer tail of which they're made, and this material has always been plentiful. Because of its texture, consistency, and length, it is valuable for many wet-fly effects. In a way, its versatility makes it more valuable than that special hair from a vixen. The deer hair that's being displaced nowadays in streamers is popping up in, of all places, dry-fly dressing. Many of the shaggy but effective Wulff flies have bucktail tails and wings. Harry Darbee's inspired Rat-Faced MacDougal and the series of variations that have followed it sport bodies of clipped deer hair.

These flies may be a bit chunky for delicate mayfly imitations, but they are the only flies that will float in a downpour. And since a pelting rain can knock enough insects out of the bushes to make a pool boil, such flies represent another deadly set of lures.

In wet flies, fluorescent flosses are also appearing these days—particularly in the bodies of salmon flies. They give off a glow on dark days or in the depths, causing many anglers to swear by them. Synthetics aren't really new; J. W. Dunne of England popularized them back in the Twenties. In *Sunshine and the Dry-Fly*, he advocated a series of artificials with bodies of cellulite floss over white-painted hook shanks. When annointed with oil, these bodies had a succulent translucency. They haven't been on the market since World War II, but new types of brightly glowing synthetics are being tied into wet patterns.

These changes in materials and in flies tell a lot about trends in fishing. Most of Halford's original split-wing floaters were winged with dun-colored starling primary feathers and epitomized the ultrarealistic approach. Theodore Gordon leaned toward bunched wood-duck flank feathers glimpsed through the hackle. He was an impressionist. Darbee's Rat-Faced and the Wulff flies are highly utilitarian and offer a good mouthful. Experimenting with shapes can probably go just so far, but experimenting with materials, from the dullest to the most garishly fluorescent, will probably never end.

Happily, the materials used for wet flies, nymphs, and streamers, whether new or old in dressing style, remain in good supply. A Royal Coachman, for instance, utilizes golden-pheasant tippet, peacock herl, red silk floss, red-brown cock or hen hackle, and white primary goose or duck quill. A fly-tyer has little trouble obtaining these items.

Salmon-fly materials felt the pinch early in this century when many feathers were proscribed by international treaties. Indian crow, cock of the rock, toucan, and bustard disappeared from the salmon-fly repertory, but suitable and effective substitutes have been found, and the fully dressed fly of today is hard to distinguish from its nineteenth-century prototype (though smaller, less fully dressed salmon flies have also gained wide acceptance).

Fortunately, the banned feathers were used mainly as color accents. The most widely used exotics—golden pheasant, English jay, summer duck, florican, European kingfisher, blue-and-yellow and red-and-yellow macaw, silver pheasant, and the rest—are still available to fly-tyers even though they can be quite expensive.

The demand for these materials is not increasing, because salmon-fishing tactics have changed considerably. In the good old days, it was mainly an early spring and late fall sport. Salmon were considered uncatchable in low water and warm weather. The British now use smaller, less colorful, more sparsely dressed flies during the summer and have opened up a whole new season for the sport. And in Canada the fishing is mostly from late June through September, and the same small, relatively drab flies are now most popular there, too.

Most of these flies are winged with hair or with the natural plumage of various ducks like widgeon, teal, and mallard. Usually such feathers are relatively easy to obtain from hunting friends, but bulk shipments from overseas are under continuous attack by the National Audubon Society. While the Society's main objection is to the use of the feathers by the millinery trade, tyers feel threatened, too.

The Audubon people are worthy opponents. A few years ago an Audubon friend of mine told me with some satisfaction that a member of his chapter was head inspector of feathers for the New York customs department. "You fly-tyers can't fool him," he claimed. "Why, he can tell what kind of bird almost any feather comes from, and you can bet he catches lots of contraband shipments." I had the last word, though. I told him that a fifth-generation salmon-fly tyer I knew who came from Ireland could do that dead drunk. And, when sober, this man could tell which square inch of the bird the feather came from and estimate the bird's age accurately! He really could, too.

Of course, these economic and legal tugs of war that plague the fly-tyer are little noticed by the world at large. Only once, to my knowledge, did fly-tying hit the headlines. Late in the last century, a man was killed in northern Ireland following a heated discussion about the precise shade of dyed seal's fur that should be used in dubbing the body of Michael Rogan's Fiery Brown salmon fly. However, one has to suspect that some fiery brown liquid may have been more to blame for this crime of passion than the fly itself.

When fly-tyers and flyfishermen do make news, it is generally conservation news which appears in publications devoted to the subject or is, unfortunately, relegated to the back pages of the papers. For these men are extremely active in conservation groups that fight pollution, wanton industrial development of wild areas, and similar threats to wildlife. And even though flies are so deadly in expert hands that they may, as Hewitt stated, take every trout in a stream, the flyfisherman is the trout's best friend. He may catch ninety percent of the trout that are netted on our hard-fished streams, but he understands that running water will support only so many fish, and he knows of the scarcity of running water itself. He releases most of the fish he catches, to avoid depleting a limited population.

His sport allows him to do so, and this is another angling advance that is virtually unique to the fly. A fly-caught fish is almost always lip-hooked and easy to release. Treble-hook plugs and spoons and bait hooks which are easily swallowed are another matter. Studies have shown that nearly half of all worm-hooked, undersized trout soon die. The comparative figure for fly-hooked fish is three percent, and this estimate is not restricted just to barbless flies; the figure would be much lower for the many flyfishermen who carefully remove the barbs from their hooks.

So, even though the lure may be deadly, the man may be merciful. And there's wisdom in this. It's better to enjoy golden eggs than to eat goose.

14

The Curious Case of the Caddis

"The little log cabin that walks" seems to fascinate young children more than any other common animal. I think it was the first of nature's great mysteries pointed out to me when I was very young, and I was astounded when I discovered there was a "bug" inside the bundle of twigs. I also remember being told this crawling creature was a caddis, but that was about the sum total of my knowledge about these insects until I'd waded well into my trout-fishing adulthood.

Surprisingly, most fishermen I talk to today know little more than that, and yet, if mayflies may make up the butter in trout diets, caddis flies are certainly their daily bread. Many of the larval forms — especially the log cabin that walks and similar species—are readily available to trout, day and night, winter and summer, as they crawl slowly over the rocks without cover or camouflage. Mayfly nymphs, on the other hand, are more a feast-or-famine proposition, for most of them hide under rocks or debris or burrow in the sand during the greater part of their lives until they have to expose themselves in hatching.

In early spring, especially, the trout's dependence on caddis larvae has become part of our folklore. An old-time Yankee mountain-brook fisherman once gave me the word on trout behavior while he was cleaning his mess of opening-day brookies.

"See all that sand and gravel in the gut? That's ballast. Keeps him from being washed downstream in this high water. That's why you got to get down to them in April. You can't put on too many split shot. Their bellies got them anchored to the bottom."

The man's remedy may have been right, but his diagnosis was all wrong. Trout aren't smart enough—or dumb enough—to eat pebbles and gravel. They don't need it for their crops as wildfowl do, and they have no use for that much roughage to keep regular. You find such stuff in trout stomachs along with pine needles and small twigs only because that's what the meal of the day comes packaged in. And the cased caddis larva is by far the most readily available form of insect food in nearly all our running waters.

Mayflies may be the foundation of our fly-fishing practices, but the much-neglected caddis flies play at least as important a part in the trout's scheme of things. On many acid Eastern streams they far outnumber the mayflies. On the limestone streams of eastern Pennsylvania and in some mineral-rich waters of the West the balance may tip the other way, but the caddis never come out worse than a close second to the mayflies and are far more important than the stone flies and the true flies put together.

Even the number of separate species seems to rival the range of the mayflies. In the British Isles alone some 189 species of caddis have been identified. And here in North America, where we have many more disparate ecological regions, the count is far higher: 568. This tally was made back in the Thirties, but the dean of caddis collectors, when he added them up at that time, admitted that his own research—and the work of others he quoted—had all been done before 1910 and they had probably only scratched the surface. It seems reasonable to suppose that we have nearly a thousand species here, though we won't know for certain until the taxonomists pay more attention to the order of Trichoptera. And that, in case you want to dazzle your friends, is the official Latin name, meaning hairy-winged, for the entire order of caddis flies. But there are far more useful things fishermen should know about them.

Caddis flies are close relatives of the moths. Both orders of insects have pronounced antennae and both have wings covered with small scales; they advance through similar life-stages, they look much alike in their adult forms, and they're both attracted to bright lights at night. Moths, however, are usually heavier in the body, their antennae are fancier, they tend to fold their wings in a horizontal plane rather than in the inverted "V" of the caddis, and, of course, they spend their formative days on land instead of under water.

In the beginning, all caddis flies are minute eggs which quickly separate from one another after they've been deposited as a cluster by the mated female. At this stage in life, and at this stage alone, the insect is probably safe from the hungry trout. The speck-like eggs are far too small to be picked off the bottom if the fish notice them.

Once they have hatched out and started to grow as worm-like larvae, caddis are eaten by trout at every opportunity. Caddis, for some reason, appear to be especially delicious. I have seen some stone flies that are carefully avoided by trout and I know of some mayflies that the trout feed on only occasionally and indifferently, but I have yet to see a caddis that wasn't gobbled with relish. Caddis are so tasty and nutritious that trout are not deterred by the abrasive houses of sticks and stones most species stick together with a silklike secretion, though these protective casings may help fend off smaller minnows and carnivorous stone flies.

During this longest stage of their lives, caddis show a great diversity in color, size and lifestyle. Most species are vegetarians, feeding on live algae or on dead forms of larger vegetable matter such as leaves and blades of sedge grass, but a few are definitely carnivorous, preying on fellow caddis and on other aquatic insects. Some types manage without the protection of the "cabin," or turtle-like carapace, never building any cases at all for themselves. They live under rocks or in crannies, and a few of these highly specialized varieties spin small, spider-like nets to strain food out of the passing current.

All these types of caddis larvae are undoubtedly eaten by trout, but the case-builders, the ones that lead relatively exposed lives, probably contribute most heavily to the trout's diet. Fishermen have been imitating these cases for years, yet the artificials have never been very popular. One of the earliest and most famous is the long, bristly "Strawman" which is tied out of deer hair and is a good general replica of many large, case-building caddis species.

The problem with case-builder imitations is that they are

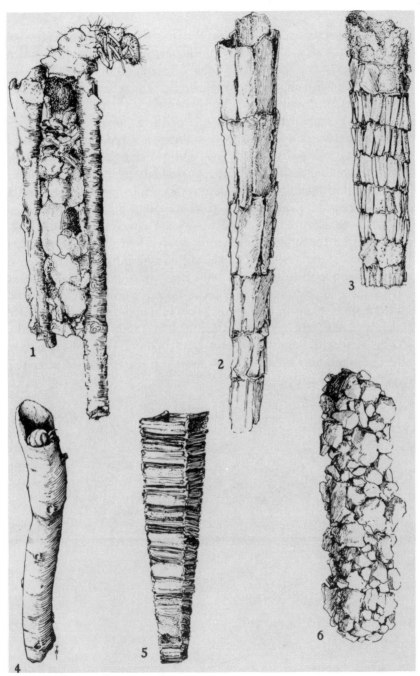

Case-building caddis construct their houses in many shapes and out of many materials. The prevalent shad fly lives in #5.

difficult to present realistically in flowing water. It may be easy to drag them slowly along the bottom with a sinking line when fishing ponds and lakes, but how can you mimic this bottom-creeping behavior in a river when the current keeps hurrying your line and leader downstream? And when the river is high and roily — the very time when caddis are drifting down-current in an easy-to-imitate manner — the less-abrasive large stone flies and mayflies are being dislodged, too, and most anglers prefer to fish with the popular artificials of these suddenly available nymphs.

The caddis larva itself, when removed from its case, has a strong enough appeal to trout so that it is a highly popular live bait all over Europe. The great American naturalist, John Burroughs, used the stick-caddis worm as live bait for brook trout as his first choice whenever fly-fishing became unproductive — or so a friend who knew and fished with him once told me. Why trout have such a hearty appetite for the naked worm they never see without its clothes on baffles me. A while ago the outdoor writer Raleigh Boaze sent me some beautiful imitations of large caddis worms tied with semitranslucent latex bodies. They're extremely effective, another proof of the trout's phenomenal if puzzling appetite for the caddis.

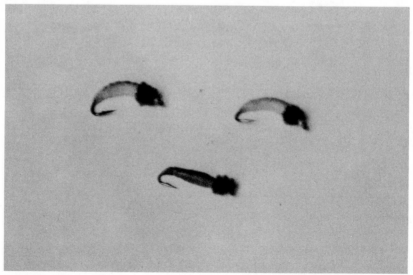

Caddis larvae imitations with latex bodies as tied by Raleigh Boaze. Trout never see them this naked—yet they work.

Once the larva is fully grown, which usually takes a year, it anchors its case firmly to a rock with silk threads and covers up the open end of its house. At this stage it becomes semidormant, taking no food for a week or two. It has now entered the semifinal, or pupal, form and is starting to look a little more like the winged insect it will become. If you pull the animal out of its case at this point, you will see its embryonic wings drooping small and dark along its sides and the long adult antennae wrapped elaborately around its body. In this walled-up, motionless state, the caddis is less tempting to the trout (and is difficult for the angler to imitate) but this armistice doesn't last long.

When the pupating caddis is finally ready to advance to its final stage in life it must run the gauntlet again. It then chews off the cover of its case and shoots rapidly to the surface, propelled by its long, oar-like middle legs and given a further upward assist by a bubble of gas that's forming between the pupal skin and the rapidly developing adult, winged insect inside.

This combination of buoyancy and swimming proficiency makes the emerging caddis a difficult target for even the nimblest trout. In fact, because fish miss so many at this time, one of the surest signs that trout are feeding on caddis instead of the more easily captured mayfly is the sight of an insect zigzagging upward from a boil on the surface. An emerging caddis is tantalizing, and trout can't resist chasing it, even though it's one of the few insect foods they miss with great regularity.

If the trout are having trouble with the caddis at this stage, the fisherman is in an even worse predicament. How can he make his sunk imitation perform like a small rocket taking off for the surface? The only way I've found to duplicate this is to wade directly up-current of feeding fish, stop the cast so that the line falls in a series of loose curves in front of me, and wait till the current pulls the line straight. If I've estimated the distance to the trout's lie accurately, the fly, which has been sinking on the slack line, will start for the surface when the line pulls tight. This is an exacting presentation, however, that calls for perilous wading, and you put down a lot of good fish stumbling down the middle of the current trying to execute it.

And this is only the beginning of your problems. What should your imitation look like? Even if you're familiar with the species of caddis that's hatching out, having studied both the pupae and the winged adults, which form should your artificial favor? How rapidly is the fly developing as it shoots up toward the surface? How does its color appear to the fish when viewed through the gas bubble that lies between the gray, chitinous skin and the living insect inside? These are questions that few anglers can answer. I've never met anyone who's actually observed an emerging pupa making its explosive trip to the surface, and I've talked to many dedicated anglers who've raised larvae in their aquaria in the hope of just such a sighting.

Imitation of this stage in the insect's life, and of its mercurial behavior pattern, is the least explored frontier of fly-fishing and perhaps the most promising one. I have been experimenting for several years with imitations of a few of the more common species and I have to admit I've had no great successes to date. I have had best results with gray- or gray-brown-bodied imitations, though I hesitate to give this as a general prescription. I know one caddis species that has a bright green body as a pupa but acquires a brassy dun color a few seconds later as a mature adult. I've had good fishing with both colors at different times during this hatch, but neither one works well all the time and I sometimes wonder if it isn't the presentation rather than the imitation itself that's responsible. I'm afraid I'll have to bring you more problems than solutions at this time, but I know several expert flyfishermen who are working in this area and perhaps there will soon be a pool of knowledge available on emerging caddis.

Although the most important species of caddis I'm acquainted with seem to emerge in this manner, not all the many species do. I know of at least one early-season caddis that crawls out on rocks or logs to hatch the way most stone flies do. And I have every belief that some types hatch under water, as the Quill Gordon mayfly does, making the trip to the surface as mature, winged insects. There seems to be no pat solution to imitating emergers, and perhaps that's a blessing. Fishing might not be so much fun if we knew all the answers.

Many emerging caddis probably never make it to the air, even though they temporarily escape the trout. As we have all observed in the case of hatching mayflies, a considerable proportion are malformed or damaged in the act of emerging from their nymphal

Imitation of the emerging caddis pupa with low-slung, short wings. Is this the way they look to trout under the surface?

cases, and these unfortunates drift downstream till they are eaten or drowned in a rapids. Then, too, since weaker specimens of the smaller species probably have difficulty in fighting their way through the rubbery film of surface tension, many must drown at the edge of success. Perhaps for this reason, a great addition to our fly boxes during caddis hatches would be accurate imitations of adult insects patterned on the old wet fly which could be fished dead drift.

We must suppose, however, that at least a majority of the pupae hatch successfully and present the fisherman with another challenge. Some specimens seem to shoot out of the water, fully fledged like a Poseidon missile, while others don't make such a clean getaway. They buzz and flutter on the surface erratically for a moment or two before they become airborne. To a trout that has probably recently missed an emerger right at the surface, this is too much to resist. And this is where presentation of the adult, winged imitations takes over. But before we look into imitations and the methods of presenting them, it's important to realize that there are other times, too, when trout will be looking for and feeding on adult caddis flies. Once they've hatched, these flies don't die in a day or so the way mayflies do. Adults of some species seem to take nourishment or at least water during their winged state and live for several weeks in this form instead of the day or so allotted to the mayflies. This is important, for the caddis that have hatched out on previous days will probably return in flights to the river in the evening whether or not this is the night when their mating and egg-laying will take place. Admittedly, many of them remain several feet above the water on the upstream flight, but a significant number also fly just off the surface and occasionally touch the water. Can you imagine anything more exciting to trout than a cloud of flies easily visible overhead? When a fly does make a mistake and come within reach, the rise is usually explosive.

Then, of course, there are the mated adults that have finished with their nightly water-play and are nearing the end of their lives. Many of the males probably fall dead or dying on the surface, while the females buzz, hop, or skitter on the surface in the act of egg-laying. Again the trout feast on easily available adults. Why most fishermen have neglected dry imitations of the various caddis species over the years baffles me. Trout look for these flies, rise to them, then look for more. And the major caddis hatches last longer than mayfly hatches. The emergers, water-players, and egg-layers of some species appear on or over the water night after night for more than a month.

The dry fly at these times is the logical choice and yet very little attention has been paid to floating caddis imitations. Frederick M. Halford, who launched the dry fly in Britain nearly 100 years ago, included five caddis patterns in his final selection of 33 dry flies recommended for the chalkstreams of southern England. But when his flies and theories crossed the Atlantic a few years later, only the mayfly imitations seemed to survive the passage.

Fortunately, caddis imitations of sorts did spring up in several regional forms here in America, but most were far less accurate and effective than Halford's original quill-winged replicas. All-hackle flies, including bivisibles and variants were, perhaps, intended to be loose imitations of caddis with their wings aflutter. The Adams from Michigan is said to represent a caddis, but, though it's one of the few great all-purpose flies, its outline looks much more like a mayfly to me. It is from the free-wheeling West rather than from the effete East that our best early caddis imitations came. I've recently seen high-floating patterns with down-wings of elk or deer hair which appear to be true regional innovations that have been used in the Rockies and the Far West for years. As impressionistic artificials for fast-water fishing they are hard to fault, except, perhaps, for the limited color-range.

No matter how realistic the artificial, however, it can't do the whole job by itself. The caddis silhouette is certainly unique and needs accurate duplication to deceive the trout, but the *behavior* of the insect on the surface is equally distinctive, and classic dry-fly presentation makes no accommodation to this fact. Caddis flies are far more active than mayflies are, and the purist's dead-drift approach doesn't seem to telegraph the caddis message to the trout.

Caddis hop, flutter, and bounce on the surface. Duplicating this behavior with a dropper fly danced on the surface was easy for our great-grandparents with their 10-foot-plus rods and light lines, but you can't begin to do this job with the stubby sticks that modern flyfishers use. The most likely tactic with modern tackle is to cast to a fish across and downstream and give the fly a little "nudge" just before it passes over the fish's lie. This "sudden

The most popular caddis imitation in past years has been the killing Adams. Tail and wings seem mayflyish to me.

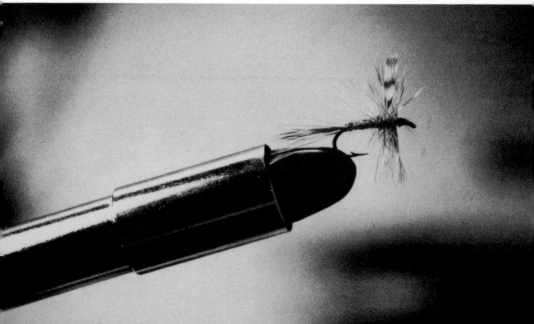

inch" will more than double your rises when fishing a caddis imitation if—and this is an all-important *if*—this staccato minimotion is in an *upstream* direction. Caddis always fly upstream, whether they're hatching out, returning for the fun of it, or egg-laying, so any motion in any other direction shouts "fake" to the trout.

I realize that moving a dry fly in any way or in any direction is in strict violation of the classic dry-fly code laid down by Frederick M. Halford. I was given a vivid reminder of this fact a few years ago. Shortly after publication of my book, *Fishing the Dry Fly as a Living Insect*, I ran across Sparse Grey Hackle at a famous fly-tying-materials emporium. Sparse, in case you've never met him in person or through his books, is so universally acknowledged as the dean of fly-fishing writers that it is rumored he has connections with our patron, St. Peter. He is very definitely a man to be listened to. Sparse, on this occasion, walked up and said, "Congratulations, Len. I hear you've just written an entire book devoted to the ancient art of trolling." He is the kindest as well as the wittiest of men and there was a twinkle behind those bottle-cap glasses he wears. Nevertheless, I got the message loud and clear. I have not given up my sinful ways, though. I still twitch my caddis imitations and sometimes even my floating mayflies.

Since the caddis dry fly is best fished with vigor, it obviously must be tied in a style that floats extremely well. Variants and bivisibles fit the bill, but their silhouettes aren't realistic enough to fool many trout in slow or even streamy water. Bodies of clipped deer hair or cork aren't the answer even though they float well. Both types lie low in the water and leave a sizable wake in the surface film when moved — a behavior pattern that in no way resembles the tip-toeing caddis adult. The most effective fly I've found is built with stiff fiber wings — either of top quality spade hackles or of high-floating guard hairs of aquatic animals like the mink. This type of wing may sound a lot like the wing of the Western elk-hair caddis but, fortunately, I'd never seen those imitations when I started work on my designs or I'd probably have adopted the existing pattern and perpetuated their two shortcomings.

The first problem with elk or deer hair is that it greatly limits your choice of colors, while hackle and mink tail can be obtained, undyed, in almost any shade the tyer wants. More important, these fibers will lie absolutely straight and flat when tied in, whereas elk and deer hair, being hollow, will splay when pinched by the tying silk. This upward and outward flaring doesn't affect floating quality but it does alter the silhouette significantly. Next time a caddis lands on the outside of your window-pane at night examine it closely. What you'll be seeing is the "fish-eye view" from directly below—precisely what the trout sees when a caddis floats overhead. I think you'll be surprised at how trim and slim a caddis appears from this viewpoint when its wings are folded.

I named my patterns the *Fluttering Caddises* (because they should be fished with a slight motion, as if they were fluttering) and they are now advertised in the catalogs of several large suppliers and are obtainable at some retail tackle stores. Although most orders, I'm told, have come from Easterners, friends of mine who have experimented with these patterns out West say they're every bit as effective on the fast-water streams out there.

So, whether you consider them welcome friends or poor relatives, the caddises are very much with us. And as some authorities

The fluttering caddis gives up a point or two on exact imitation, but gains them back in mobility and floatability.

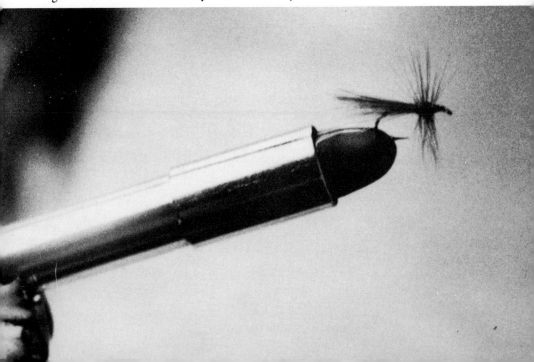

have pointed out, they're likely to increase in importance because they're a hardy tribe and aren't decimated by floods, marginal pollution, and stream erosion as are the more delicate mayflies.

Caddis flies differ from mayflies in many ways—in their life-cycle, in their longer seasonal availability to trout, and in their habits and appearance as adults. In their first several months of life they're important as trout food but a difficult proposition for flyfishers to duplicate in running water. During those split seconds when they're zooming toward the surface to hatch, they present problems both to the trout and to the angler who would imitate them. But once they hatch out, they're on or just above the surface for portions of many days—not just hours—or 10 to 20 times as long as mayflies are. Isn't this just what the dry-fly fisherman ordered?

15

Take Your Pick

Fly-fishing wouldn't be half the game it is without the alibi, the reason why not. The big one may have got away (he almost always does), he may have refused—definitely—our most choice offerings, but that is never the end of it. The angler takes defeat hard. When forced to admit that he has indeed lost at Armageddon, he rises to the occasion—with an explanation. Drag. The leader—too long or too short, too heavy or too light. The fish—highly intelligent. But we overlook perhaps the best—and most valid—excuse: the fly itself. I know I did, until that morning on Colorado's Gunnison River.

It was a beautiful June day, and this was my first trip after four wartime, fishless years. The hatch was on, the fish were rising, and I was working a long, gliding pool that looked as if it should produce something extra special in the way of trout. I tied on a #12 Ginger Quill and proceeded confidently to the business at hand. Five casts and no fish later, it was apparent that something was wrong. Puzzled, I picked an insect out of the eddy behind my waders and checked it against my imitation. In size and color it was a close double. Must be drag, I thought, and started casting a wavy line. It was five minutes before I got any attention. A fish came up under the fly, followed it back, and dropped down again. But he had taken a good close look at my fly, and, for the first time, so had I.

What was it doing? Well, it was riding tail down, eye pointing skyward. I tried another fly. This one was better. A fish even nosed it once. But it had flaws. On almost every cast it lay flat on its side, wings touching the water, a far cry from the tiptoe-prancing naturals that were coasting down from the riffle. And so it went. I got some good fish, but it wasn't a star performance.

Since that long-ago trip I've examined thousands of flies and worked out a set of standards for the ones I use. The average trout-fisher, who doesn't tie his own flies and who therefore probably doesn't scrutinize each imitation very carefully, may find these criteria helpful. Remember: All flies are *not* created equal—not even those tied by the same man and displayed in the same compartment on the tackle-store counter. And this is just as true of flies you've tied yourself, by the way. Some will definitely be better than others. How do you pick out those that are most likely to succeed?

A good dry fly is a thing of beauty and a joy on the stream. But it's easier to get a dud in this category than in any other. Little things are magnified when it comes to floaters. Only the very best cock properly. The first thing to check is the wings. Are they the same length? The same width? Are they unsplit? Turn the fly so

Left: a good dry fly. *Right:* all the mistakes—skimpy tail, uneven body, short, scraggly hackle, and uneven wings.

that you're looking it straight in the eye, which, by the way, must be closed properly. It can cut a leader or slip off if it isn't. From this angle, the wings should be just two curved lines. If one or both are slanted off to the sides, the fly will behave like a propeller—and that's bad.

Are the wings directly on top of the hook? I don't mean they shouldn't form a V—and how wide a V is purely a matter of taste—but if you extend the line formed by the bend of the hook to the top side of the hook, it should bisect the angle made by the two wings. If it doesn't, the fly will probably ride off-kilter.

Now take a look at the hackle. It's pretty hard to judge the quality of hackle without a lot of experience. Chances are all flies in the same box were hackled from the same rooster anyway, so don't worry much about hackle stiffness unless you're shopping from store to store. Some flies may be more heavily hackled than others, though. I pick bushier hackles for fast water and sparse ones for slower streams. Beware of the short-hackled fly. Sometimes the tips of the hackle extend no farther from the shank of the hook than the point does. Try to pick out flies that have a hackle length that measures from 1½ to 1¾ the width of the hook gape. Flies that are too short in the hackle have the habit of lying on their sides.

Moving back toward the tail of the fly, give the body a casual check, even though this part is the least likely to fail. If it's made of quill or fur, it should be wound smoothly, without bumps or bare spots. Sharp trout teeth can catch on bumps and bare spots and start unraveling the body.

Now to the tail itself, a prime danger spot. A defect there can cause a lot of woe. Flies from the same lot may show a great resemblance in tail length and tail bushiness, but if you look closely, you'll find a certain amount of variation. Pick the longest and the bushiest—within reason, of course. It's hard to overdo on this point; for every fly that lands on its head (too much tail), there are ten that land tail down. One final check. Drop the fly on the counter from the height of a foot or so. If it lands just the way you'd like to see it on the water, you're in. Even if it doesn't, the odds are pretty good if it answers in all other respects.

Follow the same general procedure for other types of dry fly. With hairwings, like the Wulff flies and the Irresistibles, your

Splayed tail fibers of this dry fly (seen on water surface) add to floatability and proper cocking without bulk.

special interest should be concentrated on the wings; after all, they're at least twice as big. If they aren't perfect, you're in for it! Be sure that the hair bunches are closely matched in amount of fiber and in length. I always avoid the flies with the longest wings, no matter how perfectly matched they may be. Too much wing can make the fly top-heavy, so that it rolls on its side after hitting the water.

Watch the tail section on variants and spiders. With all that long hackle up front, it stands to reason they need a longer and thicker tail than usual to make a perfect two-point landing. Bivisibles seem to be the easiest to pick out, the hardest to miss on. No matter how they're tied, they seem to float perfectly. I like them evenly hackled, though, and tapered toward the tail.

One last point on this category. Nothing, not even a woman's mind, is changed as often as a man's dry fly. It makes sense to choose one with some shank showing between the hook eye and the winding. This space will make it easier to pick off that little piece of leader left when you snip off a fly and prevent it from unwinding at the head.

Any fly will sink, after a fashion, but that doesn't mean you shouldn't be careful when you choose a wet fly, though I grant you an error here isn't nearly so fatal. Check the eye of the hook for perfect closure. Look for smooth heads, well lacquered against inadvertent unwinding. Inspect the body carefully. You can pretty nearly disregard the size and shape of the tail, though. As long as it's there it will do the job. Wings aren't crucial either, but they should be evenly matched and dead-centered for better swim. Don't short-change yourself on tinsel. Pick the shiniest; it's put there to glitter.

Hackle problems are few and far between on sunken flies. Do choose sparse flies, though. (After all, an insect has only six legs.) They sink better and they ride better in the current. I learned this fundamental a few years back on New York's Beaverkill River. My bushy March Brown wet looked plenty buggy to me, and the fish seemed to agree. They kept hitting it, anyway. Trouble was, I wasn't hooking many. A check of the hook point proved that sharpness had nothing to do with failure. Frustrating hours later I hit on the culprit—the fly. It was riding flat on its side. When I slacked off, it sank, hook down, as it should. But when I pulled on it, the fly went over on its side.

A poor wet fly: lumpy body, hackle too long, wings oversized and so uneven that fly will not swim properly through water.

Good wet-fly design: even, low-lying wings, sparse hackle, and slim body promise good entry and good travel in current.

I began pruning with a vengeance. The next time that fly hit water it had only a few wisps below the shank, and the point of the hook keeled it perfectly even in the swift current. I started to fill the creel then, and every fish was hooked firmly in the lower jaw.

The same reasoning should be applied to nymph selection. The sparser the hackle the better. Be sure also to check the eye of the hook and the head and to look for smooth, even bodies — unless it's one of those shaggy beasts.

With streamers and bucktails I go for the sparser models, too, mainly because they sink quicker. Otherwise I simply check the head and eye. If the body is tinseled, I go for the biggest shine. It's not a bad idea to look over the feathers or hair; they should be centered on top. If they're too far off, a streamer won't keel well either.

It's hard to go wrong on a big bass fly. They're usually tied on such heavy hooks that they ride perfectly, no matter how bushy. Besides, they're retrieved a lot slower and in much slower current. Again, head, eye, and body are the key places to inspect.

I don't know whether deer-hair bass and trout bugs should be classified as flies or not, but here are a few pointers, anyway. Be on the lookout for bald spots when you check the bodies. They'll float better and they'll be less likely to shed and unravel if they're uniform. And by all means pick the ones that are clipped closest to the hook shank on the underside, added insurance that they'll land right side up every time. More important, it gives clearance to the hook point, which means more fish per strike.

So much for the rules. Let's go one step further. Check on your judgment when you get to the stream. Suppose you are working with wet flies, streamers, and nymphs. When you tie on a new one, dangle it in the current close to you and see how it rides. Twitch it and see if it starts to flip over on its side. Now's the time to adjust with minor surgery, not after missing the best fish of the day. If you're a dry-fly man you can save hours of fruitless casting if you follow this one rule. Every time you put on a new fly, cast it straight upstream on a slack line and watch it carefully as it floats past you. Give it a few trials. If it's a chronic misbehaver, take it off and try another.

Remember, the perfect fly has probably never been tied. If it has, it was an accident. But most flies will work and work well. The idea is to choose the best from the better. Theodore Gordon, the father of American dry-fly fishing, advised the angler to "cast your flies with confidence." That's a lot easier to do when you know you've really *picked* them.

16

The Blue-Nosed Fly

Today it seems hard to believe that barely sixty years ago the English-speaking world was reveling in the strictest sporting code that man has ever imposed upon himself. Yet well within the memories of men still actively fishing in these days of as-you-like-it morals and will-o'-the-wisp values, the loftiest and most rigid sportsman's dogma of all time — the dry-fly purist ethic — held sway in America, in Britain, and in Britain's then-vast colonies.

So passionately were these rules of sporting honor upheld by Victorian and Edwardian gentlemen that breaking them was as unthinkable as striking a woman in public. A transgressor could expect to be called a blackguard, sent to Coventry, or even asked to resign from his club.

There had been rules governing sport for centuries, of course, but these were easy to understand and explain. They had evolved gradually from the code of chivalry which had swept out of southern France during the Middle Ages and had exerted a wide influence on all rituals and behavior. Since sports in those days were essentially war games for aristocrats, many forms of the chase had adopted the protocols that knights considered proper in combat.

In falconry, for example, there was as distinct a pecking order governing the ownership of birds as there was for position on the battlefield. The large and rare gyrfalcon was reserved for emperors and the like, while lesser nobility had to be content with lesser birds. Overstepping your bird-rank in those days promised even sterner social penalties than those meted out to today's junior executive who drives a Rolls-Royce up to the country club and parks it beside his president's Buick.

By the early nineteenth century, however, ancient war sports like falconry and chasing the stag on horseback had nearly died out, and war itself had become less chivalrous as shrapnel replaced the sabre. The knight's code did not die with him, though. It merely fastened onto other, newer sports, whether or not such behavior had any use or meaning, and here it continued to flourish as if it had a life of its own.

The accelerating technology that had made war more terrible had also brought new weapons into the sportsman's arsenal: reliable shotguns for fowlers, split-cane rods, waterproof silk lines, and light-eyed hooks for anglers. These advances made bird-shooting and fishing true sports, and even if these gentler activities didn't need rigid rules, the rising middle class that began taking to the fields and streams most certainly did. They were not to be cheated out of the delicious agonies of etiquette simply because the age of elegance had passed. They would do the proper thing at any cost, and archaic posturing made a pursuit just that much more "pukka."

Hardly more than a hundred years ago, these sports — in their modern forms — were still new. It was not long ago, for example, that game birds that had escaped the stoop of the falcon were rather crudely butchered for food after teams of spaniels drove the birds to nets. It was a far cry from the ritual of a modern Scottish grouse shoot. Fishing, too, had long been considered only a pleasant food-gathering activity. The revered Izaak Walton used live baits for all kinds of fishing quite unabashedly, and his *Compleat Angler* is more a picture of pastoral enjoyment than of formal sport.

Young queen Victoria and her friends found diversion in spearing salmon by torchlight on the rivers of her Scottish estates; this now-heinous activity was thought quite proper until the middle of her reign.

Even after the outlawing of salmon-spearing, salmon fisheries escaped the full force of the onrushing "sporting revolution" because salmon rivers were the jealously guarded properties of the nobility. To this day in Europe there is no stigma attached to using spoons, spinners, wobbling plugs, or even minnows, prawns, and worms sewn onto a murderous gaggle of treble hooks when angling for salmon — practices that would get you thrown off any decent trout water on any other continent.

Until Victorian times, a trout fishery was not considered to be of much value. The harvest of trout and other fish by countrymen was tolerated as long as the noble salmon was left alone, just as the gamekeeper might wink at a snared rabbit or two as long as

A century ago, fly-fishing on private Long Island preserves was a social

the hares, gamebirds, and stags were not molested. And yet this lesser fish, the trout, was to become the prime quarry, not only because it was more accessible to the new sportsman but because a trout feeds more on stream-bred insects — and is therefore more catchable on small artificial flies with fine tackle — than any other game fish of decent size.

And this is what modern trout fishing is all about: delicacy, refinement, artistry. Few anglers aspire to catching a blue whale on a power winch. But to take a five-pound trout on an artificial fly less than a quarter-inch long and tied to a leader that will break under a pound of pull — now that's an accomplishment. The

ritual. Elegant clothes were part of the scene.

trout's preference for an insect diet makes this feat a distinct possibility, while a pike, bluefish, or barracuda of similar size wouldn't even notice such a token lure.

Fortunately, the trout's habitat is populated by thousands of species of insects that spend most of their lives in or above or under the water. The mosquito and the mini-vampire black fly of the North Woods are probably the best-known members of this group because they bite innocent non-fishermen. The vast majority of these insects, however, such as the mayflies, caddis flies, and stone flies are fragile, harmless, delicious (to trout), and are recognized only by dedicated flyfishers and entomologists.

These insects spend ninety-nine percent of their lives in underwater forms, hiding under stones and debris, living on algae and other small organisms while breathing through external gills. Once they are fully grown, they swim, crawl, or float to the surface, split their skins, and emerge suddenly and miraculously as glistening, winged insects. In this form they take to the air, breed, lay eggs, and die in a few brief hours or, at most, days. Although the trip to the surface and the float downstream before take-off may require only seconds after a full year of grubbing and growing on the stream-bottom, this is the time when trout feed on them with abandon. When many flies are hatching out at the same time, as is often the case, a passable imitation of these small, delicate insects concocted out of fur and feathers can be very effective indeed.

And this is the ritual of modern fly-fishing. Insects are collected, studied, counterfeited, and presented on ultrarefined tackle. Outwitting the fish with cunningly contrived artificials is more important than the size or the quantity of the catch. Yet the game didn't start this way at all. The use of artificial flies for trout goes back nearly two thousand years, though it is seldom remembered that the original invention was in no way an affectation. The aquatic insects on which trout feed are simply too small and fragile to remain impaled on a hook when they are flung out over a river and so ersatz flies were devised that could take more punishment.

Primitive flies, or those in general use until the miracles of modern metallurgy came to the rescue, had to be fished "wet," or under the surface. When fish were seen snatching adult, winged insects directly off the surface, these primitive artificials may have been dangled or dapped on the water surface below the tip of a long rod, but the fly itself did not, and could not, float.

All this began to change when someone discovered that, by using the stiffest, most waterproof feathers (fighting-cock hackles) and ultralight hooks, flies could exploit the phenomenon of surface tension and float by themselves. The first printed record of this development occurs in 1841, but it wasn't until 1886 when Frederick M. Halford published *Floating Flies and How to Dress Them* that the dry—or floating—fly reached the world at large.

The most significant entomological discovery of the nineteenth century — to proper Victorians, at least — was not the malaria mosquito or the tsetse fly, but the dry fly that was pioneered on the chalkstreams of Hampshire. And its concept, its form, its manner of presentation, its every aspect was infused with the attitudes of the proper English gentleman. Even now there lingers an ultrapurist school of fly-fishing that offers a curious kind of snob-appeal to those who were not to the manor born. The Halfordian dry fly was very much a blue-nosed fly, a change-resistant emblem of what was then a new sporting peerage, a new but congenitally conservative fishing establishment.

Halford was an English gentleman who had fished with the less-remembered men who had pioneered this technique for trout: Henry Sinclair Hall, Dr. Thomas Sanctuary and George Selwyn Marryat. Halford was so taken with the beauty and delicacy of this new sport that he forsook money-grubbing in all its forms at a relatively young age to devote his life to the perfection and promulgation of the dry fly. Though his only original contributions to fly-fishing were several sets of exquisite and increasingly refined dry-fly patterns, his voice was soon considered second only to thunder over Mount Sinai.

As chief spokesman for dry-fly practice and its exclusive use, Halford laid out the rules in no uncertain terms. It was damnably thoughtless, he argued, for a chap to wade down the center of a stream setting up a miniature tidal wave and thrashing the water, left and right, with a team of wet, or sunk, flies and then ripping them back through the current. This time-honored practice might work at times, but it appealed to the noble trout's baser instincts,

A floating mayfly imitation tied with split, quill-section wings in the classic Halford manner. Still a killing fly.

it ruined the next angler's chances by frightening the fish, and it lightly hooked and lost many fish that would soon become so suspicious as to be virtually uncatchable.

The drill every gentleman should follow out of respect for both fish and fellow-fishermen, Halford argued, was the following. The angler should walk slowly along the stream-bank (no wading) until he saw a trout breaking the surface by feeding regularly on mature, winged insects that were floating overhead. A sample of the species of fly being taken should be captured, identified and an exact (as nearly as possible) imitation should be knotted onto the fine, tapered leader.

Now, from a carefully chosen position on the bank (preferably a kneeling one to avoid detection), the angler should cast this counterfeit in an upstream direction so that it will alight delicately a few feet directly up-current of the trout's feeding position. The upstream direction of casting is pivotal, for the fly must now float down-current completely unimpeded by the attached leader and line, just as the natural flies have been doing.

If there are any disruptive, intervening tongues of current between the angler and his fly, a further refinement in technique must be added to ensure a "dead-drift" presentation. The line must, in this event, be made to land in a curve, or in a series of curves, so that the resulting slack must first be straightened out before the pull of the line can exert itself—thus allowing the fly

The more impressionistic fly advocated by the Catskill school of tyers after Gordon. Wings, veiled by hackle, seem to buzz.

time to drift over the trout's nose before it is dragged unnaturally off course. The recipe ends up: Repeat at regular intervals until the fish grows suspicious and stops rising or makes a fatal mistake in judgment due to the flyfisher's (or fly-tyer's) consummate artistry.

To anyone who has ever yanked a hapless sunfish out of a pond on a hunk of worm threaded onto a penny hook, the imperatives of this method make the Ten Commandments seem as permissive as *laissez-faire*. Consider for a moment the "Thou-shalt-nots" this technique imposes.

First, you must *not* pay any mind to trout feeding underwater, but rather locate a fish feeding regularly on surface flies. Second, you must cast only to this fish and *not* prospect in likely places. Third, you must *not* appeal to the fish's carnal instincts by pitching in a succulent worm, minnow, crawfish, or any imitation of these. Fourth, you must *not* merely observe the general type of insect present in the habitat but must ascertain which species of fly and preferably which sex of this species (there are usually slight size and color differences between males and females) the fish is taking. Fifth, you must *not* concoct any impressionistic artificial that could represent a general type, for only an exact replica of this insect of the moment may be knotted onto your leader. Sixth, you must *not* multiply your chances by using two or more flies. Seventh, you must *not* better your casting position or angle of attack by now entering the water. Eighth, you must *not* let the situation dictate your angle of attack—your presentation— for your fly must be cast in an upstream direction. Ninth, it must *not* dip underwater but must be presented "dry," or on the surface only. Tenth, it must *not* be jiggled to attract the trout's attention or manipulated in any way to cater to the trout's killer instinct. Anything but dead drift is bad form and utterly unmannerly.

Can you imagine a longer or more blue-nosed list of blue laws? And would you consider applying them all to the pastoral pastime that Walton called "the blameless sport"? Yet this is precisely what the authorities decreed that trout fishing should be, and they were followed for decades.

Admittedly, this ultrarefined method disturbs the water little and it can, indeed, account for some notable catches on the clear chalkstreams where Halford and his friends cast their flies. But this type of water makes up less than two percent of Britain's total trout fisheries and a far smaller percentage in most other trout-producing countries.

These special streams in southern England (and a very few smaller ones across the Channel in Normandy) are unusual examples of the perfect environment for both trout and dry-fly fishers. All the water entering them is filtered through several hundred feet of pure chalk and then metered out from deep springs with a nearly constant flow and temperature, winter or summer, flood or drought. The advantages of this rare type of river system to both fish and their food are phenomenal.

During its six-month travel through the organic chalk, rain water absorbs rich carbonates and other minerals to the maximum of its carrying capacity. As a result, chalkstream water, gallon for gallon, is twenty times as fertile and productive of trout food as water from the average mountain stream. But that's only the beginning.

Since deep springs discharge water that's nearly the same temperature all year around, it's never too hot or too cold to put off the feeding and digestion of the trout or the rapid growth of their insect food. And, because this flow is nearly always constant in volume as well, there are no destructive floods to hurl fish and food downstream, nor are there punishing droughts to diminish the size or the amenity of their habitat. If trout had ever been granted the divine power to create their own promised land, the weed-paved chalkstreams that slide through the water meadows of Hampshire would have more than filled the bill.

These precious few streams were considered paradise by elegant anglers too. One didn't apply for a rod privilege here any more than one invited oneself to a Duke's party. One waited and hoped to be asked. Fishing rights, whether owned outright or leased by a club, seldom changed hands, and when they did the price was likely to be far higher per yard of bank than on even the choicest salmon rivers to the North.

From this trout-fishing Eden, the high priest, Halford, and his acolytes sent out their pronouncements to Wales, Scotland, Canada, New Zealand, America—to all points of the trout-bearing world. Did it matter that northern tribesmen or Colonials had few water-meadow banks, placid pools, hatching mayflies, or rising trout in their tumbling and unfertile mountain streams? Not a whit. A gentleman fished the dry fly for trout, upstream and drag-free, and that was that.

Fashionable Americans in the Northeast, taking their cue from Britain, as was their custom, quickly embraced the floating fly. Large portions of streams and pond-studded forests were leased or bought up by individuals or groups so they could practice their sport without competition from bait or wet-fly fishers.

In the early years of this movement, before lodges and summer residences had been completed, elite New Yorkers worked out an exclusive system for trout fishing without tears. On Friday nights these gentlemen would dine elegantly at Delmonico's and then head for Grand Central Station where a special Pullman car had been reserved. Here they bedded down, presumably at a reasonable hour, and slept while their hotel on wheels was taxied up to the Catskills or Adirondacks and parked on a siding. This was their clubhouse for the weekend and, on Sunday night, they were towed back to the city in time to appear at their brokerages or businesses at the proper hour on Monday morning. No traffic, no wear-and-tear.

Many of these estates and clubs exist intact to this day. The dry-fly code is still followed on many choice, private sections of New York and Pennsylvania streams where sunk-fly fishing in any form is looked upon as a mucker's or fish-monger's game.

In defense of Halford, it must be noted that he never condemned the use of the sunk fly as categorically as his followers did (at least not in print) and the excesses that ensued may have been due more to the fanaticism of the disciples than to the preachings

Frederick M. Halford was the supreme authority for three decades. His pronouncements rivaled those from Mt. Sinai.

Although he went to all the right schools—
and rivers—Skues was pitched out for one
small deviation from Halfordism.

of the master. Whatever its origin, dry-fly exclusivity became an
ethical issue and the wet-fly forces, despite occasional rebuttals
from the North Country and the Colonies, were excoriated in
issue after issue of *The Fishing Gazette* and in the elite Journal of
The Fly-Fisher's Club of London. Purists quickly gained the upper
hand, for theirs was obviously a position of superior moral
rectitude.

Then, in 1910, when the Halfordians were at the peak of their
power with no new worlds to conquer, a man in Halford's peer
group and one who also fished the chalkstreams began to rally the
routed wet-fly anglers. In that year, G.E.M. Skues published
Minor Tactics of the Chalk Stream pointing out what the trout's
stomach contents had proclaimed for years: Trout take over
ninety percent of their insect food in its underwater, or nymphal,
form and less than ten percent as winged adults off the surface.
Why not, Skues proposed, cast an exact imitation of the various
mayfly nymphs to fish that were seen feeding on the naturals
rising toward the surface to hatch?

Consider, for a moment, the modesty of this proposal. Skues

had no intention of flogging the water indiscriminately, and he agreed to cast only to fish seen feeding actively on insects. He didn't ask license to wade. He promised to present only an exact imitation of the nymph in question—not the old, winged wet fly that was considered a lure or at best a nondescript—and he agreed to fish it drag-free or without any enticing motion. But couldn't he just fish it slightly *below* the surface film where trout took ninety percent of their insect food instead of on top?

He most certainly could not!

The battle raged anew. Sunk-flyfishers came out of hiding to rally around their champion. But the establishment had the last word and it was a crushing one. Poor Skues was forced to resign his rod-privilege on a choice river (for which he had been paying a handsome annual fee) and was exiled to find his fishing wherever he could!

World War I, which was then looming, changed Britain beyond all recognition—at least from a Victorian point of view. And World War II, a cruelly few years later, ushered in an era of even more accelerated change. Today the thrust of English angling innovation and literature has turned toward still-water trout fishing on the many new reservoirs and hydroelectric impoundments. Modern British trout books concentrate on midge pupae, diving beetles, stickleback minnows, and the like—a ragtag assortment of sunk flies that would have shocked even the liberal nymphman, Skues.

The chalkstreams are still there, of course. Their clear, cool, fertile waters continue to flow over beds of curling waterweed, and they are still the choicest, most expensive trout waters in the world. But they no longer dominate trout-fishing thought and theory. Not in Britain nor anywhere else.

Today, Halford's grandson lives in the valley of his ancestor's beloved River Test—the greatest of the chalkstreams. Skues left no descendants. But his spirit would be content in this valley. His appeal for a more sensible fly-fishing policy had already begun to prevail before his death in 1949. His once-radical theory is accepted establishment doctrine now.

You will be told about this if you're ever invited to fish one of the great chalkstreams (though your chances of this are still slim, no matter whom you know). The fishery rules have been changed slightly, yet significantly, since Halford's day to read: "No wading. Dry fly *and nymph* only."

And nymph? Yes, British purism is no longer ramrod rigid. It has bent a bit in response to the fishing realities of the present century. And who knows how permissive it may become in another fifty years? Perhaps a new pundit will arise and "discover" what his great grandfather took for granted: that the classic, down-winged sunk fly is actually the best possible imitation of a drowned mayfly or caddis fly. Then, perhaps, the 2,000-year-old wet fly will be considered respectable and will be countenanced on these holy waters, too. And we'll be right back where we started.

17

More Trout Per Mile

Trout fishing that lies within one-day driving distance of our population centers is mostly bad and, let's face it, getting worse. Unfortunately, the situation is much like the weather in Mark Twain's day: Everybody talks about it, but nobody does anything about it.

Admittedly, sportsmen's groups, state governments, and private owners pour a lot of hatchery trout into our Eastern streams. But most of these innocents find few places to hide and have little chance for long-term survival. For example, a lady of my acquaintance who owns a stretch of small stream lost all her spring stocking, a few years ago, due to a late-May flood. Undaunted, she ordered another batch for the end of June. By this time, the water was catastrophically low and, when the fish were dumped in, she and the hatchery man watched in horror as $500 worth of trout stampeded downstream like a school of bonefish, never to be seen again.

Stocked fish may not always be such a sudden and total loss, but it's a dubious policy to try to stockpile trout where they don't want to live. Hatchery fish are expensive, too. Perhaps trout fanciers should take a tip from suburban birdwatchers. When the binocular boys want to attract and hold song birds, they plant protective shrubs or bushes and set out bird houses. Why shouldn't trouters build trout houses on their favorite streams?

What our run-down running waters really need is not more trout but more trout-holding places. Much has been learned and written about improving the richer, more stately flowing streams of the upper Midwest. Yet the problems of the acid, rocky spate rivers of the East have been largely neglected — despite the fact that these are the very waters that support the most fishermen and the fewest trout per mile.

Our larger streams — those that are eighty feet or more wide — are able to sustain fair fishing through sheer volume of water and depth, even when they are severely damaged. Smaller streams and brooks, however, show the effects of erosion more dramatically. And these cooler waters, which start nearer the springs and flow at higher altitudes, are the mainstays of both our summer fishing and our resident watershed trout populations. They, in particular, need all the help they can get. The question is, what sort of help?

The solution lies first in finding out what fish-producing characteristics these waters used to have before they were trampled by civilization, and then restoring them. When old-timers tell you about all the big fish they used to catch from your favorite stream, they're not necessarily lying.

A picture pool with rock-cliff sides and boulder-strewn bottom. No need to try to improve on nature here.

Timbering and farming started our streams on their downward path. Thinning, even stripping, our watersheds of trees has caused not only pronounced summer droughts, but destructive floods as well. Perhaps stream-beds could have handled this challenge if they had been left intact. But the banks came tumbling down when farmers tried to stretch their acres by removing trees right down to the edge of the stream.

Once the climax trees, with their massive root structures, were removed, floods began to tear out the margins. If you've ever watched a large tree, with its twelve-foot-diameter root structure, plow its way down a swollen stream-bed you'll understand why so many river banks are now composed of shallow, treeless gravel. After years of this chain-reaction bulldozing and uprooting, most of our running waters are two streams wide and half a stream deep.

When you examine the resulting shallow, unproductive flats (no longer pools) and riffles (no longer runs), the remedy may seem deceptively simple. You'll probably suggest that a dam, raising the water level two or three feet, could make the whole stretch into a promised land.

But you'd be wrong on four counts. First, effective dams are damnably expensive. In many areas, a Hewitt ramp-dam sixty to eighty feet wide may cost several thousand dollars. Second, dams tend to heat up water, making it intolerable to trout. Third, there's now so much unstable sand and gravel in most streams that it will soon fill in your dream pool above the dam, leaving only the limited plunge-pool below for fish-holding. And fourth, damming creates slow water which produces only one-tenth as much food per square foot of bottom as running water does. Eastern spate streams, by their character and chemistry, are food-short to begin with, and we shouldn't reduce their larders even further.

The answer lies, not in direct confrontation with the current, but in using its sudden, destructive power to heal the stream. As a *jujitsu* expert converts his opponent's strength to his own advantage, you can make a river's floods serve your purpose. You can, that is, if you use the proper techniques.

During the past thirteen summers I have spent at least as much time tinkering with running water as I've spent fishing it and over

Flat, shallow water has been speeded up by cribbing (right) which is soon deeply undercut and will hold large trout.

that period I've made all the obvious mistakes. On the other hand, I have had a few heartening successes, and if you think catching a fish on a fly you tied yourself is a thrill, just wait till you take a good trout from a productive spot you've created out of waste water with your own two hands.

I'll discuss several other improvement schemes later on, but first I'd like to describe the most versatile and durable stream-improvement device I've ever seen: the log cribbing. Essentially, this is a low-lying structure of horizontally placed logs anchored securely into the bank on the upstream end, jutting out into the current below, and ballasted with large rocks for flood insurance. Although the cribbing is far from new and I certainly didn't invent it, I may have improved it some.

Careful planning and foresight must go into the positioning of these structures. They should be built only on the strong side of

Lower logs and screening in place for simple cribbing. Be sure to place the biggest rocks nearest the logs.

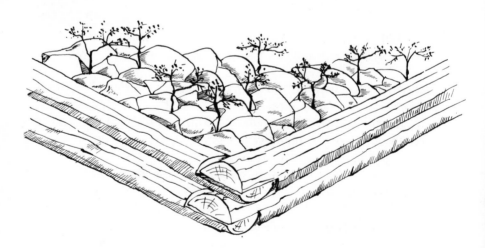

Same cribbing completed, two logs high and ballasted against flood-waters. Willow roots soon make it a permanent peninsula.

the current or at least where they will be nearest to the dominant feed-lane. Don't place them over ledge-rock — no matter how permanent such a location may appear to be. A cribbing can't possibly scour fish-holding undercuts there, and trout don't like to lie over uninterrupted sheet-rock, anyway. Choose a place with a gravel or rubble bottom in a shallow riffle or unproductive flat.

Pivotal to your future success is the embedding of the first log — the bottom one on the upstream end. It must be dug into the bank or neighboring gravel deeply enough — two or three feet on tight, tree-lined banks, but up to six or eight feet on unstable, shelving shores — so that high waters can't work in behind it and scour it out. At this stage, a little extra digging is money in the bank; and it will help you sleep better during those nights later on when the river is in flood.

Logs should be of hemlock, larch, or cedar — woods that can withstand alternate wetting and drying without rotting. Pine is virtually useless, and even the choicest hardwoods will disintegrate in a few seasons if they're not totally submerged all the time. Hemlock is usually easy to get in most parts of the Northeast, and it's light enough to handle. Twenty-foot logs measuring a foot across the butt can be moved short distances by one man with a crowbar or cant hook and are the best all-round size. Try to select smooth-trunked and knot-free logs so that debris won't find a place to hang up. Finally, before you lower the first one into its resting-place, slice the downstream end in half and remove the top section for twelve to eighteen inches much as you would in building a log cabin. This will allow the next log, if a bottom section is removed, to fit in like one continuous log.

Before filling in the trench you have imbedded the end of this log in, cut some willow switches slightly longer than the final depth of burial and poke their butts in as far as possible along both sides of the log. Willows planted in saturated sand or gravel are almost sure to take and, once established, are great insurance against the loss of this key log.

The face of the cribbing formed by this log should be slanted out into the current at an angle of no more than forty-five degrees and in some cases as little as thirty degrees, depending on the location. Large cakes of ice or whole trees tend to hang up on structures that confront the flood waters too directly, while more gradual inclines will shrug off menacing objects, deflecting them harmlessly down-current.

Whether you build a simple or complex cribbing will depend on the location you have chosen. A complex cribbing is merely one that is continued down-current with a second section jutting out into the current at a sharper angle. Construction principles are essentially the same, but a simple one is sooner completed and may make a better choice for your first efforts. The complex one may hold twice as many trout, but only in special situations—either at a bend in the river or below a diagonal riffle where the current angles sharply towards one bank. (On a straight stretch, this longer structure would have to jut out perilously far into the river and the angle of the second log, to continue the current deflection, would have to be placed at nearly ninety degrees to the flow.)

The second log, which forms the lower arm of a simple cribbing (which is just a widened A-frame skeleton) should be equally well trenched and anchored into the bank, then mortised and spiked into the first one. To be sure you won't lose your future rock ballast when the cribbing has been deeply undercut by high water, attach heavy-gauge, wide-mesh (eight-inch or more) wire fencing of four-foot or more width to the inside of these logs before you start to pile on the rocks. Fasten at six-inch intervals with either the largest-size staples or three-inch nails. If you use nails, bend the top inch down over the wire.

Next, place the heaviest rocks available on the part of the fencing that's nearest the logs, laying two rows horizontally. Be sure they're too large to fall through the wire mesh, and the bigger the better. Pull these rocks out of the nearby water, never from the bank which needs all the protection it can get. Removing them from within a few feet of the face of the cribbing helps in another way, too. It reduces the stability of that portion of the stream-bottom, helping the current to scour deeper and to produce a more pronounced cut for fish-holding.

The upper layer of logs should be placed exactly on top of the first and fastened in the same manner—except that a second layer of wire is seldom necessary. Top logs should barely break the surface even at low water so that most flood-borne objects will

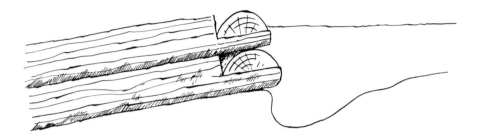

Side view from water level of newly finished cribbing.

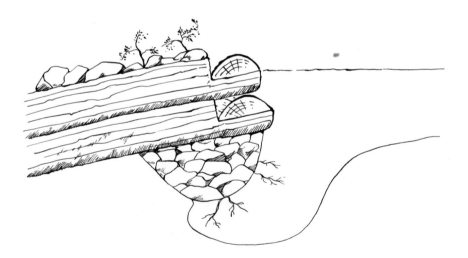

Same cribbing after high water has created deep undercut.

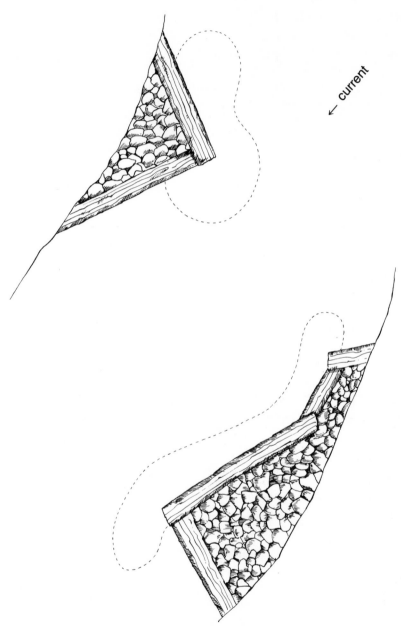

Top views of simple (left) and complex cribbings. Areas inside dotted lines will soon be scoured deep by floods.

pass over them. This final position has to be precalculated when digging the trenches for the lower logs.

Once again, place the largest rocks you can handle adjacent to the logs, then slant the rock-fill back so it is higher near the bank. It will pay you to fit the big, marginal rocks as carefully as you would a dry wall, for they, too, will have to shed high-water flotsam. Finally, plant willow shoots in the rock interstices all over the cribbing and repeat this every spring until you have a dense stand established. In two or three years, these fast-growing plants will catch debris with their trunks and branches and actually increase current deflection in high water. This not only adds to the scouring action, but also helps force destructive objects to swerve away from your cribbing.

Properly positioned, constructed, and planted, a cribbing should last for many years with only minor maintenance or repairs. Several that I have built on a good-sized river in New York's Catskills came through the Act-of-God flood of the summer of '69 with flying colors. However, less well-conceived and built structures from earlier experiments were lost, and this experience has given me some insight into which improvement schemes will—and which will not—stand up.

Gabions (fine-mesh wire cages filled with rocks) have very little value as improvers of flood-prone streams. When they deflect enough water to scour a good trench, they tumble into their own handiwork and disappear. They just aren't rigid enough to withstand much undercutting.

Simple deflector and current-directing logs that have proved themselves on more stable waters won't work here, either. They may produce the desired effect at low or medium flow, but under full flood conditions the water roars over them and attacks the bank behind them, increasing the destruction. The inflexible law that water will run off at a precise right angle to any surface it flows over is the very reason why down-current ends of all cribbings must be finished off at an obtuse — never an acute — angle to the bank.

There are, however, some less Herculean labors you can perform for a stream that will help it little by little. Willow-planting along banks is always good practice since these small trees are water-loving and strong-rooted. Riprapping the sand banks

Driving in a spike for willow-planting on an eroded shore. Nature may heal herself, but you can hurry the process.

with large, flat slabs can halt further erosion and siltation downstream.

Large rocks and boulders are always a welcome addition to a stream-bed, but the biggest you can roll are barely big enough. By all means don't steal them from the nearby banks. Large boulders usually produce short, deep scours on their down-current side while insect-food debris—dead leaves and twigs—will tend to catch under their front edges.

If you and your friends or your club decide to try to help your favorite streams, there are certain procedures you should follow. Ask permission from your state fish and game commission before you start. Many require permits to tamper with flowing water— even if you're the riparian owner. However, if your plans are sound, they'll usually give you their blessing and often some helpful advice.

If you lease the water or merely have permission to fish it, by all means get the owner's approval as well. Again, if your projects offer real improvement, he can hardly object.

When you've been given the go-ahead, resist the temptation to rush into construction. First, draw up a master plan for the area you're going to improve. Observe and take notes on this water at least once when it is in flood or running extremely high. This will not only impress you with the forces your future structures will have to contend with, but it may also give you a whole new understanding of which direction the river tends to cut when it's actually working. And there's much to be learned from studying productive pools and runs, even in low water, analyzing the high-water forces that dug them and keep them scoured clean.

Finally, start your first project at a tight-banked, relatively stable location. It's heartbreaking to slave over a cribbing only to discover, the following season, that the river has cut itself a new channel, leaving your good works high and dry on the gravel. For the same reason, work in a progressive downstream direction. Your first cribbing may deflect the current to the opposite bank and it's vital to know this before starting your next structure.

I have built several cribbings singlehandedly (despite what my children and weekend guests may tell you), but extra hands make the work quicker and pleasanter. Machinery can do wonders if

Rock-ballasting by the highway department on the far shore holds riverbank and trout. Rocks must be five-hundred pounds or more.

you're willing to pay the price. A back-hoe can dig deep trenches in a short time and a payloader can pile on all the ballast you'll need (*after* you've hand-fitted the big, outside rocks) in a few hours. With this sort of help — and expense — it's possible to complete an entire cribbing in a single day if you have pre-arranged all the materials and planned the construction sequence properly.

What sort of return, in terms of actual fish, can you expect from the finished product? It all depends on the stream you're working with and on the existing head of fish in the river available for attraction. Even a simple cribbing can hold several good (over 12-inch) fish despite the territorial aggressiveness of trout. On a rare, perfect evening, I have caught five in a row without moving my feet from one such structure, and I'm not sure there weren't even more that were put down before I could cover them. A compound cribbing, as I've said, may hold twice as many.

My all-time favorite fishing place was created by this latter type of structure. Facing upstream from where I like to stand, the water breaks over a diagonal riffle which bunches the thread of the current sharply toward the bank to my right. While the water is still dancing and deepening, it meets the first log which angles out slightly from the bank. The flow hugs this log for twenty feet or more, slowing down into a smooth glide, then hits the second log which juts out more sharply. The current gradually quickens again until it boils out past the end of this last log and shallows out into another riffle. For nearly fifty feet, the water near the logs is three to three and a half feet deep and it fishes like a short pool in low water, like a deep run when the river's up.

This place has everything a trout could ask for. There's a food-producing riffle directly above, a concentrated feed lane of drift food, and cover enough under the logs and between the rocks to hide even some full-grown salmon. It's ideal for the fisherman, too. Your presentations here are almost drag-free, for the current moves past you like a turning wheel—slowest at the hub where you stand and fastest out on the rim where your fly is cast.

Cribbings have one other big advantage: They can stretch the length of your good-fishing season. Brown trout have two main migration periods. They move upstream for cooler water and safer depths during the first hint of drought in early summer. A good undercut can hold some of these fish all summer, keeping them from pushing on through to spring-holes and feeder creeks. And in the fall, during September and October, all the mature fish in the stream seem to play musical chairs. Your fishing season may now be over, but cribbings provide ideal wintering spots and will hold large fish upriver for your early-spring fishing. These big trout might otherwise head down to the big water after spawning.

Is this sort of work worth all the backaches and blisters? It all depends on your available time, temperament, and long-range commitment to trout fishing. The number of fishermen is increasing every year by leaps and bounds while the amount of available trout water is probably shrinking. Don't let the antipollution bills —good as they are—mislead you. Even if they're carried out to the letter, they will do far more to reclaim larger rivers for warm-water species than they will to expand upland trout waters. In the meantime, we'll probably keep losing water to the dammers and developers.

Probably every generation has complained about the fishing, wishing for the good old days. An Elizabethan poet 375 years ago wrote:

> Fishing, if I, a fisher, may protest
> Of pleasures is the sweetest, of sports the best, . . .
> But now the sport is marde, and wott ye why?
> Fishes decrease, and fishers multiply.

He had no idea how good he had it! But lamenting and viewing-with-alarm are no answer. Obviously, as a trout fisherman, you should support all good conservation measures and ecology-minded candidates. Certainly you should join Trout Unlimited, the Federation of Fly Fishermen, and any organization dedicated to the future of your sport.

But perhaps you should get even more deeply involved with some local grass-roots — or rather, willow-roots — work on your favorite stream. This is the only way to produce more trout per existing mile of stream. And, if you shuttle the current back and forth from bank to bank artfully enough, you just might create a few more miles of trout fishing, too.

18

A Dry-Fly Philosophy

Socrates gave his wife all the credit for his success as a philosopher, but not in the usual I-owe-it-all-to-the-little-lady sense. He claimed Xanthippe was such a shrew and all-around five-letter girl that she had driven him into the arms of abstract thought.

I think Socrates was putting us on, though. If his theory held water, sheer frustration would also drive dry-fly fishermen to embrace pure logic and, as a result, they would surely quit fishing. Instead, they head for the stream at every opportunity armed with new flies, new theories, and new hopes even though sad experience has proved that for every small sip of success there are many cupfuls of hemlock to be choked down. I always get depressed by the top-heavy failure/success ratio when I reread my own fishing diary, and the disastrous day of July 5, 1964, is a typical example.

The previous evening had set me up for the coming defeat. In the hour before pitch darkness I had raised, pricked, or caught every rising fish I had cast to with a new imitation of a pale-yellowish dun that had long been one of the most baffling hatches on my river. I was especially pleased with this performance because the sudden-death imitation had been created in the classic manner — duplicated from live, captured specimens. I won't go into the whole dressing, for reasons that will soon become obvious, but the major change I had made from previous recipes was in the body, where I had substituted porcupine hair dyed the color of creamery butter for the usual, much duller fox-belly fur. With this inspired concoction I had given a dozen and a half trout a good toothache before darkness and a sudden downpour had driven me from the river.

By the next day, the infamous 5th of July, the river had risen six inches and, since it was still drizzling, I spent most of the morning tying up a boxful of my new "Yellow Perils." The sun came out at two o'clock and by four I was on the river—playing a hunch that cooling rainwater might start the flies hatching several hours early.

Again, my touch was pure magic. At four-thirty the same pale-yellow duns started pouring down my favorite flat and despite the bright sunlight the trout came strongly on the feed. This was going to be ridiculously easy. Higher, faster water would make the fish far less shy and I had a whole boxful of my new secret weapons. I fully expected to walk away within an hour, fed up with fishing that was too murderous to be fun.

As it turned out, it was more than three hours later when I finally left the river and my hands hardly smelled fishy. I had caught only two six-inchers and had been totally ignored by all the fish old enough to spawn. What had gone wrong? How could trout have savaged an imitation one evening then acted like militant consumerists when presented with the identical fly the very next day? The higher water, which had actually relieved near-drought conditions, should have been strongly in my favor. The critical difference appeared to be available light — heavily clouded skies at dusk versus bright afternoon sun.

Up to that point, I had thought of light as a basic commodity that could be measured on a simple scale of more or less. After all, an artificial fly in the hand looks much the same to us at dusk as it does in sunlight except for the brightness of the colors. This is true, however, only because we tend to view it in terms of the light it reflects back to our eyes.

Unfortunately, the trout's world and his modes of perception are quite different and far more complicated. He sees a mayfly floating overhead in at least three distinct ways and in many combinations of the three. In extremely poor light the fly probably blocks out all the rays reaching the trout's eyes and appears as a colorless silhouette. In bright sunlight the same insect seems mainly translucent, the light passing through the body, wings, and legs with only slight refraction, and the color of its internal organs may be even more distinctive than the color of its skin. Then, of course, when perceived by reflected light, the fly may look to the trout much as it does to us, but I believe this is only for relatively short periods of time between the translucent and opaque light conditions.

I think this explains my ups and downs on the July 4th and 5th I mentioned earlier. The imitation fooled the fish at dusk because it was being seen by reflected light at first, perhaps, and then as a pure silhouette. However, this same artificial had none of the translucence of the natural when viewed against the bright sky the following day and may well have been passed up as an inedible hemlock needle.

If you hold a live mayfly between your eye and a bright light, then at a right angle to the light and finally against a very dim light, your eye may well convince you that you have been looking at three separate insects, and if you move the fly slowly through all three stages you may see an almost infinite number of grada-tions in the appearance of that same fly. This nearly duplicates what a trout probably sees during the various hours of a single day and when you consider this enormous variety of perceptions, you may easily, and rightly, despair of ever creating, or finding, the perfect artificial of any insect.

What we often tend to forget is that all dry flies are a com-promise between the true appearance of a natural insect and what we can manage to spin on a relatively heavy hook and then float over a fish. Each type, or even tying, of an artificial is based on the premise that some of the things a trout perceives are more important than others in convincing him that this is lean red meat and not just a bundle of fluff. These aspects are emphasized while others, deemed less important, are necessarily sacrificed. With this in mind, let's look at some of the most popular schools of dry-fly tying, restricting our scrutiny to mayfly artificials since, for some inscrutable reason, ninety-nine percent of all floaters sold imitate this form of aquatic insect.

To make things simpler, let's break flies down into their four basic parts: tail, body, hackle, and wing. I'm sure trout don't do this, but fly-tyers do and this piece-by-piece approach helps put some order into centuries of fly-tying chaos.

Tails are the least controversial and worried-over part of the classic dry fly. Many of the most effective wet flies omit them altogether so it's easy to conclude that these hairlike and un-nourishing appendages aren't the focal point of the trout's attention. The earliest dry flies on record sported only two or three whisks—exactly the number of tails (or *setae*) the naturals themselves possess. However, this number was soon increased for practical reasons and, since trout apparently can't count, the more fully fibered tails are the norm today.

Don't let this mislead you into thinking that tails are just so much excess baggage, though. These few fibers are called upon to support and float nearly two-thirds of the total hook-weight—the heaviest portion over the bend and barb—and a short, sparse tail can condemn the rear end of a floater to sink below the surface film and leave your imitation pitched at an improbable angle. To prevent this, I tie my flies with the tail fibers splayed out in a horizontal fan, spreading thirty to forty degrees, the way most naturals flair their tails. I have no great faith that trout appreciate this small gesture towards realism, but this does help prevent tail-sinking and it has other advantages, too. This fanned-out position offers much more air resistance and helps the imitation flutter down to the surface in the horizontal plane we hope for. And, since the fibers are spread out perpendicular to the hook-bend, it helps to cock the fly in a bolt-upright position once it hits the water.

Many years ago I showed one of our most famous fly-tyers a series I had tied up in this manner, asking his professional appraisal. "Sure it floats a fly better, and presents it better, too. We've known that for years," he added, dashing my hopes for immortality as the Thomas Edison of fly-tying. "But they'd never sell. People expect flies to have a straight, bunched tail and that's what they get." He was right, of course. I have since seen fan-tailed flies illustrated in books and articles, but I have never seen them offered in tackle shops. However, I think it will pay you to tie up some flies like this or to get a friend to create some for you. They're that much better.

When we come to fly bodies we enter the eye of a storm that has been raging for centuries. The first dry flies had spun-fur bodies as did the ancient wet patterns described by Charles Cotton in *The Compleat Angler*. Nearly ninety years ago, Frederick M. Halford, the English genius who launched and popularized the dry fly, decided that these fuzzy-bodied imitations weren't realistic enough—at least not from a photographic point of view. In line with his doctrine of "exact imitation" he redesigned these flies with glistening, segmented bodies of horsehair dyed to a precise color. Although these same patterns are sold and used on Britain's chalkstreams to this day, the pendulum has swung back toward the older style in recent years and you now have a wide choice of body-types in even shop-tied flies.

One of the more interesting rebuttals to Halford's hard-nosed theory was launched by an English mathematician in 1924. J. W. Dunne, along with many fellow dry-fly fishers, had long felt that Halford's patterns, though ultrarealistic when viewed under side-lighted conditions, were opaque and lifeless when seen against a strong light. Dunne's "Sunshine" flies were designed with bodies made of a special synthetic fiber wound over a white-painted hook-shank. When these flies were dipped into a flask of special "Sunshine" oil, they suddenly took on both the color and transparency of the naturals.

"Sunshine" flies have not been on the market since World War II, as far as I can tell, but they may have been a giant step in the right direction. Their disappearance from the catalogs was not due to their lack of killing properties, though. Like so many other demonstrably better flies both before and since, they were just too difficult and time-consuming to tie. And the synthetic body-material was extremely fragile. One sharp trout-tooth could unravel and ruin the laborously created body.

Hard bodies of quill, stiff hair, and other opaque materials are still popular. But many tyers have taken the cue from Dunne and developed translucent bodies of simpler, tougher materials. The old fur-dubbings, particularly those spun from the underfur of aquatic mammals, are reasonably water-repellant, show a lifelike sparkle, and allow enough light to refract through their fuzzy margins to give some hint of transparency. Seal's fur is probably the best of all since it has the most lustre and changes color least when wet. This type of body has gained popularity in recent years and so have those made of fine herls, which also give a translucent appearance.

In selecting bodies of this sort it is best to hold them up to the light (preferably when wet) to choose the shade you hope the fish will see. Over three hundred years ago, Charles Cotton pointed out that the only way to tell a fur dubbing's true color was to hold it up to a strong light. It seems to take a discouragingly long time to rediscover what was common knowledge years ago.

There is one situation in which hard, slim quill bodies may be a better choice, though, and that's when imitating the mayfly spinners that fall spent on the surface at dusk. This second, and less important, stage of the mayfly's flying life has a characteristically thinner body than the earlier dun stage and since it is usually viewed against the fading light of late evening, a slim body of durable quill or hair may present a more realistic silhouette. You can usually discount the factor of translucence under such light conditions. Remember Gilbert and Sullivan's description of the rich attorney's elderly ugly daughter? "She'd well pass for forty-three in the dusk with the light behind her." You, too, can probably fool a poor fish under these flattering conditions, but I doubt that you'd want to be wed to that style of tying for the harsh, unforgiving light of midday.

Hackle is the most important part of any dry fly as far as keeping it afloat is concerned. In classic theory, it is supposed to represent the legs of the insect, but that isn't necessarily the case in modern practice. Spiders, variants, bivisibles, and conventional wingless patterns use hackle to represent both legs and wings and so, in part, do some of the most famous Catskill patterns like the Quill Gordon and the Hendrickson. The wings of bunched wood-duck fibers in these popular patterns are not at all the color of the mayflies' wings they are supposed to imitate. These barred yellow feathers are used to represent the venation of the wings, and their true gray color is recreated only when they are viewed through many turns of dun hackle.

All-hackle flies are popular because they are tough and are high floaters. This latter quality makes them ideal for prospecting in fast runs or in swirling pockets, but I find they're only so-so on the glassy surfaces of pools or flats. Here trout often drift back

The Quill Gordon (Epeorus pleuralis) with impressionistic wings and hackle as tied by the Catskill school . . .

. . . with quill-section wings in the Halford manner . . .

. . . with Baigent's long, watery outer-hackle . . .

. . . with sparse hackle clipped for a spent fly. . .

. . . with Marinaro's splayed hackle and formed wings . . .

. . . as a long-hackled, Catskill-style variant . . .

... as a no-hackle tie with buoyant body-dubbing ...

... and as a parachute fly with horizontally-wound hackle.

under a fly for quite a ways before taking it, and these more stylized patterns are often rejected when studied by good-sized, heavily fished trout.

An interesting attempt at creating a high-floating yet realistic imitation was launched by an Englishman, Dr. Baigent, in the early part of this century. The good doctor must have had a bit of the advertising man in him since he named them "Refractra" flies. They looked much like the standard British dressings of his day with this difference: One short hackle only was used to represent the legs while a second hackle, two or three times as long in the fiber and of a neutral shade, was wound over this, giving a high-floating fly without the usual appearance of too much bulk.

According to Baigent, they had another great advantage. The long, nearly invisible over-hackle produced dimples in the surface-tension over a wider area, creating extra distortion and refraction so that even the most sophisticated trout couldn't get a sharp look at the fly.

The concept of these flies, like Dunne's "Sunshine" theory, is excellent, and the only reason I can imagine for their disappearance from our inventories is the scarcity of the good-quality, pale-dun hackle needed to create the desired illusion. "Refractra" flies have all the good floating qualities of our standard variants and are far more killing on smooth, slow water. I can only hope that with our accelerated interest in new theories and new patterns that someone will "discover" them again very soon.

Believers in all-hackle flies are convinced that no artificial can fool a trout when it can be seen clearly and that it is mainly the sparkles and dimples set up in the surface tension by the hackle points, creating much the same patterns made by an insect's legs, that deceive the fish. There's considerable evidence to support this premise. Until an artificial enters a trout's relatively small window or direct, above-surface vision, these twinkles in the mirror-like water surface give the fish his only advance warning of approaching food. This stimulus seems sufficient in fast or turbulent water where trout are forced into making a hair-trigger decision but, in my experience, it leaves something to be desired when the water is slow and slick.

Vincent Marinaro, of Pennsylvania's limestone country, has come up with an ingenious compromise: a type of fly that should produce a more realistic light pattern outside the trout's window yet one that also deceives when viewed directly by the trout. He accomplishes this by splaying the hackle toward the head and tail of the fly when winding it on. This gives the fly two other advantages: more area of surface tension for the hackle to work on and a more accurate representation of the natural fly's spraddled legs.

I don't know why this style of hackling hasn't caught on. Is it because it looks untidy? After all, one of the hallmarks of a well-tied conventional fly is the close, even turn of hackle at the head, and from this criterion Marinaro's tie looks like a botched job. Whether or not this type of hackling offends your esthetic sensibilities, I can assure you that the result is extremely killing— especially in sizes #16 and smaller.

Parachute flies, those with their hackle wound in a horizontal rather than vertical plane, have been on and off the market for over forty years. They, too, spread their hackle over a larger part of the surface the way a mayfly splays its legs. However, they have one distinct drawback. With the hackle wound above the body, as is customary, the body is presented below the surface film which is uncharacteristic of mayflies. It seems a case of win one, lose one, here.

Flies without any hackle at all have reappeared after a number of years and they certainly deserve a long, hard look. One of the most popular and effective British flies of all time, the Gold-ribbed Hare's Ear, has always been tied in this manner, relying on a few picked-out guard hairs for flotation. This fly is still considered the best dry imitation of the Medium Olive Dun—one of the most important spring flies on England's legendary chalkstreams.

No-hackle flies are unquestionably accurate and deadly imitations under the conditions they were designed for. On English chalkstreams, where this tie originated, most naturals are quite small, averaging to sizes #16 and #18, and artificials of this size are quite easy to float with a minimal grip on surface tension. The water is glassy smooth, here, and few presentations are made since only rising fish are cast to. Unfortunately, we have very few rivers in this country with similar conditions and opportunities. Where these do exist, no-hackle flies are superb. However, on our usual, more turbulent waters where steady casting and prospecting for unseen fish is standard practice, these flies won't float long enough or high enough to be practical.

Imitations of spinners, or spent mayflies, are a different matter, of course. These are traditionally fished to rising trout at dusk on glassy water, and we want them to float flush in the surface film. The best of these imitations have always been tied without conventional hackle. The easiest and most effective tie, I've found, is made by winding on one hackle, then clipping off all the top and bottom fibers, but you can produce this same, spent-wing effect in many other ways.

Some sort of wing is usually preferred by anglers who concentrate on slow, clear waters and these upright "sails" of the mayfly dun can be represented in three basic ways. The classic method is with matching slips of primary feathers. A more impressionistic style is created by using split bunches of plumage as many Catskill flies do or by tying in stiff fibers of hair as in the popular Wulff flies. A relatively new school advocates wings formed of whole hackle feathers clipped to a precise mayfly-wing shape.

Using winged flies for slow-water conditions is sound practice. The top of the wing is the first part of a mayfly that a trout can see directly as it starts to enter his window of direct vision. In slow water this preview of the approaching fly may well be the stimulus that starts a fish gliding up to the surface.

Slips of primary quill, from dark to palest dun, will duplicate the wing-color of most flies you'll encounter. On small flies—size #16 and under—these wings are extremely realistic and they are highly visible to both the trout and the angler. This latter advantage is not to be taken lightly when you're trying to keep track of a #18 fly forty or more feet distant on the surface. Many anglers complain that these quill wings are too fragile and that they break up after a fish or two, but if they have been tied on properly (which, admittedly, is not always the case) the parted fibers can usually be zipped back into a solid wing in seconds.

Medium-sized flies (#16s, #14s, and #12s) are logical candidates for clipped-hackle wings. In sizes smaller than these such wings probably represent a lot of hard work that will be appreciated only by the angler. In fact, these wings are so time-consuming to prepare in all sizes that few professional tyers can afford to offer them. On the positive side, they are realistically translucent, tough and, in larger sizes, they are less likely than quill slips to wind up your tippet while casting.

Flies larger than size #12 are probably best tied with bunched-fiber or hair wings. These are less lifelike, of course, but they are also less rigid. Even clipped-hackle wings over a certain size tend to hum and whirr during high-velocity casting, and they may then wind up your tippet like the rubber band in a model airplane. The largest mayflies—the Green Drake, the March Brown and others —are the hardest naturals to imitate successfully, and I feel that winging realistically is only a small part of the problem. Trout act as if they see larger objects in a different manner than they see smaller ones. Their eyes seem able to pick big flies to pieces, and even the most realistic imitations of the larger naturals are taken with regularity only in fast water or when trout are on a feeding spree.

This phenomenon is hard to explain, but is attested to by the century-long struggle of Britain's most gifted theorists and fly-tyers to come up with an effective imitation of their large Green Drake, usually referred to as *The* Mayfly. There are hundreds of different dressings on the market and yet none of them is considered a reliable killer. In my experience, we have the same problem with our largest insects. This difficulty in deceiving trout with larger floating patterns is so pronounced that I doubt that dry-fly fishing would be at all popular if the average aquatic insect were size #8 or #10 instead of size #14 or #16.

When these giants of the insect world are being taken regularly in slow water (where, unfortunately, most of them hatch out) I usually abandon my faith in the sleight of hand of fly-tying. I then put on a higher-floating, but less realistic, variant of similar size and color and give it a slight twitch in an across or upstream direction just before it passes over the rising fish. Easy does it here: just a wiggle. This mini-motion, I've found, is often more effective in convincing the trout that your artificial is a living insect than the most inspired fly-tying efforts.

Many years ago, when I first started tying flies, I dreamed I might someday invent a pattern that no trout could resist. A little experience put an end to that fantasy, but soon another one popped up in its place. Why couldn't I design a floating imitation of, say, the March Brown dun that no fish feeding on the naturals would ever refuse?

My fly box bears witness that I have now given up even this more modest ambition. These days I tie up several imitations of the more common mayflies I expect to see during the daylight hours on the waters I fish. To stay with the March Brown, for example, I now carry some long-hackled variant imitations for fast water or to twitch slightly on flat water when all else fails. I have some standard Art Flick imitations with yellowish-cream bodies that work well most of the time. But some days, when the overhead light is especially bright, I do far better with this same dressing tied with a body of rusty-orange seal's fur that suggests the gut color of the natural instead of its yellow skin color. And yet, even with this battery, I sometimes do so poorly during a good March Brown hatch that I'm convinced I'm still missing a trick—or several.

One reason for this is that light conditions vary widely and constantly. Then, too, entomologists tell us that the aquatic insects themselves change color gradually and continually after they've hatched out. And mayflies of the very same species differ considerably in color — and in size — from one river to another even though they may be hatching out in the same ecological region. The more I learn about insects, flies, and fly-tying, the more certain I become that the one perfect imitation can never exist.

All this conspires to make fly-tying an absorbing occupation of trial and error punctuated by occasional, temporary successes. Many flies, especially those that hatch out during the bright hours of the day, seem to call for several distinct patterns. Larger specimens continue to defy predictable results with any or all imitations. And so far we've only looked into the problems of duplicating adult mayflies. Floating caddis flies, stone flies, midges, and terrestrials have their own sets of problems. And then there's another universe of nymphs, wet-flies, streamers, bucktails, and the other subsurface imitations to look into.

Obviously, trout aren't as gullible as people. You can't fool all of the fish some of the time or even some of the fish all of the time. If you can manage to fool some of the fish some of the time you'll probably be accused of being an expert. Decades of trial and error have forced me to accept this philosophy. It may have helped me *understand* dry-fly problems, but it hasn't helped me *solve* too many of them.

However, from all reports, philosophy didn't help Socrates solve his problems, either. To begin with, he was extremely ugly. After he married, his wife tried to make his life a hell on earth. And when the citizens of Athens told him to drop dead, they meant it literally. Things might have been worse, though. Think of the added grief he'd have gone through if he'd been addicted to dry-fly fishing.

19

The Perfect Fish

Although I had been a compulsive fisherman ever since I could walk, I never saw a specimen of "the perfect fish" until I had reached the advanced age of five and a half, going on six. I can still remember that moment. I was standing on a dusty dirt road, peering into a trickle—certainly not a brook—that dribbled out of a culvert, when I noticed a slight movement in the pan-sized pool below.

There couldn't be a fish in *there*, I thought. Fish, in those days, were sudden shadows that disappeared in front of me as I waded through the shallows of seashores and lakes. Then a creature slowly assembled itself in front of my eyes. First, white-tipped pink fins fanning the yellow sand—probably the motion that had caught my eye in the first place. Then, below, a cigar-shaped shadow and above this a dark-green body laced with paler markings. If I close my eyes today I can still see it in glorious full color, hovering there under the midday sun.

This was a fish I had never seen before—neither in the water, in picture books, nor in fish markets—yet I knew with utter certainty what it was. I had heard my father's friends talk in respectful tones about catching them on trips to Maine and Canada. This was a trout!

Admittedly, that six-incher was a Lilliputian sample, but it did qualify as "perfect." It was a member in good standing of a small, select group of closely related fishes that offer the angler everything he could wish for. This elite list is limited to the flowing-water, insect-eating trouts and, as we shall see, only a few species carry all the necessary credentials.

The Atlantic salmon (*Salmo salar*) and its landlocked form, which is no longer considered a subspecies, deserve the place at the very top of this honor roll. Both spend major parts of their lives in running water and are really just large trout, as their first name, *Salmo*, indicates. They are mainly insectivorous during their lives in rivers and, even though the sea-run form does not feed at all during its return to fresh water, its insect-eating reflexes are reactivated at this time and it is usually caught on artificial flies.

The major species of what are usually called the trouts qualify, too, even though they may chase a lot of minnows and crayfish during the gluttony of old age. The brown trout (*Salmo trutta*) is an excellent example, feeding mostly on insects during its first five or six years of life and often after that when the supply is abundant. So does the rainbow (*Salmo gairdneri*) and the cutthroat (*Salmo clarki*). Taxonomists keep declaring (and undeclaring) new species and subspecies from time to time, but there's not much point in making finer distinctions as a fisherman.

Of the trout-cousins called chars, perhaps only the speckled (brook) trout (*Salvelinus fontinalis*) should be included. The Dolly Varden (*Salvelinus malma*) of the West Coast is not principally an insect feeder, nor is the Arctic char (*Salvelinus alpinus*) of the North. The lake trout (*Salvelinus namaycush*) is unfortunately fond of deep water, and so are the several lesser-known chars of Europe.

Grayling, though they are even more distant relations of the true trouts, still deserve some consideration because they, too, sport the distinctive adipose fin of the tribe. They certainly prefer running water and they feed mainly on insects till they fall dead of old age. But, as we shall see, they fall short in other qualities and probably should be excluded. The Pacific salmons, six *Oncorhynchus* species, should be disqualified, too, since most are caught on heavy tackle in salt water and only a few are taken on insect imitations in fresh water.

From a scientific point of view, this grouping of fishes by habits makes little sense even though it does to the angler. Scientists might further point out that the selected fishes are not particularly smart, but merely shy, and that their place on the evolutionary ladder of fishes is down near the bottom rung, far below the relatively advanced catfishes. While I hold in great respect and awe any mental discipline that can put a man on the moon, I have to subtract a few points when it raises the catfish above the trout.

I am also aware that this selection may not exactly endear me to the army of trollers, surfers, bait-casters, or spin-fishers, either. In fact, I expect to hear accusations like "effete feather-fisherman," "trout chauvinist pig," or worse. And at this point, my chances of winning my case may seem as hopeless as Perry Mason's in the opening chapters. But stick around, there may be a surprise ending. I have a few expert witnesses and some devastating evidence.

First is the appraisal of history itself. Angling literature—which can boast of far more volumes than any other sport—has devoted more than half the pages in its library to this small group of fishes. For every book that has been written about bass, pike, stripers, or sailfish, there are two, three, or more on salmon and trout, and most of the famous books — and famous authors — throughout history have concentrated on these latter species.

Artists and illustrators seem to share this preoccupation with these same fishes. Trout and salmon are drawn and painted more often than any other species. They are, that is, if you can disregard the stylized carp that appears on so many oriental plates and vases (and I, for one, am perfectly willing to disqualify all crockery from the category of art).

A third field has also focused on this group of fishes. Fish culturists have devoted, by far, the greater part of their efforts, both in research and in actual propagation, to trout and salmon. Habitat-improvement attempts have also dealt almost exclusively with bettering their streams and rivers. Today probably eighty percent of all hatcheries—I mean true hatcheries, not commercial fish farms—raise these fish exclusively.

How has this select group of fishes managed to capture the imagination and inspire the efforts of the world of letters, art, and science for several centuries? And why have the trouts always been most prized by fishermen — at least in the countries where they occur in reasonable numbers? Simply because the list of virtues these fish possess is longer and more illustrious than the Boy Scout Oath.

The first quality that sets these fish apart is the manner in which they feed. To a very large extent, they subsist on insects and are readily caught on artificial imitations of these small, nutritious animals. Forgetting, for the moment, the joys and skills of fly-tying, this preference in food makes delicate, sporting tackle not only possible but nearly mandatory. You can't fish a small fly successfully on a heavy leader and you can't, in turn, keep from breaking a fine leader with a stiff, heavy rod. As a result, fly tackle is the most refined, most worried-over tackle in the world and because of its delicacy it is the least fatiguing to the angler and the most sporting in terms of magnifying the fish.

For example, I once killed a salmon of over twenty pounds on a small #10 wet fly. I had first rolled him on a sensible #6 and then gone to a #8, but under those low-water conditions he preferred to wait for the #10 before fastening firmly. Actually, I deserved to lose that fish because I choked and played him far too lightly and too long, but my point still stands. That's an awfully large fish to hook on a fly about a half-inch long.

Similarly, I once hooked a trout of between eight and ten pounds on a tiny #18 dry fly, and this was no fluke, either. I had seen him rising steadily to small naturals in the clear water and he wouldn't take till I gave him the correct color and size. In this case, however, I was robbed. I'm still convinced I deserved to land that fish, as I very nearly did, but that's a story in itself.

Nearly as important, it seems to me, is the fact that these fish live and feed in relatively shallow running water most of the time. The joy of small lures and light tackle would be canceled out if these fish hid themselves in the depths. The fight would bog down, and you certainly wouldn't dare use that three-ounce rod if your flies had to be lowered a hundred feet or more on metal line or with a sinker the size of a sash-weight. Then, too, you would miss the thrill of seeing the fish take as you usually do when fishing shallow runs and flats.

Another seldom-mentioned blessing of this type of fishing is that the game is usually played alone and on foot. The law may state that non-residents must hire a guide for salmon fishing in

Canada, but this is more a local employment scheme than a necessity. And, even though a few very large rivers are more easily fished from a boat for both salmon and trout, this is the exception rather than the rule. This ability to fish effectively without guide, crew, boat, outriggers, depth-finders and other intruding paraphernalia adds greatly to the joy and intimacy of fishing. There's a reward to this sort of one-on-one confrontation that is hard to describe, but veteran surf-casters will understand instinctively. Most of them would rather catch one good fish from the beach than a dozen from a boat. So would that small group of dedicated bonefishermen who prefer to stalk the flats on foot even though they know their chances would be better in a skiff with a good guide.

Certainly, any game fish deserving a top rating must have strength, style, and heart. The trouts rank very high in all three. Most species are acrobatic performers—salmon and rainbows especially. Yet browns and brooks, especially those in their early prime measuring twelve to eighteen inches, take to the air with surprising regularity when they're in peak condition. Admittedly, no trout will jump as high or as often as a tarpon. None will run as fast or as far as a bonefish. And none may give you the long, dogged, tugging fight of a jack. But even if trout don't win any particular event, they are all-round performers—probably the decathlon champions among fishes.

Trouts have one enormous energy source that is denied to almost every other freshwater fish: the ability to utilize the boundless pasturages of the oceans. Very few fish can migrate from fresh to salt water and back, but this is precisely what all the trouts, including the brook trout, can do. Running water has little or no plankton—a primary food-source at the bottom of the chain — and is, therefore, much less productive than still water. To make up for this, these fish will run out to sea, grow at a fantastic rate, and then obligingly deliver themselves back to your doorstep several times as large as they could ever get on river food.

Dams and pollution have cut off so many trout populations from the ocean that it's easy to forget this bonus, but all species will make this migration where and if this opportunity still exists. The mighty steelhead of the Pacific Northwest are only sea-going rainbows. The famous sea trout of Europe are merely sea-run

The Atlantic Salmon (*Salmo salar*), the fish that outshines all others, even its close and princely *Salmo* relatives.

browns. And the "salters" of Cape Cod and the "sea-trout" of Canada's Maritime Provinces are just brookies that have packed on the poundage during a season in the Atlantic.

This type of fishing rewards skill and punishes error because the quarry is shy and feeds selectively. This makes the capture of a trout especially rewarding. Yet if you choose the right fly and present it with delicacy and imagination after a cautious approach, you can succeed with pleasing regularity.

A complete novice might well hook into a near-record bluefish or striper on his first outing in a charter boat, but I'll lay you ten to one he couldn't catch a trout worth keeping his first day astream and he'd be lucky to catch a really decent one in his first full week.

Another amenity of trout fishing is that the fish tend to distribute themselves fairly evenly throughout a river, with every good lie holding at least a fish or two. When you approach a

Speckled Trout

The speckled trout (*Salvelinus fontinalis*), beautiful native of our eastern streams, from Georgia to the Arctic Circle.

productive-looking pool or run, you can be almost certain trout are there. It's up to you to figure out when, how, and on what they will be feeding. On the other hand, fish that school up make for feast-or-famine fishing—a lucky angler may make a killing by stumbling onto a wandering school while a more skillful one may go blank because the schools decided to avoid him that day.

Best of all, fishing for the trouts tends to become a way of life and leads the angler into more related hobbies and interests than any other sport. Certainly trout gear is talked about and tinkered with more than any other type of tackle, but that's just part of the game. I mean full-fledged hobbies in their own right. Fly-tying is a notable example. So is rod-building — especially for those few who still experiment with tapers and actions by planing their own raw bamboo. Entomology has been taken up by thousands of enthusiastic fly-tyers and flyfishermen. The truly dedicated even get involved in hydrology, geology, chemistry, botany, and the other disciplines that make up ecology in an attempt to understand more about their favorite waters, the life-systems they support, and how they can be protected or improved.

Even if you're not an angler, but merely a fish-watcher or fish-eater, you will still be drawn to the trouts. They live in the most beautiful waters of the world—cool, unspoiled streams and rivers. It's true that some mountain lakes are jewels, too, but these are usually trout lakes. Though an increasing number of our waters of all kinds have become soupy and shabby-looking, I have never seen a first-rate salmon or trout river that was not lovely to look at. For when man has butchered the trees the water is no longer cool. Where he has allowed dwellings to clutter and fester, the water is no longer pure. At this point salmon and trout quietly disappear as if they were part of an ethical boycott.

The outward beauty of the trout has been described so often that I need add little here. You may well think this praise has been overdone if you have seen these fish only in restaurant windows or in the baskets of friends who have followed the hatchery truck to your local creek. All these are hatchery fish, raised in sluggish tanks on artificial food, and they are cheap counterfeits, easily detectable on the line, in the hand, or on the table. Then, too, colors of all fishes fade soon after they die. To eyewitness these fish in their full splendor you must hold the wild ones in your hands at the moment of capture. Then, to steal a phrase from Izaak Walton, they are "Too pleasant to be looked upon, but only on holy-days."

The shape, or conformation, of the trouts is another joy to behold. We say a pickerel is skinny, a bass is deep, a carp is fat or a flounder is flat. But compared to what? Compared to a trout, of course. Unconsciously, we take the shape of the trouts as the yardstick against which all other fish are measured.

This may be hard to believe, but trout even smell good — at least they do when compared to most other fishes. Pike are notoriously slimy and bass have a skin odor that only a fisherman could love—which is why they are usually skinned before cooking. But I have never heard even a fastidious non-fisherman complain about the stench of a fresh-caught trout or salmon. A small point, perhaps, but add it to our total reckoning.

Index

Foreword

◆ Thoughtful observers of current political trends cannot help but note a fundamental but largely undebated change in our national agenda. Without much fanfare, mindless spending that was once associated with the "cold war" is being replaced by that for a new war: the "war on crime."

Susan L. Miller's timely collection of essays *Crime Control and Women* suggests that women have an important, though often unrecognized, stake in this new war, and that women's concerns must be placed at the center rather than at the periphery of any discussions of crime and crime control. That is precisely what the essays in this volume accomplish.

What is women's stake in what seems, on the surface, a set of policies driven by a public and well-publicized agenda to get tough on crime, particularly violent crime, which virtually all acknowledge is an almost exclusively male problem? Indeed, given that women are far more likely than men to fear criminal victimization, it would seem at least superficially that women would welcome the protection offered by the renewed focus on criminal victimization.

Well, as this excellent set of readings illustrates, things are not quite that simple. First, crime is down, not up, in U.S. society. A recent study by the American Bar Foundation (1995) found, for example, that with reference to rates of violent crime, "in no instance is the rate higher than 20 years ago and in most categories it is now substantially lower." Murder rates, as an example, were higher in 1933 than in 1992 (American Bar Foundation 1995, p. 4). Similarly, recent data released by the U.S. Department of Justice show that murder, rape, robbery, and aggravated assaults are at a 23-year low (Bureau of Justice Statistics, 1997a, p. 1).

Although crime levels have remained relatively stable or decreased, the public perception is clearly that crime is out of control. Between 1989 and 1994, for example, the proportion of citizens who reported that they were "truly desperate" about crime increased from 34% to 62% (Madriz, 1997, p. 6). As Lynn S. Chancer notes in this collection, the public fear of crime is driven more by media constructions and political grandstanding about the crime problem than it is by direct, personal experience. And as Mona J. E. Danner notes about one of the high profile "solutions" to the crime problem—"Three Strikes and You're Out"—women definitely need to ask what we will pay for this pitch.

Well, for starters, the pitch is for prisons and prison construction, and the cost here, both socially and fiscally, is staggering. In 1930, the number of U.S. citizens in state and federal prisons stood at just over 100,000. It took about five decades for that figure to double. Then, in 1980, the U.S. love affair with incarceration began in earnest; in that decade alone, the number of men and women in prison nearly tripled. By 1996, the number of men and women in U.S. prisons stood at a staggering 1,182,169, with about another 500,000 of our citizens in jail (Bureau of Justice Statistics, 1997b, p. 1).

The bill that we are paying for the current imprisonment binge is also immense. Mauer (1994) estimates that the cost of incarceration is $26.8 billion annually. A conservative estimate is that each new prison cell costs about $100,000 to build and about $22,000 per bed to operate (Donziger 1996, p. 49). As a direct result of the building boom in corrections, corrections budgets are by far the fastest growing segment of state budgets—increasing by 95% between 1976 and 1989. During this same period, state expenditures for lower education dropped slightly (2%), higher education dropped by 6%, and state expenditures for welfare (excluding Medicare) dropped by 41% (Donziger 1996, p. 48). This means that monies that once went to support low-income women and their children in the community, as well as the dollars to provide them with educational opportunities, are being cut back dramatically to fund jails and prisons.

Political and media constructions about crime are clearly racialized, which has laid the political groundwork for both the "solution" to the crime problem as well as those who are constructed as the "criminals." *Crime* has become a code word for *race* in the United States. Currently, nearly 1 out of 3 African American boys and men between the ages of

20 to 29 are under some form of correctional supervision (Mauer & Huling, 1995, p. 3).

As a result, correctional supervision, especially detention and imprisonment, seems increasingly to have replaced other historic systems of racial control (slavery, Jim Crow laws, ghettoization) as ways of keeping women and men of color in their "places" (Schiraldi, Kuyper, & Hewitt, 1996). This clearly has consequences for both girls and boys, women and men who are born nonwhite in a country with a lamentable history of racism. One scholar, commenting on this trend, observed, " 'prison' is being re-lexified to become a code word for a terrible place where blacks reside" (Wideman cited in Schiraldi, Kuyper, & Hewitt 1996, p. 5). And this is not an understatement.

And as Bush-Baskette clearly documents in this volume, although the public construction of the criminal is male, the hidden victims of many of the get-tough policies have been women, particularly women of color. Increases in women's imprisonment have outstripped male increases for every year, largely because, although "violent" crime captures the headlines, the upcriming of drug offenses, combined with dramatic changes in sentencing guidelines, has resulted in a huge increase in the imprisonment of women of color, particularly African American women.

Have these changes, though, brought about a safer world for women? Well, actually, not. A closer look, even at the victimization data mentioned earlier shows that the great reduction in criminal victimization has occurred in areas of male victimization, whereas women's victimization has either remained stable or actually increased (Bureau of Justice Statistics, 1995, p. 1). Why? Because the violence women experience is often at the hands of someone they know, and macho crime policies (whether they invoke the images of boot camps or wars) do little to protect women; in fact, most of the widely accepted understandings of women's vulnerability, as Elizabeth A. Stanko observes in this volume, tend to mislead women completely.

What will make for a safe society? Certainly, as the editor suggests in her opening essay, a return to a concern for social justice is an essential starting point. We also need to look past punitive and masculinist methods such as punishment-imprisonment to other forms of restorative justice, such as the community conference methods described in this volume by Braithwaite and Daly. In addition to healing rather than harming the social fabric, such interventions are also far more afford-able. This collection ably demonstrates that women do have a stake in redirecting the current macho war on crime, which more often than not harms women while also fueling racial tensions and exacerbating poverty. Our work can, in fact, lay the groundwork for more humane ways to reduce both crime and victimization by putting justice first and hatred last.

MEDA CHESNEY-LIND
Professor, Women's Studies,
University of Hawaii at Manoa

References

American Bar Foundation. (1995). Reducing crime by increasing incarceration: Does this policy make sense? *Researching Law, 6*(1), pp. 1, 4-7.

Bureau of Justice Statistics. (1997a). *Changes in criminal victimization, 1994-1995.* Washington, DC: U.S. Department of Justice.

Bureau of Justice Statistics. (1997b). *Prisoners in 1996.* Washington, DC: U.S. Department of Justice.

Donziger, S. (Ed.). (1996). *The real war on crime.* New York: Harper Perennial.

Madriz, E. (1997). *Nothing bad happens to good girls.* Berkeley: University of California Press.

Mauer, M. (1994). *Americans behind bars: The international use of incarceration, 1992-1993.* Washington, DC: The Sentencing Project.

Mauer, M., & Huling, T. (1995). *Young black Americans and the criminal justice system: Five years later.* Washington, DC: The Sentencing Project.

Schiraldi, V., Kuyper, S., & Hewitt, S. (1996). *Young African Americans and the criminal justice system in California: Five years later.* San Francisco: Center on Juvenile and Criminal Justice.

Acknowledgments

♦ The idea for this book began over coffee conversations at the American Society of Criminology conference in Boston. A group of criminologists wondered aloud why no one is looking at the consequences of the popular crime control policies and how they will affect women. Feminist scholars have, in fact, been contributing to this dialogue, yet these ideas and research are not collected in any single forum. It has been a joy to gather and solicit the chapters that comprise this collection. Together, they provide a road map of issues to continue examining and raising questions about—over more coffee, in classrooms, in journals, and in the public discourse.

Books cannot be written in isolation from the encouragement and feedback of others. I have been fortunate to have such support. Most important, I would like to thank the contributors to this collection, for without their enthusiasm and thoughtful scholarship, the book would not have come to fruition. I owe a big intellectual debt to other criminologists whose work embraces the discussion of policy implications of criminological theory and research. I also want to thank my students at Northern Illinois University and at the University of Delaware for their eagerness to understand the relevance of policy development and implementation. I am sure they can recite this refrain in their sleep: "What are the ramifications of this policy? Who is left out? What can we do to improve on this?" Claire Renzetti, Kay Forest, and Dan Curran were all optimistic and upbeat sounding boards as I navigated my way through this project. Terry Hendrix and Dale Grenfell had faith in the value of this book and helped greatly with the operational end of the process.

Last, I would like to thank my parents for raising me to value social justice and for encouraging my efforts to seek answers to complicated issues.

RAND study concludes that the law will not be applied equally, which may lead to unplanned consequences, such as nonviolent petty offenders being incarcerated for decades, decreased reliance on plea bargaining (causing backlogs and huge increases in court costs), as well as racial disparities in enforcement practices (see California Legislative Analyst's Office, 1995; Donziger, 1996; Schiraldi, Kuyper, & Hewitt, 1994).

In Chapter 2, James Massey, Susan L. Miller, and Anna Wilhelmi explore the issues of civil forfeiture of property as a valuable weapon used by the government to quickly and efficiently confiscate assets from suspected drug traffickers. Since the turn of the century, the federal government has become increasingly involved with criminal cases, with drug cases in 1990 representing the largest category (Friedman, 1993, p. 268). The federal government has "the muscle and the jurisdiction to make a big noise, to mount campaigns, to wage 'wars,' with airplanes, Coast Guard cutters, and all sorts of paraphernalia" (Friedman, 1993, p. 275), but its impact is limited and often futile. Prison populations continue to grow with convicted drug dealers, so, next, civil forfeiture of assets was embraced as a weapon in the war on drugs's arsenal. However, the forfeitures of so-called guilty property punishes not only the alleged guilty party involved, but also innocent third parties, specifically women (and sometimes, children). Women as spouses, owners, or girlfriends are victimized by the government's forfeiture of property. Massey et al.'s analysis focuses on the complexities of civil forfeiture, the negative impact on women as innocent third parties, and the stated justifications offered for the punishment of these women through an examination of federal court cases involving this issue.

Merry Morash and Lila Rucker, in Chapter 3, address the popular intermediate sentencing option of boot camps, designed as a shock incarceration strategy for first-time nonviolent offenders to instill discipline and respect for authority. The authors suggest that following a military boot camp model creates the antithesis of producing prosocial, empathetic, rehabilitated offenders. Rather, through the practice of demeaning treatment and meaningless physical tasks and punishments, it promotes a climate of masculinity that emphasizes aggressiveness, power abuses, and insensitivity to others' pain. Indeed, research has shown that although boot camps remain publicly popular and cost less than traditional prisons, offenders' recidivism is not dramatically different from incarcerated offenders unless a meaningful vocational or educational training component is included in addition to aftercare support on release (see MacKenzie, Layton, Brame, McDowall, & Souryal, 1995). Given the contradictions raised by providing training designed to prepare men for war within a correctional setting, Morash and Rucker thus question the efficacy of the boot camp as a sound punishment strategy.

In Chapter 4, Elizabeth A. Stanko explores the area of women's fear and safety concerns in Britain. No less relevant to U.S. issues about the communication of fear to women, Stanko reveals that police advice to women continues to follow misguided offender stereotypes by highlighting stranger danger, causing women to fear the infrequent offender. Police give advice admonishing women to protect themselves—which puts the onus on women to prevent crimes. The social and political climate in the United States today emphasizes offenders' low self-control, evilness, immorality, and lack of a work ethic (see Gottfredson & Hirschi, 1990; Messner & Rosenfeld, 1994, for examples) while simultaneously holding individuals (particularly women) personally responsible for avoiding victimization. Stanko challenges these practices and exposes the consequences for women of such police behavior and advice.

Lynn S. Chancer, in Chapter 5, offers a provocative analysis of media representations of the confluence of race, class, gender, and ethnicity in high profile violent crimes. She addresses these issues through local and national newspapers' coverage of three cases: the New Bedford gang rape, the Central Park jogger rape, and the Bensonhurst "mistaken identity" murder. As her work reveals, these cases play out scenarios in which there is rampant victim blaming or victim exoneration (and hence, offender bashing) depending on one' position in society and in his or her community. Chancer's concern is that the media accounts can act as inanimate players in creating public opinion and support for social control efforts. When competing claims collide, infighting occurs, relegating systemic changes to the background and reinforcing conservative approaches to crime control (see also Elias, 1993). In addition, acceptance or rejection of issues aired in public forums also influences how the criminal justice system treats women and how these women are treated within their local communities.

In Chapter 6, Susan L. Miller, with her work "The Tangled Web of Feminism and Community Policing," explores feminist thought and controversies related to a traditionally masculinized component of the criminal justice system—the police. She raises the philosophical issues and contradictions contained in the tension between traditional policing styles and beliefs and alternative policing strategies, such as community policing. Her argument is that traditional policing has emphasized a more autonomous, efficient, impersonal model, and this image has been used to prevent women from equal participation in the institution because of their (stereotypical) tendency to value relational connections, care, and personal connections. Yet the new genre of policing, community policing, stresses the "feminine" side of justice. Miller explores the consequences of what happens when traditionally female traits are elevated to desirable characteristics and how this might affect male and female officers' skills and job performance evaluations. This notion of gendered skill in the community policing context is reminiscent of recent work on gender and technology in which "skill" remains differentiated by gender under circumstances when it is advantageous for organizations to draw these distinctions (see Acker, 1992; Cockburn, 1991).

In the seventh chapter, "The War on Drugs as a War Against Black Women," Stephanie R. Bush-Baskette provides a set of questions to guide future research on the topic of racial disproportionality and the incarceration of black women. Too little research has been conducted on black female criminality and the treatment of black women by the criminal justice system. Bush-Baskette begins her chapter by noting the increase in the numbers of female offenders incarcerated between 1980 and 1990 for nonviolent property crimes and drug offenses, and asks: Has the well-publicized "drug war" resulted in these increases in female incarceration, as opposed to simply greater drug use by females? And are black women more likely to be disproportionately incarcerated relative to white females for the same offenses? The chapter examines how the interactive effects of racial stereotyping and gender may be embedded in criminal justice system treatment. In other research, Chesney-Lind (1995), looking only at gender, found that mandatory sentencing for drugs had a profound effect on women, although women's involvement continues mostly to be with minor offenses compared to their male counterparts. Tonry (1995), examining only black men, revealed that black men have been disproportionately affected by the war on drugs compared to similarly situated white male offenders. Bush-Baskette asks whether the goals of the war on drugs and the mandatory sentencing initiatives are to decrease drug use and reduce violent crime and how these efforts relate to black female offenders.

In Chapter 8, Zoann K. Snyder-Joy and Teresa A. Carlo address the destructive emotional and social costs related to family life when parents—mothers in particular—are separated from their children because of mothers' imprisonment. They remind us that when fathers are locked up, their children are typically cared for by their girlfriends, wives, or their own mothers. Yet when women are incarcerated, important bonds that have been empirically demonstrated to be related to lower truancy, less promiscuity, better grades, and higher self-esteem of children disintegrate. The state, in acting as the punitive parent, trains women to become "better" parents in their prison programs, whereas no such attempt is made with incarcerated fathers. Thus, the burden of maintaining and improving parental bonds in the face of punishment becomes a goal that often seems out of reach. Snyder-Joy and Carlo's analysis of a program designed to lessen the deleterious effects of mother's imprisonment, with a Michigan women's prison children visitation program, offers hope for what the future *could* look like if we were to take the importance of familial bonds seriously.

An alternative strategy to the traditional criminal justice system response to violent men is explored by John Braithwaite and Kathleen Daly in Chapter 9. They discuss the failure of current punishment methods in addressing the masculinist structures that facilitate violence and turn instead to what they feel is a more promising approach, namely, community conferencing. This approach combines shaming elements and ritualized reintegration ceremonies as well as other key principles of republican criminology, such as victim and community empowerment (see Braithwaite, 1989; Braithwaite & Pettit, 1990). Although some feminist researchers have criticized the use of mediation-type efforts in addressing intimate violence because it privileges, or equalizes, relationships already characterized by power imbalances and patriarchal structures, Braithwaite and Daly discuss how these asymmetries can be addressed within the communitarian conference approach (see Fineman, 1991; Rifkin, 1989),

Last, in Chapter 10, Claire M. Renzetti provides a synthesis of the issues raised in this collection. She examines the broader connections between crime control policies, violence against women, and how these issues are not just about crime control but, rather, share similar features that guide social policy in general, such as welfare reform. Renzetti's chapter also provides a valuable set of questions to examine when using a feminist approach to evaluate the strengths and weaknesses of crime control policies.

As we fast approach the 21st century, criminal justice policy makers and the public will face skyrocketing expenditures; new prisons will soon be filled. We can learn from experience, failures and successes, and research. Crime, and our social reaction to it, touches us all—there are myriad interconnections among and between women, whether as the children of inmates, sharing the fear that keeps women from being as autonomous and independent as men, or looking at the employment opportunities that exist for women and men in this crime control industry explosion. We need to move beyond stopgap, after-the-fact solutions; reducing crime is about getting smart, not about getting tough. And within this framework, social control and punishment must remain just and humane, with commitments to prevention, education, and treatment. Thus, this book is a collection of chapters written by individuals committed to looking beyond popular rhetoric and slogans. In light of this, the authors' works offers hope in forging a new path to future, *wiser* criminal justice policy making.

References

Acker, J. (1992). The future of women and work: Ending the twentieth century. *Sociological Perspectives, 35,* 53-68.

Bertram, E., & Sharpe, K. (1996, January 6). War ends, drugs win. *The Nation, 264*(1), 11-17.

Braithwaite, J. (1989). *Crime, shame and reintegration.* Sydney, Australia: Cambridge University Press.

Braithwaite, J., & Pettit, P. (1990). *Not just desserts: A republican theory of criminal justice.* Oxford, UK: Oxford University Press.

California Legislative Analyst's Office. (1995). *The "three strikes and you're out" law: A preliminary assessment.* Sacramento, CA: Author.

Caringella-MacDonald, S. (1988). Parallels and pitfalls: The aftermath of legal reform for sexual assault, marital rape, and domestic violence victims. *Journal of Interpersonal Violence, 3*(2), 174-189.

Chesney-Lind, M. (1995). Rethinking women's imprisonment: A critical examination of trends in female incarceration. In B. R. Price & N. J. Sokoloff (Eds.), *The criminal justice system and women.* New York: McGraw-Hill.

Cockburn, C. (1991). *In the way of women: Men's resistance to sex equality in organizations.* Ithaca, NY: ILR.

Donzinger, S. R. (Ed). (1996). *The real war on crime: The report of the National Criminal Justice Commission.* New York: HarperCollins.

Elias, R. (1993). *Victims still: The political manipulation of crime victims.* Newbury Park, CA: Sage.

Fineman, M. (1991). *The illusion of equality: The rhetoric and reality of divorce reform.* Chicago: University of Chicago Press.

Friedman, L. M. (1993). *Crime and punishment in American history.* New York: Basic Books.

Gottfredson, M. R., & Hirschi, T. (1990). *A general theory of crime.* Stanford, CA: Stanford University Press.

Greenwood, P. W., Fydell, C. P., Abrahamse, A. F., Caulkins, J. P., Chiesa, J., Model, K. E., & Klein, S. P. (1994). *Three strikes and you're out: Estimated benefits and costs of California's new mandatory sentencing law.* Santa Monica, CA: RAND.

MacKenzie, D., Layton, R. Brame, R., McDowall, D., and Souryal, C. (1995). "Boot Camp Prisons and Recidivism in Eight States." *Criminology. 33*(3), 327-357.

Messner, S. F., & Rosenfeld, R. (1994). *Crime and the American dream.* Belmont, CA: Wadsworth.

Rifkin, J. (1989). Mediation in the justice system. *Women & Criminal Justice, 1,* 41-54.

Schiraldi, V., Kuyper, S., & Hewitt, S. (1994). *Racial disparities in the charging of Los Angeles County's "third strike" cases.* San Francisco: Center on Juvenile and Criminal Justice.

Tong, R. (1984). *Women, sex, and the law.* Totowa, NJ: Rowman & Allenheld.

Tonry, M. (1995). *Malign neglect.* New York: Oxford University Press.

Weatheritt, M. (1987). Community policing now. In P. Wilmot (Ed.), *Policing and the community* (pp. 7-20). London: Police Studies Institute.

CHAPTER ONE

Three Strikes and It's *Women* Who Are Out

The Hidden Consequences for Women of Criminal Justice Policy Reforms

Mona J. E. Danner

✦ The 1994 Federal Crime Control Act marks the 26th year of the "get tough on crime" movement initiated with the passage of the 1968 Crime Control and Safe Streets Act (Donziger 1996, p. 14). The 1984 crime bill increased penalties for drug offenses, thereby engaging the "War on Drugs" and initiating the centerpiece of law-and-order legislative efforts to control crime—mandatory minimum and increased sentence lengths. "Three Strikes and You're Out" laws in particular captured the imagination of the public, press, and politicians. State legislators in 37 jurisdictions proposed Three Strikes laws in 1993 and 1994, often as part of their own state crime bills. By February 1995, 15 jurisdictions had enacted these laws, and California voters had made

This chapter was originally prepared as the 1995 Women's Studies Junior Faculty Lecture, Old Dominion University; I thank Anita Claire Fellman, Director of Women's Studies, for that invitation. Thanks to Marie L. Van Nostrand (Virginia Department of Criminal Justice Services) and Lucien X. Lombardo (Old Dominion University) who were most gracious in providing me with materials. An earlier version was presented at the 1995 American Society of Criminology meetings, Boston, Massachusetts. The members of Our Writing Group and COOL provided much encouragement and entertainment.

Three Strikes part of their Constitution (Turner, Sundt, Applegate, & Cullen, 1995). The new sentencing laws contained in the federal and state crime bills increased the dramatic expansion of the criminal justice system already underway, especially in corrections.

In 1995, the United States of America recorded over 5.3 million adults in the correctional population (U.S. Department of Justice, 1996). Our nation now incarcerates over 1.5 million of its citizens in federal and state prisons, more than a fourfold increase in just 20 years; another one-half million people are in local jails. Over 120,000 of those imprisoned are women (Gilliard & Beck, 1996). In the 1980s, the rate of women's imprisonment increased nearly twice as much as that of men's, and 34 new women's prison units were opened (Immarigeon & Chesney-Lind, 1992). African Americans, who account for 13% of the population, are 48% of those incarcerated (Maguire & Pastore, 1995, p. 546); 20 years ago they were 35% of those locked up (Maguire, Pastore, & Flanagan, 1993, p. 618). Black men and women are 7 times more likely to be imprisoned than are white men and women (U.S. Department of Justice, 1995); the expansion of mandatory and increased sentences for drug law violations accounts for much of the increase (Mauer, 1990). Young African American men are particularly hard hit by the rhetoric and ensuing policies associated with the war on drugs and Three Strikes laws (Tonry, 1995). Nearly all of those behind bars are poor.

The result of "lock 'em up" policies is that U.S. prisons currently operate at 114% to 126% capacity (Gilliard & Beck, 1996). Across the country, federal and state governments are engaged in an enormous and costly prison construction program. In fact, prisons represent "the only expanding public housing" in our country (*The Nation*, 1995, p. 223). One truism of prison and jail construction remains: If you build it, they will come. And so, the costs associated with maintaining these facilities and incarcerating citizens—especially geriatrics as lifers age—will quickly dwarf the costs of construction.

The rationale behind the crime bills and the resulting expansion of the criminal justice system cannot be found in the crime rate. Despite political rhetoric at the national and state levels and the carnage shown daily and repeatedly in all forms of news and entertainment media, the violent crime rate has remained relatively stable over the past 20 years as measured by the National Crime Survey (Bureau of Justice Statistics, 1994a).

Throughout it all, however, the consequences for women of the expansion of the criminal justice system remain largely unconsidered and invisible in public policy discussions. This chapter makes women visible in the identification of the hidden costs to women of the expansion of the criminal justice system. In brief, I argue that, one way or another, it is women who will pay the lion's share of criminal justice reform.

Looking for Women

The feminist revolution in society and the academy is about making women visible, interrogating and deconstructing the manner in which women do appear, and calling for progressive action to benefit women. In criminal justice, feminist analysis has largely focused on women as offenders, victims, and workers (Price & Sokoloff, 1995) with the issues and debates centered around building theory, containing men's violence against women, and the equality-difference concern (Daly & Chesney-Lind, 1988). This chapter, indeed the entire volume, advances feminist perspectives in criminal justice in the analysis of the ways in which supposedly gender-blind crime control writ large affects all women.

Women are not readily visible in current criminal justice policy debates. The use of a baseball analogy—Three Strikes and You're Out—to refer to the policy of mandatory life sentences for those persons convicted of three felonies illustrates the exclusion of women from the crime debates. Although it's called the national pastime, women don't identify with baseball much, have no significant presence in the sport, and reap few of its economic benefits (facts true of all professional sports). Yet it is in this sense that baseball represents an excellent analogy to the crime bills because women remain largely invisible from the debates surrounding criminal justice reforms. When women do appear, it is often as diversionary props that only barely resemble the realities of the lives of women and girls. Recent public debates in some states regarding increasing the availability of concealed weapons provide one illustration of this phenomenon.

During the 1995 legislative year, Virginia enacted a "right to carry" law requiring that judges grant permits for concealed weapons to nearly anyone who applies (Snider, 1995). Lobbyists for the National Rifle Association (NRA) along with sympathetic legislators repeatedly invoked the image of the lone woman walking to her car at night who might need a gun to protect herself from the lurking stranger ready to pounce on her at any moment. This image of a woman served as a diversionary prop to obscure the protests of police and judges who objected to the law because of safety concerns and the restriction on judicial discretion. The image also diverted attention away from the vested interests of the NRA and state politicians who benefit from NRA contributions.

This is simply one example of the way in which women are used in debates surrounding criminal justice policies. Women's lives and the realities of potential dangers are distorted, and in the process, women are left out of the debate and policies are enacted that will not only *not* benefit women, but will, in fact, harm women.

Nearly all of the political rhetoric about crime focuses on making our streets and neighborhoods safe again and protecting our homes from vicious, dangerous intruders. The focus on stranger crimes ignores the fact that it is the ones whom they know and love who represent the greatest danger to women's lives.

Although women are much less likely than men to become victims of violent crimes in general, when women are assaulted, robbed, or raped, the best guess is to look to loved ones (Bachman, 1994). Of these violent crimes that women experience, the perpetrator is a husband, boyfriend, ex-husband, or ex-boyfriend 28% of the time; the comparable figure for men is 2%. Adding in other relatives increases the figure for women to 34%; for men, it is 5%. Expanding the definition to include other persons known reveals that 72% of the times that women are the victims of violent crimes, the assailant is known to the victim either as an acquaintance, a relative, or an intimate partner; for men, this figure is 54%. The offender is a stranger in just one quarter of the occasions when women are victims of violent crime. In violent crimes occurring between spouses, lovers, and ex-spouses and ex-lovers, 90% of the time, the victim is a woman. And a woman is the victim in 70% of murders between intimate partners (Bureau of Justice Statistics, 1994b).

Women need far less protection from strangers than from supposed protectors, especially intimate partners, relatives, and acquaintances.

But the debates surrounding the crime bills and recent research demonstrate that women are also at risk from the lawmakers and even some law enforcers (Kraska & Kappeler, 1995), most of whom are men, nearly all of them white, and with respect to politicians, legislators, and judges, members of the elite social classes. Law makers do not pay attention to the data but, like the public, fall victim to popular myths about crime, especially the myth that it is strangers who are most responsible for violent victimizations, particularly those committed against women. The result is that this myth and others like it are used to shape public debate and craft public policies that ignore women's lives and force women to bear the brunt of the financial and emotional costs of such policies.

The *New York Times* called women the "quiet winners" in the U.S. Crime Bill because of the inclusion of the Violence Against Women Act (Manegold, 1994). This portion of the national crime bill budgets $1.6 billion for a national hot line for domestic violence victims and education programs aimed at police, prosecutors, and judges. It includes provisions that encourage mandatory arrests in domestic violence complaints, sex offender registration programs, the release to victims of the results of rapists' HIV tests, and it allows women to file civil suits in cases of sex bias crimes.

The Violence Against Women Act makes women's victimization visible and crafts public policies to assist women. The act represents an important step in public recognition of, and response to, male violence against women. But examination of the crime bills and their accompanying public debate reveals no sign of women other than as victims of domestic violence.

Feminist interrogation about how criminal justice policies affect women's lives calls us to make visible more of the ways in which criminal justice policies affect women. Considering the unintended consequences and hidden costs of the crime bills and current public policies suggests that women are less likely to be quiet winners in criminal justice reforms as a whole than to be quiet and big-time losers.

And so we return to the baseball analogy. "Three Strikes and You're Out" doesn't just refer to the policy of mandatory life sentences following a third felony conviction. "Three Strikes and You're Out" also refers to three ways in which women will be hurt by, and forced to pay for, criminal justice reform.

Strike One–Off the Rolls

The first strike against women comes in the decisions regarding which government services will be sacrificed to pay for the expansion of the criminal justice system. The emphasis on budget balancing and deficit reduction at the national and state levels means that money targeted for tough-on-crime proposals comes at the expense of other government programs. RAND researchers concluded that implementation of California's Three Strikes law would require cuts in other government services totaling more than 40% over 8 years—a move that would leave the state of California "spending more money keeping people in prison than putting people through college" (Greenwood et al., 1994, p. 34). The hardest-hit programs, however, are those in social services, especially those targeted to the poor, most of whom are women and children.[1]

Discussion about entitlements to the poor is to some extent a separate debate about the causes of poverty and the state's responsibility, or lack thereof, to help alleviate misfortune and suffering. But it is also a debate that remains close to the debates about crime and criminal justice. Like criminal offenders and prisoners, women on welfare and their families are demonized as lazy, unwilling to work for their keep, immoral, and criminal. Both groups—composed disproportionately of poor and minority persons—are scapegoated as the source of numerous social ills while public attention draws away from inequitable economic and political conditions (Sidel, 1996). Blaming the victims of structural conditions justifies cutting welfare for the poor and funneling savings elsewhere.

Social services that benefit women are sacrificed to accommodate the expenditures associated with the expansion of the criminal justice system. Chesney-Lind (1995) notes that New York continued to build beds in women's prisons at the same time that it had an insufficient number of beds for women and children in shelters. Adequate social services can reduce those life stressors associated with criminality; legal changes and battered-women's shelters helped reduce the rates of women's homicide of male partners (A. Browne, as cited in Chesney-Lind, 1995).

The rhetoric surrounding cuts in social programs reveals class, as well as racial-ethnic and gender, bias. The Welfare Reform Bill of 1996 imposes a limitation on the length of time that poor women may receive AFDC (Aid to Families with Dependent Children). After 2 years, most women will be kicked off the rolls under the assumption that they will find work. Overall, few provisions are made for ensuring that either jobs or day care are available. We see social class bias operating here. Politicians, pundits, and religious leaders commonly argue that children should be cared for at home by the mother. Apparently, this is true, however, only for middle-class mothers and their children; poor mothers are admonished and will be legally required to leave their children so that they may return to work in order to save the tax coffers.

In 1994, at the same time that Virginia first instituted welfare reform, the state also passed its crime bill and accompanying criminal justice reforms. Plans called for the building of 27 new prisons at a cost of $1 billion over 10 years (later estimates placed these costs at $2-4 billion) as well as Three Strikes and other provisions for increasing the length of sentences for violent offenses and repeat offenses. The bill also called for the abolition of parole as of January 1, 1995, but the governor's new parole board had already, in effect, abolished parole as it drastically reduced the number of paroles granted—at a cost of $77 million in just 6 months (LaFay, 1994). Virginia prisons remain so overcrowded that they cannot accept new inmates to be housed in local jails awaiting transfer to the state system. This, in turn, has led to such pressures in the jails that sheriffs sued the state to force it to assume its responsibility and take custody of its charges (Jackson, 1995). One way in which Virginia, like many states, deals with the problem of overcrowding is to ship inmates to other states and pay them the costs associated with incarceration (LaFay, 1995).

The expenditures associated with the expansion of the criminal justice system are being paid for in part by the savings to come from reforms that cut the social safety net of welfare. Furthermore, an "iron triangle" of interests—politicians, job-starved communities, and businesses that build and service prisons—benefits from tough-on-crime rhetoric and policies (Thomas, 1994). Neither military, corporate, nor middle-class subsidy programs are targeted for payment in support of the prison industrial complex; rather, social service programs—with their disproportionately poor, minority, and female recipients—remain those responsible for picking up the check.

Women are the majority of direct beneficiaries of various social service programs, but we know that they steer nearly all of those benefits to their dependents, especially their children but also the elderly and disabled adults in their lives. Simply put, women and those who depend on them will lose their social security, in part so that politicians can appear to be tough on crime and imprison more men and women. It is poor women—who are also disproportionately minority, especially African American women—and their families who in this way will pay a disproportionate share of the hidden costs associated with the wars on crime and drugs.

Strike Two–Jobs for Whom?

Women are not only more likely than men to be the recipients of social services, women are also more likely to be employed in social service agencies as social workers, case workers, counselors, and support staff. The implications of this fact represent the second strike against women.

Sixty-nine percent of social workers are women, and women comprise an even larger portion of front-line case workers and clerical personnel (U.S. Bureau of the Census, 1994, p. 407). Thus, as social services are cut back, women workers will be disproportionately affected.

Critics will respond that the expansion of the criminal justice system means increased employment opportunities for women. After all, 24% of law enforcement employees in the United States are women (Maguire & Pastore, 1995, p. 55). Even greater opportunities appear to exist in corrections, where 30% of employees in adult corrections are women (Maguire & Pastore, 1995, p. 92). However, most women employed in law enforcement and corrections agencies work in traditional pink collar ghettos as low wage clerical or support staff. Practically speaking, the *only* way to advance to upper levels of administration in either policing or corrections is through line employment as a police or correctional officer. And although 72% of law enforcement employees are police officers, only 9% of police officers are women (Maguire & Pastore, 1995, p. 55). And, women make up just 18% of correctional guards (Maguire & Pastore, 1995, p. 92).

There remains a long-standing bias against women in policing and corrections. Even after women's more than 20 years of proven effectiveness as officers on the streets and in the prisons, male coworkers and supervisors persist in their bias against them. They use harassment and masculine work cultures that marginalize women to resist efforts to increase the representation of women on these forces (Martin & Jurik, 1996; Morash & Haarr, 1995).

The attacks on affirmative action in the current political climate further endanger women's employment possibilities in the criminal justice system (Martin, 1995). In addition, the definition and nature of work in criminal justice is being restructured to emphasize punitiveness and dangerousness. In Virginia, probation and parole counselors were renamed officers and may now carry weapons (53.1-145 of the Code of Virginia). Virginia's Director of Corrections since 1994 insists that probation and parole clients as well as inmates be called "convicts" or "felons." These moves emphasize punishment and the untrustworthiness of offenders; they stand in sharp contrast to the need to develop positive relationships to encourage social adjustment. Such practices also emphasize masculinity as a requirement for the job, thereby creating a climate that further discourages women in the work.

Three Strikes and no-parole policies have at least three implications for police and correctional officers. For the police, Three Strikes may influence people likely to be caught in the web of these laws to take more desperate measures to evade arrest than ever before. For correctional guards, abolishing parole first means overcrowding in the prisons; it also means the loss of incentives and rewards for good behavior and the loss of faith in the future. In turn, these conditions produce an increase in the likelihood of prison violence and uprisings.

Thus, real increases in fear and the loss of hope among offenders become coupled with politically inspired attitudes about the dangerousness of offenders and the punitive goals of the work. Combined with attacks on affirmative action, bias against women in traditionally male occupations, and the resulting stress on women employees, these factors may be surprisingly effective in bringing about actual *decreases* in women's employment in precisely those positions in policing and corrections that lead to advancement and higher pay.

The crime bills represent a government jobs program—criminal justice is, in fact, "the only growing public-sector employment" (*The Nation*, 1995, p. 223)—but the new jobs created come at the cost of other public sector jobs, such as those in social services, which are more likely to be held by women. And the new jobs created by the expansion of the criminal justice system are overwhelmingly jobs for men.

Strike Three–Family Values?

Men and women who commit crimes for which they are convicted and sentenced to prison have not lived their lives solely in criminal gangs; they do not structure their entire days around illegal activity; they are not *only* criminals. They are also sons and daughters, fathers and mothers. In short, they are responsible for caring for others who depend on them, and most of them do their best to meet these responsibilities because they do, in fact, love their families.

In 1991, 67% of women and 56% of men in state prisons had children under the age of 18; most of these women (72%) and men (53%) lived with their children before entering prison (Maguire & Pastore, 1994, p. 616). Imprisoned adults cannot contribute to their families' financial or psychological well-being. In a very few cases, children are committed to foster homes or institutions (Maguire & Pastore, 1994, p. 616). But most of the time, another family member takes over the care of those children and any elderly or disabled adults left behind—and that family member is usually a woman. This fact represents the third strike against women.

Because most of those imprisoned are men, it is the women in their lives—wives, girlfriends, and mothers—who are left with the responsibility for providing for the economic and emotional needs of the children and any dependent adults, a task these women must accomplish on their own. And when women are imprisoned, it is generally their mothers who take over the care of the children.

As we imprison increasing numbers of men and women, we saddle more women with sole responsibility for care of the next generation. The problem is exacerbated when the state, due to overcrowding, moves prisoners out of its system and to other states, thereby leaving women and children bereft of even emotional support from incarcerated parents.

Today in the United States, "there are at least 1.5 million children of prisoners and at least 3.5 million children of offenders on probation or parole" (Johnston, 1995a, p. 311). The women who care for these children, as well as the children themselves, must be recognized as paying some of the hidden costs of punitive criminal justice policies. Parental arrest and incarceration endures as a traumatic event for all involved. It can lead to inadequate child care due to persistent and deepening poverty. In addition, children may suffer from problems with which the women who care for them must cope: developmental delay, behavioral and emotional difficulties, feelings of shame and experiences of stigmatization, distrust and hatred of police and the criminal justice system, and subsequent juvenile delinquency (Carlson & Cervera, 1992; Fishman, 1990; Johnston, 1995b). In effect, children suffer from post-traumatic stress disorder when their parents are imprisoned (Kampfner, 1995). Effective programs to address the needs of children of incarcerated parents and their caregivers remain few in number and endangered.

As politicians get tough on crime, it is women and children who do the time, alone. Remembering the first two strikes against women discussed earlier, it emerges as strikingly clear that women will not be able to look to the federal or state governments for either public assistance or public employment. Strike three. It's *women* who are out.

Final Thoughts:
An Every Woman's Issue

It remains far too easy to be lulled into complacency when it comes to women and criminal justice. After all, women represent a very small number of offenders. And in spite of male violence against women, most victims of crime are men. Yet the social construction of crime and criminals and the political nature of their control are neither gender blind nor gender neutral. We are finally and fully confronted by the harsh reality that criminal justice *is* about women, *all* women. Although it occasionally operates as an important resource for women, the criminal justice system most frequently represents a form of oppression in women's lives. It attacks most harshly those women with the least power to resist it. As Jean Landis and I wrote several years ago,

> It is time to recognize that in real life . . . offenders do not exist as exclusive objects. They are connected in relationships with other people, a major portion of whom are women—mothers, wives, lovers, sisters, and daughters. Any woman who fights to keep her wits, and her roof, about her as she helplessly experiences a loved one being swept away by the currents of criminal justice "knows" the true brutality of the system and the exten-

siveness of its destruction. If she is a racial/ethnic minority person, which she is likely to be, and/or if she is poor, which she surely is, she intuitively knows the nature of the interaction between criminal justice practices and the racist and/or classist [as well as sexist] structure of her society, as well as its impact on her life, her family, and her community. (Danner & Landis, 1990, p. 111-112)

She also knows that precious little assistance exists for her, and those who depend on her, in the form of either welfare or employment from the larger community as represented by the state. In addition, it is every woman, no matter who she is, who will pay for the dramatic expansion of the criminal justice system. Clearly, criminal justice *is* a women's issue.

The current get-tough, lock-'em-up, and Three Strikes policies will not reduce crime nor women's pain associated with crime. They will only impoverish communities as they enrich politicians and those corporations associated with this new prison industrial complex. Although women have been largely left out of the debate, it is women who are the quiet losers—the big-time losers—in the crime bills. Criminal justice reforms such as these are politically motivated, unnecessary, ineffective, and far, far too costly. And last and most important, it is women who receive the least from the wars on crime and drugs, and it is women who bear most of their hidden burdens.

Note

1. Entitlements to the poor include AFDC; the Women, Infants and Children nutritional program; food stamps; school breakfast and lunch programs; Medicaid; public housing and emergency grants; and social security for disabled and dependent persons as well as other programs. Each of these programs is under attack and will almost certainly be cut back, just as has welfare.

References

Bachman, R. (1994). *Violence against women: A national crime victimization survey report*. Washington, DC: U.S. Department of Justice.

Bureau of Justice Statistics. (1994a). *Criminal victimization in the United States: 1973-92 trends.* Washington, DC: U.S. Department of Justice.

Bureau of Justice Statistics. (1994b). *Violence between intimates.* Washington, DC: U.S. Department of Justice.

Carlson, B. E., & Cervera, N. (1992). *Inmates and their wives: Incarceration and family life.* Westport, CT: Greenwood.

Chesney-Lind, M. (1995). Rethinking women's imprisonment: A critical examination of trends in female incarceration. In B. R. Price & N. J. Sokoloff (Eds.), *The criminal justice system and women: Offenders, victims, and workers,* (2nd ed., pp. 105-117). New York: McGraw-Hill.

Daly, K., & Chesney-Lind, M. (1988). Feminism and criminology. *Justice Quarterly, 5,* 497-538.

Danner, M., & Landis, J. (1990). Carpe diem (seize the day!): An opportunity for feminist connections. In B. D. MacLean & D. Milovanovic (Eds.), *Racism, empiricism and criminal justice* (pp. 109-112). Vancouver, Canada: Collective Press.

Donziger, S. A. (Ed.). (1996). *The real war on crime: The report of the National Criminal Justice Commission.* New York: HarperPerennial.

Fishman, L. T. (1990). *Women at the wall: A study of prisoners' wives doing time on the outside.* New York: State University of New York Press.

Gilliard, D. K., & Beck, A. J. (1996). *Prison and jail inmates, 1995.* Washington, DC: U.S. Department of Justice.

Greenwood, P. W., Fydell, C. P., Abrahamse, A. F., Caulkins, J. P., Chiesa, J., Model, K. E., & Klein, S. P. (1994). *Three strikes and you're out: Estimated benefits and costs of California's new mandatory-sentencing law.* Santa Monica, CA: RAND.

Immarigeon, R., & Chesney-Lind, M. (1992). *Women's prisons: Overcrowded and overused.* San Francisco: National Council on Crime and Delinquency.

Jackson, J. (1995, January 11). Sheriffs suing state to relieve overcrowding in city jails. *Virginian-Pilot,* pp. A1, A6.

Johnston, D. (1995a). Conclusion. In K. Gabel & D. Johnston (Eds.), *Children of incarcerated parents* (pp. 311-314). New York: Lexington Books.

Johnston, D. (1995b). Effects of parental incarceration. In K. Gabel & D. Johnston (Eds.), *Children of incarcerated parents* (pp. 59-88). New York: Lexington Books.

Kampfner, C. J. (1995). Post-traumatic stress reactions in children of imprisoned mothers. In K. Gabel & D. Johnston (Eds.), *Children of incarcerated parents* (pp. 89-100) New York: Lexington Books.

Kraska, P. B., & Kappeler, V. E. (1995). To serve and pursue: Exploring police sexual violence against women. *Justice Quarterly, 12,* 85-111.

LaFay, L. (1994, December 9). New, low parole rate has cost Va. $77 Million. *Virginian-Pilot,* pp. A1, A24.

LaFay, L. (1995, February 17). State sends 150 inmates to Texas. *Virginian-Pilot,* A1, A9.

Maguire, K., & Pastore, A. L. (Eds.). (1994). *Sourcebook of criminal justice statistics 1993.* Washington, DC: U.S. Department of Justice, Bureau of Justice Statistics.

Maguire, K., & Pastore, A. L. (Eds.). (1995). *Sourcebook of criminal justice statistics 1994.* Washington, DC: U.S. Department of Justice, Bureau of Justice Statistics.

Maguire, K., Pastore, A. L., & Flanagan, T. J. (Eds.). (1993). *Sourcebook of criminal justice statistics 1992.* Washington, DC: U.S. Department of Justice, Bureau of Justice Statistics.

Manegold, C. S. (1994, August 25). Quiet winners in house fight on crime: Women. *New York Times,* p. A19.

Martin, S. E. (1995). The effectiveness of affirmative action: The case of women in policing. *Justice Quarterly, 8,* 489-504.

Martin, S. E., & Jurik, N. D. (1996). *Doing justice, doing gender: Women in law and criminal justice occupations.* Thousand Oaks, CA: Sage.

Mauer, M. (1990). *Young black men & the criminal justice system: A growing national problem.* Washington, DC: The Sentencing Project.

Morash, M., & Haarr, R. N. (1995). Gender, workplace problems, and stress in policing. *Justice Quarterly, 12,* 113-140.

Price, B. R., & Sokoloff, N. J. (1995). *The criminal justice system and women: Offenders, victims, and workers* (2nd ed.). New York: McGraw-Hill.

Sidel, R. (1996). *Keeping women and children last: America's war on the poor.* New York: Penguin.

Snider, J. R. (1995, December 13). Have gun, will travel . . . *Virginian-Pilot,* Isle of Wight Citizen section, p. 6.

The Nation. (1995, February 20). The prison boom. Pp. 223-224.

Thomas, P. (1994, May 12). Making crime pay. *Wall Street Journal,* pp. A1, A6.

Tonry, M. H. (1995). *Malign neglect: Race, crime, and punishment in America.* New York: Oxford University Press.

Turner, M. G., Sundt, J. L., Applegate, B. K., & Cullen, F. T. (1995). 'Three strikes and you're out' legislation: A national assessment. *Federal Probation, 59,* 16-35.

U.S. Bureau of the Census. (1994). *Statistical abstract of the United States 1994.* Washington, DC: Government Printing Office.

U.S. Department of Justice. (1995 December 3). *State and federal prisons report record growth during last 12 months.* Press release.

U.S. Department of Justice. (1996, June 30). *Probation and parole population reaches almost 3.8 million.* Press release.

CHAPTER TWO

Civil Forfeiture of Property

The Victimization of Women
as Innocent Owners and Third Parties

James Massey
Susan L. Miller
Anna Wilhelmi

✦ Although it has assumed various forms, the tendency to include secondary social others as responsible for the crime, deviance, and the sins of family members, friends, and significant others is well-established in the human experience (Jacoby, 1983). As far back as the 7th century B.C.E., the prophet Jeremiah of Hebrew scripture chastised the people of Judah for their tradition of blood guilt: "The fathers have eaten the unripe grapes;" the prophet observed, "the children's teeth are set on edge" (Jeremiah 31:29). This was to change, however, under the new covenant of Yahweh proclaimed by Jeremiah: "Every man who eats unripe grapes is to have his own teeth set on edge" (Jeremiah 31:30).

The idea of individual culpability for wrongdoing, especially in the case of criminal behavior, forms the very foundation for the administration of justice in modern Western societies (Israel, 1993). The rigor of this ideal and the sensitivity of communities to the secondary suffering of those who become enmeshed in the social network of deviant

15

actors is, itself, a function of the prevailing tolerance limits within a community. As tolerance limits expand, the tendency toward strict accountability slackens by definition and, with it, any desire to ensnare the families and friends of the deviant actor. Conversely, during epochs in which policies of "zero tolerance" are enshrined, there occurs a corresponding expansion in the scope of the deviance designation process, the rigor of norm enforcement, and the severity (but often not the certainty or celerity) of punishment apparatuses.

The last several years of the 20th century is such an epoch. At a time when violent crime rates have shown significant decline, it is still considered astute for political candidates to inveigh ever more severe applications of the criminal sanction ("Clinton, Dole Focus," 1996). The punitive mind-set has drawn tolerance limits inward along several venues: increased criminalization, harsher sanctions for existing crimes, restrictions in discretionary decision making (e.g., "truth in sentencing" legislation, legislative attempts to restrict the exercise of civil rights and civil liberties, and the extension of the powers of law enforcement [police and prosecutors]). It is important to note that all of this activity has occurred without any convincing evidence that the threat of criminality or deviance-based social disorder has generally increased.

The goal of this present analysis is to provide an illustration of the inevitable side effects that accrue during epochs of expansive punitiveness. Our specific concern is with the callousness and indifference that the legal system must assume toward the family and friends of criminal actors within such epochs. It is our argument that the structure of the social web necessitates the wisdom that it is not always possible to give individuals what they deserve (Schwartz, 1978; Selznick, 1992). To do otherwise not only taxes societal resources beyond the point of social utility but provides the context to promote distributive injustice in the interest of retribution.

The focus of the analysis dwells on the practice of civil forfeiture and its effect on innocent owners, specifically women. The civil forfeiture of property has been described as one of the so-called new weapons in the ongoing war on crime (Aylesworth, 1991). Although it is perceived to serve a variety of penal purposes, the primary intent of civil forfeiture is to deny criminal actors use of the proceeds and instrumentalities of criminal enterprise (Larson, McLaughlin, & Badger, 1989). As is soon discovered, however, the right to claim ownership of property is a highly complex phenomenon, equal in effect to the value that property rights assume within a materialistic culture. In short, the prerogative of government to seize property collides with the obvious fact that property can be co-owned, loaned, leased, and, in any of a variety of ways, shared.

To accommodate to this fact, the federal and state governments have established rules to assess the culpability of secondary others in the illegal acquisition or use of shared property. There has emerged from this process the idea of "innocent owners" who can claim immunity from forfeiture procedures. Our concern revolves around the fate of women as a recurring class of so-called innocent owners. Women involved in relationships with deviant males, typically husbands, are among the most frequent claimants in legal proceedings initiated to recover property identified by the government as forfeitable. The intimacy of such relationships creates a unique challenge to women who claim innocent ownership given the current structure of forfeiture proceedings. The nature of this challenge will be examined with reference to the following four questions:

1. What does the law require of secondary others in order for them to establish themselves as innocent?

2. To what extent are these procedures neutral in gender-coded social contexts?

3. Under ordinary circumstances, how are the interests of the female innocent owners balanced against governmental interests?

4. To what extent are these outcomes consistent with the larger aims of the justice process?

In sum, this analysis is concerned with the potential effects of what Goffman (1963) has referred to as "stigma fallout," besmirching the identity of persons who are members of a deviant actor's social web, with the attendant suffering that can be imposed on these people in the wake of socially sanctioned punishments for the wrongdoers. As we will attempt to show, civil forfeiture is a practice that not only produces such effects but cannot escape from doing so if it is to achieve its principal policy objective.

Case Selection

This analysis is based on an examination of 53 federal court cases drawn from a purposive sample of 195 innocent-owner forfeiture cases identified using Westlaw Database. Specifically, these cases, heard by federal appellate courts between 1986 and 1995, involve female appellants who sought to reclaim property seized through civil forfeiture. Although a small percentage of these cases involves mothers, girlfriends, or daughters of alleged criminal offenders, the vast majority (77%) are wives presenting an innocent-owner defense. Cases dropped from the original sample consisted of those cases wherein the innocent-owner defense was advanced by a criminal defendant or where the same defense was employed by a third party unrelated to the alleged criminal offender. Thus, the cases are representative of cases where the application of the law is controversial, where the stakes are relatively high, and where women as significant others are parties to the case.

Background

The innocent-owner defense is a highly circumscribed claim that is in no way equivalent to a simple demonstration of a legal interest in property by a noncriminally culpable claimant. To understand the ways in which forfeiture law places women in special peril, a brief overview of these laws is needed.

There are two distinct legal avenues that state and federal governments use to seize property as an adjunct to law enforcement: (a) criminal, *in personam,* proceedings and (b) civil, *in rem,* proceedings. Criminal forfeiture proceedings are actions brought against a person charged with an illegal act and are considered a criminal sanction (Atkins & Patterson, 1991; Aylesworth, 1991; Dombrink & Meeker, 1986; Goldsmith & Lenck, 1992; Linscott, 1990; McClure, 1991). Civil forfeiture is an action directed against the proceeds and instrumentalities of crime. It is based on the legal fiction that the property itself is culpable of wrongdoing (Linscott, 1990; Palm, 1991; Taylor, 1990; Yoskowitz, 1992). Because the assets seized under authority of civil forfeiture statutes presumably "compensate" governments for the cost of law enforcement, these actions have been widely argued to be remedial in nature (Atkins & Patterson, 1991; *Austin v. U.S.,* 1993). Civil forfeiture has the added advantage of permitting governments to move against property without a finding of criminal culpability on the owner's part. This opportunity extends even to cases where criminal forfeiture proceedings have been foreclosed by the acquittal of the owner on criminal charges (Linscott, 1990).

There are at least 16 major federal statutes that authorize asset forfeiture; 10 of these authorize civil forfeiture specifically. The target behavior runs the gamut of vice, white-collar, and organized crime, including drug trafficking, money laundering, gambling and racketeering, child pornography and obscenity, auto and electronic communication theft, illegal arms dealing, copyright violations, smuggling of aliens, and possession of drug paraphernalia (Larson et al., 1989).

The federal civil forfeiture statute that is used in the "theatre of illegal narcotics" is incorporated in 21 U.S.C. Sec. 881 (Linscott, 1990). Section 881 allows certain property to be subject to forfeiture on conviction of the defendant-property owner in violation of the Controlled Substance Act (Linscott, 1990). This statute was originally enacted in 1970 as part of the Comprehensive Drug Abuse Prevention and Control Act. A subsequent amendment to the statute that is highly pertinent to the present discussion was enacted by Congress in 1984. Here, as described by Wilson (1991-92), Section 881 was amended

> to provide for the forfeiture of vehicles used or intended to be used in drug trafficking, of money or things of value exchanged for narcotics and of real property "which is used or intended to be used, in any manner or part, to commit or to facilitate the commission of drug-related offenses." (Wilson, 1991-1992, p. 135)

Prior to 1984, Section 881 did not authorize civil forfeiture of real property (Yoskowitz, 1992). Such property could only be forfeited through actions sanctioned under the Racketeer Influenced and Corrupt Organizations statute (RICO) or the Continuing Criminal Enterprises statute (CCE). Later, in 1988, Section 881 was again extended to include the property of leaseholders within the sweep of the forfeiture provisions (Yoskowitz, 1992).

Under federal law, persons whose property was used to commit or facilitate an act proscribed by the Controlled Substances Act without the owners' knowledge or consent can petition to retain a legal interest in property subject to forfeiture (21 U.S.C. s881 (a) (7) [1995]). What is critically important to understand in this regard is that the so-called innocent-owner claimant (a) has the affirmative obligation to initiate legal proceeding to reclaim property, (b) must often defeat a government bid for summary judgment against the property, (c) must demonstrate the legitimacy of the proprietary claims, and (d) must provide evidence that neither consent nor knowledge that property was being used to facilitate crime or that the property was, itself, a product of criminal enterprise. The burden that this places on female owners whose property has been misused by a (typically male) significant other will be demonstrated in the analysis that follows.

The Innocent-Owner Gauntlet

Legal procedure is stacked against the claimant who seeks to recover property subject to civil forfeiture and intentionally so. This in turn has led to a cavalier disregard for the effects of forfeiture on third parties. "The compelling and insistent enigma of drug abuse and its attendant ramifications," observes one author (McClure, 1991, p. 447), "far outweigh the few toes on which the civil forfeiture of assets will inevitably and harshly step." Valukas and Walsh (1988), in turn, point approvingly to the government's ability "to seize money, businesses, real estate, and vehicles from criminals, not-so-criminals, *innocent relatives* [our emphasis], and even defendants' unsuspecting counsel" (p. 31). For women, this involves negotiating the intricacies of forfeiture and property law within a milieu premised on the assumption that intimate relationships with criminal defendants bias one toward knowledge of or consent (or both) to use property in an illegal fashion.

Procedural obstacles that lie in the path of the owner-claimant begin with the government's power to seek transfer of property through summary judgment. Property targeted for forfeiture may be legally seized by the mere showing that there is probable cause to believe that the item in question was either a proceed or instrumentality of crime. Summary judgment, when rendered, brings closure to a forfeiture proceeding without a formal hearing regarding facts related to the complicity of the claimant regarding use of contested property. To stay a summary judgment, a claimant must file an affidavit with the court that disputes the government's contention regarding the claimant's role in the case. But even if a claimant is successful in preventing summary judgment against the contested property, this alone does not prove innocent ownership. Only if a subsequent hearing is granted will the claimant have the chance to address the criteria of innocent ownership by presenting evidence and, hopefully, meeting the burden of proof in support of her claim.

These hurdles, in essence, provide the government with two opportunities to defeat the claimant's legal challenge while providing the claimant with only one binding use of judicial process. Specifically, the courts have shown a capability to weigh the merits of disputations before a claimant has had a change to present evidence. The case of *U.S. v. 755 Forest Road* (1993) provides an apt example of this. In this case, the court ruled that the circumstances regarding a husband's drug use in the home could only have been unknown to his wife through her own "willful blindness." The court rejected the claimant's affidavit and awarded summary judgment to the court.

The dissenting judge in this case demonstrated a remarkable sensitivity to the manner in which legal procedure was used to circumscribe the opportunity to challenge forfeitures and to the untenable position that wives may face within the domestic setting:

> The wife's affidavit of denial should have been enough to prevent summary judgment forfeiture and give her an opportunity to be heard. The wife . . . should have at least been entitled to show that she had made reasonable efforts to eliminate the presence of narcotics in her home. . . . [W]e are dealing here with a wife and a mother, not a Cosa Nostra godfather (*U.S. v. 755 Forest Road,* 1993)

Should a claimant succeed in obtaining a hearing on an innocent-owner defense, the intimacy that is assumed to adhere to marital and other familial relationships makes it especially difficult for a female claimant to demonstrate either lack of knowledge regarding the criminal use of property or to launch a credible defense regarding an absence of consent to use property in an illegal fashion. The preceding case is illustrative of the pattern of rulings that the courts render when adjudicating an innocent-owner defense; the greater the extent to which illegal activity occurred within or near the home, or the greater the extent to which a wife was demonstratively active in joint business ventures with her spouse, the less likely it is that courts will define the female spouse as an innocent owner.

In *U.S. v. 3756 W. 106th Street,* (1992), for example, a husband was found not to have been an innocent owner of an alleged crack house by conveying to complaining neighbors that "he did not care how his tenants made their money as long as they paid their rent." In the lower court hearing, it was ruled that the wife, asserting a half-interest community property claim, lost her interest in the property through the inference that the husband acted as his wife's agent in the management of property. The appellate court reversed the judgment, claiming that the husband's agency, given neither the wife's apparent knowledge nor consent regarding the use of the property, was a question of fact to be determined by the trial jury.

Not so fortunate was the wife of a man engaged in laundering money through her personal bank account in *U.S. v 21090 Boulder Circle,* (1993). She lost a house that she had purchased for her parents subsequent to placing $100,000 in the account through which the husband's illegal proceeds had been laundered. The court held that the wife was "a sophisticated business woman" who knew "exactly what was going on." Similarly, in *U.S. v. 9818 S.W. 94 Terrace,* (1992), the court held that the claimant failed to establish by a preponderance of the evidence that she did not know that her home was used by her husband to negotiate drug transactions. In *Terrace,* the claimant testified that she had no knowledge of her husband's activity and that on the day of his arrest in their home, she had been away for most of the day running errands. Although the court conceded that there was no evidence that the property was purchased with drug proceeds and that no evidence was found that their lifestyle was inconsistent with their lawful income, it held that *"the nature and circumstances of the marital relationship* [italics added] may give rise to an inference of knowledge by the spouse claiming innocent ownership," (*U.S. v. 9818 S.W. 94 Terrace,* 1992).

Even more pointedly, the court, in *U.S. v. 5.382 Acres* (1994), held that the proliferation of drugs in and around a property, combined with evidence of drug use within the home, defeated the claim that the wife did not have knowledge of her husband's drug dealing. More important, the court held that "unless an owner with knowledge can prove every action, reasonable under the circumstance, was taken to curtail drug-related activity, consent is inferred and the property is subject to forfeiture."

Given the inference of consent in intimate relationships, evidence of submission to a husband's power over his wife has been defined as insufficient to sustain a claim of nonconsent. In the case of *U.S. v. 107.9 Acre Parcel of Land* (1990), a wife-claimant acknowledged participating in her husband's drug operation but argued that such cooperation was involuntary—that she had pleaded with her husband to stop his illegal activities, threatened to leave him, was afraid of him, and had to do whatever he told her to do. When asked specifically whether her husband had threatened her, she conceded that her husband had not threatened her directly but indicated that she perceived that carrying out his "commands" was a "normal thing that wives did," aggravated by the fact that she was isolated from others who might have provided models of behavior more appropriate for the situation in which she found herself: "I was all by myself, I don't have no friends. I was always by myself. I went shopping by myself, I did everything by myself" (*U.S. v. 107.9 Acre Parcel of Land,* 1990). The court ruled in this case that submission to the demands of a husband involved in crime was not sufficient to reach the rigorous standard of legal duress and, as such, was insufficient to forestall forfeiture of jointly owned property to the government.

The case *U.S. v. Sixty Acres* (1990) illustrates a common theme that emerges in these cases that is reminiscent of victim-blaming ideology present in domestic violence cases. Blaming the victim who is seen to be in an unsavory domestic situation and does not leave is not uncommon. For some of the same reasons a female victim of domestic violence does not leave the relationship, so is it for the female innocent owner who is victimized in civil forfeiture procedures. Narcotics, which is the reason for forfeiture in most of these cases, are associated with crime, violence, threats, danger, risk, and weapons. A person who lives with another individual who sells or uses drugs is indeed already a victim, subjected to, at the very least, emotional abuse from the user or dealer. In *U.S. v. Sixty Acres,* attribution of blame to the victim spouse is apparent: In January of 1989, Evelyn Ellis's husband sold marijuana to an undercover informant and subjected their 60 acres of property to forfeiture. She made a claim for the property, asserting the innocent-owner defense, claiming that she knew nothing of her husband's current drug dealings. As part of her defense, Ellis said that she lived in fear of bodily harm from her husband, but the court rejected this because she chose to take no action except to make verbal objections in "a bland and ineffective way, or to 'nag' her husband until he told her to 'mind her own business.' " The court held that because she was generally aware of the illegal activity, she did not meet the burden of proving she was an innocent owner; perhaps, the court explained, she was required to seek a divorce to escape the forfeiture. Although the appellate court had evidence demonstrating that Ellis's husband had been with her in the past and threatened her, *and* had beaten to death his previous wife, she could not claim lack of consent under duress because the threat was not "immediate." The court explained: "We may not substitute . . . a vaguely defined theory of 'battered wife syndrome' for the showing of duress." There must be immediate threat of harm to be considered duress. Although the court held that her fear was "genuine and pro-found," and it evoked the court's sympathy, this did not excuse her conduct.

Complete disregard or significant bias by the courts in domestic violence cases is not new. Despite major statutory reforms, courts often show callous disregard and lack of empathy or understanding of the circumstances under which an abused woman may live. Courts routinely ignore sociological data that suggest that the "cycle of violence, eco-nomic dependence, lack of support from family and community, and fear" combine to keep women from leaving these types of situations (Schafran, 1995, p. 336).

One of the most common property relationships between husband and wives in this arena involves homes that are owned in tenancy by the entireties. The *entireties* concept as applied to property ownership is unique to marital relationships. At its core is the tenet that husbands and wives have an indivisible tenancy interest that is tantamount to their owning the property as if they were a single individual. Hence, neither spouse can divest his or her interest in the property without the consent of the other spouse. Similarly, both spouses have a sole survivorship interest in the property should one of the spouses die.

Tenancy by the entireties creates an opportunity for governments to establish a 100% interest in a property, even in instances where a wife has successfully pressed an innocent-owner claim. The case of *U.S. v. 44133 Duchess Drive* (1994) is an illustrative case. In this case, a husband was arrested for selling cocaine from the couples' home, and in fact, cocaine was found on the defendant's property. In her innocent-owner affidavit, the claimant testified that she had no knowledge of her husband's use of the home for drug trafficking, and if she had known, she would have moved to terminate the marriage. The court ruled that the wife could retain 100%, tenancy by the entireties, interest in the property as long as death, divorce, or a court order did not intervene to severe the relationship.

It is interesting, however, that the court also stipulated that the government was free to seek an attachment and thereby establish its own legal interest in the property. If the government so moved, it would mean, as a practical matter, that the wife would ultimately retain her 100% interest only if she were preceded in death by her husband. Should she attempt to dissolve the entireties by divorcing her husband or by obtaining a court order breaking the entireties, the government would be empowered to force the sale of the property and retain the husband's 50% interest in it. Should the wife precede her husband in death, the government could claim the entire property, effectively disabling the wife from willing any portion of the property to beneficiaries.

The doctrine of tenancy by the entireties grows out of a very specific theory of the marital relationship, one marked, if not by bliss, at least by harmony and a mutuality of interest that is obviously not present in seizure through forfeiture. Given the hostile interests of the government, it is fairly evident that within the context of civil forfeiture, tenancy by the entireties, rather than providing a benefit to a surviving spouse, becomes, instead, the vehicle of her exploitation. Thus, even in situations where innocent ownership is affirmed, an attenuated claim to property is the end result of the claimant-spouses' brush with justice.

The courts also recognize a *straw owner* concept. In *U.S. v. Henry* (1995), the court held that the sole-owner wife claimant was forced to sell her house because most of the money used to purchase the house was found to be "drug money" of her husband, and that this made her in essence a straw owner. Although the property was not used to facilitate the commission of a crime, the substitute asset provision (21 U.S.C. 853 (p) West Supp. 1995) statute provides that other assets can be substituted for forfeiture. The wife was held to be a straw owner and not a real owner of the property, even though she lived in the house, paid part of the purchase price of the house ($23,000 at time of purchase), and wanted to keep the house for her children. The court forced a sale and gave the wife claimant her $23,000 back from the purchase price of a home worth $195,000.

Although we cannot draw generalizations regarding how *all* judges think in forfeiture cases, nonetheless, this illustrative material supports a broader claim, which is that the criminal justice system has the *capacity* to exacerbate the victimization of women. It is to this issue and related ones we now turn.

Discussion and Conclusion

The patterns revealed by court decisions raise serious questions about consequences faced by so-called innocent owners—women, and by extension, their children. The most striking defect in legal reasoning in this arena involves the naive social assumptions made by the judiciary on how women *ought* to have behaved in their relationships. Contained within the court rulings is a nested assumption of symmetry of resources and power dynamics within marriage or intimate relationships. We know that this symmetry is fallacious: Social and economic power simply is *not* equally distributed. Yet, repeatedly, judges imply that wives should be accountable for their husbands' behavior—that wives share culpability by their "failure" or inability to control their husbands. This judicial misunderstanding and condemnation facilitates wives' claims of innocent-owner status—they are left with little choice, for they are even less successful with making a claim in another way. Indeed, only 5 of the 53 women in this sample were able to keep 100% interest in property because of innocent-owner claims, contingent on the entireties unbroken by death, divorce, or court order. It is not insignificant to note that federal judges deciding these cases are almost exclusively white males, appointed during the Reagan and Bush administrations at the height of the punitive crime control platform.

Rather than reflect the judicial reasoning used in these court decisions about women's efficacy in relationships, the extant research demonstrates an asymmetry of power in intimate heterosexual relationships, with these relationships being characterized by different controls and meanings for male and female partners. For example, Johnson (1988) suggests,

> The structure of the husband-wife relationship, considered apart from other contravening sources of power, tends to define wives as lesser partners in marriage. . . . . From a structural standpoint, marriage institutions tend to be controlled by men and serve to control and organize women's mothering. (p. 5)

Women prioritize relationships over other socially valued capital and tend to value them more than do men, even when they are inherently unstable and morally problematic (Gilligan, 1982, p. 62). If violence, or illegal behaviors, or something else occurs within relationships, women are far more likely than men to try to maintain and repair the relationships (Miller & Simpson, 1991, p. 340). As Miller and Simpson state,

> Relationships, then, have pushes and pulls for females. On the one hand, females seek the protection, intimacy, and emotional security that relationships offer. . . . On the other hand, it is within relationships that females fall under the direct control of men. (p. 340)

This has direct consequences for innocent-owner claims.

A common thread running throughout the judges' rulings is that a woman "must have known" and can control the general extent as well as the particulars of her husband's drug involvement. Her knowledge is both implicitly and explicitly granted because, after all, she lived there with him (and perhaps their children) and together created a daily life. Therefore, full responsibility or accountability is attached to her here because of shared domicile. Yet this assumption is sometimes inverted and used by judges at other times to demonstrate she does *not* share similar interests or expectations of property—as illustrated by the straw-owner concept in *U.S. v. Henry*—even though they shared the living space.

In addition, in cases in which the woman, in effect, becomes "married" to the government, the rights of her children as heirs are also compromised in these three ways:

1. On death, divorce, or court order, the entireties are broken, and the government gets the husband's value of the property.
2. If the wife dies before the husband, the government gets the entire property.
3. If the wife divorces, it becomes tenancy in common (50-50), but the government can force a sale of the property.

So, although there is a "forced marriage," the government does not recognize or "claim" the children. Wives (and husbands) lose their ability to will property to their children. Through her new "indentured" status, a woman can make no decisions without government intrusion and shared decision-making power. This assumes a benevolent and caring state that has the best interests of the children at heart, which does not appear to be the case.

These realities are reminiscent of Goffman's (1963) concept of *courtesy stigma,* in which innocent others carry a burden that is not really theirs. They did not personally earn the stigmatic role. In the case of civil forfeiture, not only are wives or significant partners affected, but their children may also suffer the emotional and financial costs of "stigma fallout." If civil forfeiture has been constructed as a deterrent-based punishment mechanism, the tenets fail here because offenders who forfeit assets typically have never considered how their drug trafficking might affect the future of their children.

Another striking pattern emerges when we examine how women are silenced by the courts when trying to assert an innocent-owner defense because of cultural stereotypes endorsed by the judiciary. In one case in which drug paraphernalia was discovered in the couple's bedroom, the wife's affidavit denied the allegations and asserted an innocent-owner defense, claiming that she knew her husband used drugs; however, she did not know he used them in her home (*U.S. v. 755 Forest Road,* 1993). The court rejected her claim of innocent owner (forfeiting the property to the government), holding that she did not take all reasonable steps to prevent the illegal use of her property. In another case (*U.S. v. 107.9 Acres Parcel of Land,* 1990), the wife was unable to proceed on an innocent-owner defense because the court rejected her claim that her participation in her husband's marijuana cultivation was obtained under duress (she stated she was afraid of him and had to do whatever he told her to do). In other legal arenas, such as with battered women who kill their abusers in self-defense, feminist legal theorists contend that relying on traditional "reasonable man" standards is problematic because the behavioral expectations are simply not gender neutral. For instance, the self-defense requirement includes elements such as imminence of threat or harm, proportionate strength, and so forth, yet women and men, on average, are *not* of proportionate size nor do they incite equal levels of fear based on threats or physical intimidation (see Gillespie, 1989). Judicial interpretations thus often ignore not only the gendered power dynamics within intimate relationships but also the structural limits to women's efficacy in disentangling themselves from such relationships that are present in these situations.

Taken as a whole, our findings suggest that the severity of judicial reasoning in civil forfeiture cases with innocent-owner claims reflects a punitive orientation, a misguided notion of equality between men and women, and a naive dismissal of how these imbalances affect social power and resource distribution.

In sum, it is not that women are routinely victimized by the criminal justice system in innocent-owner cases that concerns us; it is that they are victimized at all. The fact that wives and girlfriends are quite capable of conspiring in the use of property toward illegal ends does not excuse the callousness observed in the cases reviewed herein. The fact that an intimacy factor is defined as prima facie evidence of knowledge and consent to illegal use of property is disturbing in its implications. When coupled with the notion that duress short of an immediate threat of harm is irrelevant to the assessment of responsible ownership, one finds a pernicious logic that acts to further victimize untold numbers of women caught up in difficult relationships. Justice Clarence Thomas, in his concurring opinion in *Bennis v. Michigan* (1996), cautions that a woman's exploitation by a philandering husband followed by forfeiture of her property to the state of Michigan is "ultimately a reminder that the Federal Constitution does not prohibit everything that is intensely undesirable." In fact, the decision in *Bennis,* in a fashion similar to the cases reviewed here, is ultimately a reminder that the criminal justice system has yet to develop a coherent and just perspective on the myriad gender-based inequities that blight the administration of justice in the United States during the final years of the 20th century.

References

Atkins, D. P., & Patterson, A. V. (1991). Punishment or compensation?: New constitutional restrictions on civil forfeiture. *Bridgeport Law Review, 11,* 371-381.

Aylesworth, G. N. (1991). *Forfeiture of Real Property: An overview.* Washington, DC: Bureau of Justice Assistance.

Clinton, Dole Focus on Health, Crime. (1996, May 12). *Chicago Tribune* (p. I1).

Dombrink, J., & Meeker, J. W. (1986). Beyond 'buy and bust': Nontraditional sanctions in federal drug law enforcement. *Contemporary Drug Problems, 13,* 711-740.

Gillespie, C. (1989). *Justifiable homicide: Battered women, self-defense, and the law.* Columbus: Ohio State University Press.

Gilligan, C. (1982). *In a different voice.* Cambridge, MA: Harvard University Press.

Goffman, E. (1963). *Stigma: Notes on the management of spoiled identity.* New York: Simon & Schuster.

Goldsmith, M., & Lenck, W. (1992). *Protection of third-party rights.* Washington, DC: Bureau of Justice Assistance.

Israel, J. H. (1993). Cornerstones of judicial process. *Kansas Journal of Law and Public Policy, 2,* 5-30.

Jacoby, S. (1983). *Wild justice.* New York: Harper & Row.

Johnson, M. M. (1988). *Strong mothers, weak wives.* Berkeley: University of California Press.

Larson, C. W., McLaughlin, M. J., & Badger, S. M. (1989). *Federal asset forfeiture: Law enforcement's guide to preparing a case for judicial forfeiture.* Washington, DC: U.S. General Accounting Office.

Linscott, M. S. (1990). Asset forfeiture (modern anti-drug weapon): Is bankruptcy a defense? *Tulsa Law Journal, 25,* 617-637.

McClure, K. (1991). Federal civil forfeiture of assets: How it works and why it must. *Bridgeport Law Review, 11,* 419-447.

Miller, S. L., & Simpson, S. S. (1991). Courtship violence and social control: Does gender matter? *Law & Society Review, 25*(2), 335-365.

Palm, C. W. (1991). RICO forfeiture and the eighth amendment: When is everything too much? *University of Pittsburgh Law Review, 53,* 1-95.

Schafran, L. H. (1995). Overwhelming evidence: Gender bias in the courts. In B. R. Price & N. J. Sokoloff (Eds.), *The criminal justice system and women* (2nd ed., pp. 332-342). New York: McGraw-Hill.

Schwartz, B. (1978, August). Vengeance and forgiveness: The uses of beneficence in social control. *School Review, 86,* 655-668.

Selznick, P. (1992). *The moral commonwealth: Social theory and the promise of community.* Berkeley: University of California Press.

Taylor, W. W., III. (1990). The problem of proportionality in RICO forfeitures. *Notre Dame Law Review, 65,* 874-895.

Valukas, A., & Walsh, T. P. (1988). Forfeitures: When Uncle Sam says you can't take it with you. *Litigation, 14,* 31-37.

Wilson, D. (1991-1992). Drug asset forfeiture: In the war on drugs, is the innocent spouse the loser? *Journal of Family Law, 30,* 135-153.

Yoskowitz, J. (1992). The war on the poor: Civil forfeiture of public housing. *Columbia Journal of Law and Social Problems, 25,* 567-600.

Legal References

Austin v. U.S., 509 U.S. 602 (1993)
Bennis v. Michigan WL 88269 Y.S. (1996)
21 U.S.C. s881 (a) (7) (1995)
21 U.S.C. 853 (p) West Supp. (1995)
U.S. v. 755 Forest Rd., 985 F.2d 70 (1993)
U.S. v 21090 Boulder Circle, 9 F. 3d 110 (1993)
U.S. v. 3756 W. 106th Street, 940 F. 2d 1537 (1992)
U.S. v. 9818 S.W. 94 Terrace, 788 F.Supp. 561 (1992)
U.S. v. 5.382 Acres, 871 F. Supp 880 (1994)
U.S. v. 107.9 Acre Parcel of Land, 898 F. 2d 396 (1990)
U.S. v. Sixty Acres, 727 F. Supp.1414 (1990)
U.S. v. 44133 Duchess Drive (863 F. Supp. 492 (1994)
U.S. v. Henry _____F. 3rd_____ (1995)

CHAPTER THREE

A Critical Look at the Idea of Boot Camp as a Correctional Reform

Merry Morash
Lila Rucker

Introduction: The Boot Camp Idea

In several states, correctional boot camps have been used as an alternative to prison in order to deal with the problem of prison overcrowding and public demands for severe treatment (Parent, 1988). Correctional boot camps are styled after the military model for basic training, and, similar to basic training, the participants are primarily young males. However, the "recruits" are offenders, though usually nonviolent and first-time ones (Parent, 1988). Boot camps vary in their purpose, but even when they are instituted primarily to reduce overcrowding, the implicit assumption is that their programs are of equal or greater deterrent or rehabilitative value than a longer prison sentence.

By the end of 1988, boot camps were operating in one county (Orleans Parish, Louisiana) and in eight states (Georgia, Oklahoma, Mississippi, Louisiana, South Carolina, New York, Florida, and Michigan), they were planned in three states (North Carolina, Kansas, and New Hampshire), and they were being considered in at least nine other states (Parent, 1988). The model was also being considered for a large

Reprinted from *Crime & Delinquency,* Vol. 36, No. 2, April 1990. Used with permission.

number of youthful Detroit offenders. And in the summer of 1989, the boot camp model was put forth by the House Crime Subcommittee chairman as a potential national strategy for treating drug abusers (Gannett News Service, 1989).

The National Institute of Justice is supporting evaluations of correctional boot camp programs, and other evaluations without federal support are also underway. Such formal evaluations will no doubt provide invaluable evidence of the effect of the problems on participants and, in some cases, on the correctional system (e.g., the resulting diversion of offenders from more restrictive environments). The purpose of this article is to provide another type of assessment, specifically, a critical analysis of the history and assumptions underlying the use of a military model in a correctional setting.

The popular image of military boot camp stresses strict and even cruel discipline, hard work, and authoritarian decision making and control by a drill sergeant. It should be noted that this image does not necessarily conform to either current practices in the U.S. military or to all adaptations of boot camp in correctional settings. However, in a survey of existing correctional boot camp programs, Parent (1988) found commonality in the use of strict discipline, physical training, drill and ceremony, military bearing and courtesy, physical labor, and summary punishment for minor misconduct. Some programs have combined selected elements of the military boot camp model with more traditional forms of rehabilitation. In Oklahoma, for example, the paramilitary structure, including the use of regimentation, has been only one aspect of an otherwise "helping, supportive environment" that is considered by the administration to be a prerequisite if "change is to last or have any carry over" (Kaiser, 1988). In Michigan, the major emphasis has been on developing the "work ethic" by utilizing various motivational tactics (e.g., chants), strong discipline, and rehabilitation (Hengish, 1988). All participants work from 8:00 a.m. to 3:30 p.m. daily; evenings involve educational and therapeutic programs. When more traditional methods of rehabilitation are included, a consideration of the boot camp idea is more complex, requiring an analysis of both the costs and benefits of mixing the imagery or the reality of a boot camp approach with other measures.

Regardless of the actual degree to which a militaristic, basic training model has been emphasized, the press has taken this emphasis as primary and usually has portrayed it in a positive light. Numerous stories have been printed under titles such as "Boot Camp—In Prison: An Experiment worth Watching" (Raspberry, 1987, p. H21), "New York Tests a Boot Camp for Inmates" (Martin, 1988), " 'Squeeze You Like a Grape': In Georgia, A Prison Boot Camp Sets Kids Straight" (*Life,* 1988), and "Some Young US Offenders Go to 'Boot Camp'—Others Are Put in Adult Jails" (Sitomer, 1987, p. 1). The text similarly has reflected a positive evaluation of the approach. For example, Raspberry (1987) wrote of the Louisiana boot camp that "[t]he idea [is] to turn a score of lawbreakers into disciplined, authority-respecting men." He quoted the warden: "[W]e're giving an inmate a chance to get out of prison in 90 days instead of seven years. But you're making him work for it. . . . We keep them busy from the time they wake up until they fall asleep with chores that include such sillinesses as cleaning latrines with a toothbrush." The warden concluded that the approach "teaches them self-discipline and self-control, something many of these men have never had" (Raspberry, 1987). Similarly, Martin (1988, p. 15) wrote about the New York program:

> Days are 16 hours long, and two-mile runs and calisthenics on cold asphalt are daily staples. Work is chopping down trees or worse. The discipline recalls Parris Island. . . . those who err may be given what is genteelly termed 'a learning experience,' something like carrying large logs around with them everywhere they go or, perhaps, wearing baby bottles around their necks.

Life's (1988, p. 82) coverage of the Georgia program included the following statement by one of the sergeants: "[Here] being scared is the point. You have to hit a mule between the eyes with a two-by-four to get his attention . . . and that's exactly what we're doing with this Program."

The journalistic accounts of boot camps in corrections have celebrated a popular image of a relatively dehumanizing experience that is marked by hard, often meaningless, physical labor. The inmate has been portrayed as deficient, requiring something akin to be beaten over the head in order to become "a man."

The imagery of the people that we send to boot camp as deserving of dehumanizing treatment is in itself troubling, but even more so in light of the fact that the inmates are disproportionately minorities and underclass members. The boot camp idea also raises the disturbing question: Why would a method that has been developed to prepare people to go into war, and as a tool to manage legal violence, be considered as having such potential in deterring or rehabilitating offenders? Wamsley (1972, p. 401) concluded from a review of officers' manuals and prior research that military basic training is designed to promote fundamental values of military subculture, including

(1) acceptance of all-pervasive hierarchy and deference patterns; (2) extreme emphasis on dress, bearing, and grooming; (3) specialized vocabulary; (4) emphasis on honor, integrity, and professional responsibility; (5) emphasis on brotherhood; (6) fighter spirit marked by aggressive enthusiasm; and (7) special reverence for history and traditions.

In another summary of the values stressed in military basic training, Merry Finch (1981, p. 9) identified "a commitment to organized violence as the most effective way to resolve conflicts, a glorification of 'hard' emotions (aggression, hatred, brutality) and a strict channeling of 'soft' emotions (compassion, love, suffering). . . ." Clearly, many of the objectives of military basic training are not shared by the policymakers who promote correctional boot camps. What is even more striking is that none of them make sense as a means to promote either rehabilitation or deterrence, and the emphasis on unquestioned obedience to authority and aggression is inconsistent with prosocial behavior.

What Has Been Tried and What Works in Corrections?

The correctional boot camp model has been touted as a new idea. However, militarism, the use of hard labor, and efforts to frighten offenders—most recently surfacing in the "Scared Straight" programs— have a long history in prison settings. We will focus first on militarism. In 1821, John Cray, the deputy keeper of the newly constructed Auburn Prison, moved away from the use of solitary confinement when suicides and mental breakdowns increased. As an alternative, he instituted a military regime to maintain order in overcrowded prisons (McKelvey, 1977, p. 14). The regime, which was based in part on his experiences as a Canadian army officer, required downcast eyes, lockstep marching, no talking or other communication among prisoners, and constant activity under close supervision (McKelvey, 1977). The issue for Cray and his contemporaries was the prevention of crime "through fear of punishment; the reformation of offenders being of minor consideration" (Lewis, 1983, p. 226).

Neither Cray's attempts nor those of his Pennsylvania cohorts, however, achieved either deterrence or reform (Cole, 1986, p. 497). During the Progressive Era, there was a shift away from the sole emphasis on punishment. At Elmira Reformatory, Zebulon Brockway added a new twist to Cray's militaristic regulations, certain of which (lockstep marching and rules of silence) had fallen into disrepute because they were now seen as debasing, humiliating, and destructive of initiative (Cole, 1986, p. 497). By 1896, the industrial reformatory at Elmira had ". . . well coordinated discipline which centered around the grading and marking system, an honest application of the indeterminate sentence, trade and academic schools, military organization and calisthenic exercises" (McKelvey, 1977, p. 137). Similar to many of the contemporary boot camps, at Elmira the philosophy was to combine both rehabilitation approaches and work with military discipline and physical activity to, among other things, improve self-esteem. However, the legacy of Brockway's Elmira Reformatory was not a move toward rehabilitation (Johnson, 1987, p. 41). Instead, the militaristic atmosphere set the stage for abusive punishment, and the contradiction between military discipline and rehabilitation was apparent (Pisciotta, 1983, pp. 620-21).

Some might counter the argument that the militaristic approach opens the door for abusive punishment by pointing out that in contemporary correctional settings, physical punishment and harm are eliminated. However, as Johnson (1987, p. 48; see also Christie, 1981) noted, nonphysical abuse can be viewed as a "civilized" substitute. Also, in some cases physical abuse is a matter of definition, as is seen in the accounts of dropouts from one contemporary boot camp. They reported being treated like "scum," working 18-hour days, being refused permission to use the bathroom, being provoked to aggression by drill instructors, being forced to push a bar of soap along the floor with their noses, and being forced to participate in an exercise called "air raids" in which trainees run and dive face down, landing on their chests with arms stretched out to their sides (Bellew, 1988, p. 10). At least in some settings, the military model has provided a legitimization of severe punishment. It has opened the door for psychological and even physical abuse that would be rejected as cruel and unusual punishment in other correctional settings.

Turning now to work in correctional settings, its persistent use has been supported by its congruence with alternative objectives, including punishment, incapacitation, rehabilitation, and control inside the institution (Lejins, 1970, pp. 309-10). However, the form of work at a particular time has not been influenced just by ideals and objectives, but by basic economic forces (Rusche and Kirchheimer, 1939). For example, in order to protect private enterprise, the treadmill was used to occupy offenders following prohibitions against the use of prison labor (Morse, 1973, p. 33; see also Morash and Anderson, 1978). Also, in the nineteenth century, a major purpose of imprisonment was to teach the regular work habits demanded by employers (Rusche and Kirchheimer, 1939; Melossi and Pavarini, 1981). In contemporary discussions of correctional boot camp programs, work has been justified as both punitive and rehabilitative, as both exemplifying the harsh result of breaking the law and teaching the "work ethic." However, the economic constraints imposed by limited budgeting for rehabilitation efforts and the shrinking number of jobs for unskilled workers have shaped the form of work. Thus, hard physical labor, which has no transfer to the contemporary job market, has been the choice in correctional boot camps.

Further criticism of the form of work used in the boot camp settings rests on empirical research. The literature on work programs in general has not supported the conclusion that they produce a decrease in recidivism (Taggart, 1972; Fogel, 1975, pp. 114-16; Lipton, Martinson, and Wilks, 1975). Especially pertinent to the present analysis, in a recent article Maguire, Flanagan, and Thornberry (1988) showed that labor in a correctional institution was unrelated to recidivism after prisoner differences were taken into account. The exception was work programs that actually provided employment (e.g., Jeffrey and Woolpert, 1974; Rudoff and Esselstyn, 1973). Based on an extensive review of the literature, Gendreau and Ross (1987, p. 380; see also Walter and Mills, 1980) further specified the characteristics of correctional work programs that were related to lower recidivism: "Work programs must enhance practical skills, develop interpersonal skills, minimize prisonization, and ensure that work is not punishment alone." Clearly, the evaluation literature contradicts the idea that hard, often meaningless, labor in the boot camp setting has some positive effect.

Moreover, although negative attitudes and lack of the work ethic might be one influence on the choice of economic crime instead of a job, structural arguments have provided alternative explanations. For example, Wilson (1987) documented that low-skilled minorities have been hardest hit by deindustrialization of the national labor force and changes in the geographic location of industries. The labor surplus in low-technology fields, and the strength of general social and psychological factors thought to cause criminal behavior, have been found to counteract most offender work programs (Maguire et al., 1988, p. 16). In a supporting ethnography, Sullivan (1983) showed that the slightly greater availability of jobs in white, working-class neighborhoods explained residents' lesser criminality; in black, lower class neighborhoods where there were no work opportunities, males in their late teens used robbery as a regular source of income. Altering men's attitudes toward work does nothing to combat these structural deficiencies.

The "Scared Straight" programs, a contemporary version of correctional efforts intended to deter offenders through fright, also are not supported by empirical research. In a San Quentin program of this type, older adolescent participants were arrested less often but for more serious crimes than a comparison group (Lewis, 1983). An evaluation of a similar New Jersey program showed that participants were more seriously delinquent than a control group (Finckenauer, 1982). On the surface, an evaluation of a "tough" detention regime in British detection centers suggests that though there were no increases in recidivism, there also were no decreases (Thornton et al., 1984). However, although the British detention center programs incorporated such "military" approaches as strict discipline, drill, and parades, a primary focus was on staff being personally helpful to the youth. Also, humiliating and punitive staff reactions were prohibited by general guidelines. Thus, the British detention center model departed markedly from many of the U.S. models. In general, then, the program elements of militarism, hard labor, and fear engendered by severe conditions do not hold much promise, and they appear to set the stage for abuse of authority.

Military Boot Camps

The idea of boot camp as applied in correctional settings is often a simplification and exaggeration of an outdated system of military training that has been examined and rejected as unsatisfactory by many experts and scholars and by the military establishment itself. The difficulties that the military has discovered with the traditional boot camp model, and the resulting implications for reforms, could be instructive to people in search of positive correctional measures.

A number of difficulties with what will be referred to as the "traditional" military boot camp approach that is now mimicked in correctional settings were uncovered by a task force appointed in the 1970s (Raupp, 1978; Faris, 1975). The first difficulty with the traditional boot camp approach involved inconsistent philosophies, policies, and procedures. Ten years after the task force report was published, a follow-up study provided further insight into the problem of inconsistency and the related patterns of unreasonable leadership and contrived stressful situations. The study documented the "severe effects" of lack of predictability in such areas as standards for cleanliness and how cadence was called (Marlowe et al., 1988, p. 10). According to the study, "predictability and reasonableness contribute to trainee self esteem, sense of being valued by the unit and commitment to the organization." Further "when authority is arbitrarily imposed, or when leaders lead strictly by virtue of their power or authority, the result is often anger and disrespect" (Marlowe et al., 1988, pp. 11-12). Also, "dysfunctional stress [which results when work is irrelevant or contrived], heightens tensions, shortens tempers, and increases the probability of abuse while generally degrading the effectiveness of training" (Raupp, 1978, p. 99). By contrast, "functional" stress is legitimate and work-related, resulting from such instances as "the mental and physical stress of a tactical road march" (Raupp, 1978, p. 98).

The second difficulty that the task force identified with traditional boot camp training was a widespread "we-versus-they" attitude and the related view that trainees were deserving of degrading treatment (Raupp, 1978, p. 9). The we-versus-they attitude was manifested by different behavioral and/or dress standards for trainees and for other personnel. Specifically, trainees were given "skin-head" haircuts and were prohibited from swearing and shouting, and physical training was used as punishment.

Aside from the investigative reports sponsored by the military, empirical studies of the effects of military boot camps, the effects of physical training (which is a major component of many correctional boot camp programs), and learning in general have provided relevant findings. Empirical evidence regarding the psychological impact of traditional military basic training on young recruits between the ages of 18 and 22 has demonstrated that "there was no increase in scores on ego-strength, or any other evidence of beneficial psychological effects accruing from basic training" (Ekman, Friesen, and Lutzker, 1962, p. 103). Administration of the MMPI to recruits revealed that "the change in the shape of the [MMPI] profiles suggests that aggressive, impulsive, and energetic features became slightly more prominent" (Ekman et al., 1962, p. 103). The authors concluded that the changes on the subscales imply that

> more callous attitudes, a tendency to ignore the needs of others, and feelings of self-importance increase slightly during basic training. The recruits appear less prone to examine their own responsibility for conflicts, and more ready to react aggressively. (Ekman et al., 1962, p. 104)

The importance of this finding is heightened by the conclusion of Gendreau, Grant, and Leipciger (1979, p. 71) that components of self-esteem that were good predictors of recidivism include the very same characteristics, namely, "self-centered, exploitive of others, easily led, and anxious to please." Sonkin and Walker (1985; see also Walker, 1983; Eisenberg and Micklow, 1979) also speculated that basic training in the military can result in the transfer of violent solutions to family settings. Eisenberg and Micklow (1979, p. 150) therefore proposed that military basic training be modified to include classes on "communication skills, stress reduction, and anger management." Although correctional boot camps do not provide training in the use of weapons or physical assault, they promote an aggressive model of leadership and a conflict-dominated style of interaction that could exacerbate tendencies toward aggression.

In another empirical study of military basic training, Wamsley (1972) contrasted the effects of Air Force Aviation Cadet Pre-Flight Training School with Air Force Officer's Training School. The Cadet

School employed harsh techniques—including such activities as head shaving, marching miles in stiff shoes, and impromptu exercises as physical punishment—to inculcate basic values and eliminate the "unfit." After one week, 33% of recruits left. Wamsley (1972, p. 401) wrote that "Those with low capacities for anxiety, insufficient self-esteem to withstand and discredit abuse, inability to control or suppress anger, or those with latent neuroses or psychoses literally 'cracked' under the stress, and attempted suicides and psychiatric referrals were not uncommon." The purpose of constant exhortations to "get eager, mister" or "get proud, Raunch" was to promote an aggressive fighter spirit, and the "common misery and despair created a bond" among the trainees.

Increased aggression and a bond among inmates are not desired outcomes of correctional boot camps, so again the efficacy of using the military boot camp model is in question. Moreover, it is unlikely that the offenders in correctional boot camps are more mentally healthy than Air Force recruits. What is the effect of using such techniques when there is no escape valve through dropping out of the program? And, if only the best-adjusted stay, what is accomplished by the program? The contrast of the Cadet School with the Officer's Training School, which did not use humiliation and severe physical conditions and punishment, provides convincing evidence of the ineffectiveness of such an approach to training people. Wamsley (1972, p. 418) concluded that there was a "lack of a clear utility for Pre-Flight's intense socialization" and that the "socialization process was brutally expensive in human terms and produced exaggerated forms of behavior which were not clearly related to effective task accomplishment."

Additional research has shown that positive improvements in self-esteem result from physical training primarily when the environment is supportive. For example, Hilyer and Mitchell (1979, p. 430) demonstrated that college students with low self-concepts who received physical fitness training in a helpful, facilitative, supportive environment demonstrated an increase in self-concept scores. The improvement was two and one-half times as great as that of low-concept peers who received physical fitness training and no support.

Also contradicting the negatively oriented training strategy that is characteristic of the old-style military boot camp model, virtually no empirically supported criminological theories have suggested that aggressive and unpredictable reactions by authority figures encourage prosocial behavior. The opposite has been promulgated by most learning theorists. For instance, Satir (1972, p. 13) concluded that learning happens only when a person feels valued and is valued, when he or she feels like a connected part of the human race (see also Rogers, 1975, p. 6). Feelings of self-worth can only flourish in an atmosphere in which individual differences are appreciated and mistakes are tolerated; communication is direct, clear, specific, and honest; rules are flexible, human, appropriate, and subject to change; and links to society are open (Satir, 1972, pp. 4-6). Finally, there has been considerable theory and research showing that antisocial behavior is increased when authority figures provide aggressive models for behavior (e.g., Bandura, 1973, pp. 252-53). Research in the sociology of sport has provided further evidence that physical training under the direction of an authoritarian trainer increases aggression (Coakley, 1986).

There is no systematic evidence of the degree to which the problems in traditional-style military boot camps are manifested in correctional settings, but there is evidence that they do occur. The introductory descriptions of the correctional boot camp model clearly reveal a tendency for some of the "drill sergeants" to use negative leadership. Telephone interviews with representatives of nine correctional boot camps show a tendency to focus on "tearing down the individuals and then building them back up." Reflective of this philosophy are negative strategies alluded to earlier, such as the utilization of debasing "welcoming speeches," the "chair position," and "learning experiences" that require men to wear baby bottles around their necks or to carry tree limbs with them all day.

Correctional boot camps also provide settings conducive to high levels of unpredictability and contrived stress. In one program (Bellew, 1988, p. 5), dropouts, current trainees, and parolees who had completed the program all reported that "differences between DI [drill instructor] styles made it tough to avoid trouble. Trainees' beds may be made to satisfy DI 'A,' but at shift change, if DI 'B' doesn't approve of that particular style, trainees are punished." As further illustration, another inmate reported that on the first day of participation in the boot camp, he was told that he had quit and could not participate. When the inmate sat down for the rest of the day, he was reportedly "kicked out for sitting down," and his having left the program was listed as voluntary. The inmate reported that he had tried to participate but that the drill instructor kept telling him that he had quit. The interviewer reported that at the time of the interview, the offender was "still confused as to what actually had happened that day" (Bellew, 1988, p. 10).

It is true that, as proponents of correctional boot camps claim, many military recruits feel that their survival of basic training is evidence of maturity and a major achievement in their lives (Gottlieb, 1980, pp. 166-67). However, the sense of achievement is linked to the notion that the experience is the first step in preparing them for the unique role of a soldier. Moreover, military boot camp is intended as just a prelude to acquaint the recruits with their new environment, in which they will take more control of their lives (Rabinowitz, 1982, p. 1084). It is not obvious that the boot camp experience alone, including elements of capricious and dehumanizing treatment, would be seen in such a positive light by inmate participants.

Clearly, the view that boot camp is just the first step in a socialization process has not been carried over into the correctional setting. While nearly all programs reported either regular or intensive probation or parole periods following release (Parent, 1988), none of the postrelease programs have had the capability to provide the continuous and multifaceted support network inherent in being a member of the military "family" or process. Postrelease programs are not designed to provide either the tightly knit structure or the guaranteed work that characterize military life.

It could be argued that the purpose of correctional boot camp is not to bind soldiers to their leaders or to develop group solidarity. Thus, the failure of the outmoded military boot camp model to achieve these results may not be a serious concern. Even if we accept this argument, the research on military basic training raises serious questions about the potential for undesirable outcomes, including increased aggression.

Stereotypes of Masculinity and Correctional Measures

The very idea of using physically and verbally aggressive tactics in an effort to "train" people to act in a prosocial manner is fraught with contradiction. The idea rests on the assumption that forceful control is to be valued. The other unstated assumption is that alternative methods for promoting prosocial behavior, such as the development of empathy or a stake in conformity (e.g., through employment), are not equally valued. Feminist theorists (Eichler, 1980; Bernard, 1975) have noted the societywide valuation of the stereotypically masculine characteristics of forcefulness and aggression and of the related devaluation of the stereotypically feminine characteristics of empathy and cooperative group behavior. Heidensohn (1987, p. 25) specifically wrote that programs like boot camp have been "designed to reinforce conventional male behaviour" and that they range from "quasi-militaristic short, sharp shocks to adventure training."

There is little doubt that the military is a male-dominated institution (*Defense*, 1987) and that there is a military ideology that rejects both women and stereotypically female characteristics (Yuval-Davis, 1985; Yudkin, 1982; Larwood, Glasser, and McDonald, 1980; Stichm, 1981, p. 57, 1989, p. 226; Enloe, 1983). As Enloe (1983, p. 7; see also Ruddick, 1983; O'Brien, 1979) wrote, there is a common assumption that "the military . . . is a *male* preserve, run by men and for men according to masculine ideas and relying solely on *man* power." In some military settings, terms such as "little girl," "woman," and "wife" have been routinely used to negatively label a trainee who is viewed as having failed in some way (Eisenhart, 1975; Stiehm, 1982, p. 371). Traditional marching chants have included degrading comments about women, and sexist terms for women and their body parts have been common in military settings (Ruddick, 1983, p. 231). Stiehm (1981, p. 257) concluded from her research that even after the mandated inclusion of women in the U.S. Military Academy, considerable derogatory name calling and ridicule of women were common. The implication is that to fail is to be female, or, conversely, to succeed is to be aggressive, dominant, and therefore unquestionably "male."

One might argue that name calling is not used in correctional settings. Given the military background of many correctional staff involved in the reforms and the popular image of boot camp experiences, the degree to which such an antiwoman attitude exists is an important empirical question. Aside from overt rejection of women and femaleness, the boot camp model, with its emphasis on unquestioned authority and aggressive interactions and its deemphasis on group cooperation and empathy, promotes a limited image of the "true man."

It is not surprising that few have questioned the distorted image of masculinity embodied in the idea of boot camp, for this imagery is implicit in the assumptions of many criminological theories (Naffine, 1987), and it is shared by many offenders. Focusing on criminologists, Naffine (1987) showed how several major theories have presented male offenders' aggression and assertiveness in a positive light while they have devalued characteristics associated with women. To be more specific, major theories have accepted the stereotypical characteristics of men as normal and have presented women as dependent, noncompetitive, and passive. Naffine's (1987, p. 126) analysis revealed the "curious result of extolling the virtues of the male, as a good criminal, and treating conforming women as if they were the socially deviant group." This result has been echoed in the use of a military model that similarly extols the virtues that are often associated with both masculinity and aggression in our society.

Writing about images of masculinity among economically marginalized men, who are overrepresented in the offender population, Messerschmidt (1986, p. 59) built on the notion that in our society "both masculinity and power are linked with aggression/violence while femininity and powerlessness are linked with nonviolence" (also see Schwendinger and Schwendinger, 1985, p. 161). He went on to note that as a result of the unavailability of jobs that are not degrading, powerless men seek out alternative avenues through which to exercise their masculinity. Other supports of criminality include an orientation toward "exploitative individualism," as opposed to any caring ties to group members, and male bonding, which is the ritual rejection of "weakness" associated with femininity. This rejection is demonstrated through activities like gang fights. Again, there is a parallel with the stereotype of masculinity embodied in the boot camp model. Specifically, Eisenhart (1975) has described military training's emphasis on self-sufficiency and the avoidance of attachment to others.

The irony in emphasizing an aggressive model of masculinity in a correctional setting is that these very characteristics may explain criminality. Theorists working in the area of crime causation have focused on both the identification with male stereotypical traits and roles, which are consistent with illegal behavior (Oakley, 1972, p. 72; see also Tolson, 1977), and the frustration that males feel when they cannot achieve these stereotypes because of low social status (Messerschmidt, 1986, pp. 59-68). The empirical support to link stereotypical masculinity with criminality has been inconsistent (Cullen, Golden, and Cullen, 1979; Norland, James, and Shover, 1978; Thornton and James, 1979; Loy and

Norland, 1981). There is some evidence, however, that female stereo-typical characteristics predict prosocial behavior (Morash, 1983; Gilligan, 1982; Hoffman, 1975; Eisenberg and Miller, 1987).

An additional irony is found in the inclusion of women in correctional boot camps. Holm (1982, p. 273) observed that in the military, "women . . . suffered from role identification problems when put through military training programs designed traditionally " 'to make men out of boys,' " programs that had "more to do with the rites of manhood than the requirements of service jobs." There is serious doubt about the efficacy of placing women in a militaristic environment that emphasizes masculinity and aggressiveness and that in some cases rejects essentially prosocial images and related patterns of interaction associated with the stereotype of femininity.

Alternative Models in Corrections

Correctional policymakers and program staff are not alone in their application of the traditional boot camp model as an approach for training people outside of military settings. Looking again at news reports, we see that the boot camp type of training has been accepted in a variety of organizations as a means to increase the productivity, skill levels, efficiency, and effectiveness of participants. Such enterprises are as diverse as the Electronic Data Systems Corporation (Klausner, 1984, p. 17), the Nick Bollettieri Tennis Academy (Arias, 1986, p. 107), and Japan's Managers' Training School (Bueil, 1983). In keeping with the boot camp model, participants are made to endure humiliation so that a bond can develop with the teacher (Klausner, 1984, p. 17). There appear to be social forces supporting acceptance of the general idea that the boot camp model is appropriate as a method for promoting training and human development. In spite of the societal pressures to use such a model, our assessment has a number of negative implications for the application of boot camps in correctional settings.

The first implication is based on the research on boot camp and the development of human potential in a military setting. At certain times and in certain geographic locations, military personnel have been charged with training and employing populations that are not markedly dissimilar from the economically marginalized young men and women that populate the prisons. They also have been engaged in the imprisonment of people for the violation of criminal laws. A continued examination of their techniques and outcomes could provide further instruction. As a starting point, it might be noted that in the military, the version of boot camp used in correctional settings is not commonly viewed as an effective correctional measure. Furthermore, through *Project 10,000,* the military has been successful in integrating poorly educated recruits into their own workforce, though often in relatively low-skill positions that restricted transfer to the civilian workforce (Sticht et al., 1987). Contrary to critics' anticipation of disciplinary problems with poorly educated recruits, less than 5% of the participants failed to conform to military rules and regulations. The approach to integration involved traditional methods of literacy training coupled with individualized teaching geared to a specific job assignment. This approach is consistent with the findings that we have reviewed on effective work programs in correctional settings.

A second implication of our analysis of the idea of boot camp is that we need to reconsider correctional alternatives. Harris (1983, p. 166) wrote that the "development of a more humane, caring and benevolent society involves a continuing quest for higher standards of decency and good will and an ever decreasing resort to . . . degrading sanctions." For her, the continued and fundamental interdependence of self and other is primary, and she thinks in terms of "persuasion, nonviolent action, positive reinforcement, personal example, peer support and the provision of life-sustaining and life-enhancing services and opportunities" (Harris, 1983, p. 166). It is noteworthy that the rehabilitation models of corrections that many experts have publicly rejected reflect a deemphasis on the questionable stereotypes of "how to be a man" that are promoted by the boot camp model.

A third implication has to do with the evaluation of existing and planned boot camp programs. A number of potential, negative outcomes of a boot camp environment have been identified. One of these is increased aggression, including physical and nonphysical punishment, directed against offenders by prison staff. Also included are increased offender aggression, a devaluation of women and so-called feminine traits (e.g., sensitivity), and other negative effects of an unpredictable, authoritarian atmosphere. In addition to considering these effects directly, program evaluation should monitor the degree to which the environment is characterized by inconsistent standards and expectations, dysfunctional stress, a we-versus-they attitude, and negative leadership styles. Furthermore, because correctional boot camp programs mix the elements of a military model with less coercive methods of human change, it is important to design research that reveals the actual program elements that produce both desired and undesired program outcomes.

Our review and analysis suggest that even when the elements of the military boot camp model are mixed with traditional rehabilitative approaches, there can be negative outcomes. Thus, the boot camp model is unlikely to provide a panacea for the needs of rehabilitation or for the pressures arising from the problems of both prison overcrowding and public demands for severe punishment. Whether the point is to provide rehabilitation, to deter, or to divert people from prison, alternatives other than boot camp should be given careful consideration.

References

Arias, Ron. 1986. "At Nick Bollettieri's Florida Boot Camp, Tennis is Played Only One Way, To Win." *People Weekly* October 20:107.

Bandura, Albert. 1973. *Aggression: A Social Learning Analysis.* Englewood Cliffs, NJ: Prentice Hall.

Bellew, Deena C. 1988. *An Evaluation of IMPACT Using Intensive Interviews: The Inmate perspective.* Unpublished manuscript. Baton Rouge: Louisiana State University.

Bernard, Jesse. 1975. *Women, Wives, Mothers: Values and Options.* Chicago: Aldine.

Bueil, Barbara. 1983. "Corporate Boot Camp in Japan." *Life* September:40.

Christie, Nils. 1981. *Limits to Pain.* Oxford: Martin Robertson.

Coakley, J. J. 1986. *Sport in Society: Issues and Controversies.* St. Louis, MO: Mosby.

Cole, George F. 1986. *The American System of Criminal Justice."* Monterey, CA: Brooks/Cole.

Cullen, Francis T., Kathryn M. Golden, and John B. Cullen. 1979. "Sex and Delinquency: A Partial Test of the Masculinity Hypothesis." *Criminology* 17:301-310.

Defense. 1987. "Almanac: People in Active Duty." September/October:32.

Eichler, Margrit. 1980. *The Double Standard: A Feminist Critique of Feminist Social Science.* New York: St. Martin's Press.

Eisenberg, Nancy and Paul A. Miller. 1987. "The Relation of Empathy to Prosocial and Related Behaviors." *Psychological bulletin* 101:91-119.

Eisenberg, Sue E. and Patricia L. Micklow. 1979. "The Assaulted Wife: 'Catch 22' Revisited." *Women's Rights Law Reporter* 3:138-161.

Eisenhart, R. Wayne. 1975. "You Can't Hack It Little Girl: A Discussion of the Covert Psychological Agenda of Modern Combat Training." *Journal of Social Issues* 31:13-23.

Ekman, Paul, Wallace V. Friesen, and Daniel R. Lutzker. 1962. "Psychological Reactions to Infantry Basic Training." *Journal of Consulting Psychology* 26:103-104.

Enloe, Cynthia. 1983. *Does Khaki Become You? The Militarization of Women's Lives.* Boston: South End.

Faris, John H. 1975. "The Impact of Basic Combat Training: The Role of the Drill Sergeant." Pp. 13-24 in *The Social Psychology of Military Service,* edited by E. Goldman and D. R. Segal. Beverly Hills, CA: Sage.

Finckenauer, James O. 1982. *Scared Straight and the Panacea Phenomenon.* Englewood Cliffs, NJ: Prentice Hall.

Fogel, David, 1975. . . . *We Are the Living Proof* . . . Cincinnati: Anderson.

Gannett News Service. 1989. "Boot Camp Prisons." *Lansing State Journal* 135 (June 19): 11.

Gendreau, Paul, Brian A. Grant, and Mary Leipeiger. 1979. "Self-Esteem, Incarceration, and Recidivism." *Criminal Justice and Behavior* 6:67-75.

Gendreau, Paul and Robert R. Ross. 1987. "Revivification of Rehabilitation: Evidence from the 1980s." *Justice Quarterly* 4:349-396.

Gilligan, Carol. 1982. *In a Different Voice.* Cambridge, MA: Harvard University Press.

Gottlieb, David. 1980. *Babes in Arms: Youth in the Army.* Beverly Hills, CA: Sage.

Harris, M. Kay. 1983. "Strategies, Values, and the Emerging Generation of Alternatives to Incarceration." *Review of Law and Social Change* 12:141-170.

Heidensohn, Francis. 1987. "Women and Crime: Questions for Criminology." Pp. 16-27 in *Gender, Crime and Justice,* edited by P. Carlen and A. Worral. Milton Keynes, England: Open University Press.

Hengish, Donald. 1988. Michigan Bureau of Correctional Facilities, Community Alternatives Program. Telephone interview, December 1.

Hilyer, James S. Jr. and William Mitchell. 1979. "Effects of Systematic Physical Fitness Training Combined with counseling on the Self-Concept of College Students." *Journal of Counseling Psychology* 26:427-436.

Hoffman, Martin L. 1975. "Sex Differences in Moral Internalization and Values." *Journal of Personality and Social Psychology* 32:720-729.

Holm, Jeanne. 1982. *Women in the Military.* Novato, CA: Presidio.

Jeffrey, Ray and Stephen Woolpert. 1974. "Work Furlough as an Alternative to Incarceration: An Assessment of its Effects on Recidivism and Social Cost." *Journal of Criminal Law and Criminology* 65:404-415.

Johnson, Robert. 1987. *Hard Time.* Monterey, CA: Brooks/Cole.

Kaiser, Steven. 1988. Warden, Lexington Assessment and Reception Center. Lexington, Oklahoma. Telephone interview, November 16.

Klausner, Michael. 1984. "Perot's Boot Camp." *Wall Street Journal* (August 3): 17.

Larwood, Laurie, Eric Glasser, and Robert McDonald. 1980. "Attitudes of Male and Female Cadets Toward Military Sex Integration." *Sex Roles* 6:381-390.

Lejins, Peter P. 1970. "Ideas Which Have Moved Corrections." *Proceedings of the One Hundredth Annual Congress of Corrections of the American Correctional Association:* 308-322.

Lewis, Roy V. 1983. "Scare Straight—California Style: Evaluation of the San Quentin Squire Program." *Criminal Justice and Behavior* 10:209-226.

Life. 1988. " 'Squeeze You Like a Grape': In Georgia, A Prison Boot Camp Sets Kids Straight." July:82.

Lipton, Douglas, Robert Martinson, and Judith Wilks. 1975. *The Effectiveness of Correctional Treatment.* New York: Praeger.

Loy, Pamela and Stephen Norland. 1981. "Gender Convergence and Delinquency." *Sociological Quarterly* 22:275-283.

Maguire, Kathleen E., Timothy J. Flanagan, and Terence P. Thornberry. 1988. "Prison Labor and Recidivism." *Journal of Quantitative Criminology* 4:3-18.

Marlowe, David H. James A. Martin, Robert J. Schneider, Larry Ingraham, Mark A. Vaitkus, and Paul Bartone. 1988. *A Look at Army Training Centers: The Human Dimensions of Leadership and Training.* Washington, DC: Department of Military Psychiatry, Walter Reed Army Institute of Research.

Martin, Douglas. 1988. "New York Tests a Boot Camp for Inmates." *New York Times* March 4:15.

McKelvey, Blake. 1977. *American Prisons: A History of Good Intentions.* Montclair, NJ: Patterson Smith.

Melossi, Dario and Massimo Pavarini. 1981. *The Prison and the Factory: Origins of the Penitentiary System.* London: Macmillan.

Merryfinch, Lesley. 1981. "Militarization/Civilization." Pp. 9-13 in *Loaded Questions: Women in the Military,* edited by W. Chapkis. Washington, DC: Transnational Institute.

Messerschmidt, James W. 1986. *Capitalism, Patriarchy, and Crime: Toward a Socialist Feminist Criminology.* Totowa, NJ: Rowman and Littlefield.

Morash, Merry. 1983. "An Explanation of Juvenile Delinquency: The Integration of Moral-Reasoning Theory and Sociological Knowledge." Pp. 385-410 in *Personality Theory, Moral Development, and Criminal Behavior,* edited by S. S. Laufer and J. M. Day. Lexington, MA: Lexington Books.

Morash, Merry and Etta Anderson. 1978. "Liberal Thinking on Rehabilitation: A Work-Able Solution to Crime?" *Social Problems* 25:556-563.

Morse, Wayne. 1973. "The Attorney General's Survey of Release Procedures." Pp. 23-53 in *Penology: The Evolution of Corrections in America,* edited by G. C. Killinger and P. F. Cromwell, Jr. St. Paul, MN: West.

Naffine, Ngaire. 1987. *Female Crime: The Construction of Women in Criminology.* Sydney: Allen and Unwin.

Norland, Stephen, Jennifer James, and Neal Shover. 1978. "Gender Role Expectations." *Sociology Quarterly* 19:545-554.

Oakley, Ann. 1972. *Sex, Gender and Society.* London: Temple Smith.

O'Brien, Tim. 1979. *If I Die in a Combat Zone, Box Me Up and Ship Me Home.* New York: Dellacorte.

Parent, Dale. 1988. "Shock Incarceration Programs." Paper presented at the American Correctional Association Winter Conference, Phoenix.

Pisciotta, Alexander W. 1983. "Scientific Reform: The New Penology at Elmira, 1876-1900." *Crime and Delinquency* 29:613-630.

Rabinowitz, Stanley. 1982. "Inauguration for Adulthood: The Military System as an Effective Integrator for Adult Adaptation: An Israel Air Force Base Perspective." *Psychological Reports* 51:1083-1086.

Raspberry, William. 1987. "Boot Camp—In Prison: An Experiment Worth Watching. Washington Post March 21: Section H, 21.

Raupp, Edward R. 1978. *Toward Positive Leadership for Initial entry Training. A Report by the Task Force on Initial Entry Training Leadership.* Fort Monroe, VA: United States Army Training and Doctrine Command.

Rogers, Carl R. 1975. "Empathic: An Unappreciated Way of Being." *Journal of the Counseling Psychologist* 5:2-10.

Riddick, Sara. 1983. "Drafting women: Pieces of a Puzzle." Pp. 214-43 in *Conscripts and Volunteers: Military Requirements, Social Justice and the All-Volunteer Force,* edited by R. K. Rullinwinder, Totowa, NJ: Rowman and Allenheld.

Rudoff, Alvin and T. C. Esselstyn. 1973. "Evaluating Work Furlough: A Follow-Up." *Federal Probation* 37:48-53.

Rusche, Georg and Otto Kirchheimer. 1939. *Punishment and Social Structure*. New York: Columbia University Press.

Satir, Virginia. 1972. *Peoplemaking*. Palo Alto, CA: Science and Behavior Books.

Schwendinger, Julia R. and Herman Schwendinger. 1985. *Adolescent Subcultures and Delinquency*. New York: Praeger.

Sitomer, Curtis J. 1987. "Some Young U.S. Offenders Go to 'Boot Camp'—Others are Put in Adult Jails." *Christian Science Monitor* October 27:1.

Sonkin, Daniel Jay, Del Martin, and Leonard E. Aurbach Walker. 1985. *The Male Batterer: A Treatment Approach*. New York: Springer.

Sticht, Thomas G., William B. Armstrong, Daniel T. Hickey, and John S. Caylor. 1987. *Cast-Off Youth Policy and Training Methods from the Military Experiences*. New York: Praeger.

Stiehm, Judith H. 1981. *Bring Me Men and Women: Mandated Change at the U.S. Air Force Academy*. Berkeley: University of California Press.

1982. "The protected, the Protector, the Defender." *Women's Studies International Forum* 5:367-376.

1989. *Arms and the Enlisted Woman*. Philadelphia: Temple University Press.

Sullivan, Mercer. 1983. "Youth Crime: New York's Two Varieties." *New York Affairs: Crime and Criminal Justice*. New York: New York University Press.

Taggart, Robert III. 1972. *The Prison of Unemployment*. Baltimore: Johns Hopkins University Press.

Thornton, David, Len Curran, David Grayson, and Vernon Holloway. 1984. *Tougher Regimes in Detention Centres: Report of an Evaluation by the Young Offender Psychology Unit*. London: Her Majesty's Stationery Office.

Thornton, William E. and Jennifer James. 1979. "Masculinity and Delinquency Revisited." *British Journal of Criminology* 19:225-241.

Tolson, Andrew. 1977. *The Limits of Masculinity: Male Identity and the Liberated Woman*. New York: Harper & Row.

Walker, Lenore. 1983. "The Battered Woman Syndrome Study." Pp. 31-48 in *The Dark Side of Families: Current Family Violence Research*, edited by D. Finkelhor, R. J. Gelles, G. Hotaling, and M. Straus. Beverly Hills, CA: Sage.

Walter, Timothy L. and Carolyn M. Mills. 1980. "A Behavior-Employment Intervention Program for Reducing Juvenile Delinquency." Pp. 185-206 in *Effective Correctional Treatment*, edited by R. R. Ross and P. Gendreau. Toronto: Butterworths.

Wamsley, Gary L. 1972. "Contrasting Institutions of Air Force Socialization: Happenstance of Bellwether?" *American Journal of Sociology* 78:399-418.

Wilson, William Julius. 1987. *The Truly Disadvantaged: Inner City, the Underclass, and Public Policy*. Chicago: University of Chicago Press.

Yudkin, Marcia. 1982. "Reflections on Wolf's *Three Guineas*." *Women's Studies International Forum* 5:263-269.

Yuval-Davis, Nira. 1985. "Front and Rear: The Sexual Division of Labor in the Israeli Army." *Feminist Studies* 11:649-675.

CHAPTER 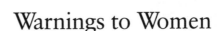 FOUR

Warnings to Women

Police Advice and Women's Safety in Britain

Elizabeth A. Stanko

Common sense tells you that not every man approach-ing you in a lonely place will do you harm. But it still pays to be wary.

Positive Action (1995)

✦ Through the traditions of an approach to women's safety as developed in Britain from radical feminist critiques of violence against women (Kelly, 1988; Stanko, 1985, 1990b), I raise concerns with the assumptions about women, violence, and crime avoidance embedded in police and other governmental crime prevention literature that ulti-mately find their way into the popular press. This article offers a textual analysis of police advice literature to women on crime and its avoidance. During the years, I have watched as this advice has been reproduced by the media in its coverage of violence against women. Do the public

Positive Action, now titled *Stay Safe,* is a publication of the Directorate of Public Affairs, Metropolitan Police Service, New Scotland Yard, 10 Broadway, London SW1H OBG.

Reprinted from *Violence Against Women,* Vol. 2, No. 1, March 1996. Used with permission.

police and popular media converge in their views of men's violence to women? Do such views give advice to women that may assist them in avoiding or minimizing (or both) men's violence?

I ask: Have women's experiences of sexual and physical violence and its avoidance been used to inform women's safety pamphlets issued by the police, who are credited for finally taking violence against women seriously? What are the lessons about safety we can glean from media accounts of violence against women? Is such advice likely to assist in assuaging women's fear of crime (Stanko, 1990b; Young, 1992) or women's avoidance of men's violence?

Some Contextual Backgrounds

Women's Fear of Crime

During the 1980s, women's fear of crime, as measured by the influential British Crime Survey (Hough & Mayhew, 1983), opened up another dimension of the debate about women and violence in the United Kingdom. Stanko (1987) suggested that women's fear of crime is an expression of women's fear of men and of men's violence. Radical feminists interpreted women's fear of crime as a barometer of our actual and perceived vulnerability to men's physical and sexual violence (Hanmer & Maynard, 1987; Hanmer & Saunders, 1984; Kelly, 1988; Stanko, 1987, 1990a, 1992; in the United States, see Young, 1992). As such, we began to document our anticipation of men's violence, which results in "policing ourselves" (Radford, 1987). Accumulated research suggests that (a) women are more likely to restrict their activities in public because of anxiety about encountering the potential of men's violence (Burgess, 1995; Crawford, Jones, Woodhouse, & Young, 1990) and (b) women use more safety precautions than men do (Stanko, 1990b; for the United States, see Gardner, 1980, 1990; Gordon & Riger, 1988).

The British Home Office, the government ministry responsible for all domestic affairs including law and order in Britain, also became concerned about fear of crime, and women's greater fear was acknowledged. It convened a working group in 1989 to consider the problem and recommend solutions to people's fear of crime.[1] One of the findings of the Working Group on the Fear of Crime was that the media exaggerated the fear of crime and, as part of a concern for public responsibility, the media were asked to be "more responsible" in their coverage of crime and violence. Although some media (such as the BBC) adopted guidelines for their handling of crime, there is little evidence that the media have muted their spotlight on violence, in particular sexual violence.

Policing and the Crisis of Protection

In the early 1980s, the police came under public scrutiny for their treatment of women as victims of violence (Radford & Stanko, 1991). The police were criticized for their handling of women who complained of rape. Public pressure initiated internal police reforms (Blair, 1985). Police suddenly seemed to be taken by a zealous concern about violence against women: They established domestic violence teams; initiated training about sexual assault; and became active spokespeople, advising women about criminal assault. Today, many of these reforms are still in place, and police crime prevention literature remains an important component in an overall publicity strategy to involve individuals, and especially women, in crime avoidance.

Women's Safety and the Agendas
for State Responsibility

In Britain, the Conservative government was elected in 1979. One central component of their campaign was a "law and order" agenda (Downes & Morgan, 1994). Concern for victims, and the development of a national agenda to meet their needs, was given special emphasis with the establishment of a National Association of Victim Support Schemes (see Rock, 1990). The Women's Movement was also active; refuges for battered women arose in the early 1970s and most major conurbations had rape crisis centers (see Dobash & Dobash, 1992).

By the late 1980s, local government authorities hosted a variety of women's units, equality units, or community safety units, many of which put women's fear of crime, domestic violence, and sexual violence on the agendas for innovative social policy. Although not exclusively in Labour authorities,[2] many of the mostly women working on issues of women's violence and safety were informed by radical feminist campaigns and were theorizing about violence against women. Underpinning the work on women's safety, therefore, was a commitment to confront the climate of victim blame so prevalent within the criminal justice approaches to violence against women (Dobash & Dobash, 1979; Stanko, 1985; see, in particular, Dobash & Dobash, 1992, for a history of the rise of domestic violence as a social problem in Britain).

A decade later, by the 1990s, many local authorities, police forces, and central government departments had taken on the issues of women and violence, in its broadest sense.[3] The Association of Women's Units in Local Government released *Responding With Authority* (National Association of Local Government Women's Committees, 1991) as a call to action for local governments to become actively involved in discovering support systems to alleviate all kinds of violence against women, including women's fear of crime. Edinburgh City Council sponsored a highly visible public education campaign, *Zero Tolerance*, which confronted myths about rape, child sexual abuse, domestic violence, and women's safety from a feminist perspective (see Stanko, 1995). All of these initiatives served to reinforce the importance of catering to the needs of women in the communities—and violence was shown to be high on the agenda of the needs of women.

However, the mid-1990s find Britain, after 16 years of Conservative party rule,* amid a cash crisis in public expenditure, with a decline in the welfare state (with severe cutbacks in basic provision of services such as health, education, social services, transportation, and public policing). It is essential to view police advice within the context of the wider changes in British public services—and as a metaphor for the abdication of the state for collective responsibility toward its subjects. Crime prevention advice is a centerpiece of the Conservative government's campaign against crime; advice to women flourished in the context of the developments in prevention of crime (Pease, 1994), not the prevention of violence against women (Stanko, 1990a).

My ongoing research suggests that police advice dominates community safety work. As part of a nationwide crime prevention initiative, crime avoidance and safety have become popularized, with the so-called active citizen taking center stage (O'Malley, 1992; Pease, 1994).[4] Indi-

---

*In May 1997, a Labour government was elected.

vidual prudence (O'Malley, 1992) prevails;[5] as individuals, we are responsible for our own safety.

A Methodological and Theoretical Approach for Analyzing Safety Advice

---

As a feminist academic, I am consciously trying to influence change through a radical feminist perspective (see, e.g., Stanko, 1985). How we think about violence against women involves devising strategies for local government officers to introduce programs addressing violence against women and for the training of police on issues of rape and domestic violence.[6] I am interested in discovering ways of changing police practice, thinking, and attitudes toward violence against women. My critique of this literature is in the spirit of such activism.

Since 1991, I have collected safety advice generated by government bodies, statutory and voluntary agencies, and the police. The initial study began in 1991 when I contacted more than 80 local governments in England, Scotland, and Wales to discover whether these bodies distributed information about women and safety to their local residents.[7] I asked for pamphlets, posters, and other relevant material to advise women about issues of their safety. I received information from 66 separate agencies.[8] A significant proportion of these local authorities forwarded the literature produced by their local police or by the Home Office's crime prevention campaign, *Practical Ways to Crack Crime,*[9] or had local models adapting these official approaches.

The analysis in this article first examines the literature distributed by police, then illustrates how this advice appears within the press coverage of men's violence against women. I am using content analysis, choosing particular passages of the texts to illustrate the approach to crime prevention advice that permeates this literature. The advice contained within these documents cannot be read with indifference to gender. To analyze them, police must be treated as socially situated within legal and ideological structures that take the provision of safety and its distribution as gender neutral. In many ways, women—the supposed audience of these booklets—are largely silent, presumed unified in their needs, and are treated as simultaneously needlessly frightened, yet rationally wary, the voiceless objects in the negotiation of our own safety. It is an ambivalence that, I suggest, can only arise because the theoretical basis of such crime advice removes women from their position as intentional targets for men's violence (Stanko, 1990b). As such, my interpretation of these booklets is necessarily my own, informed by my 20 years as a radical feminist criminologist and an analyst of the everyday practices of personal safety of women and men.

Advising Caution:
A Look at the Safety Advice

My 4-year collection of available advice literature can be assigned to five categories:

1. Advice concerning sexual assault, rape, or both.
2. Advice concerning personal safety for women, notably a pamphlet that first appeared in 1982 titled *Positive Steps,* produced by the London Metropolitan Police and reproduced by numerous local police forces. In 1995, such pamphlets were still being used and were often available at front desks of police stations, distributed at neighborhood meetings, or posted as general advice from community police officers.
3. General advice about crime prevention in the community, including personal and household safety. Although some communities authored their own guidelines, by and large the central government crime prevention document *Practical Ways to Crack Crime* (known in Scotland as *Don't Give Crime an Open Invitation*) was the literature provided.
4. Advice concerning domestic violence. Some of this information was directed at women themselves; other information received included information to workers in local government, such as housing officers, social workers, or teachers.
5. Guidelines and advice concerning sexual harassment, aggression at work, or both.

As such, women's safety from men's violence has become divided into discrete problems, which are fragmented, with advice about domestic violence separated from that of crime, and particularly, rape avoidance. Kelly (1988) warned us against separating forms of women's abuse at the hands of men, preferring instead to remind us of the "continuum of sexual violence." Without such an understanding, I believe, thinking about violence against women becomes a distortion of individual men's behaviors, when, according to a radical feminist analysis, such behavior is indicative of women's subordinate status to men.

A word about the booklets: Their structures are similar; the types and kinds of illustrations show remarkable likenesses. Men are shadowy characters, police are kind and reassuring figures, and women deserve to be reassured. These booklets (and there were many different booklets issued in Scotland, England, and Wales) tend to be organized around three sections:

1. Suggestions about how to conduct oneself when home alone, fending off exterior intrusion.
2. Advice about how to walk on the street, carry one's handbag, and how to travel by car or public transport.
3. Reassurance if an assault happens, with a description of the partnership the victim has with the police to solve the crime.

I will explore each of these in turn.

Home Alone: Women Beware

Section 1 of *Positive Steps* (PS), an example of the first (and current) booklet specially devised for women and safety by the London Metropolitan Police in the early 1980s, and *Practical Ways to Crack Crime* (PWCC), the Home Office's crime prevention guide, emphasize the special risks of being at home, at risk to strangers. States PS: "You probably think that you are only at risk when you're out—in side streets or up dark alleys. . . . Many incidents occur just where you might expect to feel safest—at home."

The safety suggestions revolve around the fitting of security hardware: chains on doors, windows, and so forth. The booklet gives tips on safe courses of action: Ask for identification of callers who wish access to the house; dial 999 if you are at all suspicious of the caller;

and seek special advice if you are trying to sell a house ("Try not to show people around on your own"). The booklet continues:

> You can never be too careful. Every woman living alone should be especially safety conscious, and take these simple precautions to improve her security. Get into the habit of "doing the rounds" before you leave home. Lock every outside door and window— *one lapse could put you at risk.* (emphasis mine)

Similarly, "Although attacks on people do occur in their own homes, many citizens fail to take precautions to reduce such risks" (*Taking Care*).

Directed at women living alone, the suggestions include keeping the fact that one lives alone as obscure as possible. The pamphlets add that one might "wish to keep a dog," "draw curtains at night and remove clothes from outside line to deter peeping toms," keep a whistle by the telephone for pestering callers, and demand identity cards of strangers at the door. At every stage, reminders about the availability of the police to provide advice and protection appear. Throughout, there are constant references to join a Neighborhood Watch group, advice that ignores the research that suggests that Neighborhood Watch participants report higher levels of fear of crime (Mayhew, Dowds, & Elliot, 1989) and are confused about how to participate (McConville & Shepherd, 1991), and that overall such schemes have a doubtful effect on crime reduction (Bennett, 1990).

The view of "woman" is a reflection of assumptions about which women are likely to be frightened unnecessarily: single, home owning, incompetent, perhaps elderly, and naive about strangers, and especially women living outside of the supposed individual protection from individual men. Two points to emphasize here: First, the research about women and safety (Gardner, 1980, 1988, 1990; Gordon & Riger, 1988; Stanko, 1990b) suggests that most women already have fairly elaborate strategies to minimize risk of danger from strangers and are already wary of male strangers (Burgess, 1995). Of course, women could always learn different, creative strategies, but many of the ones suggested—for example, do not walk in dimly lit alleyways—are ones women already adopt (Burgess, 1995; Stanko, 1990b), and if we do not, we do so for our own reasons (e.g., we may live down dimly lit alleys!).

Second, as all the research suggests, it is known that men, partners or former partners of women, pose the greatest threat to women. Advice about this type of violence is limited in these booklets: Women, it is proposed, might ask for police or court interventions, but there is no recognition that women are already actively negotiating men's violence day in and day out. The fourth and current edition of *PWCC* suggests:

> If the violence is within your family, the courts have powers to help you, regardless of whether you press criminal charges. They can, for example, require a husband not to enter your home, and in some cases, even your neighborhood.

The actual protection provided by civil injunctions has been questioned by research (Barron, 1992). The focus on strangers found in the safety literature continues to capture the imagination of the advisers as they turn to tips for women walking and driving in public. Moreover, it is also interesting to note that we ourselves have strongly held beliefs that we are most at risk in public places (Pain, 1993). Such beliefs, suggested from an overall evaluation of my collection of safety advice, influence the literature produced by local government women's units as well as by the police. As more women live outside male control/protection by choice, is it possible to advise women about men's violence without somehow belittling different women's perceptions and experiences of dangerous men?

Out and About: Women Keep Vigilant

> Obviously, no one deliberately puts themselves at risk, but the thought of becoming a victim can still be a constant worry. (*Positive Steps*)

Consolation for women's anxieties begins the next major section on women-in-public. Women are told to walk confidently, to avoid lingering at darkly lit bus stops, to keep to well-lit roads, to walk facing the oncoming traffic—all practical steps the advisers assume women do not already do. Women are encouraged to plan ahead if they are going out for the evening: Have taxi numbers on hand or trusted friends and acquaintances for company on the way home and, if walking, keep hands free for self-defense. Booklets state that handbags, carried carelessly, expose women to the opportunistic thief, as does the wearing of expensive-looking jewelry. Precautions about how to travel on public transport, how to travel in a car, and how to park safely in well-lit public areas are also included.

This advice is especially ironic, given the ruthless abandonment of public expenditure to services such as transport and the staff employed by transport. The wholesale privatization of bus companies has resulted in limited and unpredictable provision of bus services and in the elimination of staff on underground trains in London and on British Rail (which is itself scheduled for privatization, hence the reduction of more staff).

The pamphlets attempt to reassure women by alerting them to their potential as targets of theft, personal assault, or worse, in public places. Returning to the sanctuary of one's home is presumed. Are homeless women or women fleeing violence in the home merely overlooked? Having options, choices, daily plans, and detailed strategies are obligations: These are the armaments of the responsible woman. But many of us are excluded from being responsible before we start. What if we feel we are targets for men's violence? What happens if a man really wants to hurt us because we are women?

If the Worst Happens:
Sympathetic Partnership

It is sensible to think about what you would be prepared to do if you were physically attacked. Could you fight back or would you play along and wait for a chance to escape? Preparing yourself for all possibilities could provide a split-second advantage. (*Taking Care*)

If the worst happens and you are raped or sexually assaulted, turn immediately to the police. It's vital to report quickly what has happened, and you can do so in complete confidence. You will need all the special care and attention the police are anxious to give. (*Positive Steps*)

The booklets encourage the woman to report the assault to the police and assure her that she will be treated sympathetically. Police practice, however, does not ensure such sympathetic treatment. More than 10 years after this booklet was first issued, the police practice of "unfounding" rape complaints—in effect, nullifying the crime report— still exists (Lees & Gregory, 1993). No matter how sympathetic the police, if the woman gives evidence in court, she is still likely to be aggressively cross-examined by a defense attorney in a way that relies on stereotypical images of "the responsible woman" (Matoesian, 1993) and that contributes to the likelihood that her assailant will be acquitted.

Inspector Shirley Tulloch, "personal safety adviser" of the London Metropolitan Police, recently commented in a 1994 article in the widely read popular London weekly guide *Time Out* that women's fear of crime is unrealistic ("Cosh or Cheque," 1993). She noted that most women imagine potential attackers as strangers who jump out at them from bushes but this type of crime is actually rare.

She suggested that police advise women to be on their guard and avoid potentially dangerous situations: Do not take shortcuts and stay in well-lit areas. She also recommended that women carry rape alarms. Her comments are meant to comfort, but they illustrate both the confusion in the way women's safety is promoted by the police and their actual concern about it. On one hand, there is an effort to debunk the stereotype of women's danger (see Stanko, 1988; Young, 1992)—the stranger—whereas on the other hand, offering advice about how the prudent woman should behave to avoid the potential danger of the (presumably) male stranger.

This contradiction, I suggest, can be understood through an analysis of the creation of the responsible woman. Police advice exists within a context that takes for granted the responsible woman—the woman who commonsensically takes all necessary precautions to avoid the violence of men and treats the violence of men to women as encounters that can, given responsible precautions, be avoided.

In addition, the conscious use of pictures and sketches of women and children in the care of women officers invites women's trust in the police as sensitive interviewers of women reporting rape or sexual assault, as crusaders in child protection, or as dedicated domestic violence workers. Clearly, these images illustrate how the police are using women police as a public relations tool, the acceptable face of police protection, and aim specifically at reassuring women they will be treated sympathetically should they need to contact police. What is important here is the use of imagery about victims. Only the deserving and unfortunate victim is the legitimate recipient of care. Presumably, she is responsible.

Over the past few years, police have extended this approach to advising women in highly publicized crimes against women. For instance, when a young mother was brutally killed in a London park, police suggested women avoid parks until the killer was arrested.[10] In one recent study of the use of urban fringe woodland (Burgess, 1995), all of the women interviewed mentioned this horrific murder, some adopting precaution without police advice.

Long-standing allies of the police in their fight against crime, the media cover much crime within a legacy of its own distortions (see, e.g., Ericson, Baranek, & Chan, 1991; Saward, 1991; Soothill & Walby, 1990). Police advice to women appears as part of the story, as a public service cautionary tale. How this assuages women's fear is unclear, for the fact that women are attacked, and are attacked because they are women, is a subtext, within both the safety pamphlets and, as I argue next, in the news.

Popularizing Danger:
Media and Police Advice

Clearly, women's fear of crime has captured, and continues to capture, the imagination of the popular press. Images of women walking down dark alleys clutching their handbags abound; news stories of women attacked in parks, cabs, and dimly lit streets mirror these images of danger. Within this arena of crime, prevention initiatives embrace individual obligation and specify the burdens of individuals to protect themselves and their property from the opportunist thief and assailant. Within this opportunity-reduction initiative, gender has particular salience. Women—the generic audience of the advice about personal safety—represent a stereotypical, gendered vulnerability. There is, for instance, no special advice for young men, the population, according to official data, that is most at risk from assault in public.

The production of news has metaphorical import: It presents the police as sympathetic, caring professionals who are knowledgeable about what frightens women. It is only recently that police public relations officers have spotlighted the symbolic import of women police as protectors of women and as specially qualified to service the needs of women's emotional turmoil (Soothill, 1993).

The use of the police by the media as experts in women's safety stems in part from the ideological import of the police in societal protection, which is based in their crime fighting abatement, their role as gatherers of evidence and apprehenders of suspects, and their moral obligation to protect the public from the vagaries of those dangerous few, who the police, given their ownership of expertise, can identify. This is paradoxical because the media have also spearheaded the discussion of the role of policing and public confidence in that role in contemporary Britain. Concerns about confidence in the police to protect the public against crime—fostered by the civil disturbances of the 1980s, feminist campaigns about police responses to rape and domestic violence, Black people's campaigns about racial harassment, escalating crime statistics, and a host of miscarriages of justice—have been raised by the popular press in Britain.

However varied the explanations of the decline in confidence in the police though, such coverage uses the police forces throughout the country to assuage women's anxiety. In doing so, the news media actively give credence to police as servicers of the needs of vulnerable or victimized women. Although the police may privately assail the media for focusing on the most salacious of crimes against women—murder or sexual assault of young, often White women—and for raising women's anxiety about safety, police also use the publicizing of such crime as occasions for issuing encouraging advice about how to avoid similar misfortunes and for confirming their position in the public's eye as the experts on women's safety and protection. But what they suggest as responsible precautions are usually safety measures that women already take (Stanko, 1990a) or that may increase women's fear of crime. Pain's (1993) study of women in Edinburgh found that 1 in 6 said they worried more about their safety because of police advice.

Ironically, radical feminists are still being accused of unnecessarily frightening women by publicizing the prevalence of violence against them (Roiphe, 1993). To me, though, the awareness of men's violence through a radical feminist perspective intends to spotlight the problem of men, not the problem of individual, imprudent women. The police advice fails to condemn male violence as indicative of women's subordinate position in society. As such, it individualizes responsibility, without collective comment on *the problem of men.*

So, too, the media individualizes the problem of violence against women. Violent crime committed by male strangers against women is a popular folktale of danger. The police use publicity to appeal to the public for clues to the identity of an unknown attacker. Take, for instance, a story that appeared in the *Daily Telegraph* ("Don't Go Out Alone," 1992). An Oxford undergraduate who was raped on her way home from a party was interviewed about the incident in an attempt to catch the attacker. The attack, it was noted, had created an atmosphere of tension among the thousands of women students in the city. With a victim-support counselor and a "specially trained police woman at her side," the young woman warned others not to walk alone at night. She praised the police for treating her well, and a detective working on the case advised students to avoid walking alone at night, because the crime appeared to be opportunistic and "spur of the moment."

What then are women to do? Do such news stories reassure women that the police are on the suspect's trail? This story contains a standard recipe: a random attack, an innocent victim grateful for her sympathetic treatment at the hands of police and for victim support, a police search for the perpetrator, and offers of public service follow-up to women, such as advice and police seminars on self-defense.

Another tale in *The Independent* ("Taxi Driver," 1992) reported on a taxi driver jailed for rape in a cab. The news story reported the conviction of a man for rape of a passenger. The final paragraph of the story contained a statement by the detective who headed the investigation, reassuring women that they should not be afraid to take a black cab, because this was an isolated incident.

An August 1992 story in *The Guardian* contained an appeal by police for a witness to an attack on a woman by a "bogus" minicab driver (Johnson, 1992). The detective heading the investigation stated that he was sure that the rapist had found the woman by listening to calls to the firm she had phoned, and he warned other women to be on their guard against rogue cabbies who may eavesdrop, telling women readers to always use a reputable firm and to check that the driver who arrives is from the company they called. *The Independent* also carried a story about this incident in which the final paragraph also contained a warning to women to be vigilant, to always use reputable taxi companies, and to be certain that when a cab arrives, it is from the firm called (Braid, 1992). This article also stated that there had been no publicity about this case until this point because police feared that reports might hamper their investigation. Here, it is interesting that the requirements of the police—catching the suspect—may collide with the need to warn women about similar incidents. What is the message about safety here?

Finally, consider a story that appeared in *The Independent* in July 1992 with the headline "Fantasy World of a Murderer." In a journalistic biography of Scott Singleton, recently convicted killer of a 17-year-old woman, cautionary advice for young job applicants was included in the story. The last two paragraphs were devoted to lessons about men's tactics for luring women for abuse. The detective leading the murder investigation was quoted as saying that he was disturbed by the number of phone calls the police had received from women who had had experiences similar to the victim, but had managed to escape. He noted that this made the police realize how widespread the practice of recruitment is, especially during a period of economic recession. His advice to women applying for jobs through agencies was to check the credentials of all prospective employers by using such techniques as looking for agency letterhead, taking the agency's phone number and calling back to see if it really exists, and being suspicious of any job that sounds "too good to be true."

When I asked senior police officers at a recent seminar on service to women given at Bramshill Police College about the appearance of the above advice in the newspapers, they suggested that the reporters ask police "what advice they have for the public" subsequent to an act of random violence. The scripts for the social construction of the responsible woman are readily available: Prudent women avoid men's violence.

The messages contained within the advice booklets and the news stories suggest that we should, and can, be individually accountable for our own safety. To be a responsible woman is to display a healthy suspicion of men who appear to be ordinary men: cab drivers, potential employers, passers-by, doctors, coworkers and so forth.[11] Such wariness is never-ending and resonates in the questions we ask ourselves when we have been attacked: if only I did not walk home, open the door, shop at this store, and so forth. Even more curious, all of this advice is supposed to ease our anxiety about our safety-in-public.

Concluding Remarks

In this article, I have argued that police advice to women about personal safety fails to question why we are at risk. The feminist efforts to put violence against women on the state's agenda has also led to police turning the problem back on us. Although the police may be taking violence against women seriously, the form of their practice and thinking often reinforces the assumption that we can, given correct and responsible behavior, avoid the violence of men. As the research continues to verify, violent men want to attack a woman, whether at random or with foresight. Even assailants rationalize their behavior by blaming us for bringing on the assault ourselves (Scully, 1990; Smythman, 1978), or minimize the actual harm they cause us (Hearn, 1993).

Police advice to women implicitly reflects an understanding of our risk to men's violence: Presumably, we are vulnerable because we are women. What continues to be ignored, however, is the feminist-inspired interpretation of our vulnerability, embedded in an appropriation of our sexuality: "that which is one's own, yet most taken away" (MacKinnon, 1982, p. 515). We take many precautions because we acknowledge such potential violence as a condition of being a woman. Publicized advice, generated by in-house police publicity or through media attention to salacious crime, reinforces the message of our sexual vulnerability. It does so without the wider context that radical feminism sought to expose. Our anxiety may be raised: By placing the responsibility for avoiding men's violence once again on our shoulders—for it is our behavior that can minimize the chances of becoming a target of men's violence—we are responsible for sorting safe from unsafe men.

Given that much abuse arises within women's friendship, intimate, kinship, and daily relationships with men (Stanko, 1990a; Young, 1992), women routinely risk misjudging men's trustworthiness. Given that we may wish to live our lives without constantly thinking about our protection, we are questioned about being prudent and sensible when we stray from the rigid guidelines that will never entirely assure safety. The failure to recognize the contradictions within the subtext of police advice and the daily media accounts of violence to women, I suggest, diminishes the potential to assuage women's "fear of crime." Police are not guaranteeing—and can never guarantee—us safety within a world that takes for granted our perceptions and our experiences of sexual vulnerability. But the police are trying to do just that, resulting in a failure to truly confront the devastating personal consequences of our subordination (nor do I think they can). Thus Inspector Tulloch's advice mentioned in this article is not meant to aid us in eluding violence, but is meant to reassure. So if personal alarms make some of us feel better, regardless of whether they actually work in attracting assistance ("Calls for Alarm," 1994) or fending off attackers, then alarms work as long as they reduce our anxiety.

In sum, the advice booklets and the media accounts of police advice following horrific incidents subscribe to a standard narrative: Women are unduly afraid; if we were to adopt a set of basic safety precautions, we would reduce an already small risk of crime; police are our protectors and will treat us seriously and sympathetically; men, when they encounter us "duly protecting ourselves," will not act on impulse and foresight and attack, rob, beat, or rape us.

What would radical feminist-inspired safety advice look like? If we suggest women-only parking lots, women-only buses, or women-only bars, would we be ridiculed? Is this even realistic, given the many differences among us? How would we offer advice about minimizing the violence within intimate relationships? If we drew up a list of the "dos" and "don'ts" of safety, would it minimize the violence of men we experience? Certainly, women-designed environments, which increase the likelihood that other people "look out for them" (Burgess, 1995), are contributing to more woman-friendly environments in public. But we are still left with the problem of men. I welcome any and all suggestions to find some method of discovering collective ways to minimize our encounters with violence. After all, the research suggests that ultimately it is men who decide to attack us—and we need to find ways of stopping them collectively, not individually.

Notes

1. The working group was convened in 1989, chaired by Michael Grade, chief executive of Channel 4 Television. I was a member of the working group, which was dominated by members of the media.

2. Three parties dominate the political scene in mainland Britain: Labour, Tory, and Liberal Democrat. From 1979 onward, the Tory party has controlled Central Govern-

ment, but local authorities were controlled largely by either the Tory or Labour parties. Much of the so-called progressive work took place within Labour authorities, who incorporated special units within the local government, such as women's equality units or police units (which monitored the activities of police delivery of community protection.)

3. See, for instance, Smith (1989a, 1989b). The Home Office issues two circulars to police concerning their treatment of women complainants of rape and domestic violence. Home Office Circulars 69/1986 and 60/1990 were issued to the police forces of England and Wales, serving as guidance in their responsibilities to provide more adequate care and attention to violence against women. A handful of local authorities, for instance, hosted conferences bringing together local agencies, interested women, and the police to discuss available remedies to domestic violence, women's fear of crime, or sexual safety.

4. Not only is such advice available throughout Britain, but I have seen versions of this crime prevention document in Australia, Canada, and the United States (see DeKeresedy, Burshtyn, & Gordon, 1992, for an analysis of the Canadian pamphlet).

5. As both Stanko (1988, 1990b) and Young (1992) argued, traditional approaches to women's fear of crime neglect the domestic nature of a vast majority of men's violence to women, which may contribute to women's fear and anxiety about their own safety.

6. These training sessions took place at the Hendon Police Training College, home of the Metropolitan Police training operations. Later, I participated in the training of senior officers at Bramshill Police College, a national training ground for officers facing promotion.

7. I did so as a prelude to a national conference on women's safety, bringing together then junior Home Office Minister John Patten (Tory) and the late Shadow Minister for Women Jo Richardson (Labour)—a demonstration that both parties treat the issue of violence against women high on their agendas.

8. I did not receive replies from 10 queries; 4 responded, informing me that they did not distribute any information to women.

9. First published in 1988, this pamphlet is the premier crime prevention literature produced by central government and distributed through local police stations throughout England, Scotland, and Wales.

10. A man was arrested and acquitted of this murder. The police were accused of entrapment.

11. Even more curious, when radical feminists suggested that all men could be rapists, they were castigated for tarring all men with the same brush.

References

Barron, J. (1992). *Not worth the paper.* Bristol: Women's Aid.

Bennett, T. (1990). *Evaluating neighbourhood watch.* Aldershot: Gower.

Blair, I. (1985). *Investigating rape.* Aldershot: Gower.

Braid, M. (1992, August 18). Woman raped by bogus cab driver. *The Independent,* p. 1.

Burgess, J. (1995). *Growing in confidence.* Walgrave, Northampton: Countryside Commission.

Calls for alarm. (1994, December). *Which? The Independent Consumer Guide,* pp. 12-13.

Cosh or cheque. (1993, September 8-15). *Time Out,* pp. 29-30.

Crawford, A., Jones, T., Woodhouse, T., & Young, J. (1990). *The second Islington crime survey.* Middlesex, UK: Middlesex University.

DeKeseredy, W., Burshtyn, H., & Gordon, C. (1992). Taking Woman abuse seriously: A critical response to the Solicitor General of Canada's crime prevention advice. *International Review of Victimology, 2* 157-168.

Dobash, R. E., & Dobash, R. P. (1979). *Violence against wives.* Milton Keynes: Open University Press.

Dobash, R. E., & Dobash, R. P. (1992.) *Women, violence and social change.* London: Routledge.

Don't go out alone, warns rape victim. (1992, June 9). *The Daily Telegraph,* p. 3.

Downes, D., Morgan, R. (1994). "Hostages to fortune?" The politics of law and order in post-war Britain. In M. Maguire, R. Morgan, & R. Reiner (Eds.), *The Oxford handbook of criminology* (pp. 183-232). Oxford: University Press.

Ericson, R., Baranek, P. M., & Chan, J. B. L. (1991). *Representing order: Crime, law and justice in the news media.* Milton Keynes: Open University Press.

Fantasy world of a murderer. (1992, July 23). *The Independent,* p. 3.

Gardner, C. B. (1980). Passing-by: Street remarks, address rights and the urban female. *Sociological Inquiry, 50,* 328-356.

Gardner, C. B. (1988). Access information: Public lies and private peril. *Social Problems, 35,* 384-397.

Gardner, C. B. (1990). Safe conduct: Women, crime and self in public places. *Social Problems, 37,* 311-328.

Gordon, M., & Riger, S. (1988). *The female fear.* New York: Free Press.

Hanmer, J., & Maynard, M. (Eds.). (1987). *Women, violence and social control.* London: Macmillan.

Hanmer, J., & Saunders, S. (1984). *Well-founded fear.* London: Hutchinson.

Hearn, J. (1993). *How men talk about men's violence to known women.* Conference Report, Masculinities and Crime, Centre for Criminal Justice Research, Brunel University, Oxbridge, Middlesex, UK.

Hough, M., & Mayhew, P. (1983). *The British crime survey.* London: HMSO.

Johnson, A., (1992, August 18). Rapist driver intercepted radio cab call. *The Guardian,* p. 5.

Kelly, L. (1988). *Surviving sexual violence.* Oxford: Polity.

Lees, S., & Gregory, J. (1993). *Rape and sexual assault: A study of attrition.* London: Islington Council.

MacKinnon, C. (1982). Feminism, Marxism, method and the state: Toward a feminist jurisprudence. *Signs, 8,* 515-544.

Matoesian, G. M. (1993). *Reproducing rape.* Oxford: Polity.

Mayhew, P., Dowds, L., & Elliot, D. (1989). *The 1988 British crime survey.* London: HMSO.

McConville, M., & Shepherd, D. (1991). *Watching police, watching communities.* London: Routledge.

National Association of Local Government Women's Committees. (1991). *Responding with authority: Local authority initiatives to counter violence against women.* Manchester: Author.

O'Malley, P. (1992). Risk, power and crime prevention. *Economy and Society, 21,* 252-275.

Pain, R. (1993). Crime, social control and spatial constraint: A study of women's fear of sexual violence. Unpublished doctoral dissertation, University of Edinburgh.

Pease, K. (1994). Crime prevention. In M. Maguire, R. Morgan, & R. Reiner (Eds.), *The Oxford book of criminology* (pp. 659-704). Oxford: Oxford University Press.

Radford, J. (1987). Policing male violence—policing women. In J. Hanmer & M. Maynard (Eds.), *Women, violence and social control* (pp. 30-45). London: Macmillan.

Radford, J., & Stanko, E. (1991). Violence against women and children: The contradictions of crime control under patriarchy. In K. Stenson & D. Cowell (Eds.), *The politics of crime control* (pp. 186-202). London: Sage.

Rock, P. (1990). *Helping victims of crime.* Oxford: Clarendon.

Roiphe, K. (1993). *The morning after.* London: Chatto & Windus.

Saward, J. (1991). *Rape: My story.* London: Pan Books.

Scully, D. (1990). *Understanding sexual violence.* London: Unwin Hyman.

Smith, L. (1989a). *Concerns about rape.* London: HMSO.

Smith, L. (1989b). *Domestic violence.* London: HMSO.

Smythman, S. D. (1978). *The undetected rapist.* Unpublished doctoral dissertation, University of California.

Soothill, K. (1993, January). Policewomen in the news. *The Police Journal,* pp. 25-36.

Soothill, K., & Walby, S. (1990). *Sex crime in the news.* London: Routledge.

Stanko, E. (1985). *Intimate intrusions: Women's experience of male violence.* London: Routledge.

Stanko, E. (1987). Typical violence, normal precaution: Men, women, and interpersonal violence in England, Wales, Scotland and the USA. In J. Hanmer & M. Maynard (Eds.), *Women, violence and social control* (pp. 122-134). London: Macmillan.

Stanko, E. (1988). Fear of crime and the myth of the safe home: A feminist critique of criminology. In K. Yllo & M. Bograd (Eds.), *Feminist perspectives on wife abuse* (pp 75-88). Beverly Hills, CA: Sage.

Stanko, E. (1990a). *Everyday violence.* London: Pandora.

Stanko, E. (1990b). When precaution is normal: A feminist critique of crime prevention. In L. Gelsthorpe & A. Morris (Eds.), *Feminist perspectives in criminology* (pp. 171-183). Milton Keynes: Open University Press.

Stanko, E. (1992). The case of fearful women: Gender, personal safety and fear of crime. *Women and Criminal Justice, 4,* 117-135.

Stanko, E. (1995). Women, crime and fear. *Annals of American Political and Social Science, 539,* 46-58.

Taxi driver jailed for rape in cab. (1992, July 23). *The Independent,* p. 4.

Young, V. (1992). Fear of victimization and victimization rates among women: A paradox? *Justice Quarterly, 9,* 421-441.

CHAPTER FIVE

Gender, Class, and Race in Three High-Profile Crimes

The Cases of New Bedford, Central Park, and Bensonhurst

Lynn S. Chancer

◆ As Kimbele Crenshaw (1992) noted in a brilliant essay about Anita Hill's historic confrontation with Clarence Thomas in 1991, a language sophisticated enough to embrace the multileveled forms of discrimination that operate in U.S. society has yet to be forged. Although other social critics have made a similar point, the question of what happens in the meantime—in the absence of adequately complex analytic tools and in the course of developing them—has been much less explored. Yet, perhaps one consequence of such a conceptual void is that it facilitates subtle processes through which potential forces of protest in a particular society come to be counterposed and divided against each other. Instead of three-dimensional understandings of gender-race-class biases and their complicated interactions emerging, much more two-dimensional frameworks unfold: It begins to seem as though addressing issues of gender must necessarily be counterposed against sensitivities toward problems of race or ethnicity; it seems as though race must compete against class, or ethnicity against race, in an only apparently zero-sum game. Unfortunately, one effect of such falsely dichotomized perceptions is that they come to comprise subtle forms of social control.

The energies of social-movement protesters become directed at each other rather than aiming collectively at more systemic changes. And in such a cultural climate, it is not surprising if criminal justice policies may benefit from resultant outcomes that lean toward, and support, conservative outcomes.

Feminist criminology, reflecting developments in feminist theory as a whole, has become increasingly concerned about the complex ways in which prejudices based on gender, class, race, and ethnic discrimination combine to affect and structure social experience. Although radical feminists of the contemporary "second wave" first analyzed patriarchy as a social structure affecting *all* women, both feminists and feminist-oriented criminologists are in the process of further refining the paradigm of gender to encompass differences between women.[1] For example, it is obvious that not only gender but class position affects whether and how particular women will be treated within the criminal justice system as well as within local communities in which they may live. Similarly, sociological factors, such as race, ethnicity, or sexual preference, often further compound the discriminatory effects of gender within U.S. culture.

This chapter attempts to illuminate these refined feminist concerns by focusing on a specifically criminological question: How is the role of gender affected in highly publicized instances of violent crime when considerations of class, race, and ethnicity are also taken into account? In each of the three cases I have selected for purposes of analyzing this question, sexist attitudes were present in a given situation and then either hardened, nourished, or mitigated by the coming together of several factors. In each of the three selected cases, women's sexual freedom was limited, either directly and violently or much more indirectly and subtly. But three other factors were commonly present in each case as well: (a) media saturation of a violent crime, meaning that each case was covered on a daily or near-daily basis, both when initial incidents occurred and over the course of ensuing trials; (b) preexisting conflict and potential competition between sexual, ethnic or racial, and class forms of oppression in a given community or urban area; and (c) a felt exigency among community members to respond in some fashion or another to this now highly publicized "event," an event that refers both to an actual crime and a media construction. First, the New Bedford case, with which I begin, involved a gang rape of a young woman that took place in a bar in New Bedford, Massachusetts, in

March of 1983. The second case was just as clearly coercive: the "Central Park" rape case in which a young woman was attacked by a group of young men while jogging in Central Park on the evening of April 19, 1989. In the last example, cited for comparative purposes, the racist killing of young Yusef Hawkins in Bensonhurst, Brooklyn, on August 23, 1989, a gang of white youths shot Hawkins to death; he was allegedly mistaken for a local woman's boyfriend. Although the third case involves homicide rather than rape, a sexual component was nonetheless entailed: The Bensonhurst case involved young men incensed that the local woman in question preferred to date an African American or Hispanic man over a white in their predominantly Italian American neighborhood.

As I will show, television and newspaper coverage picked up each event and saturated the media with it, devoting front-page or top-story local TV news attention to the incident for weeks after the crime had actually occurred. In all three instances, social variables came to be pitted against one another. The New Bedford case involved a conflict between two sociological dimensions—sexual and ethnic forms of discrimination (class did not play a noticeable role, because most of the persons in the Portuguese community were either working or lower middle class). The Central Park case entailed the confluence of three biases: Here, class, gender, and race were invoked through the circumstances and media coverage of the case. Last, the Bensonhurst case brought all the variables into play, suggesting not only the presence of sexism and racism but class and ethnic antagonisms as well.

To facilitate this analysis, I have read newspaper accounts in both local and national sources. In the New Bedford case, I looked at news coverage in the New Bedford *Standard Times* and *The New York Times* from March 6, 1983, through March 22, 1984, the year following the rape, until verdicts were reached in the trial. With regard to the Central Park incident, I perused all newspaper coverage in the *Daily News* and *The New York Times* from April 19, 1989 (when the incident occurred), until August 1990 (the end of the first Central Park trial). I used the same two newspapers for the Bensonhurst case, scanning the period between August 23, 1989 (the date of the incident), until the end of the first trial in December 1990. I have supplemented newspaper coverage by looking at magazine reportage for the three cases, particularly weekly news magazines, such as *Time* and *Newsweek*. In the Central Park and

Bensonhurst cases, more local news coverage as presented in *The Village Voice* and *Newsday* were also analyzed.

My interest in studying high-profile crimes, such as New Bedford, Central Park, and Bensonhurst, stems from a desire to incorporate contemporary developments in cultural and literary theory of media into criminology, an incorporation I believe to be a much-needed effort. As will become apparent, cases such as New Bedford and Bensonhurst suggest that media coverage can become a part, virtually an inanimate "player," in the unfolding of community response to instances of crime. People in a town or city where a so-called notorious crime has occurred seem to be reacting not only to the crime and their feelings about it but also to how they feel that crime is perceived by others, given media saturation of the event. (Of course, a semiotically or postmodern-oriented observer might contend that these two levels of response frequently cannot be differentiated experientially, even if it is possible to do so analytically.) Even more specifically, I am particularly interested in the implications of highly publicized crimes occurring in communities where, as is frequently the case, the social atmosphere is already divided by sexual, class, ethnic, and racial tensions. Media coverage may harden preexisting sexist and racist sentiment, or other divisions, by shaping them in particular directions so that one form of prejudice is highlighted at the expense of another as reaction to a case unfolds over time.

New Bedford, Massachusetts: A Case of Gender Versus Ethnicity

That I start with the New Bedford case is not accidental. Having already written an article on the subject (Chancer, 1987), the conclusions of the earlier analysis may provide a framework of possible insights that can then be expanded to include similarities with, and divergences from, the Central Park and Bensonhurst cases. In the New Bedford incident, a young woman was raped on a pool table in a bar of cheering men. Although the community's initial reaction was sympathetic toward the rape victim and condemning of the rapists, it changed over the course of the year following the rape into hostility toward the victim and sympathy for the rapists. This sympathy manifested itself in public demonstrations against the latters' conviction and petitions of protest to the local judge signed by as many as 16,000 to 18,000 people (Chancer, 1987). This shift was apparently inseparable from the fact that the case involved not only sexism and the blaming of a rape victim for her own victimization but also a long history of discrimination against the Portuguese in the town of New Bedford and neighboring Fall River. The Portuguese were a majority in the town (approximately 60%-65%) and were beginning to feel a greater degree of acceptance and economic and political respectability at around the time the rape occurred.

Following the rape, however, people in the Portuguese community began to feel incensed at media descriptions of the "Portuguese" rapists. In fact, media coverage was extremely intense and focused on the horrifying fact of a woman being raped in a bar full of people. Stories abounded in both local and national newspaper and television accounts, and the trial was the first criminal trial to be televised nationally on cable TV. As the publicity reached a saturation level—initially, in the immediate aftermath of the rape and then later, before and during the trial of the rapists—members of the Portuguese community became concerned that the case was reviving prejudice against the Portuguese population as a whole. Defense committees were formed, and, slowly but surely, community reaction shifted toward defense of the rapists and, concomitantly, toward condemning the rape victim who had allegedly caused the incident to occur in the first place. During a large protest march that followed the trial and the conviction of four out of six indicted men, the two defendants who were not convicted were given a hero's welcome by the crowd.

That the young woman who was raped in New Bedford came to be blamed for her own victimization, however, cannot be viewed as entirely a by-product of anti-Portuguese discrimination. For one thing, neither the press nor the community paid any attention to the seemingly important fact that *the rape victim herself was of Portuguese descent*— why was there so much hostility toward her when she, too, could have been perceived as a member of the Portuguese community in New Bedford? (Her name, Cheryl Araujo, became a matter of public knowledge when she died in a Florida car accident several years after the rape and publicity of the rape led her to leave New Bedford because of threats she and her family received.) One of the conclusions I reached was that, given this and other suggestive information, ethnic discrimination was a necessary but not sufficient explanation of the sexism that led to the victim herself being blamed. The other factor was traditional ideology within the community itself about the respective gender roles of women versus men, assumptions the young woman had violated by entering the bar at all when she could have been home with her children. The New Bedford case conforms perfectly to the findings of attribution theory that five criteria increase a rape victim's chances of being blamed for her own victimization: The victim tends to be blamed if (a) this victim had some prior acquaintance with her attackers, (b) a reason can be found to attribute a bad reputation or nontraditional behavior to the woman involved, (c) the rape takes place in a bar, (d) alcohol was present, and (e) the rape occurred in close proximity to the victim's residence. If it is true that these factors increase the likelihood that a rape victim will be blamed for her own victimization, then it would not have been surprising if some degree of victim blaming occurred even without media saturation and a preexisting history of anti-Portuguese discrimination in the town of New Bedford.

Nonetheless, it is hard to believe that the tendency for victim blaming within a traditionally oriented community on purely sexist grounds would have manifested itself quite as explosively nor taken on the highly political dimension it did, were it not for the particular conflict of sexual and ethnic forms of prejudice the case entailed. Thus, a second conclusion I reached was that subordinate groups subjected to an invidious legacy of prior prejudice may wish to defensively deny wrongdoings committed by members of their group. Such defensiveness may be particularly facilitated when the crime in question happens to be a rape, so that the "blame the victim" ideology that has uniquely surrounded prosecution of rape cases in United States and other patriarchal cultures comes into play. This reactive tendency, I would argue, is produced by a structural no-win situation in which such groups have found themselves embedded: If they acknowledge the actual heinousness of a given crime, they fear reinforcing negative stereotypes about the group as a whole; on the other hand, if they deny the seriousness of a violent act and rationalize the actions of the given perpetrator(s), they find themselves defending criminal acts (and possibly, the objects of scorn for this latter position as well).

The media focus of the present chapter is extremely relevant here insofar as it is newspaper and television saturation of a particular crime that acts as a historically specific catalyst for the accretion of such defensiveness. Without media saturation of the event, Portuguese residents of New Bedford would have been far less concerned, if concerned at all, about the ethnically discriminatory potential of the case. Provocative references to Portuguese rapists angered the community precisely because they were encountered in print and television media and consequently publicized widely to the larger, dominant culture that was known to have been antagonistic to Portuguese assimilation.

The Central Park Jogger:
Introducing Class and Race Differences

This brief discussion sets the stage for raising several issues of comparison between the New Bedford case and the Central Park rape that took place in April 1989 when a group of youths assaulted a young woman who was out jogging in the park at approximately 10:00 p.m. Three critical differences are immediately apparent, helping to distinguish the latter case from the former. First of all, unlike New Bedford, where ethnicity could conceivably be canceled out on both sides of the equation because both victim and perpetrators were of Portuguese descent, the woman raped in Central Park was white, whereas the seven teenagers arrested for assaulting her were black. Second, the Central Park case did *not* involve victim blaming to anywhere near the degree evident in the New Bedford example (if at all). Not only was the young woman jogger not held responsible for her own victimization, but she even became something of a folk heroine, as New Yorkers cheered on and closely followed her—or, more precisely, media accounts of her—recovery. (I refer here to a public response, to hostile quotes people were *not* willing to provide reporters as they had in New Bedford, to the fact that no demonstrations or marches antagonistic to the rape victim initially occurred. I think many people wondered why a young woman would go jogging by herself in as dangerous a place as Central Park at night, but this thought did not translate into *blaming* her or in any way diffusing the responsibility of the rapists.) This is quite a marked contrast to the hero's welcome extended the rapists in New Bedford and the threats and hatred to which the rape victim there was subjected. The third major divergence is that the black community in New York does not seem to have become defensive in such a way that the guilt of the defendants was denied or somehow exonerated. In fact, just the opposite appears to have occurred. According to *The New York Times*, 600 families in the Schomburg Plaza housing project, where several of the defendants lived, sent flowers to the victim in Metropolitan Hospital in the weeks following the rape; the same group of families invited city residents to a prayer vigil "hoping that the mass display of concern could help defuse any notions that the people of Harlem are not moved by the victim's suffering" (Marriott, 1989, p. B3). How, if at all, can conclusions reached on the basis of the New Bedford incident help to explain why victim blaming and exoneration of the perpetrators unfolded in one case and not in the other?

Attribution theory may again contribute to an understanding of the lesser degree of victim blaming in the Central Park case relative to the New Bedford case. The circumstances of this second rape barely conform to the five criteria previously cited: The woman was not previously acquainted with her attackers and did not live in the same neighborhood as they nor were alcohol and a barroom setting entailed. Although one might contend she was jogging in a park that bordered her own home and therefore could be considered her neighborhood, most New Yorkers would probably agree she had strayed into strange and lonely territory at that deserted hour. Last, and perhaps most important in this case, the victim did *not* have a so-called bad reputation. Indeed, she was portrayed as an exemplary person by the standards of upper-middle-class society. Consequently, returning to feminist theory and feminist criminology, an extremely important distinction between the New Bedford and Central Park cases involves the different class backgrounds of the respective victims. That the young woman in New Bedford was a single mother receiving assistance, whereas the young woman in Central Park was an upper-middle-class investment banker certainly affected whether or not victim blaming began to occur.

Here, not just attribution theory but the way in which media coverage combined with preexisting attitudes to represent a particular picture of the class background of the victim must have been seen as a crucial factor in the way the New York City community began to actually perceive the young woman in the Central Park case. For instance, both the *Daily News* and *The New York Times* immediately began to set up a semiotic connection in readers' minds between the "young woman" and her occupation: The *Daily News* rarely reported on the story without writing comma, "an investment banker" after referring to the "victim" or "the young woman"; the *Times*'s first coverage of the story on April 21 begins with similar language: "The woman, a 30-year old investment banker" and then goes on to elaborate "who had worked at Salomon Brothers for three years and lives on the Upper East Side, has been an avid runner and bicyclist" (Wolff, 1989, p. B1). And consider one of the lead stories in the *News* on the same day, in which the young woman is described as having "lived a dream life" (Kriegel, 1989, p. 2). This American dream theme continues as we are treated to a number of details of the victim's life: that she grew up in Upper St. Clair, Pennsylvania, an affluent suburb of doctors, lawyers, and professionals 10 miles south of Pittsburgh and *far from the steel mills* (my emphasis); that she graduated Phi Beta Kappa from Wellesley, received a master's degree from Yale's School of Management and was rated one of the top new hires at Salomon Brothers; and that "she was much more than a brain. . . . in her yearbook photo she appears as a pretty blonde in a turtleneck sweater with an engaging smile and eyes gleaming with promise" (Kriegel, 1989, p. 4). Much detail is similarly devoted to information about her family background and the respectable professional occupations of her father and brothers. The comparison with the New Bedford case is telling and sad in that no such complimentary phrases were written about the young woman in the New Bedford case: Cheryl Araujo was described as a "welfare mother" if she was described at all. When a few days later, the Sunday *Daily News* front page headline indignantly told readers that the arrested youths had said of the young woman, "SHE WASN'T NOTHING" (April 23, 1989)—so that one's sympathies were appropriately directed toward a rape victim and one's anger toward the rapists—they could have been describing the relative invisibility accorded the rape victim by media reporters and the community in the New Bedford case.

This is not to say that no news coverage whatsoever focused on the potentially victim-blaming issue of why the jogger was out alone in Central Park. In fact, a *Daily News* story titled "Why Jog at Night?" (Broussard & Lubrano, 1989) hints at the "foolishness" of jogging at that hour. But it is to say that the tone is one of gentle concern rather than the harsh condemnation so apparent in the New Bedford instance: The problem here is not the woman but that "these kids have no self-discipline and do what they want without consequences. . . . If they see what they want, they take it" (p. 29). Compare this statement with a quote published in the New Bedford *Standard Times* (Hirsch & Vosburgh, 1984) and attributed to a woman marcher: "I'm also a woman, but you don't see me getting raped. If you throw a dog a bone, he's gonna take it—if you walk around naked, men are just going to go for you" (p. 1.) The young woman, moreover, is represented as part of a joggers' community, one that of course is differentially composed of middle-class and upper-class adherents. For example, one *New York Times* article was devoted in its entirety to why people with busy schedules would wish to run at that time if no other was available and would find the activity compelling and invigorating (Hays, 1989), p. B1).

Clearly, then, a major difference between the two cases revolves around class, in two senses: (a) that the young woman in the Central Park case was of a higher economic and social status than the young woman in the New Bedford instance and (b) that there was a *class distinction* between her superior status and the relatively lower standing of her attackers. In the New Bedford case, on the other hand, both ethnicity *and* class could be canceled out on both sides of the equation— Cheryl Araujo did not have this advantage on her side to potentially ameliorate and mediate the effects of blatant sexism. News coverage, of course, capitalized on and promoted this class issue by making it into an American dream story: Not only was the jogger's background a success story but so also was the portrayal of her recovery process.

Nonetheless, to point to the role of class in influencing why the Central Park victim was blamed to a relatively lesser degree, if at all, than was the young woman in New Bedford is not to deny other specific traits that distinguished the two cases. The fact that a *series* of attacks on people in Central Park took place that night may have also decreased the likelihood of victim blaming; so may the fact that the young woman in the Central Park case was beaten much more severely, to the point of near death, whereas injuries to the young woman in New Bedford were far less physically life threatening and required less post-traumatic hospitalization. At the same time, I am arguing that the class factor cannot be ignored and that the specific configuration of gender, class, race, and ethnic factors that surround particular instances of violent crimes against women must all be taken into account. In this respect, I am not only in agreement with socialist feminist criminology but even with aspects of the argument made by Herman and Julia Schwendinger

(Schwendinger & Schwendinger, 1983) in their well-known *Rape and Inequality* (a work that I would otherwise fault for its tendency to reduce gender to a function of class).[2]

Nonetheless, yet another unfortunate ramification of this preexisting class division, magnified by media coverage, between two women otherwise commonly victimized by a violent crime is that in *both cases,* the conflict contributes to a demeaning of the rape itself. That victim blaming took place in the New Bedford case meant a loss of much-needed community support and sympathy for Cheryl Araujo: That victim blaming did *not* occur in the Central Park case is far less or not at all immediately problematic for the young woman involved yet implies that her experience may come to be resented by some persons in the (New York) community who may suspect that they would not be treated nearly as sympathetically because of their own class or racial backgrounds. In both instances, the violent crimes of gang rape come to arouse a second level of hostility aimed at women, albeit in these two cases, for important and differing reasons.

This brings me to the second comparative issue raised when we began to analyze the Central Park incident. Why did the black community in New York City *not* respond as vehemently and defensively as did the Portuguese in New Bedford? Why was the culpability of the rapists *not* denied despite the potential for the same structural tendency described earlier to unfold? Several possibilities come to mind, each of which may provide a hint toward an answer. For one thing, as Joyce Williams and Karen Holmes (Williams & Holmes, 1981) reported in their study, victim-blaming attitudes in rape cases vary directly with traditional or nontraditional attitudes toward sex roles extant in a given community. According to their account of women treated for rape in San Antonio, Texas, who were either "white Anglo," black, or Mexican American, the first two groups were less likely than the latter to be blaming of rape victims. To the extent the African American community in New York City may (similarly) hold less rigidly stereotyped attitudes about sex roles than did the Portuguese community of New Bedford, this factor may form part of the explanation as may the potentially very powerful influence of the black church in discouraging denial of crimes that cause enormous human suffering.

On the other hand, defensiveness may have existed at a latent level, never becoming manifest in the way evident in New Bedford, because of the differing majority-minority, dominate-subordinate relationships in the two cases. As already mentioned, the Portuguese community of New Bedford was a majority population, whereas African Americans in New York are a large, diverse, but nonetheless minority group in the City, subject to pervasive racism within a predominantly white dominant culture. This suggests that even if a similar defensiveness to that which existed in New Bedford was likewise provoked within segments of the African American community of New York City, it is hard to imagine it taking the visible public form of huge prodefendant demonstrations in which the arrested youth are hailed as heroes and petitions signed on their behalf. Such demonstrations would be perceived (and perceived as capable of being perceived) as further exacerbating racism in the city.

At the same time, and as will be apparent when we turn to the Bensonhurst case, demonstrations of public outrage are not just conceivable but likely in instances where black Americans have themselves been the victims rather than perpetrators of crime and whites the assailants. (This argument may be buttressed by recalling that the highly publicized Bernhard Goetz case did not provoke the expression of ire or become a cause célèbre within the black community, despite expressions of racist sentiment that subtly or not so subtly surrounded that particular event. On the contrary, the reported case of Tawana Brawley did lead to public expressions of anger, as did the killings of Michael Stewart and Eleanor Bumpurs.) Yet it is interesting that in the already alluded to *New York Times* article (Marriott, 1989), Harlem residents expressed their fear

> that the crime and highly publicized arrests of black youths for assaulting a white woman would ignite smoldering racial divisions among black and white New Yorkers. A common concern was that the attack, although not termed racial by the public, would further fuel a misconception that blacks, particularly young males, are to be subjects of fear and scorn. (Marriott, 1989)

Consequently, a potential for defensiveness based on the same structural dilemma operating in the New Bedford case was present even if not historically enacted for a variety of reasons.

But it was not just differing configurations of class, and the ramifications of this difference, that distinguished the New Bedford and

Central Park cases. The fact of the defendants and victim being of different races was highly significant as well.

For indeed, based on newspaper reportage of the Central Park case, there was good reason for members of the local black community to feel defensive. Almost all of the *Daily News* coverage in the 2 weeks following the incident referred to the group of attackers as a "wolf pack" (e.g., Kriegel, 1989), language rarely used to describe violent crime committed by groups of white teenagers. (For example, it is entirely absent from coverage of the white Bensonhurst defendants.) Again, language reinforces a highly problematic semiotic connection between being black, committing violent crime in groups, and not existing in human form. (In my research, I have yet to find cases of white teenagers who moved from place to place while committing a series of crimes being similarly described.) This racist allusion to animality, so reminiscent of both social Darwinism and the worst excesses of biologically oriented criminality of the Lombroso-Hooton variety, was initially avoided by *The New York Times* but later picked up in stories quoting others using the terminology (and then eventually dropping the quotes as the story approached its denouement). For instance, note the language of a *Daily News* editorial (1989) on the subject:

> There was a full moon Wednesday night. A suitable backdrop for the howling of wolves. A vicious pack ran rampant through Central Park. . . . This was bestial brutality. . . . The only way to deter these marauding bands is to use the full force of the law against them. The kid gloves have to come off. . . . Wolf packs have been roaming the subways in increasing numbers. Assaulting and robbing passengers. They've declared the subways their turf. Wednesday's wolves declared Central Park their turf. (p. 11)

The editorial goes on to illustrate the earlier point about the rape victim remaining relatively impervious from blame. Each New Yorker, we are counseled, must make his or her own individual decision about personal safety, but *as a city,* New Yorkers can never accept the principle that some areas are off limits. It is not the *victim's* fault (I agree), but the prime responsibility for safety must fall on government to provide more police patrols, better lighting, more activities that draw crowds. . . . collectively, New Yorkers must claim the streets and the night for themselves. *Retreating behind doors* [italics added] is like telling the wolf pack: Go on, the city is yours. (Editorial, *Daily News*, 1989)

Of course, it is interesting to inquire into whether a point of view quite as sympathetic to the victim, and quite as condemning of the city's political and policing establishment, was expressed by the *Daily News* when Yusef Hawkins was killed one evening simply because he was black. That no such analogous editorial appeared on the day marchers walked through Bensonhurst to reclaim the streets of the city for all New Yorkers, black and white—and in fact, my research indicates one did not—points to the substantial role of racism in both the victim's ability to remain relatively immune from sexist attribution of culpability and the inability of the community to defensively protest racism in this case, even if such a desire had been present and provoked.

Thus, it is not just the class differences between the victim and perpetrator that distinguishes the Central Park from the New Bedford examples but in fact this racial element as well. Once again, I would argue that this juxtaposition of mediated circumstances not only feeds on preexisting racism in a community where whites remain in a dominant and majority position, but it also reinforces sexist attitudes in an insidious fashion. If one listens closely to the very language employed even in writing this account, a "story" that I think accurately portrays the way class and racial discrimination accrued to the benefit of the rape victim, one nonetheless cannot be immune to an almost inescapable tendency to at once deflect attention from the very real suffering the woman in the Central Park case experienced, *regardless of her class or race.*

In this respect, a radical feminist treatment of rape, such as that found in Susan Brownmiller's (1975) *Against Our Will: Men, Women, and Rape,* is useful insofar as it calls attention to rape as an act of sexual politics aimed at exercising social control over *all* women. As a violent act of forced sexual intercourse, rape reflects sexual oppression in a society still brimming with patriarchal fear and intimidation. Although it may affect women differently depending on the class and race of the victim, it nevertheless poses a threat to all women. At the same time, that the plight of the Central Park rape victim becomes compared with other victims' plights in rape cases must be seen as a structural dilemma bequeathed when sexism, racism, and class-based discriminations coexist in an explosive and uneasy juxtaposition. The effect of media coverage is often to act as a catalyst amid this sociological maze, forcing comparisons and competition between these factors to appear as though inevitable by its characteristic lack of analytical precision.

Bensonhurst: Similarities and Differences in a Homicide Case

In turning to my third example, the murder of Yusef Hawkins on August 23, 1989, the sociological maze is raised to yet another level of complexity. The New Bedford example involved conflicts between gender-based and ethnic-based discrimination; Central Park's highlighted divisions based on gender, class, and race: Arguably, Bensonhurst's suggests the presence of all of the forms of oppression referred to so far—gender, class, race, *and* ethnic. This is so despite the fact that, unlike in the first two cases, homicide rather than rape was entailed. Yet if one were to rely either on media accounts or interpretations of the event presented by public officials in the immediate aftermath of Hawkins's death, gender discrimination would appear to be virtually nonexistent as a dimension of the case. Nonetheless, in addition to the case involving a race-motivated murder, the actions of the young men simultaneously amounted to coercive interference with a woman's right to sexual freedom: namely, a woman's ability to date or sleep with whomever she chose.

In early *New York Times* coverage of the case (Blumenthal, 1989), then mayor Edward Koch and then police commissioner Benjamin Ward described the case as "merely" a case of a spurned lover and mistaken identity. In minimizing the degree of race-based and gender-based discrimination involved (while absurdly suggesting that somehow the situation would have been improved if the *right* person had been identified), this depiction failed to note the victim blaming of Gina Feliciano that quickly began to occur among some members of the Italian American community in Bensonhurst. According to the *Times* on August 31 (Barron, 1989), many residents (including women), believed that "Miss Feliciano's friendships with Black and Hispanic men in the neighborhood increased the racial tension that the police say erupted in the attack" (p. B2). (Virtually identical quotes were mentioned in the *Times*'s coverage of the New Bedford case, similarly attributed to both female and male members of the Portuguese community in describing the so-called culpability of the young woman who had been raped.) On September 1, the *Times* (Kifner, 1989) similarly noted that "the fault, in the eyes of much of the neighborhood, lies with Gina Feliciano, who violated the mores of the Italian American community by dating black and dark-skinned Hispanic men . . . [Again] 'She provoked everybody, . . . it's a sin' said Carmen Mercado" (Kifner, 1989). When the case came to trial, the *"cherchez la femme"* theme rose even more noticeably to the surface as attorneys explicitly built Feliciano's alleged role into their defense of Joseph Fama, one of the young men on trial for homicide. At the same time, community antagonism toward this young woman continued to mount in a way that is again, sadly, reminiscent of New Bedford.

That another form of gender-based victim blaming occurred in the Bensonhurst example suggests the potential applicability of attribution theory even to cases where overt physical violence has not occurred and a woman is only secondarily victimized by an actual crime. As did the situation of the young woman in New Bedford, Gina Feliciano's circumstances also conform with attribution theory findings that women are more likely to be blamed if a crime occurs close to their places of residence and if they are acquainted through neighborhood ties with a given group of assailants. In addition, the likelihood that victim blaming will increase if there is evidence of a previous so-called bad reputation or nontraditional behavior on the part of the woman is borne out here by the perception that dating black or Hispanic men violated community mores. On the other hand, the Bensonhurst case can likewise be distinguished from the Central Park case in that Gina Feliciano had no class status to mitigate or neutralize perceptions of her own culpability in the public eye. Early newspaper accounts of the Bensonhurst homicide do not mention Feliciano's occupation or economic status: As in the New Bedford case, class exerts an influence by its very absence and presumed inferiority.

But what about the issue of community response to the murder of Yusef Hawkins, victimized by the ultimate act of violence? For the second time, events in Bensonhurst are so strongly reminiscent of those in New Bedford that one suspects that a virtual genre of such high-profile crimes may exist. Perhaps a more general criminological pattern involving a distinctive mix of media exposure and traditionally oriented subcultural attitudes toward gender, class, and race or ethnicity takes recurring forms. For just as in the aftermath of the New Bedford gang rape, so *The New York Times* ran similarly formulaic features on the characteristics of Bensonhurst as an Italian American community, in the aftermath of Hawkins's killing. The resentment felt by members of the Portuguese community at the fact that their Portuguese identity was being broadcast by the media and that Portuguese defendants were shown wearing headphones they needed for translation is echoed in a September 1 *Times* story titled "Bensonhurst: A Tough Code in Defense of a Closed World" (Kifner, 1989). To quote it,

> This is a closed, insular world, this enclave in Brooklyn where Italian is as likely to be spoken as English, a world of tight-knit families and fear and hostility toward the outside. It is a world, too, where the young men who gravitate each night to a specific street corner or candy store to hang out with their friends grow up with a macho code. . . .
>
> But there were blunt expressions of racism, too, a feeling that their neighborhood was being maligned by the news media and, above all, talk of defending their world. (p. A1)

Another article described Bensonhurst as a neighborhood of "one- or two-family houses that line the tree-lined streets" where little had changed since *The Honeymooners* was set there in the 1950s (Bohlen, 1989, p. A1).

Similar accounts abounded in the *Daily News*, and the case made national and local television broadcasting on virtually a nightly basis. Preexisting racist sentiment, then, was aggravated and exacerbated by the defensiveness incumbent on such coverage. This defensiveness was based only partially on the community's sense that the social boundaries of its own neighborhood were being invaded (an observation that harks back to social ecology theory). In addition, one suspects that class sensitivities of the kind Richard Sennett and Jonathan Cobb (Sennett & Cobb, 1972) astutely described in *The Hidden Injuries of Class* were also stung as predominantly working-class residents of Bensonhurst (or New Bedford, for that matter) were reminded of their lack of upper-class, gentrified status in capitalist America.

Thus, when a group of 60 to 70 marchers (of whom about half were black) marched through the streets of Bensonhurst less than a week after the killing to "reclaim the streets of New York," (Ravo, 1989, p. B1) it is horrifying but not amazing that they were met with an enraged response: À la New Bedford, it was the protesters who became recast as the intruders, the troublemakers, the *victimizers,* whereas members of the Italian American community (including, as we shall see, the defendants themselves) saw themselves as *victimized*—those who were truly under siege. And so, in a counterdemonstration so redolent with overt racism that some journalists compared it to 1960s Mississippi, local white residents shouted "Niggers, go home," "You savages," and "Long Live Africa," holding up hate-filled signs and watermelons. Simultaneously, and confirming Jack Katz's (1989) phenomenological thesis of how "self-righteous slaughter" comes to be rationalized,[3] the arrested young men were seen as "good boys . . . they were defending the neighborhood" (Kifner, 1989); at the same counterdemonstration, the white crowd shouted "Central Park, Central Park!" (Ravo, 1989, p. B1). It is interesting that the Central Park rape case—a case familiar to the Bensonhurst residents largely by virtue of their exposure to it as a media representation—thereby came to be placed in competition with the murder of Yusef Hawkins, used as yet another vehicle for transforming a sense of collective defensiveness and guilt into collective anger and blaming of the black demonstrators qua "other."

Obviously, then, it was not only Gina Feliciano who was blamed for instigating the incident but, by extension of the counterdemonstrators' angry logic, even Yusef Hawkins as well. Ultimately, one suspects many members of the community must have felt that it was *their* neighborhood that had been invaded, *their* turf that had been exposed. Organized hostility was aimed much more openly, and publicly, at the black and white marchers who protested Hawkins's killing than it was at Ms. Feliciano; after all, it was the former group who dared to collectively protest, just as in New Bedford, the young woman who was the object of so much hostility had dared to prosecute her attackers. In both cases, painful media exposure was produced, and the vulnerability of the community to vestiges of ethnic and class discrimination was reignited. Thus, I would argue that the Bensonhurst case did indeed involve multilayered dimensions based on the intersection not only of gender discrimination, but class, race, and ethnically based prejudices as well.

Conclusion

In the New Bedford and Bensonhurst cases, media saturation created a specific variety of community defensiveness that fed into preexisting sexist and racist sentiments in traditionally oriented communities. In and of itself, this media saturation played a role in the unfolding of events to the extent it that aroused anger at the community's helplessness and inferiority vis-à-vis its perceived class and ethnic position in the surrounding world. Television and news coverage are uncontrollable, rendering the community powerless; as in both the New Bedford and Bensonhurst cases, they magnified ethnic sensitivities by subjecting these communities to microscopic inspection. However, because no concrete outlet for rage against media exists, it may become displaced toward victims who themselves come to be seen as, instead, the so-called real perpetrators of a given violent crime. In New Bedford, it was the young woman who shouldn't have been in a bar away from her children in the first place; in Bensonhurst, it was Gina Feliciano who ought not to have been bringing in men from outside her neighborhood and race and demonstrators (symbolically, black persons) who ought not have been crossing the territorial boundaries of the neighborhood. Consequently, media saturation can inflame and give new collective shapes to already existing prejudices.

Second, whether a group enacts the potential for defensiveness created by media exposure of violent crime committed by one of its members also depends on particular configurations of dominant-subordinate relationships between a given local community and the larger society of which it is a part. Despite the discriminatory identification made between "wilding" and the activities of young black men and the racist usage of "wolf pack" language to describe black rather than white teenage group violence, public sympathy for the defendants may be much more difficult in this instance than it was in New Bedford. The extremity of continuing racism in U.S. culture and the minority status of African Americans in New York City would raise the fear of public defense reinforcing this form of oppression. At the same time, studies such as that done by Williams and Holmes (1981) suggest that victim blaming in rape cases may not be as severe within the black community as it would be in Portuguese or Italian American communities, where more rigid gender divisions persist. On the other hand, the Portuguese community in New Bedford was a majority population, whereas the Italian American community in Bensonhurst does not face nearly as severe a legacy of continuing discrimination and powerlessness as do blacks in the United States. Consequently, it would not be surprising if protesting racism may be deemed much more socially permissible in cases where blacks have been the *victims* rather than the *perpetrators* of highly publicized violent crimes. (In other words, it may be easier to protest the killings of Eleanor Bumpurs, Michael Stewart, or Michael Griffith than to call attention to racist treatment accorded teenagers out wilding or those young black men shot by Bernhard Goetz.)

Last, with regard to highly publicized rape cases and questions of gender, the young woman raped in Central Park may have managed to escape much of the victim blaming foisted on the young woman in New Bedford, and Gina Feliciano in Bensonhurst, because of her upper-class background. This conclusion verifies and validates the concerns of socialist feminists and socialist feminist criminologists (including Herman and Julia Schwendinger; see Schwendinger & Schwendinger, 1983) about taking both class and gender factors into account when trying to understand the full complexity of women's life experiences.

At the same time, this analysis suggests that when highly publicized violent crimes involve the complex intersection of gender with simultaneous dimensions of class, race, and ethnic biases, an uneasy potential for competition between these variables is created. In the case of the Central Park incident, this meant that members of New York's black community might secretly resent the young woman for reinforcing stereotypes of young black men or for the fact that her rape was publicized, whereas stories of minority women's victimization go far less often told (if told at all). Or returning for a moment to the Bensonhurst case, accounts of Gina Feliciano's victimization can appear as though measured against the murder of Yusef Hawkins when indeed no comparison can or should have to be made nor resentment need to be aroused. Yet the *cherchez la femme* theme continues to be so deeply embedded in patriarchal societies that its presence is sometimes barely noticeable.

In sum, then, one major task of a socialist feminist criminology must be to account for the confluence of gender-related, class-related, race-related, and ethnicity-related factors in the unfolding of crime. But it must also, and at the same time, be scrupulous lest focusing on these other factors would obfuscate the specifically sexist nature of victim blaming still so common in U.S. culture. Both dimensions need to be considered if we are to untangle and clarify these complicated layers—as though peeling back the layers of a sociological onion—evoked when the spotlight of high-profile media coverage stirs deeply embedded community anxieties. But coming back full circle to the question of social control from which we started, the three case studies considered also illustrate the pitfalls—not only for academic accounts engaged in understanding the social world but for social movement participants eager to develop a more complex language that embraces gender, class, and race discriminations. Somehow, strategies must emerge that compel the media itself to incorporate a necessarily deeper sense of complexity into its day-to-day understandings. Without the kind of furthered sophistication that feminist criminology can aid in promoting, subtle forms of social control are able to thrive with far too much ease and effectiveness. The New Bedford, Central Park, and Bensonhurst cases all took place in the mid-1980s and 1990s, when conservative policies toward crime were emerging alongside high-profile crime cases centered on gender, race, and class discriminations. Thus, the more we insist on analyzing such cases with the multifaceted considerations they require, the more we may contribute simultaneously to breaking forms of social control that depend on simplistic or "either-or" frames of mind.

Notes

1. With regard to the question of class within socialist feminist thought as a whole, see Zillah Eisenstein (1979), *Capitalist Patriarchy and the Case for Socialist Feminism,* and, more recently, Hansen and Philipson (1990), *Women, Class and the Socialist Imagination.* Eisenstein's argument is applied in a particularly explicit fashion to criminology in James Messerschmidt's (1986) *Capitalism and Patriarchy: Toward a Socialist Feminist Criminology.*

2. In *Rape and Inequality,* Herman and Julia Schwendinger (Schwendinger & Schwendinger, 1983) criticize Susan Brownmiller's (1975) radical feminist work, *Against Our Will: Men, Women and Rape,* for ignoring the historical specificities introduced when rape is placed not only in the context of gender but class and race variables as well. Nonetheless, I think the Schwendingers' work tends to be reductionistic in its eagerness

to ignore gender as an autonomous source of oppression. Thus, the Schwendingers have difficulty explaining the persistence of rape and domestic violence against women *across* class lines. This was also taken up in Messerschmidt's work.

3. See Jack Katz's (1989) account of self-righteous slaughter in his interesting book, *The Seductions of Crime*. Katz argues that the slaughterer frequently sees himself (or herself?) as defending the "good." I would add to this that communities' perceptions of killings can be equally defensive.

References

Barron, J. (1989, August 31). 2 indicted for murder in racial attack. *The New York Times*, p. B2.

Blumenthal, R. (1989, August, 25). Black youth is killed by whites: Brooklyn attack is called racial. *The New York Times*, p. A1.

Bohlen, C. (1989, August 28). In Bensonhurst, grief mixed with shame and blunt bias. *The New York Times*, pp. A1, B3.

Broussard, S., & Lubrano, A. (April 21, 1989). Why jog at night? *Daily News*, p. 29.

Brownmiller, S. (1975). *Against our will: Men, women and rape*. New York: Simon & Schuster.

Chancer, L. S. (1987). New Bedford, Massachusetts, March 6, 1983-March 22, 1984: The "before and after" of a group rape. *Gender and Society, 1*, 239-260.

Crenshaw, K. (1992). Whose story is it anyway? Feminist and anti-racist appropriations of Anita Hill. In *Race-ing justice, en-gendering power: Essays on Anita Hill and the construction of social reality*. New York: Pantheon.

Editorial. (1989, April 22). 'Juvenile delinquency' does not apply. *Daily News*, p. 31.

Eisenstein, Z. (Ed.). (1979). *Capitalist patriarchy and the case for socialist feminism*. New York: Monthly Review Press.

Hansen, K. V., & Philipson, I. J. (Eds.). (1990). *Women, class, and the feminist imagination*. Philadelphia: Temple University Press.

Hays, C. L. (1989, April 29). The ethos of the late-night jogger. *The New York Times*, p. B1.

Hirsch, A., & Vosburgh, M. (1984, March 24). 10,000 fill the streets, press blasted for publicity. *Standard Times* (New Bedford, MA), p. 1.

Katz, J. (1989). *The seductions of crime*. New York: Basic Books.

Kifner, J. (1989, September 1). Bensonhurst: A tough code in defense of a closed world. *The New York Times*, p. A1.

Kriegel, M. (1989, April 21). Lived a dream life. *Daily News*, p. 2.

Marriott, M. (1989, April 24). Harlem residents fear backlash from park rape. *The New York Times*, p. B3.

Messerschmidt, J. (1986). *Capitalism and patriarchy: Toward a socialist feminist criminology*. Totowa, NJ: Rowman & Littlefield.

Pitt, D. E. (1989a, April 25). Gang attack: Unusual for its viciousness. *The New York Times*, p. B1.

Pitt, D. E. (1989b, April 24). More crimes tied to gang in park rape. *The New York Times*, p. B1.

Ravo, N. (1989, August 27). Marchers and Brooklyn youths trade racial jeers. *The New York Times*, p. B1.

Schwendinger, H., & Schwendinger, J. (1983). *Rape and inequality.* Beverly Hills, CA: Sage.

Sennett, R., & Cobb, J. (1972). *The hidden injuries of class.* New York: Vintage.

She wasn't nothing. (1989, April 24). *Daily News,* pp. 2-3.

Williams, J. E., & Holmes, K. A. (1981). *The second assault: Rape and public attitudes.* Westport, CT: Greenwood.

Wolff, C. (April 21, 1989). Youths rape and beat Central Park jogger. *The New York Times,* p. B1.

CHAPTER SIX

The Tangled Web
of Feminism and
Community Policing[1]

Susan L. Miller

✦ In 1987, the actresses who portrayed two New York City police women in the title roles of the television series *Cagney and Lacey* were featured on the cover of *Ms.* as two of the magazine's Women of the Year. A popular show, *Cagney and Lacey* made people nervous, for it introduced two competent, hardworking police women with strong friendship bonds and thus challenged viewers' ideas of gender, femininity, and feminism in the male world of policing (D'Acci, 1994). Rather than relying on physical attractiveness or superhuman qualities as in earlier police women shows (e.g., *Police Woman, Get Christy Love, Charlie's Angels,* and *Wonder Woman*), with the stars ultimately rescued by male costars or magic powers, *Cagney and Lacey*'s characters used their own blend of bravado, humor, toughness, and empathy in resolving situations week after week.

The tension that exploded on the television screen in weekly episodes of *Cagney and Lacey* mirrored similar tensions faced by real women who had entered police forces: Could women do "men's" work? How would citizens respond to female officers? How would male colleagues perceive and treat female officers? In fact, women did not make significant inroads into the male world of police patrol until the late 1960s and 1970s. For well over a century, traditional policing remained an occupation that elevated the traits of the aloof professional by glamorizing and emphasizing the masculinity and machismo of the profession. Women were unwelcomed into the institution, for they were seen not to have what it takes to be crime fighters; women's roles were constrained to ones of matron in the precinct jail, to performing clerical duties, and to responding to the needs of juveniles and women who became entangled with the criminal justice system (Schulz, 1995).

The criminal justice and legal system overall is viewed by many as operating with a uniquely masculine voice—a detached and impersonal one that emphasizes the rational above the relational. Others maintain, however, that a feminine voice is also present, particularly when decisions are made based on contextual or affiliational factors. Given the ideological preoccupation with masculinity in policing, however, any behavior that appears tied to femininity, weakness, or subjectivity is suspect and denigrated. Officers who express care and connection beyond superficial niceties have been trivialized or dismissed as too emotional for proper policing. In particular, these beliefs have been used historically to justify the exclusion of women as police officers. With the advent of a "new" genre of policing, community policing, so-called feminine constructs (such as an emphasis on cooperation and the maintenance of connections) have been reintroduced. The ideal community police officer has a more social worker orientation, a style that traditionally has been beyond the purview of acceptable police action. To be accepted by police, however, these feminine traits must be appropriated as masculine traits and reshaped to appear powerful and desirable (see Cockburn, 1991; Hunt, 1990; Jurik, 1988; Martin & Jurik, 1996; Myers & Chiang, 1993; Young, 1991). Hence, what follows in this chapter are the various contradictions that emerge when a recalcitrant institution is challenged to change and expand its ideology and practice.

In particular, this chapter explores the ambiguities that surround the feminine voice of care and its appropriation by community policing in contrast to the rejection of the feminine voice by traditional policing. The chapter represents the beginning of a feminist conceptual framework of community policing, which also introduces questions and develops ways to empirically test the ideas contained here. Community policing, with its potential for forging closer connections and deeper trust between police and citizens, epitomizes "ethic of care" concerns. Although the promises of community policing are laudable—and some rules and structures of the police organization have changed to accommodate these promises—many officers remain resistant to these changes. Changing the masculinist bias requires a paradigmatic shift of policing itself. Certainly, the ideological anxieties of the policing institution need to be resolved so that the gendered nature of traditional policing does not sabotage the potential success of community policing. The questions this raises are varied: How can policing be transformed to honor the values of care, connection, empathy, and informality (the so-called female voice) within the paramilitary, masculinist police organization? What changes must occur to reconcile the contradictions between male-identified and female-identified activities? What matters more: the genders of the officers, or whether the officers of either gender actively integrate the ethic of care within their social control–policing ideology? Will policing still be gendered in terms of who is seen as the expert? Are there other officer characteristics besides gender that increase community policing effectiveness? These questions will be explored in this chapter.

Community Policing of the 1990s

Community policing has captured the hearts (as well as the political and budget-allocating souls) of the nation.[2] Its promises are vast. They include "an emphasis on improving the number and quality of police-citizen contacts, a broader definition of 'legitimate' police work, decentralization of the police bureaucracy, and a greater emphasis on proactive problem-solving" (Rosenbaum, 1988, p. 334). In addition, community policing encourages the police to be "responsive to citizen demands" and committed to "helping neighborhoods help themselves" (Skogan, 1990, p. 92). Community policing introduces major role reorientation among police officers themselves and, if successful, relies on the ability to implement both philosophical and organizational change within an institution that is characterized by "rigid bureaucratic procedures [and] fear of change among employees" and hypermasculinity (Rosenbaum & Lurigio, 1994, p. 303).

Foot patrol officers—one of the most popular forms of community policing (and the form most heavily favored by federal funds)—are challenged to do more than duplicate the "walk-and-talk" styles of past community policing practice. Officers today are expected to interact with community members, not just respond to merchants and political leaders, and to move beyond the surveillance and arrest functions of traditional patrol officers (Rosenbaum & Lurigio, 1994). Rather, foot patrol officers are expected to engage in more nontraditional activities, such as participation in community meetings and identification of community problems coupled with strategies to address these needs. Officers are encouraged to organize community initiatives, resolve disputes among residents, establish connections, and actively make referrals to appropriate social service agencies (Trojanowicz, 1986). These activities are expected to occur through a decentralized process, which brings police closer to the neighborhoods in ministations or storefront offices within the community (particularly the more troubled areas). Decentralization, in particular, increases community police officers' autonomy from the larger police organization. At the same time, this decentralization may exacerbate negative feelings toward neighborhood officers by the actions and attitudes of routine patrol officers who misunderstand community policing and see these efforts as "*social work rather than real policework*" (Rosenbaum & Lurigio, 1994, p. 306; see also Skolnick & Bayley, 1988).

Before exploring the contradictions with feminism and community policing, this essay begins by examining the gendered culture of policing and the ways this masculinist culture manifests itself in the everyday reality of policework. In doing this, the essay explores how stereotypically feminine traits once used to exclude women's participation from patrol or to separate the "real" crime fighters from the "office cops" have now been resurrected and elevated to the pinnacle of community policing agendas and practice. The success of this resurrection, however, depends on the reshaping of unacceptable traits (associated with femininity) to acceptable traits (associated with masculinity, or so-called real policework). This reversal can possibly only be accomplished under the guise of police policy initiatives that treat these qualities as important (and masculine). We turn now to these issues.

"Different-Voice" Perspectives and Justice Issues

A logical first step is to explore the ways "doing gender" in policing is shaped by feminine and masculine voices or expectations. This is relevant to community policing because, regardless of departmental model or philosophical change, policing as a social institution is still largely a male institution. Carol Gilligan (1982) introduced the "different-voice" approach to moral development,[3] and her concepts easily lend themselves to look at the male voice of law and legal practice, although the law is ostensibly gender neutral (Daly, 1989, p. 1; see also Menkel-Meadow, 1985; West, 1988). Gilligan casts female and male voices as opposing ethical styles used in resolving conflict or dilemmas: Men prioritize individual rights, autonomy, and impartiality, whereas women reject male values of objectivity and detachment and instead honor and emphasize care, responsibility, and affective connections. This places moral problem solving in a contrast of "conflicting responsibilities [the female voice = ethic of care] rather than competing rights [the male voice = logic of justice]" (Gilligan, 1982, p. 17). Resolution of conflict, then, follows different paths if we were to adopt the values associated with the female voice, based on the "contextual and narrative, rather than formal and abstract" (Gilligan, 1982, p. 17).

Gilligan, however, is not without her share of critics, stemming from methodological criticisms based on her mostly white, middle-class sample to more substantive conceptual attacks. For instance, some argue that her different voice constructs are ahistorical and apolitical (see MacKinnon, 1989). The constructs fail to take into account that women's exclusion from public life virtually dictated their affiliational reliance on caretaking and relational traits, for "women acquired status and power only in a derivative sense through their relationships with men" (Menkel-Meadow, 1985, p. 40; see also MacKinnon, 1984). This fallacy is viewed as reintroducing the stereotype that men think and are rational, whereas women feel and are relational (Lloyd, 1983). Thus, this perpetuates the myth that there exists an "everywoman," an essentialist argument that for many is untenable (see Code, 1983). Or, in a related vein, different-voice approaches promote women's moral superiority rather than championing her intellect. Regardless of these criticisms, however, Gilligan's concept of different voices has permeated the discourse across a wide range of feminist academic disciplines, such as education, psychology, and the law.

Kathleen Daly (1989) has found it useful to use Gilligan's different-voice constructs to highlight traditional and ongoing criminology debates surrounding the ideologies of punishment. For instance, Daly sees proportionate punishment, when applied in a depersonalized context and when stressing deterrent or retributive purposes, as reflective of a male justice model. She sees the female care model operating when treatment and rehabilitation concerns are raised, based on the potential to reform individuals and reintegrate them back into communities. Daly (1989) takes issue with "Gilliganites" who believe that only the male voice operates within the criminal justice system. She argues that "the relational, contextual, and concrete reasoning which Gilligan associates with the female voice *is* the voice of criminal justice practices" (p. 2). She explains that this is because prior and ongoing victim-offender relationships *are* routinely taken into account with culpability assessments, sentencing practices, and so on, which provide evidence of a strong ethic-of-care approach to case processing.[4] Daly also raises the point that this personalized approach, the so-called ethic-of-care model, competes with current sentencing reform efforts designed to reduce disparity and put limits on judicial discretion (exemplifying the logic-of-justice model). This practice promotes sanctions that are fair, rational, equal, and tied to a crime control orientation as well as—quite ironically—being tied to notions of equality in treatment (Daly, 1989).[5]

Daly contends that it is not "that the female voice is absent, but that certain relations are presupposed, maintained, and reproduced" (Daly, 1989, p. 2) in ways that hurt or oppress those least powerful and most marginalized in society (usually women, children, and people of color). So merely adding more female judges to the bench or further changing the current system to resemble an ethic-of-care model would not necessarily change currently existing legal or criminal justice system practices. Others (MacKinnon, 1989; Menkel-Meadow, 1985; West, 1988) disagree, stating that law is created, enforced, interpreted, and punished by men who cannot begin to fathom women's experience and knowledge.[6] Consequently, a number of feminist legal theorists contend that increased representation of women in policing or in the practice of law—or in any institution that has been historically comprised of mostly men and used male values as gatekeepers and membership rules—may transform those institutions by readjusting the rules to accommodate alternative approaches to "doing justice." Menkel-Meadow (1989) argues that this "transformative potential derives from women's experiences of exclusion which create an outsider's critical perception; oppression which engenders greater empathy for subordinated groups; and the learned attention to caring and relationships" (pp. 312-313).

This discussion of police practice and ideology and different voices raises some additional important issues: Will male and female officers be evaluated differently because of gender-based assumptions? For example, if women are seen as doing great work with kids, it is because of women's so-called natural nurturing abilities, whereas if men do great work with kids, it is because they are great cops and have gone above and beyond the traditional parameters of policing. Can these questions be empirically tested? Studies by Acker (1990), Acker and Ask (1989), Baran (1990), Cockburn (1988, 1991), Cockburn and Ormrod (1993), and Hacker (1990) found that although computerization and new technologies upgraded women's skills (across a variety of occupations, such as engineering, banking, and insurance), men remained in charge. Male workers were perceived as having more skills than female workers, and women's skills were undervalued; women workers remained at the lower levels of the organization's status and hierarchy. Given the gendered skills inherent in community policing, future performance evaluations will reveal whether female-identified skills have been upgraded to be perceived as more highly valued masculine skills and how skill assessment will be interpreted for male and female officers who exhibit such skills.

Policing as a Male Institution and Site of Gendered Action

Feminist researchers, such as Acker (1990), Connell (1987), Martin and Jurik (1996), Messerschmidt, (1993), and West and Zimmerman (1987) frequently write about the gendered nature of organizations and how these structures shape behavior of the men and women in such a way that their responses are also conditioned by gender role expectations. This process of doing gender describes the activity of practicing such behavior.[7] In his theoretical treatment of structured action and the construction of masculinity, James Messerschmidt (1993) uses the police as an example to illustrate "how gender, specifically masculinity, is socially constructed and resultingly institutionalized" (p. 174). In his work, Messerschmidt discusses the male-dominated nature of the police workforce: Despite inroads made in assigning women police officers to routine patrol activities (since the 1970s), the gender division of labor within the force remains segregated. Nationally, 10% of police departments are comprised of women (Martin, 1989), and "women are virtually excluded from upper-level management . . . just as they are in corporate boardrooms and law partnerships" (p. 6), thus reproducing gendered power relations that exist in society at large. Messerschmidt (1993) contends,

> Within police agencies, men's power is deemed an authentic and acceptable part of social relations. This legitimacy of the power by men in police work adorns them with greater authority. Indeed, gender relations of power promote and constrain the social action of men and women police officers. . . . Police work is defined culturally as an activity only "masculine men" can accomplish. As Allison Morris (1987, p. 111-144) shows, police work is viewed by the police and public as a masculine pursuit: the imagery is "of the armed man of action fighting crime and criminals," the Clint Eastwood model. (p. 175)

Accepting women as equal police officers to men challenges the "masculine association with police work—if women can do it, the value of the practice as a means for exhibiting masculinity is cast into question" (Messerschmidt, 1993, p. 175).[8]

Barriers to Women as Police Officers: Moving Beyond Women, Children, and Typewriters

To summarize what at this point is well documented at length elsewhere, women were excluded from the traditionally male world of police work because others saw them as too soft to do the job. Women officers were seen as mother figures in skirted uniforms, dispensing care and guidance (see Schulz, 1995). Women's job responsibilities reflected their emotional, compassionate, and cooperative temperaments. Thus, women's domain included helping runaway, lost, or abused children; or prostitutes (because of women's perceived higher moral standards of behavior vis-à-vis men's moral standards); or (of course) performing stereotypically female clerical roles. Despite the historical fact that women police had higher educational backgrounds and more training than male officers did, women's perceived physical deficiencies (lack of strength and mettle to intimidate crooks or be willing to fight) and so-called fragile emotional composition prevented them from movement away from proscribed roles focusing on women, children, and typewriters (Milton, 1972).

Whereas women were excluded from policing based on the justifications just discussed, men were celebrated as paragon police officers: brave, suspicious, aloof, objective, cynical, physically intimidating, as well as willing users of force and brutality. Women's femininity, by contrast, stressed a less masterful, more submissive style: partiality, subjectivity, gentleness, conciliation, and a focus on affective connections. Take a look at Table 6.1; it does several things. First, it summarizes the typical traits women presumably share that would prevent them from being good or real police officers (see column 1). These perceptions are based on constructions of femininity and have been used to devalue women's potential contributions and to limit women's equal access to patrol jobs and challenging assignments within policing hierarchies. Second, Table 6.1 (column 2) provides some interpretations or responses these traits typically generate from male police officers, which reinforce the (male) rejection of women as police officers. Note that not all women possess these traits (or that all men do not have some of these) but that these are gender role stereotypes and assumptions that exist and that have been used to exclude women from becoming fully participating, vested police officers with similar job roles and responsibilities as have their male officer counterparts. Last, Table 6.1 (column 3) illustrates the co-optation, if you will, of traits previously labeled feminine and undesirable and the traits promoted as desirable for community police officers today.

Yet the community policing model ironically rejects the "aloof, authoritarian, detached" police officer model and also rejects the traditional policing style "structured around random patrols and response to service calls . . . respond[ing] 'by the book,' [and] carrying out policies as directed in a mechanical fashion" (Metchick & Winton, 1995, p. 115). Community policing has instead embraced the feminine qualities (contained in the chart) as *ideal* or *superior* traits for neighborhood officers to possess, although the words that have been used in the past to characterize these qualities as feminine (and therefore unwel-

TABLE 6.1 Comparison of Policing Styles

Styles Women Bring to Policing	Criticisms These Styles Generate	Community Policing Styles and Goals
Peacemaker, naive and caring style, negotiator, cooperative style	Ignores need to assert authority, make judgment calls, particularly because authority is the backdrop of efficiency and coercive force (see Bittner, 1967; Van Maanen 1978); indecisiveness, which would translate into an inability to achieve respect and control over situations	Cares about the residents and community, peacemaker, negotiator, cooperative style
Informal style of interaction; values empathy and strong communication skills	Not able to be an autonomous, aloof professional; too softhearted; it is better to be detached, cynical, and suspicious (Skolnick, 1994)	Informal style of interaction that builds on trust and interpersonal rapport
Emphasizes connections among relationships, family, and community	Needs to be able to distance oneself from human tragedy (Pogrebin & Poole, 1988); loss of ability to be fair-minded and objective	Emphasizes connections between police and community
Problem-solver; tenacious interest in knowing history of problem and causes; is reform minded (long-term)	Incorrect role: needs rapid response to symptoms and immediate action, then move on; not part of the tough-guy facade, which seeks short-term fixes	Problem-solver; tenacious interest in knowing history of problem and causes; is reform minded (long-term)

comed) have faded from the present dialogue. But they do not completely disappear. Once the previously disdained feminine qualities are elevated to a desirable status, gender-based exclusionary behavior focused on these qualities merely becomes more muted and insidious. In fact, the negative connotations associated with femininity remain present in the interpretations of neighborhood police officers by those officers who oppose or misunderstand the premise of the policy change (or are jealous because of the positive attention or presumed rewards of "fast-track" to promotion accorded to neighborhood officers; see Miller, 1996a).

A parallel construction can be drawn from research exploring the occupational cultures of "street cops" and "office cops" (see Reuiss-Ianni & Ianni, 1983). For example, in her work with New York street cops, Jennifer Hunt (1984) found that street cops' assessments of office cops were not flattering, and their assessments were based on gender-related factors. The street cops saw the office cops as

> engaged in "feminine labor" such as public relations and secretarial work. These "pencil-pushing bureaucrats" were not involved in the masculine, physical labor which characterized "real police work" on the street. High-ranking administrators were also viewed as "inside tit men," "ass kissers" and "whores" who gained their positions through political patronage rather than through superior performance in the rescue and crime-fighting activities associated with "real police work." (p. 287)

What is the relevance of these renamed traits to the tenets of community policing? Community policing stresses communication, familiarity, the building of better rapport and trust between police and residents, informal problem solving, and the fostering of citizen-police cooperation. Community police officers are taught to use conflict resolution and mediation skills and to go beyond immediate crisis responses to focus instead on more long-term solutions to problems that will facilitate greater connections between police and citizens. The informal styles of policing are perceived as more effective tools in enhancing recognition, trust, and support that citizens develop for their neighborhood cop. Yet, one must ask, if men adopt these feminine traits, does this perpetuate seeing *men* as the experts of caring in a community policing context and is this appropriation done at women's expense? Do women continue to be subordinated because, after all, it is only natural for women to have these traits?

These questions fit into a larger literature on the gendering of skill. Acker (1992) argues that the restructuring of the global capitalistic economy necessitates changes in skill demands. New technologies may upgrade skilled work, but firms or institutions may not recognize or reward increases in skill, particularly for women workers. In fact, according to job evaluations, women's jobs are typically viewed as requiring less skill than comparable men's jobs (Acker, 1989, 1992).

Similarly, Cynthia Cockburn, in her studies of gender and technology, found that skill is gendered, with boundaries redrawn and maintained "between male and female, skilled and unskilled" (Acker, 1992, p. 61; Cockburn, 1991; Cockburn & Ormrod, 1993). In regard to community policing, a similar adjustment may take place in which the feminine traits that characterize community policing objectives will be masculinized to fit into traditional policing frameworks (in other words, a readjustment of the rules to fit men only).[9]

Examining the Conflict Between Traditional Beliefs and Alternative Beliefs

---

The conceptual issues raised in this chapter facilitate a number of research questions to explore. Initially, we need to address officers' receptivity for embracing, valuing, and actively promoting a reorientation—a reconstituted role of sorts—that was previously stigmatized. This message must be supported from the top of the policing hierarchy—the chief—for the shift in policy and practice to be taken seriously (see Bayley, 1994).[10] As Lurigio and Skogan (1994, p. 316) say (in their discussion of introducing community policing to Chicago police), the next goal is to "win the hearts and minds" of police officers who will be carrying out these new policies. This goal entails the process of redefining the social work aspects of policing, in particular, those activities previously seen as tainted or so-called women's work that permitted a devaluation, a trivialization, and a dismissal of these feminine qualities and activities. These social work aspects of community policing need to be perceived by officers as rewarding to stimulate the buying in and adopting new values that reflect today's modern police officer. Resistant officers need to see this new role as carrying *more* power, because power is inextricably entangled with masculinity, rather than associated with *less* power, or femininity. Lurigio and Rosenbaum (1994), in their review of the impact of community policing on police personnel, found that job satisfaction increased, officers perceived that their occupational role expanded, relations with coworkers and citizens were improved, and officers increased their expectations for community participation in crime prevention. Playing a leading role in "saving" a neighborhood could satisfy a police officer's desire for meaningful work! To accomplish this, the feminine virtues associated with so-called women's work need to be recast and imbued with honor. This is a difficult task, as these denigrated traits previously associated with women are virtually antithetical to the masculinized construction and organization of police work. Without this reshaping of the definition and the value attached to it, however, neighborhood officers will continue to be seen by others as "pansy police."[11] This suggests using different approaches to win the hearts and minds of those officers already working in the police department and to effectively devise ways to screen applicants during the hiring process for assessing their potential for using ethic-of-care reasoning.

In addition, there is a need to examine the relevance of gender-based different-voice constructs within policing. Both women and men can apply different-voice frameworks to solving community crime problems. Women alone cannot do this job, despite the numerous feminine traits that have been associated with them as women and currently reintroduced as ideal qualities of community police officers. Different-voice constructs within a community policing model are ideally gender neutral. Community policing may be best when it can blend both justice and care models and be practiced by all men and women on the force. This raises the question, Is the promotion of the ethic-of-care voice sufficient (under the guise of a community policing philosophy)? Or does the reality of the institution of policing "constrain the possibilities or the desirabilities of different approaches" (see Anleu, 1995, p. 360)? The feminine attribute of caring may need to be deskilled and neutered before it can be embraced by a male-dominated police force. This deskilling could move us toward a more androgynous police model. It may be that the feminine attribute of caring associated with community policing will be redefined to be accepted into the existing masculinist skill framework (see in general, Martin & Jurik, 1996). Future research with community police officers and police administrators could explore these questions: How do male and female officers reconcile different voices? How does this compare between neighborhood police officers and traditional rapid response patrol officers? How do community police officers renegotiate, or impression manage, their positions, given the rejection of feminine qualities in a masculine organization and the overall resistance to community policing by the rank and file? How do gender and gender role expectations shape police evaluation practices?

Conclusion

As an institution, the police combine both social control and social service functions. Yet these services are provided against a backdrop of a hegemonic masculinity, one that elevates so-called manly pursuits and the role of the tough, aloof, detached professional, while simultaneously rejecting qualities or behaviors that are reminiscent of femininity or femaleness (Messerschmidt, 1993). As an emerging paradigm of policing, today's community policing policies stress a more community-oriented role, emphasizing increased interaction between police and citizens as well as greater accountability to the community that police officers serve. Its success seems to rest on favorable citizen evaluations of police service delivery as well as the community's acceptance of this new police role (Wasserman & Moore, 1988). By definition, this necessitates greater accountability of police behavior to community members; in fact, citizen satisfaction is tied to establishing or reinforcing police legitimacy. But, the hearts and minds of police officers aren't won yet (Lurgio & Skogan, 1994). Successful community policing programs also require a shift in how the activities of community police officers are viewed by the entire police department and seen as serious work. Community policing's connection to the fundamental goal of crime fighting and the role it plays in achieving this goal must be understood and accepted by the rank and file and administration alike. Until the police reconcile the contradictions that arise when feminine traits are appropriated by masculine experts, dismissing women officers' behavior as timid or natural while commending men's behavior, the acceptance of community policing will remain merely symbolic.

Notes

1. A modified version of this chapter is to appear in *Journal of Contemporary Criminal Justice* (in press).

2. "Community policing" emerged in the early 1980s as a result of the growing tension between police and citizens (Kelling & Moore, 1991). This so-called new approach stresses the building of closer ties between police and community members. It is hypothesized that by increasing community members' contact with police, suspicion and distrust between police and citizens would decrease, citizen satisfaction with police would increase, quality of community life would be improved, and levels of fear would

be reduced. One predicted outgrowth of community policing is that residents would also be more willing to come forward with information about crimes (as witnesses or victims) and to become more involved with prevention activities because the police officer would be a familiar, recognizable person. The driving force behind community policing is to enable police officers to fully know the community they serve: its residents, its habits, its trouble spots, its strengths.

3. Gilligan (1992) challenges Kohlberg's (1984) cognitive-developmental theory of moral development, arguing that the hierarchical stages of moral development that he delineates places girls at lower stages than boys; this placement fails to take into account that men and women follow different developmental paths, with women expressing an ethic of care rather than Kohlberg's morally superior stage of the ethic of justice, a stage more likely achieved by males. Gilligan contends that the care ethic is no less superior than the justice model.

4. There is ample empirical evidence from the past three decades to suggest that police and court officials *do* use relational and social information to guide their decision making (Black, 1980; Daly, 1989, 1994; LaFree, Resnick, & Vischer, 1985; Stanko, 1985) even though the risks in responding this way can be unacceptable (e.g., creating different standards of justice by assuming that relational connections are less needy of criminal justice interventions and control, ignoring the power and inequality dynamics involved in date rape or battering).

5. Gilligan (1982) herself has responded to gender-based a priori assumptions:

> The different voice I describe is characterized not by gender but theme. Its association with women is an empirical observation, and it is primarily through women's voices that I trace its development. But this association is not absolute, and the contrasts between male and female voices are presented here to highlight a distinction between two modes of thought and to focus a problem of interpretation rather than to represent a generalization about either sex. In tracing development, I point to the interplay of these voices within each sex and suggest that their convergence marks times of crisis and change. No claims are made about the origins of the differences described or their distribution in a wider population, across cultures, or through time. Clearly, these differences arise in a social context where factors of social status and power combine with reproductive biology to shape the experience of males and females and the relations between the sexes. (p. 2)

6. And these lawmakers (legislators), law enforcers (police and prosecutors), and law interpreters (judges) only include a certain group of men: mostly white, educated, professionals from middle to high socioeconomic classes.

7. The term *doing gender* describes an interactive social process through which assumptions about power, sexuality, and role expectations shape reactions to men and women (see Martin & Jurik, 1996). Doing gender goes far beyond the social identity of being a man or woman but, rather, involves "the activity of managing situated conduct in light of normative conceptions, attitudes, and activities appropriate to one's sex category" (West & Zimmerman, 1987, p. 127). Doing gender captures the difference in how people are treated and controlled within organizations such that "advantage and disadvantage, exploitation and control, action and emotion, meaning and identity, are patterned through and in terms of a distinction between male and female, masculine and feminine" (Acker, 1990, p. 146). Policing, as a masculine organization, assumes there are "socially gendered perceptual, interactional, and micro-political activities that cast particular pursuits as expressions of masculine and feminine 'natures' " (West & Zimmerman, 1987, p. 126).

8. Messerschmidt also suggests that, even when both men and women officers work together, their actions remain gendered: With team policing, the male partner will drive the squad car, decide the activities, and conduct interviews, whereas women officers tend to play supportive roles, recording responses and doing paperwork (Messerschmidt, 1993, p. 175). Research by Remmington (1981) found that the "women officers not partnered with men were frequently backed up on calls by males. The latter often usurped the female officer's role and dominated the encounter" (p. 117). Susan Martin's (1994) work suggests that not only sexism but also racism further divides police officers, with men of color and white men ending up more closely aligned because of shared masculinity assumptions of male power, whereas women of color remain separated from both white men and women as well as men of color.

9. Special thanks to an anonymous reviewer for the suggestion to use the literature regarding the gendering of skill.

10. This strategy has been adopted and used successfully by departments battling corruption: Only when the police chief aggressively promotes a zero tolerance for the undesired activity—with certain and serious penalties attached to the new policy—will police departments change (Murphy & Caplan, 1993).

11. This is a typical slur used by traditional patrol officers to demean neighborhood police officers (Miller, 1996b).

References

Acker, J. (1989). *Doing comparable worth*. Philadelphia: Temple University Press.

Acker, J. (1990). Hierarchies, jobs, and bodies: A theory of gendered organizations. *Gender & Society, 4,* 139-158.

Acker, J. (1992). The future of women and work: Ending the twentieth century. *Sociological Perspectives, 35,* 53-68.

Acker, J., & Ask, A. M. (1989). *Wage difference between women and men and the structure of work and wage setting in Swedish banks.* Stockholm: Arbetslivscentrum.

Anleu, S. L. (1995). Women in law: Theory, research, and practice. In B. R. Price & N. J. Sokoloff (Eds.), *The criminal justice system and women: Offenders, victims, and workers* (2nd ed., pp. 358-371). New York: McGraw-Hill.

Baran, B. (1990). The new economy: Female labor and the office of the future. In K. V. Hansen & I. J. Philipson (Eds.), *Women, class, and the feminist imagination* (pp. 517-534). Philadelphia: Temple University Press.

Bayley, D. (1994). *Police for the future.* New York: Oxford University Press.

Bittner, E. (1967). *The functions of the police in modern society.* Washington, DC: Government Printing Office.

Black, D. (1980). *The manners and customs of the police.* San Diego, CA: Academic Press.

Cockburn, C. (1988). *Machinery of dominance: Women, men, and technical know-how.* Boston: Northeastern University Press.

Cockburn, C. (1991). *In the way of women: Men's resistance to sex equality in organizations.* Ithaca, NY: ILR.

Cockburn, C., & Ormrod, S. (1993). *Gender and technology in the making.* London: Sage.

Code, L. B. (1983). Responsibility and the epistemic community: Woman's place. *Social Research, 50,* 537-555.

Connell, R. W. (1987). *Gender and power.* Palo Alto, CA: Stanford University Press.

D'Acci, J. (1994). Defining women: Television and the case of *Cagney and Lacey*. Chapel Hill: University of North Carolina Press.

Daly, K. (1989). Criminal justice ideologies and practices in different voices: Some feminist questions about justice. *International Journal of the Sociology of Law, 17,* 1-18.

Daly, K. (1994). *Gender, crime, and punishment.* New Haven, CT: Yale University Press.

Gilligan, C. (1982). *In a different voice.* Cambridge, MA: Harvard University Press.

Hacker, S. (1990). *Doing it the hard way.* Boston: Unwin Hyman.

Hunt, J. (1984). The development of rapport through the negotiation of gender in field work among police. *Human Organization, 43,* 283-296.

Hunt, J. (1990). The logic of sexism among police. *Women and Criminal Justice, 1,* 3-30.

Jurik, N. (1988). Striking a balance: Female correctional officers, gender role stereotypes, and male prisons. *Sociological Inquiry, 58,* 291-305.

Kelling, G. L., & Moore, M. H. (1991). From political to reform to community: The evolving strategy of police. In J. R. Greene & S. D. Mastrofski (Eds.), *Community policing: Rhetoric or reality* (pp. 3-25). New York: Praeger.

Kohlberg, L. (1984). *The psychology of moral development.* San Francisco: Harper & Row.

LaFree, G., Reskin, B., & Vischer, C. (1985). Jurors' responses to victims' behavior and legal issues in sexual assault trials. *Social Problems, 32,* 213-232.

Lloyd, G. (1983). Reason, gender and morality in the history of philosophy. *Social Research, 50,* 490-513.

Lurigio, A. J., & Rosenbaum, D. P. (1994). The impact of community policing on police personnel: A review of the literature. In D. P. Rosenbaum (Ed.), *The challenge of community policing: Testing the promises* (pp. 147-163). Thousand Oaks, CA: Sage.

Lurigio, A. J., & Skogan, W. G. (1994). Winning the hearts and minds of police officers: An assessment of staff perceptions of community policing in Chicago. *Crime and Delinquency, 40,* 315-330.

MacKinnon, C. (1984). The 1984 James McCormick Mitchell lecture: Feminist discourse, moral values, and the law—A conversation." *Buffalo Law Review, 11,* 20.

MacKinnon, C. (1989). *Toward a feminist theory of the state.* Cambridge, MA: Harvard University Press.

Martin, S. E. (1989). Women on the move?: A report on the status of women in policing. *Women & Criminal Justice, 1,* 2-40.

Martin, S. E. (1994). "Outsider within" the station house: The impact of race and gender on black women police. *Social Problems, 41,* 383-400.

Martin, S. E., & Jurik, N. C. (1996). *Doing justice, doing gender: Women in law and criminal justice occupations.* Thousand Oaks, CA: Sage.

Menkel-Meadow, C. (1985). Portia in a different voice: Speculations on a women's lawyering process. *Berkeley Women's Law Journal, 1,* 39-63.

Menkel-Meadow, C. (1989). Exploring a research agenda of the feminization of the legal profession: Theories of gender and social change. *Law & Social Inquiry, 14,* 289-314.

Messerschmidt, J. W. (1993). *Masculinities and crime: Critique and reconceptualization of theory.* Lanham, MD: Rowman & Littlefield.

Metchick, E., & Winton, A. (1995). Community policing and its implications for alternative models of police officer selection. In P. C. Kratcoski and D. Dukes (Eds.), *Issues in community policing* (pp. 107-123). Cincinnati, OH: Anderson.

Miller, S. L. (1996a, November). *Gender paradoxes: Reconciling informal and formal social control of battering in a community policing context.* Paper presented at the annual conference of the American Society of Criminology, Chicago, IL.

Miller, S. L. (1996b). "Real" police work or the work of "pansies?" Unpublished manuscript.

Milton, C. (1972). *Women in policing.* Washington, DC: Police Foundation.

Morris, A. (1987). *Women, crime and criminal justice.* New York: Basil Blackwell.

Murphy, P., & Caplan, D. G. (1993). Fostering integrity. In R. G. Dunham & G. P. Alpert (Eds.), *Critical issues in policing: Contemporary readings* (pp. 304-324). Prospect Heights, IL: Waveland.

Myers, L. B., & Chiang, C. (1993). Law enforcement officer and peace officer: Reconciliation using the feminine approach. *Journal of Crime and Justice, 14,* 31-41.

Pogrebin M. R., & Poole, E. O. (1988). Humor in the briefing room: A study of the strategic uses of humor among police. *Journal of Contemporary Ethnography, 17,* 183-210.

Remmington, P. W. (1981). *Policing: The occupation and the introduction of female officers.* Washington, DC: University Press of America.

Reuiss-Ianni, E., & Ianni, F. A. J. (1983). Street cops and management cops: The two cultures of policing. In M. Punch (Ed.), *Control in the police organization* (pp. 251-274). Cambridge, MA: MIT Press.

Rosenbaum, D. P. (1988). Community crime prevention: A review and synthesis of the literature. *Justice Quarterly, 5,* 323-395.

Rosenbaum, D. P., & Lurigio, A. J. (1994). An inside look at community policing reform: Definitions, organizational changes, and evaluation findings. *Crime & Delinquency, 40,* 299-314.

Schulz, D. M. (1995). *From social worker to crimefighter: Women in United States municipal policing.* New York: Praeger.

Skogan, W. G. (1990). *Disorder and community decline: Crime and the spiral of decay in American neighborhoods.* New York: Free Press.

Skolnick, J. H., & Bayley, D. H. (1988). *The new blue line: Police innovations in six American cities.* New York: Free Press.

Skolnick, J. H. (1994). *Justice without trial: Law enforcement in a democratic society.* New York: Macmillan.

Stanko, E. A. (1985). *Intimate intrusions: Women's experience of male violence.* London: Unwin Hyman.

Trojanowicz, R. C. (1986). Evaluating a neighborhood foot patrol program: The Flint, Michigan, project. In D. P. Rosenbaum (Ed.), *Community crime prevention: Does it work?* (pp. 157-179). Beverly Hills, CA: Sage.

Van Maanen, J. (1978). The asshole. In P. K. Manning and J. Van Maanen (Eds.), *Policing: A view from the street* (pp. 221-238).

Wasserman, R., & Moore, M. H. (1988). *Values in policing: Perspectives on policing.* Cambridge, MA: Harvard University, National Institute of Justice and John F. Kennedy School of Government.

West, R. (1988). Jurisprudence and gender. *The University of Chicago Law Review, 55,* 1-72.

West, C., & Zimmerman, D. H. (1987). Doing gender. *Gender & Society, 1,* 125-151.

Young, M. (1991). *An inside job: Policing and police culture in Britain.* Oxford, UK: Clarendon.

CHAPTER SEVEN

The War on Drugs as a War Against Black Women

Stephanie R. Bush-Baskette

✦ The number of Black females incarcerated for drug offenses increased by 828% between 1986 and 1991. This increase was approximately twice that of Black males (429%) and more than 3 times the increase in the number of White females (241%) (Mauer & Huling, 1995, p. 20). In Florida, Black females constituted 55.6% of the incarcerated female population in 1983. By 1993, the percentage had increased to 58.3% and by 1994, to 59.3%. In 1993, a drug offense was the primary offense of 38.9% of the Black female inmates in Florida. Drug offenses were the primary convictions for 29.5% of the incarcerated White females (Florida Department of Corrections, 1993/1994).

Although Black females generally constitute a higher percentage of the incarcerated female population than Black males do of the incarcerated male population, the Black female's presence in the criminal justice system is seldom studied. The impact of the so-called war on drugs on the incarceration of Black females is no exception. Tonry (1995), although acknowledging the apparent impact of the drug policies on

---

When referring to specific studies, the terms *Black women*, *African American women*, and *women of color* are not used interchangeably in this chapter. When not referencing a particular study, however, the terms *Black women*, *African American women*, and *women of color* are used interchangeably.

Black females, chose to focus his attention on the impact of the war on drugs on the Black male. Feminist criminologists often generalize the impact of drug policies to all women and propose that "the 'war on drugs' has been translated into a war on women" (Chesney-Lind, 1995, p. 111). As such, the experiences of Black females in the criminal justice system are often ignored or marginalized. Even when criminologists attempt to place Black females at the center of their research on the processing of females by the criminal justice system, such investigations tend to be piecemeal and incomplete. The problem often derives from the lack of data sources that provide information with regard to the intersection of race and gender throughout the criminal justice process (Mann, 1995).

The purpose of this chapter is to (a) further the study of the treatment of the Black female by personnel within the criminal justice system, (b) investigate the impact of drug law violations on the incarceration of the Black female, and (c) substantiate the need to test the impact of "war on drug" initiatives on the incarceration of the Black female.

Conceptual Framework

Although drug use had begun to decline by the early 1980s (except in the case of cocaine use, which declined in the mid-1980s), beginning in 1987-1988, the war against drugs focused on the arrests of low-level drug dealers and street-level drug offenses, such as possession and trafficking (Tonry, 1995). The drug war initiatives enacted by state and federal legislators included increased penalties, mandatory sentencing laws, and stricter enforcement for drug law violations. Coinciding with these drug law initiatives was an increase in the arrest and imprisonment of Black people. In 1976, Blacks constituted 22% of the arrest cases in the United States for drug abuse violations (as compared to 77% for Whites). By 1990, the percentage of arrests involving Blacks nationwide had risen to 41% and had decreased to 59% for Whites.

Although Blacks were disproportionately arrested for drug law violations, as indicated in Table 7.1, reported drug use by Blacks and

TABLE 7.1 U.S. Percentage of Drug Use by Race, 1990

Type of Illicit Drug	Black	White
Marijuana	31.7	34.2
Cocaine	10	11.7
Hallucinogen	3.0	8.7
Heroin	1.7	.7

SOURCE: Adapted from Bureau of Justice Statistics (1991) and Tonry (1995).

Whites did not support the racially disproportionate patterns of drug arrests.

It was only in the case of heroin that drug use by Blacks exceeded that of Whites, and then only by 1%. The drug used most prevalently by both Blacks and Whites was marijuana (31.7% for Blacks and 34.2% for Whites). Tonry proposed that the drug policies of 1987-1988 led to the increase in the racial disparity of increased incarceration for the Black male living in the inner city while having no positive impact on the drug problems in the United States (Tonry, 1995).

Some feminist criminologists posit that this war against drugs has actually been a "war against women" (Chesney-Lind, 1995; Feinman, 1994). They support their position with statistics that reveal that the increased incarceration of females coincided with the onset of the drug law initiatives. Although the incarceration rate of females has remained somewhat constant, with only a 1.6% increase, the number of incarcerated females in state and federal prisons increased from 12,746 in 1978 to 47,691 in 1991 (Feinman, 1994). Between 1980 and 1990, there was an increase of 256% in the number of females incarcerated in state and federal institutions, as compared to an increase of 139.6% for males. Incarceration data for Florida also indicate an increase in the number of incarcerated females between 1983 and 1991. The incarcerated female population in 1983 was 1,253; by 1991, the number had more than doubled to 2,687 (Florida Department of Corrections, 1993/1994).

Most of the increase in the rate of female incarceration was for nonviolent property crime and drug offenses. An analysis of individual states indicates that the percentage of women incarcerated for violent crimes is far less than that for women incarcerated for drug offenses. In

1990, Rhode Island reported that 10% of the incarcerated female population had been convicted of violent crimes, whereas one third had been convicted of drug offenses. During the same year, in Massachusetts, 22% of incarcerated females had been convicted of violent offenses, as compared to 47% who were found guilty of drug offenses (Chesney-Lind, 1995).

Drug offenses represented the single most prevalent primary offense for female inmates in Florida in both 1993 and 1994. Of the female prisoners, 35% in 1993 and 31% in 1994 were imprisoned for a drug offense as the primary charge (Florida Department of Corrections, 1993/1994, 1994/1995). This figure does not include those women who were incarcerated for drug offenses as secondary or lower offenses.

The percentage of females who were incarcerated at the federal level for various offenses significantly shifted between 1986 and 1991, as indicated in Table 7.2.

Between 1986 and 1991, the percentage of females (64%) incarcerated for drug-related offenses more than doubled.

National arrest data indicate that the nonviolent offense category of larceny-theft was the single most frequent arrest charge for women in 1983, 1987, and 1991. Furthermore, beginning in 1987, drug abuse violations consistently appeared in the top five crimes for which women were most frequently arrested in selected years from 1960 to 1991. Arrests for violent crimes were not prevalent enough to be included in these listings (Feinman, 1994).

Mann (1995) reports that much of the recent growth in the arrest and incarceration of women can be attributed to increased drug use and related offenses by women in "an era of harsher drug laws." In 1989, one out of every three women (33.6%) who were held in jails nationwide were charged with a drug offense. Property crimes (31.9%), public order violations (19%), and all other offenses (2.2%) followed (Mann, 1995, p. 129). In Mann's study of the criminal justice processing of women in California, Florida, and New York, she concluded that drug offenses were the third most frequent cause of arrests for women when the arrests of the three states were combined; larceny-theft and driving under the influence being the first and second most frequent arrest charges.

These studies and data support the assertion that the increase in the incarceration of women can be attributed to the policies incorporated

TABLE 7.2 Offenses of Female Inmates in Federal Institutions, 1986
Compared With 1991 (in percentages)

Offense Type	1986	1991
Violent	7.1	2.0
Drug	26.1	63.9
Property	28.2	6.3
Robbery	4.4	2.0

SOURCE: Adapted from Kline (1993).

in the war on drugs, namely, mandatory sentencing for drug offenses
and mandatory sentencing for felony convictions.

A Closer Analysis
of the Female Prisoner

The general profile of the incarcerated female has changed very little
over the past 20 years. Glick and Neto (1977) conducted a study of 14
states and the federal correctional systems. From their study evolved a
profile of the typical female prisoner as a woman who was (a) Black
(more than 50%), (b) unmarried (80%), and (c) the mother of at least
one child (75%). Over half of the women were recipients of welfare
prior to their imprisonment.

In 1980, a national study was conducted of federal and state
correctional facilities. As in the Glick and Neto (1977) study, the
findings of the national report concluded that incarcerated females
tended to be members of a minority group, young, poor, unskilled, and
unmarried. Furthermore, the single most frequent reason for the imprisonment of these women was their conviction for a drug-related or an
economic crime (Feinman, 1994).

The American Correctional Association (1990) conducted a national survey of state correctional facilities in 1987. They reported a
similar profile for the incarcerated female: 57% of the women were
members of minority groups, approximately 80% were mothers, and
60% were on welfare prior to their incarceration (60.1%). The single
largest crime that led to the incarceration of the female inmates was

drug law violations (20%), and the reason most often provided for the commission of women inmates' current offense was their desire or need to buy drugs (25.1%).

In a recent study, Chesney-Lind (1995) discovered an increasing relationship between drugs offenses and the incarceration of women. Between 1980 and 1986, there was an *increase* in the number of women who were incarcerated for the *possession* of drugs and a *decrease* in the number of women who were incarcerated for *drug trafficking*. Her review of a 1990 Rhode Island study indicated that the number of women who were incarcerated in that state increased from 25 to 250 in a 5-year period. Of the 250 women, 33% were incarcerated for drug offenses. In Massachusetts in 1990, nearly half (47%) of the incarcerated women were imprisoned for drug offenses. In New York between 1980 and 1986, 23.3% of the incarcerated females were imprisoned for drug offenses; by 1991, this percentage had increased to 62%. In California in 1984, 17.9% of the incarcerated females were imprisoned for drug offenses; in 1989, the percentage had increased to 37.9%. Of those females who were incarcerated for drug offenses in California in 1989, 37% were held for the possession of marijuana. Chesney-Lind (1995) concludes that "mandatory sentencing for particularly drugs has affected women" (p. 112).

A drug offense was the primary offense of 38.9% of the Black females incarcerated in Florida during 1993. Drug offenses were the primary convictions for 29.5% incarcerated White females. In 1994, 34% of the incarcerated Black females had a drug offense as the primary charge, as compared to 27.2% of the White females. The second most prevalent category of offenses for Black females in 1993 was theft, forgery, fraud (15.7%); for White females, it was murder-manslaughter (26%). The second most prevalent category of charges continued to be theft, forgery, fraud (18.7%) for Black females, and murder-manslaughter (22.9%) for White females (Florida Department of Corrections, 1993/1994, 1994/1995).

Feinman (1994) summarized the increase in the incarcerated female population as follows:

The increase from 1983 to 1991 can be attributed to the "war on drugs," mandatory sentencing for drug offenses, mandatory sentencing for second felony convictions, and more women getting involved in both the use/possession and the sale of drugs, especially the cheap, easy-to-produce "crack." (p. 47)

These studies support the hypothesis that the drug war has been a major factor in the increase of the incarceration of females. This is inferred from the increase in the number of women incarcerated for drug offenses since the early 1980s.

To summarize, it is apparent from these studies that most of the incarcerated female population are Black or members of a minority group, single mothers, and economically marginalized. Drug law violations are a major factor in the incarceration of women.

Gender, Race, and Criminal Justice System Practices

Black women constitute a greater proportion of the incarcerated female population than do Black males of the incarcerated male population. In 1993, a total of 48,170 females were incarcerated in state correctional institutions. Of this group, Black females composed 51.06% (24,595) of the incarcerated female population; White females constituted 43.9% (21,135). The Black male constituted 49.65% of the male state prison population in 1993 (Bureau of Justice Statistics [BJS], 1995). In New Jersey, 69.37% of the incarcerated female population were Black females, as compared to Black males constituting 65.58% of the incarcerated male population. The proportions were similar for New York (58.28% Black female as compared to 54.4% Black male), Florida (59.71% Black female to 58.36% Black male), and California (34.86% Black female to 32.45% Black male; BJS, 1995). These three states were selected for the analysis because of the disproportionate representation of Black females within their respective incarcerated female populations. However, this overrepresentation of the Black female is not exclusive to these states (see Table 7.3).

Considering that Black females and Black males separately comprise about 6% of the general population, these data indicate that both groups are disproportionately represented in the population of incarcerated individuals in all of the referenced jurisdictions.

TABLE 7.3 Female and Male Prisoners Under State and Federal Jurisdiction by Race, 12/31/92

Region and Jurisdiction	Prison Population	Number (and Percentage) of Female Prisoners		Prison Population	Number (and Percentage) of Male Prisoners	
		White	Black		White	Black
U.S. total	55,061	25,148 (45.67)	27,292 (49.57)	891,885	406,632 (45.59)	429,278 (48.13)
Federal	6,891	4,013 (58.5)	2,697 (39.13)	82,696	52,523 (63.51)	27,472 (33.22)
State	48,170	21,135 (43.88)	24,595 (51.06)	809,189	354,109 (43.76)	401,806 (49.66)
New Jersey	1,133	338 (29.83)	786 (69.37)	22,698	6,301 (27.76)	14,885 (65.58)
New York	3,528	1,446 (41)	2,054 (58.21)	61,041	25,508 (41.78)	33,221 (54.42)
Florida	2,699	1,080 (40)	1,612 (60)	50,349	19,949 (39.62)	29,385 (58.36)
California	7,581	4,622 (61)	2,643 (34.86)	112,370	71,139 (63.30)	36,461 (32.45)

SOURCE: Adapted from Bureau of Justice Statistics (1995).

Between 1980 and 1991, the number of Black females in state or federal prisons increased by 278%, as compared to an increase of 186% for Black males and an increase of 168% in the overall prison population. Moreover, there was an eightfold increase in the number of Black women incarcerated in state facilities between 1986 to 1991, which was the largest increase among Black, White, and Hispanic females or males, as shown in Table 7.4 (Mauer & Huling, 1995, p. 19).

Lewis (1981), in her review of the data and findings of the San Francisco jail study and Glick and Neto's national study, concluded that in the criminal justice system, racism seems to negatively affect the Black woman more than the Black man. Other researchers have concluded that Black women are treated more harshly than their White female counterparts by police officers and judges (Feinman, 1994; Mann, 1989; Odubekenon, 1992; Simpson, 1989; Young, 1986).

Based on this research and data, it would be counterintuitive to assume that the drug law initiatives have affected Black and White women similarly or that the types of drug offenses (type of drug and level of offense) for which Black and White women are arrested and convicted are the same. Research on these issues is limited. As stated earlier, it is apparent from the American Correctional Association (1990), Glick and Neto (1977), and Mann (1995) studies that the majority of the women who are incarcerated are (a) Black or a member of a minority group, (b) single mothers, and (c) are economically marginalized. Drug law violations are a major factor in the incarceration of women. However, the studies do not answer these questions: (a) Are Black women disproportionately arrested for drug offenses? (b) Are Black women disproportionately incarcerated for drug offenses? (c) Are most female prisoners Black women who are incarcerated for drug offenses?

The Need to Investigate the Effects of the Drug War on the Incarceration of Black Females

Tonry (1995) restricted his research solely to the impact of the 1987-1988 federal drug law initiatives on the incarceration of the Black male. He explained his rationale for doing so as thus:

TABLE 7.4 State Prisoners Incarcerated for Drug Offenses by Race-Ethnic Origin and Sex, 1986 and 1991

	1986		1991		Percentage Increase	
Race	Male	Female	Male	Female	Male	Female
White non-Hispanic	12,868	969	26,452	3,300	106	241
Black non-Hispanic	13,974	667	73,932	6,193	429	828
Hispanic	8,484	664	35,965	2,843	324	328
Other	604	70	1,323	297	119	324
Total	35,930	2,370	137,672	12,633	283	433

SOURCE: Mauer and Huling (1995, p. 20). Reprinted by permission.

Racial disproportions are about as bad in women's prisons as in men's. Like men, about half of female prisoners are Black. However, women make up only 6 to 7 percent of the total number of prisoners. Because one of my central arguments is that by removing so many young Black men from their families and communities, crime control policies are undermining efforts to ameliorate the conditions of life of the Black urban underclass, the focus on Black men is necessary. *The story of Black women as offenders and as prisoners is important, but it is a different story* [italics added]. (p. ix)

This researcher posits that the story of the Black female offender and prisoner is important *and* is different from that of the Black male and the White female. The imprisonment of women also has a profound effect on the family and the community, particularly because, unlike the male, most female inmates were responsible for the care of a child or children at the time of their arrest or imprisonment (American Correctional Association, 1990). Unfortunately, few criminologists have studied Black female criminality and the treatment of Black females within the criminal justice system. Furthermore, there is little understanding of the interactive effects of race and gender on the treatment of Black women within the criminal justice system. As noted by Mauer and Huling (1995) in their attempt to explain the fact that the Black female experienced the greatest increase in criminal justice control of all demographic groups studied,

> Although research on women of color in the criminal justice system is limited, existing data and research suggest it is the combination of race and sex effects that is at the root of the trends which appear in our data. (p. 18)

Existing studies support Mauer and Huling's position and have found that Black females and White females are treated differently at every stage of the criminal justice system (Daly, 1987, 1989, 1994; Mann, 1989, 1995).

For at least the past two decades, researchers have consistently concluded that the Black female has experienced harsher treatment in the criminal justice system, from the decision to arrest through sentencing, than White females. Visher (1983) concluded from her observational study of arrests by police in various cities that chivalrous treatment tends not to be displayed toward the Black female. Instead, White female suspects who are older and submissive receive the preferential treatment afforded by chivalry. Simpson (1989) confirmed these findings in her review of the literature from 1984 to 1989. Police were found to extend preferential treatment to White women as opposed to Black, married women received more lenient sentences than single women, and women with families were treated with more leniency than women who had no families. Part of the explanation for the disparity in treatment may be explained by the fact that more Black females tend to be single. Omole (1991) also found that gender statuses affected the pretrial release dispositions of federal defendants, particularly for the Black females in her sample.

Mann (1995), in a 1989 study of the female jail populations in Florida, New York, and California, confirmed that one third of these prisoners were being detained for drug offenses. When differentiated by race, 32.2% of the White females and 33.8% of the Black females were held in jail for drug offenses. Mann reports that the White female drug offenders tended to be jailed for drug trafficking, whereas the Black female drug offenders were most often detained for the lower-level offense of drug possession.

Mann (1993) noted the virtually unlimited discretion exercised by prosecutors in determining who will be charged or not charged at the very beginning of the processing of a criminal case. This unbridled discretion increases the likelihood that minorities will be "charged, overcharged, and indicted" (p. 108). Spohn, Gruhl, and Welch (1987) studied the prosecutors' rejection or dismissal of charges in felony cases in Los Angeles. Controlling for the defendants' ages, prior criminal records, seriousness of the charges, and uses of weapons, these researchers found that both White females and White males enjoyed higher rates of rejection of their charges at the initial stages, whereas the racial-ethnic minority suspects-defendants did not. They also noted that White females had a notably lower (19%) prosecution rate as compared to African American females (30%).

Foley and Rasche (1979) conducted a 16-year study in Missouri to investigate the effects of race on the sentencing of defendants. They concluded that the African American women in their study received longer (55.1 months) sentences than the White women (52.5 months) for the same crimes. They also discovered that although White women received longer sentences (182.3 months) for personal crimes than their African American counterparts (98.5 months), the latter group served more actual time for these offenses (African American women, 26.7 months; White women, 23 months). These two groups showed no significant difference in mean sentences for drug offenses; however, the African American women served more time (20.4 months compared to 13.2 months).

Kruttschnitt (1980-1981) reviewed sentencing outcomes for 1,034 female defendants in a northern California county during 1972 to 1976. She concluded that the African American female who was convicted of drug offenses or disturbing the peace was sentenced more harshly than her White counterpart. Approximately 18 years later, in 1990, Mann (1995) compared the arrest figures to the imprisonment data for women in California, New York, and Florida who were charged with major felonies (drug violations, theft, burglary, robbery). Mann found that women of color who were arrested for these crimes were sentenced to prison more often than White women with similar arrests. Furthermore, she determined that California, the state that incarcerates more women than any other state in the nation and that also has the largest incarcerated female population in the world, appears to differentiate among these women based on race. Mann pointed out that although White female felons (48.3%) were arrested more often for drug law violations, theft, and burglary, than the African American (30.5%) or Hispanic women (18.7%), the percentage who went to prison for these offenses was much less. Only 38.3% of the White females who were arrested for drug violations were incarcerated, whereas 34.1% of the African American females and 26.1% of the Hispanic American females were imprisoned for the same offenses. Unfortunately, Mann was unable to control for the prior records of the female felons in this study. She did state, however, that with such controls, she would still expect to find evidence of disparate treatment. Mann posited that it would be implausible that prior arrests could affect the three racial-ethnic groups, in the three separate states, in such a way as to explain away the disparity in sentencing (Mann, 1995, p. 129).

Mandatory imprisonment for drug offenses and for second felony convictions are integral parts of the drug law initiatives initiated by many jurisdictions (Feinman, 1994). These laws have an impact on the incarcerated female population. In Florida, the percentage of females incarcerated for drug offenses under mandatory offenders laws increased for both Black and White females between 1993 and 1994. The percentage of Black female inmates sentenced under such laws rose from 40.5% in 1993 to 54% in 1994; for White females, the increase was from 44% to 54% (Florida Department of Corrections, 1993/1994, 1994/1995). An analysis of the percentage of females sentenced under Florida's Felony Habitual Offenders statutes with drug offenses as the underlying felonies is necessary to better understand the impact of the drug law initiatives on the incarcerated female population.

Being both Black and female places Black women into two groups that are experiencing immense growth in their contact with the criminal justice system (Mauer & Huling, 1995). It has been postulated that the treatment of Black women by the criminal justice system actually mirrors the social and historical experiences of Black women in the United States. "Black women in American society have been victimized by their double status as blacks and women" (Young, 1986). Young describes the characterizations used to describe the American Black woman:

As an Amazon . . . she is domineering, assertive and masculine. *. . . In the case of the black female offender, there is no need for* only two or three female prisons were created. In the 1980s, 34 prisons for females were created. In addition to the social costs of incarcerating female offenders, there is an economic cost that is borne by the taxpayers. These costs also determine the community's ability to provide financial support for other services.

Without question, Black women have been disproportionately represented among females who are arrested, convicted, and incarcerated for drug offenses. What must now be queried is (a) if this disproportionate representation is due to race-gender effects inherent in the application of the drug law initiatives and that are operating against the Black female, and, if so found, then (b) if the costs—to individuals, communities, and society as a whole—are worth the displacement of the Black women from mainstream society to that of prison inmate.

References

American Correctional Association. (1990). The female offender: What does the future hold? Washington, DC: St. Mary's.

Bureau of Justice Statistics. (1991). Special report on women in prison. Washington, DC: Government Printing Office.

Bureau of Justice Statistics. (1995). Correctional populations in the United States, 1993. Washington, DC: U.S. Department of Justice.

Chesney-Lind, M. (1995). Rethinking women's imprisonment: A critical examination of trends in female incarceration. In B. R. Price & N. J. Skoloff (Eds.), The criminal justice system and women (pp. 105-117). New York: McGraw-Hill.

Daly, K. (1987). Structure and practice of familial-based justice in the criminal court. Law and Society Review, 21(2), 267-290.

Daly, K. (1989). Neither conflict nor labeling nor paternalism will suffice: Intersections of race, ethnicity, gender and family in criminal court decisions. Crime and Delinquency, 35(1), 136-168.

Daly, K. (1994). Gender, crime and punishment. New Haven, CT: Yale University Press.

Feinman, C. (1994). Women in the criminal justice system. Westport, CT: Praeger.

Florida Department of Corrections. (1993/1994). 1993-94 annual report: The guidebook to corrections in Florida. Tallahassee, FL: State of Florida.

Florida Department of Corrections. (1994/1995). Florida Department of Corrections annual report: Corrections as a business. Tallahassee, FL: State of Florida.

Foley, L. A., & Rasche, C. E. (1979). The effect of race on sentence, actual time served and final disposition of female offenders. In John A. Conley (Ed.), Theory and research in criminal justice. Cincinnati: Anderson.

Glick, R., & Neto, V. (1977). National study of women's correctional programs. Washington, DC: National Institute of Law Enforcement and Criminal Justice.

Hagan, J. (1985). Toward a structural theory of crime, race, and gender: The Canadian case. *Crime and Delinquency, 3*(1), 129-146.

Kline, S. (1993). A profile of female offenders in state and federal prisons. In *Female offenders: Meeting needs of a neglected population* (pp. 1-6). Baltimore, MD: United Book Press.

Kruttschnitt, C. (1980-1981). Social status and sentences of female offenders. *Law and Society, 15*(2), 247-265.

Lewis, D. (1981). Black women offenders and criminal justice. In M. Q. Warren, (Ed.), *Comparing female and male offenders* (pp. 89-105). Beverly Hills, CA: Sage.

Mann, C. M. R. (1989). Minority and female: A Criminal justice double bind. *Social Justice, 16*(4), 95.

Mann, C. M. R. (1993). *Unequal justice: A question of color.* Bloomington: Indiana University.

Mann, C. M. R. (1995). Women of color and the criminal justice system. In B. R. Price & N. J. Skoloff (Eds.), *The criminal justice system and women* (pp. 118-135). New York: McGraw-Hill.

Mauer, M., & Huling, T. (1995). *Young Black Americans and the criminal justice system: Five years later.* Washington, DC: Sentencing Project.

Miller, J. G. (1996). *Search and destroy: African-American males in the criminal justice system.* New York: Cambridge University Press.

Odubekon, L. (1992). A structural approach to differential gender sentencing. *Criminal Justice Abstracts, 2,* 343-60.

Omole, O. E. (1991). *Clarifying the role of gender in the court dispositions: A LISREL model of pretrial release.* Ann Arbor, MI: UMI Research Press.

Rafter, N. H. (1990). Partial justice: Women, prisons and social control. New Brunswick, NJ: Transaction Books.

Simon, R., & Landis, J. (1991). *The crimes women commit and the punishments they receive.* Lexington, MA: Lexington Books.

Simpson, S. (1989). Feminist theory, crime, and justice. *Criminology, 27*(4), 605-631.

Spohn, C., Gruhl, J., & Welch, S. (1987). The impact of the ethnicity and gender of defendants on the decision to reject or dismiss felony charges. *Criminology, 25*(1), 175-191.

Tonry, M. (1995). Malign neglect. New York: Oxford University Press.

Visher, C. (1983). Gender, police arrest decisions, and notions of chivalry. *Criminology, 21*(1), 5-28.

Young, V. (1986). Gender expectations and their impact on black female offenders and their victims. *Justice Quarterly, 3*(2), 305-327.

CHAPTER EIGHT

Parenting Through Prison Walls

Incarcerated Mothers and Children's Visitation Programs

Zoann K. Snyder-Joy
Teresa A. Carlo

✦ The restoration of the "American" family is a much discussed topic in the United States today. The airwaves are filled with campaign promises, media debates, and docudramas focusing on how to save this beleaguered institution. Divorce, single parenthood, and the loss of "family values" are reviled as the primary factors contributing to the destruction of the family. What is not heard is how governmental policy itself is separating parents and children, potentially destroying family structures. Contemporary criminal justice policies designed to punish law violators may also contribute to the breakdown of U.S. families. The politicians and policy makers do not discuss what happens to family relationships when parents are sent to prison.

In this chapter, we discuss incarcerated mothers and their perspectives as parents behind prison walls. Our research began as an invited evaluation of a mother-children visitation program at a women's correctional facility, thus identifying mothers as our research focus. To better understand the context of imprisoned mothers, our research draws on the extant literature to identify some of the social and emotional costs of incarceration for the child as well as the mother. Adding to the literature, our data analysis examines how parenting classes and the mother-children visitation program affect (a) communication between incarcerated mothers and their children, (b) the mothers' assessments of their relationships with their children, and (c) the parenting concerns expressed by the women. The conclusion discusses means of providing for better mother and child contact during imprisonment and the implications of such programs for the mothers' postrelease readjustment to society. To help ground the reader in numbers of mothers behind bars, the next section provides a brief demographic overview of the U.S. adult female prisoner population.

Growth in the U.S. Female Prisoner Population

Although women are still numerically the minority in prison populations, the female prisoner population is growing at a faster rate than for male prisoners. During the 1980s, the female prisoner population increased over 200% as compared to a 112% increase for male prisoners (Bureau of Justice Statistics, 1991). Drug crimes accounted for 55% of the increase in the women's prisoner population between 1986 and 1991 (Bureau of Justice Statistics, 1994).

Adding to the growth of incarcerated women are the number of children affected by imprisonment. Two thirds of the 38,658 women incarcerated in state prisons in 1991 were mothers to approximately 56,123 children under the age of 18 (Bureau of Justice Statistics, 1994). Prior to incarceration, 72% of the mothers were living with their children. In comparison, 56% of the male prisoners had minor children, and about 53% of the fathers were living with their children before entering prison (Bureau of Justice Statistics, 1994).

Although there is variation in the proportions of female and male prisoners, a more distinct difference is in who cares for the children while the parents are incarcerated. Nearly 90% of the male prisoners reported that their minor children were living with the children's mothers. Incarcerated mothers were more likely to report that their children were living with grandparents (50.5%). Fathers were caring for the children in about 25.4% of the cases, whereas other relatives

(20.3%) were also called on to care for the children during the mothers' incarceration (Bureau of Justice Statistics, 1994).

From this brief overview, it is clear that the issue of incarcerated mothers and their children is neither a small nor a contained issue. The numbers of women going to prison continue to rise. The increasingly punitive sanctions for all offenses, including drug crimes, virtually guarantee growth in the female prisoner population. As a result, the numbers of children affected by their mothers' incarceration is expected to increase.

The numbers alone do not tell all of the story. What happens to the children, and how do they feel after their mothers are incarcerated? What effect does a mother's incarceration have on her children, and how do they feel? The next section provides a brief overview of research regarding how children are affected by their mothers' imprisonment.

The Impact of Mothers' Incarceration on Children

There are alternative explanations for the increase in the number of female prisoners that cannot be accounted for solely by greater female criminality. Research findings indicate that female offenders may be viewed and judged more harshly by the criminal justice system if they are perceived to be so-called bad mothers (Beckerman, 1991; Pollock, 1995). Governmental representatives have become increasingly involved in defining the criteria for "good" parents versus "bad" parents. Agents of the state may deduce that involvement in criminal activity indicates poor parenting; therefore, incarcerating the parent should be beneficial for the child (Beckerman, 1989, 1991; Carron, 1984).

Although removing a child from the bad influence of a criminal parent may be justified as in the best interests of the child, a number of studies (see Clark, 1995; Gabel, 1992; Johnston, 1995; Kampfner, 1995) conclude that incarcerating mothers may produce serious negative consequences for the children. The forcible separation and lack of close contact between mother and child may cause psychological and behavioral problems for the children, such as aggression, poor school performance, attention deficit, anger, poor social skills, depression, and sleep disruptions (Gaudin, 1984; Johnston, 1995; Kampfner, 1995;

research design. The next section identifies the focus of our study and our data collection tools.

Methodology

The focus of the current research is a mother-children visitation program (MCVP) located in a midwestern women's correctional facility. The MCVP is maintained by a private, nonprofit corporation that arranges monthly visits for incarcerated mothers and their children in addition to regular institutional visitation provisions. The MCVP visits are conducted in a room at the prison that has been set aside for the program. Volunteers have decorated the room with donated carpeting and brightly painted walls featuring cartoon characters. The mothers and children are encouraged to participate in a number of supervised activities, such as crafts, games, reading, or simply talking quietly.

The MCVP provides transportation for many of the children who do not have any other means of traveling to the prison. The volunteer drivers are carefully screened by the program coordinators and are accompanied by volunteer aides on each trip.

The MCVP is a relatively small program that operates on donations and small grants. Its limited operating budget provides services for only about 40 women and their children. Because of the small population of program participants, personal interviews with the incarcerated mothers were used to collect the data. At the time of the research, 36 women were actively receiving visits through the MCVP. Of MCVP participants, 31 agreed to be interviewed. A control group of women waiting to enter the program were also interviewed. The women were either waiting for space availability or to complete the prerequisite parenting class to qualify for the program. Of the 36 women on the waiting list, 27 accepted the invitation to participate in the research.

All women interviewed attended a brief orientation session in which the research project was explained. A question and answer period was included to address any concerns that the women voiced. At the completion of the session, all women were given a consent letter to read and sign if they chose to participate. Due to scheduling conflicts at the institution, 8 women were excluded from participation. Six women chose not to participate. We later heard that these women thought that the evaluation project was a student's research project. Several complained that they had their own schoolwork to complete and that they did not want to give up their own study time to help a student. The majority of women who did participate spoke about the importance of the MCVP and stated that they wanted to help us with our evaluation.

The interview questions covered a range of topics, including the women's assessment of their relationships with their children, their perceptions of their parenting skills, their evaluations of the MCVP, and suggested improvements for the program. The interview schedules included 23 questions that provided for both open-ended and closed-ended responses. For the purposes of this chapter, four series of questions are included in the analysis.

Our first series of questions identified the means that mothers and children used to communicate with one another beyond the monthly MCVP visits. The women were asked how often they sent letters to their children, how often they received letters from their children, and how often they spoke on the phone with their children. All three questions had the same Likert response category of "Daily," "Once per week," "Once per month," "Less than once per month," and "Never."

Next, the women were asked what types of things they discussed with their children. They were prompted with possible responses of "school, friends, health, feelings, family, and caregiver." They were also given an open-ended response of "other" and were prompted to specify other issues discussed.

The third series of questions focused on the mothers' perceptions of their children and their relationships during their incarceration. The mothers were asked, "How do you perceive your child (or children) are doing?" Prompts included noting the children's overall health, happiness, and well-being. We also asked the mothers, "How would you rate your relationship with your child(ren)?" Both questions had Likert responses of "Very good," "Good," "Fair," "Poor," and "Very Poor."

Last, we asked about the issues that concern them as parents. The mothers were asked to identify, "What is (are) your primary concern(s) for your child(ren) while you are here?" Probes included addressing the care, love, and guidance that they perceived their children were getting or lacking. The women were also asked, "What things about being a parent cause you the most problems?"

Because of the previous research done on this issue, we wanted to examine whether participation in the program would improve communication skills, strengthen relationships between mothers and their children, and help to reduce some of the anxiety and concern felt by the mothers. We proposed that women receiving MCVP visits would have more frequent communication with their children, perceive that they had positive relationships with their children, and have fewer anxieties about their roles as mothers than did the control group of women waiting to participate in the program. The following section details our research findings.

Findings

Chi-square analyses were conducted to determine whether or not there was a statistically significant relationship between the variables, and measures of association were examined to determine the strength of association between the variables. The independent variable of MCVP participation versus nonparticipation is a nominal-level variable, and the chi-square analysis was determined to be the most appropriate form of statistical analysis.

Communication With Children

The mothers receiving regular program visits with their children noted a greater frequency of letters and phone conversations with their children than the women not in the MCVP (see Table 8.1). Women in the MCVP were more likely to write to their children than non-MCVP mothers. Nearly 97% of the MCVP participants wrote to their children at least once per month as compared to 81.5% of the non-MCVP women.

Three fourths of the MCVP mothers indicated that their children wrote to them at least once per month. About half of the mothers not in the MCVP noted receiving at least monthly letters. Nearly one third of the women not receiving regular visits reported never receiving letters from their children.

The frequency of phone contact with children was also higher for the MCVP mothers. About 10% of the women in the MCVP said they talked to their children daily, with 77% of the mothers having at least monthly phone calls. About 56% of the non-MCVP women reported at

TABLE 8.1 Communication With Children

	Not in Mother-Children Visitation Program		In Mother-Children Visitation Program	
	Count	Percentage	Count	Percentage
Frequency of letter to children[a]				
Never	4	14.8	0	0.0
Less than once a month	1	3.7	1	3.2
Once per month	7	25.9	8	25.8
Once per week	15	55.6	18	58.1
Daily	0	0.0	4	12.9
Frequency of letters from children[b]				
Never	10	37.0	2	6.5
Less than once a month	4	14.8	6	19.4
Once per month	8	29.6	14	45.2
Once per week	5	18.5	7	22.6
Daily	0	0.0	2	6.5
Frequency of phone contact with children[c]				
Never	11	40.7	6	19.4
Less than once per month	1	3.7	1	3.2
Once per month	5	18.5	13	41.9
Once per week	10	37.0	8	25.8
Daily	0	0.0	3	9.7

a. Chi-square = 8.10, $p = .09$; Cramer's $V = .37, p = .09$
b. Chi-square = 9.47, $p = .05$; Cramer's $V = .40, p = .05$
c. Chi-square = 8.01, $p = .09$; Cramer's $V = .37, p = .09$

least monthly phone calls. Phone conversations had to be made collect, and this cost may have been too much for some caregivers to afford in addition to child care costs. This may account for why approximately 41% of the non-MCVP mothers and 19% of the women receiving visits reported never having phone contact with their children.

The data analysis indicated a moderate association between involvement in the MCVP and the frequency of letters and phone calls with the children. The visitation program appeared to facilitate ongoing lines of communication between mothers and children. Several women noted that the phone calls and letters were opportunities for them and their children to reflect on the most recent visit and plan future visits. The letters and phone calls enabled the women and children to maintain the bonds established through the MCVP.

The frequency of the letters and phone calls may also have been influenced by the quality of the relationship between the caregiver and the mother. A number of women noted that their phone calls were not accepted by the caregiver or that their letters were not given to their children. Although there was not a statistically significant relationship between the mothers' participation in the MCVP and the quality of contact with their children's caregivers, conflicts between the mothers and caregivers could explain why some mothers did not have other means of communicating with their children.

Overall, mothers in the MCVP noted greater frequency of contact with their children. This contact enabled the women and children to discuss a number of different issues.

What the Mothers and Children Discussed

The MCVP mothers seemed to spend more time discussing issues central to the children and their futures as compared to the women not in the MCVP who focused more on themselves and their present situations (see Table 8.2). The subjects talked about by the mothers and children were topics of interest for most parents, including how the child was doing in school, their health, feelings, family, and friends. There were also additional concerns for incarcerated mothers, such as the child's relationship with their caregiver, and the mother's life in prison.

The majority of the women receiving regular visits talked to their children about the children's relationships with other people. More than 80% of the MCVP women reported discussing their children's friends, caregivers, and other family members as compared to slightly more than one half of the women not receiving MCVP visits. The opportunity to speak away from other family members or caregivers may provide for more open communication. Phone calls and letters can be monitored by others and inhibit dialog. Face-to-face conversations can promote greater intimacy and encourage more candid responses than letters or phone calls alone.

TABLE 8.2 Issues Discussed With Children

	Not in Mother-Children Visitation Program		In Mother-Children Visitation Program	
	Count	Percentage	Count	Percentage
School[a]				
No	8	29.6	6	19.4
Yes	19	70.4	25	80.6
Friends[b]				
No	12	44.4	6	19.4
Yes	15	55.6	25	80.6
Health[c]				
No	9	33.3	5	16.1
Yes	18	66.7	26	83.9
Caregiver[d]				
No	11	40.7	3	9.7
Yes	16	59.3	28	90.3
Family[e]				
No	12	44.4	2	6.5
Yes	15	55.6	29	93.5
Feelings[f]				
No	8	29.6	1	3.2
Yes	19	70.4	30	96.8
Other topics discussed with children[g]				
None	13	48.1	13	41.9
Friction with caregiver	1	3.7	0	0.0
Child's activities	3	11.1	5	16.1
Life in prison, mothers' incarceration	8	29.6	4	12.9
Religion, church	1	3.7	1	3.2
Concerns regarding behaviors: sex, drugs, discipline	1	3.7	7	22.6
MCVP visits	0	0.0	1	3.2

a. Chi-square = .83, $p = .36$; Cramer's $V = .12$, $p = .36$
b. Chi-square = 4.24, $p = .04$; Cramer's $V = .27$, $p = .04$
c. Chi-square = 2.33, $p = .13$; Cramer's $V = .20$, $p = .13$
d. Chi-square = 7.60, $p = .01$; Cramer's $V = .36$, $p = .01$
e. Chi-square = 11.38, $p = .001$; Cramer's $V = .44$, $p = .001$
f. Chi-square = 7.67, $p = .01$; Cramer's $V = .36$, $p = .01$
g. Chi-square = 8.10, $p = .23$; Cramer's $V = .37$, $p = .23$

Greater closeness in the relationship also provided for the ability to discuss more sensitive issues with the children. Nearly all of the MCVP mothers (96.8%) said they talked to their children about their feelings, whereas almost one third of the women not receiving visits did not discuss how their children felt. The moderate association between MCVP participation and talking about feelings may be a further indicator of how the program benefits incarcerated mothers and their children. Improving communication may ease the fears and anxieties felt by the women and children. As previous research has suggested, the reduction of stress may facilitate a stronger relationship and also reduce negative behaviors among both the women and children.

Concerns regarding the children's present behavior was another variable that showed significant differences between the MCVP and control groups. Only 4% of the non-MCVP mothers reported discussing their concerns about the children's behavior, whereas almost one fourth of the MCVP women did so. This difference should be noted because it may mean that MCVP moms were taking a more active role in the parenting of their children. The actions and choices of the children will undoubtedly affect their future chances, within or without their mothers' care. The associations found between the MCVP participants and more active parenting do need further investigation. It may be worth exploring the quality of these interactions and what specifically about the MCVP is causing the increased frequency of the discussions.

The regular visits can also help alleviate children's concerns about where their mothers are living and how they are being treated. Nearly one third of the non-MCVP women reported discussing their life in prison with their children, as compared to only 13% of the MCVP mothers. Children who visit their mothers can see the prison conditions and their mothers' physical well-being. Children separated from their mothers may have distorted fears and anxiety about incarceration and treatment of prisoners. Statements such as "Do they only feed you bread and water?" and "Are you beaten every day?" are examples of the questions asked by children not granted visitation. Regularly scheduled visits where the children can physically see and touch their mothers seem to allay these fears. This leaves time for the mothers and children to concentrate on the needs of the children and the futures of both the mothers and children. The mothers can spend the visits focused on their children and parenting responsibilities.

The MCVP does have some effects on the type and frequency of the issues discussed by mothers and children. More women in the MCVP discussed present and future issues with the children. These same mothers seemed to be more involved in the lives of their children and maintaining the mother-child bond.

Perceptions of Children's Well-Being and Relationship With Mother

Maintaining contact between the mothers and children is only one aspect of the MCVP noted as important by program participants. Many of the women said it was reassuring for them to be able to physically see and touch their children. It was important that the women be able to see for themselves that their children were well and happy. Mothers not in the MCVP stated that they would be much reassured that their children were okay if they were able to see them. These concerns are reflected in the responses women gave when asked how they thought their children were doing (see Table 8.3). A moderate association exists between program participation and positive perceptions of how the children are doing. Nearly 97% of the MCVP participants said their children were doing fair to very good compared to 74% of the nonparticipants. Nearly one fourth of the nonparticipants perceived that their children were doing poorly.

The importance of contact may be reflected in how the mothers perceived their relationships with their children. Although the test of these variables was not statistically significant, there were interesting differences in responses between the MCVP participants and nonparticipants. In comparison to 52% of the nonparticipants, 77% of the program participants reported a very good relationship with their children. Nearly 20% of the mothers not receiving visits indicated a poor to very poor relationship with their children.

The responses of the mothers not receiving visits may have reflected their own fears rather than serving as an accurate assessment of how their children were doing. As noted earlier, the mothers who saw their children through the MCVP were reassured that their children were well because they did not have to rely on a third party's report. The ability to physically see and touch the children may do a great deal toward alleviating parental concerns.

TABLE 8.3 Perceptions of Children's Well-Being and Relationship With Mother

	Not in Mother-Children Visitation Program		In Mother-Children Visitation Program	
	Count	Percentage	Count	Percentage
How children are doing[a]				
Very poor	0	0.0	1	3.2
Poor	6	22.2	0	0.0
Fair	5	18.5	6	19.4
Good	4	14.8	10	32.3
Very good	11	40.7	14	45.2
Don't know	1	3.7	0	0.0
Relationship with children[b]				
Very poor	3	11.1	0	0.0
Poor	2	7.4	0	0.0
Fair	3	11.1	3	9.7
Good	5	18.5	4	12.9
Very good	14	51.9	24	77.4

a. Chi-square = 10.80, p = .06; Cramer's V = .43, p = .06
b. Chi-square = 7.50, p = .11; Cramer's V = .36, p = .11

Parenting Concerns

Additional questions focused on what the mothers' primary concerns were for their children and their fears about their own parenting skills (see Table 8.4). When asked about the concerns they had regarding their own parenting skills, nearly one third of the MCVP participants questioned their abilities to provide adequate nurturance and emotional support for the children, as compared to 18.5% of the nonparticipants. MCVP mothers also expressed greater concern about providing for the well-being and safety of their children during their incarceration (25.8%), as compared to mothers not in the program (3.7%). One area of common worry was separation from their children, with approximately 23% of all mothers noting this as their greatest concern. Several mothers talked about how hard it was to be a parent from a distance. Mothers not in the MCVP were more likely to cite their financial responsibilities to their children and parenting skills as their primary problems with parenting.

TABLE 8.4 Concerns of Mothers

	Not in Mother-Children Visitation Program		In Mother-Children Visitation Program	
	Count	Percentage	Count	Percentage
Problems with parenting[a]				
Separation with no contact	1	3.7	0	0.0
Separation from children	6	22.2	7	22.6
Responsibility to children, nurturing	5	18.5	10	32.3
Responsibility to children, financial	4	14.8	3	9.7
Parenting skills	7	25.9	3	9.7
Child care	1	3.7	0	0.0
Well-being, safety of child	1	3.7	8	25.8
None	2	7.4	0	0.0
Primary concerns for children[b]				
Abuse, treatment of children	9	33.3	16	51.6
Emotional, behavioral state of children	7	25.9	8	25.8
Feelings, relationship with children	9	33.3	7	22.6
Separation of children	1	3.7	0	0.0
Family arrangements and impact on children	1	3.7	0	0.0

a. Chi-square = 12.72, $p = .08$; Cramer's $V = .47$, $p = .08$
b. Chi-square = 4.02, $p = .40$; Cramer's $V = .26$, $p = .40$

Although the relationship between MCVP participation and concerns for the children was not statistically significant, there was some variation in the mothers' primary worries. Slightly more than half of the MCVP participants reported fears that their children would be emotionally or physically abused in their absence. About one third of the non-MCVP mothers indicated similar concerns. MCVP participants and nonparticipants reported nearly identical worries about the emotional states of their children. Consistent with earlier findings, a greater percentage of non-MCVP participants expressed concerns about their relationship with their children (33.3%) than did program participants (22.6%).

The concerns reported by the MCVP mothers and women not in the program manifested different patterns. Although the women participating in the MCVP did express fears about their children's safety and how to provide a safe, supportive environment, they were less likely to question their parenting abilities and relationships with their children. Mothers not receiving regular visits questioned their abilities as parents and worried if they would be able to financially provide for their children. The MCVP mothers interviewed talked about the importance of communication and mutual respect in building good parent-child relationships. Learning these skills may help the women to better understand themselves and their children. At a minimum, the MCVP may help to reduce parenting fears as the mothers face institutional release. Building greater self-confidence in parenting abilities and maintaining a strong relationship with their children have already been cited as important components of women's successful reintegration into the community.

Conclusions

Our research findings indicated substantive differences in the reported interactions between mothers and children involved in the MCVP, in comparison to those families not receiving regular visits. The MCVP mothers reported more regular letter writing and telephone conversations than those experienced by the women not participating in the program. Women who were able to have regular contact visits with their children noted that other means of communication were important components for strengthening their bonds with the children.

Mothers who regularly saw their children were more likely to discuss the children's relationships with others, such as family, friends, and the immediate caregiver(s). The children and mothers in the MCVP were also able to discuss the feelings and the emotions of the children. Non-MCVP mothers spent more time communicating their physical well-being and attempting to reassure their children that they were not being harmed.

Mothers receiving visits were more likely to perceive that their children were doing well in comparison to mothers not in the program. It was reassuring for the women to be able to verify their children's well-being. The MCVP mothers also reported fewer fears about their abilities as parents and were more focused in their concerns about caring for their children. Non-MCVP mothers were more anxious about their parenting skills and their abilities to provide for their children.

Although our study is a one-shot examination of a small program, the findings provide support for the importance of maintaining mother-child relationships despite incarceration. Our findings are consistent with prior studies noting the importance of regular visits and open communications for reducing fear and anxiety for both mothers and children. The research results also indicate areas for further study.

Future research is needed to address what the long-term consequences are for women who maintain a close relationship with their children during incarceration. Are these mothers candidates for a more successful postrelease period? Are they less likely to recidivate or return to drugs? Are they able to regain and maintain custody of or contact with their children? Tracking is needed to examine what, if any, long-term postrelease effects result from participation in prison visitation programs. Such research must consider both mothers and children because previous studies indicate both are affected by the increased incarceration of women.

Children must be included in the studies of incarcerated mothers. Issues such as the children's experiences while their mothers are incarcerated and the effect of visitation programs on children's' behavior, both positive and negative, must also be examined. Anecdotal evidence suggests that both teachers and caregivers for children involved in the MCVP noted a decrease in anger, frustration, and aggressive behavior among the children following the visits. School performance quality increased, and the children were more cooperative at home. Are these children less likely to enter the juvenile or adult criminal justice system than their peers who are not allowed prison visitation with their mothers?

Research needs to assess the improvement or deterioration in mother-child relationships over the course of the mother' incarceration. Do bad relationships improve and stabilize with contact visits? Do good relationships remain positive, or do they worsen during the separation? Also needed is an examination of the variables that are most likely to indicate and promote healthy relationships.

Limited resources and the low priority of parenting provisions fragment the application of visitation programs. The lack of research funding available to the programs restricts evaluations. Without evaluation results to justify expanding the projects, additional monies are not forthcoming.

In a period of skyrocketing prison budgets and increasingly punitive stances toward crime, arguments for implementing or expanding (or both) children's visitation programs must be strong. More research is needed to expand on and clarify the importance of maintaining mother-child relationships despite incarceration. The importance of these programs as intervention must be stressed, and additional research is needed to strengthen the growing number of studies citing the responsibility of the state to provide essential services in support of the family.

References

Barnhill, S., & Dressel, P. (1991). *Three generations at risk.* Atlanta, GA: Aid to Imprisoned Mothers.

Baunach, P. J. (1985). *Mothers in prison.* New Brunswick, NJ: Transaction Books.

Beavers-Luteran, B. A. (1983, June). Mother/child retreats. *Corrections Today, 93-95.*

Beckerman, A. (1989). Incarcerated mothers and their children in foster care: The dilemma of visitation. *Children and Youth Services Review, 11,* 175-183.

Beckerman, A. (1991). Women in prison: The conflict between confinement and parental rights. *Social Justice, 18,* 171-183.

Bloom, B. (1993). Incarcerated mothers and their children: Maintaining family ties. In *Female offenders: Meeting the needs of a neglected population.* Laurel, MD: American Correctional Association.

Browne, D. C. H. (1989). Incarcerated mothers and parenting. *Journal of Family Violence, 4,* 211-221.

Bureau of Justice Statistics. (1991). *Women in prison.* Washington, DC: U.S. Department of Justice.

Bureau of Justice Statistics. (1994). *Women in Prison.* Washington, DC: U.S. Department of Justice.

Carron, L. R. (1984). Termination of incarcerated parents' rights in Massachusetts. *New England Journal on Criminal and Civil Confinement, 10,* 147-167.

Clark, J. (1995). The Impact of the prison environment on mothers. *The Prison Journal, 75, 306-329.*

Driscoll, D. (1985, August). Mother's Day once a month. *Corrections Today,* 18-24.

Gabel, S. (1992). Behavioral problems in sons of incarcerated or otherwise absent fathers: The issue of separation. *Family Process, 31,* 303-314.

Gaudin, J. M., Jr. (1984, May). Social work roles and tasks with incarcerated mothers. *Social Casework: The Journal of Contemporary Social Work,* 279-286.

Hairston, C. F. (1991). Family ties during imprisonment: Important to whom and for what? *Journal of Sociology and Social Welfare, 18,* 87-104.

Hale, D. C. (1988). The impact of mothers' incarceration on the family system: Research and recommendations. *Marriage and Family Review, 12,* 143-154.

Johnston, D. (1995). Effects of parental incarceration. In K. Gabel & D. Johnston (Eds.), *Children of incarcerated parents* (pp. 59-88). New York: Lexington Books.

Kampfner, C. J. (1991, August). Michigan program makes children's visits meaningful. *Corrections Today*, 130-134.

Kampfner, C. J. (1995). Post-traumatic stress reactions in children of imprisoned mothers. In K. Gabel & D. Johnston (Eds.), *Children of incarcerated parents* (pp. 89-100). New York: Lexington Books.

Light, R. (1993). Why support prisoners' family-tie groups? *The Howard Journal, 32,* 322-329.

Moses, M. C. (1993, August). Girl Scouts behind bars: New program at women's prison benefits mothers and children. *Corrections Today,* 132-135.

Pollock, J. M. (1995). Gender, justice, and social control: A historical perspective. In A. Merlo & J. Pollock (Eds.), *Women, law, & social control* (pp. 3-35). Boston: Allyn & Bacon.

Sach, W. H., Siedler, J., & Thomas, S. (1976). The children of imprisoned parents: A psychological exploration. *American Journal of Orthopsychiatry, 46,* 618-628.

Stumbo, N. J., & Little, S. L. (1991, August). Campground offers relaxed setting for children's visitation program. *Corrections Today,* 136-144.

Thompson, P. J., & Harm, N. J. (1995). Parent education for mothers in prison. *Pediatric Nursing, 21,* 552-556.

Weilerstein, R. (1995). The prison MATCH program. In K. Gabel & D. Johnston (Eds.), *Children of incarcerated parents* (pp. 255-264). New York: Lexington Books.

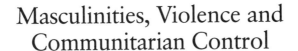

CHAPTER NINE

Masculinities, Violence and Communitarian Control

John Braithwaite
Kathleen Daly[1]

✦ Violence is gendered: it is a problem and consequence of masculinity. Contemporary state interventions to control violence are no less gendered: structures of response, from arrest through imprisonment, glorify tough cops, celebrate adversarial relations, and construct a virtuous 'protective' state by incarcerating or, in some countries, killing the 'bad guys'. What alternatives are possible in an apparently closed system, where masculinity and masculinist structures are both the cause and the putative cure of violence?

In this essay, we consider men's violence towards women and ways of responding to it. Recognising the failure of traditional justice system responses towards violent men, we outline a more promising approach, one compatible with the principles and visions of republican criminology (Braithwaite 1989; Braithwaite and Pettit 1990). This approach uses a community conference strategy adapted from the Maori culture in New Zealand as a key element in an overall regulatory ideal that repudiates exploitative masculinities (see Mugford and Mugford 1992). We elucidate the community conference, discuss its strengths, and address vexing questions about its efficacy in different contexts.

Multiple Masculinities
and Normal Violence

Multiple masculinities are implicated in the gendered patterning of violence. Men's violence towards men involves a masculinity of status competition and bravado among peers (Daly and Wilson 1988; Luckenbill 1977; Polk and Ranson 1991). Men's rape and assault of women reflects a masculinity of domination, control, humiliation, and degradation of women (Brownmiller 1975; Wilson 1978; MacKinnon 1987; Smith 1990; Alder 1991; Snider 1992). Other types of harmful conduct involve a shameless masculinity or a masculinity of unconnectedness and unconcern for others. When called to account for exploitative conduct, men's responses may be rage rather than guilt, or an amplification of non-caring identities such as 'badass' (Braithwaite 1991; Katz 1988; Miedzian 1991; Retzinger 1991). Some women may exhibit these masculine qualities, but their behaviour would likely be interpreted as pathology. They would derive little support for expressions of masculine violence from even the most marginal of subcultures.

For men, status competition through physical force, domination-humiliation of the less powerful, and knowing no shame have substantial cultural support. Few societies today contain a majoritarian masculinity that sets its face against violence. In general, women's and men's social movements have failed to nurture credible competing non-violent identities for heterosexual men.[2] When such identities are imagined or promoted, they are confined to men's potential to care for others in families, that is, to be loving or caring fathers, husbands, sons, or brothers. In fact, the caring masculine identities having some cultural support are more likely found within 'the family' than outside it. To suggest that masculine caring is featured in family life is expected and paradoxical. It is to be expected in light of the physical separation for men of 'work' and 'home' with the rise of capitalism (see Zaretsky 1976); historically, emotional life for men became centred on the home or the family 'as haven' (Lasch 1977). Yet, in the light of feminist research, it is paradoxical to associate masculine caring with family life. Evidence from the eighteenth and nineteenth centuries in Europe and the US shows that men exercised control over household members, including wives, children, servants, and slaves by physical force and violence, often with the support of the religious and secular law (Dobash and Dobash 1992: 267-9). Contemporary research indicates that women's experiences of physical and sexual violence are most likely to be within intimate relationships with men including fathers, husbands, boyfriends, and other men they know. Thus, while male identities in the family are a problem, the caring sides to those identities may be part of the solution.

Failures of Justice System Intervention

The failures of traditional justice system responses to men's violence against women can be summarised in three points.

Problem 1: Most men are not made accountable for acts of rape or violence against intimates. Women do not report the incidents (Dobash and Dobash 1979: 164-7; Estrich 1987: 13, 17; Temkin 1987: 10-12; Stanko 1985; Dutton 1988: 7; Smith 1989). There are also perceived evidentiary difficulties or police indifference leading to non-prosecution (Chappell and Singer 1977; Edwards 1989: 100-6, 172-3; Frohmann 1991; Hatty 1988; Temkin 1987: 12-15; Buzawa and Buzawa 1990: 58; Stith 1990; Zorza 1992: 71), plea bargaining, and acquittals (Kalven and Zeisel 1966: 249-54; Adler 1992: 121; Temkin 1987: 15).[3]

Problem 2: The men who are arrested and prosecuted for violence against women have likely got away with it before and may have entrenched patterns of raping and assaulting women. This follows from the evidence cited under Problem 1. When criminal conviction is a rare event for perpetrators, repeat offenders will often be hardened by the time of their first conviction. Because they are hardened offenders, rehabilitation programmes fail. They fail because they are attempted when a history of violence is so advanced; they fail because the prison that is seen as necessary for a hardened criminal is the least likely site for rehabilitation; and they fail because they occur in a context where a man is stigmatised as a fiend when he believes that he has been a normal (violent) male for many years.[4]

Problem 3: Women victimised by men's violence are re-victimised by engaging the criminal process. Complaints of intimate assault may not be taken seriously by the police or courts (Stanko 1982; Ferraro 1989; Stanko 1989). Rape survivors feel ashamed of coming forward and pursuing a complaint (Dobash and Dobash 1979: 164; Newby 1980: 115; Scutt 1983: 166; Stanko 1985: 72). The criminal process silences the victim. If the case goes to trial, the woman is denied the chance to tell her story in her own way. Rather, she becomes evidentiary fodder for a defence attorney. She is not allowed to tell the offender what she thinks of him, what he has done to her life. She has no opportunity to say what she thinks should happen to the man (Smart 1990; Real Rape Law Coalition 1991), and there is no ceremony to clear her character (Smart 1989).

For rape, the reform literature tends to concentrate on evidentiary rules at trial. Some feminists have become disillusioned with the possibility of changing rape law and procedure; they urge that energies be focused on the bigger battles against patriarchal structures rather than dissipated on the minutiae of liberal legalism (Smart 1990; Snider 1990, 1992). For domestic violence, debate has centred on the merits of the conciliation model and law enforcement model (Lerman 1984).

We acknowledge the limitations of liberal legalism as a reform agenda. Moreover, we think it important that a regulatory strategy not pitch law enforcement against communitarian forms of control. We suggest that justice system institutions can be reformed to give voice to women and to continue the struggle against men's domination of women. A radical shift of paradigm will be required: it will treat victims and offenders as citizens rather than as legal subjects, empower communities at the expense of judges, and confront exploitative masculinities with pro-feminist voices. It involves a shift from a liberal to a civic republican frame.

Republican Criminology

Defended elsewhere (Braithwaite 1989, 1993; Braithwaite and Pettit 1990), republican criminology contains the following elements and claims. Shaming is more important to crime control than punishment, and the most potent shaming is that which occurs within communities of concern. Shame has negative consequences for offenders and victims unless it is joined with a ritual termination of shame (reintegration ceremonies). The criminal process should empower communities of concern, and it should empower victims with voice and the ability to influence outcomes (Eijkman 1992). Communities of concern must negotiate social assurances that victims will be free from future predation and harm.

A reform strategy that embodies these principles, albeit in a tentative way, is the community conference. These conferences can become a key building block of a political strategy against exploitative masculinities.

The Community Conference Strategy

The idea of the community conference comes from New Zealand, where, since 1989, it has been the preferred approach in responding to juvenile crime. White New Zealanders (or *Pakeha*) adapted the idea of family group conferences from Maori culture, where it has been used for centuries in responding to sexual abuse and violence in families as well as for a variety of more minor offences. *Pakeha* have been more cautious about applying the Maori approach in response to family violence, partly because of the legitimate concern that power imbalances among family members can easily be reproduced in family conferences.

Let us describe the family group conference (FGC) approach in handling juvenile crime.[5] After an offence is detected by the state, a youth justice coordinator convenes a conference. Those invited are the offender (let us assume here a male),[6] the boy's family members (often extending to aunts, grandparents, cousins), other citizens who are key supports in the boy's life (perhaps a football coach he particularly respects), the police, the victim, victim supporters, and in some instances, a youth justice advocate.

These conferences can be viewed as citizenship ceremonies of reintegrative shaming (Braithwaite and Mugford 1993). The theory of the FGC is that discussion of the harm and distress caused to the victim and the offender's family will communicate shame to the offender. The assembling of people who care about and respect the offender fosters reintegration (or healing in Maori terms) of social relationships. In a successful conference, the offender is brought to experience remorse for the effects of the crime; to understand that he or she can count on the continuing support, love, and respect of family and friends; and to agree on a plan of action to prevent further harm. All conference participants are given the opportunity to explain how the offence affected them and to put forward proposals for the plan of action. The offender and his or her family members then propose a plan, which is discussed and modified until it is agreeable to all FGC participants, including the police.

Two features of the conference maximise its potential for reintegrative shaming. Giving voice to victims and victim supporters structures shaming into the process, and the presence of offender supporters structures reintegration into the process. These features are conducive to reintegrative shaming, though they do not guarantee it.

Those familiar with the uses of mediation in domestic assault cases, or in family law more generally (Lerman 1984; Fineman 1991; Rifkin 1989; Gagnon 1992), will immediately see the dangers in this approach. It empowers a family structure already characterised by deep imbalances of power between men and women, abusing adults and abused children. However, traditional Maori diagnoses of power imbalance, while not feminist, bear some resemblances to a Western feminist analysis. For example, in some Maori tribes an accused male abuser would have no right to speak at the conference. Any statements in his defence would have to be made through someone moved to speak on his behalf. Maori responses also challenge statist solutions to crime problems. Statist thinkers see a problem of power imbalance in the family and assume state personnel (such as social workers or police officers) are the best agents for correcting that imbalance. In Maori thinking, it is members of extended families who are in a better position to intervene against abuse of family power than the social workers or police officers. Communities of care and concern such as extended families are in a better position to exercise periodic surveillance of family violence or abuse, to talk with family members to ensure they are enjoying freedom from violence, to shame family members when abuse of power does occur, to enforce agreements such as not drinking alcohol, to negotiate understandings that an abused person has a safe haven nearby to stay (a kin member's or neighbour's house), and to negotiate the circumstances of the abuser's removal from the household until there is satisfactory assurance of violence-free family life.

Viable extended families do not exist for many abused individuals who live in Western societies. In New Zealand, the state at times has been impressively proactive on this score. If there is an aunt who has an especially loving relationship with the offender, but who lives hundreds of miles away, the state will pay for her to attend the conference. Occasionally, an agreement is reached in which an offender, who has run to the streets to escape an abusive household, can live with relatives in another community.

In 1991, a variation on the New Zealand conference strategy was implemented in Wagga Wagga (Australia), a city with a population of 60,000 a hundred kilometres west of the capital, Canberra. It has been introduced in other Australian jurisdictions, though taking variable forms.[7] One of the authors has observed the processing of twenty-three young people through conferences in Wagga Wagga and New Zealand during 1991-3; we shall draw from some of these conferences to illustrate its practice.

The genius of the Maori approach, as adapted in New Zealand and Australia, is that it is a particularistic individual-centred communitarianism that can work in an urban setting. The strategy does not rely on fixed assumptions of where community will be found. It does not assume that there will be meaningful community in the geographical area surrounding an offender's home. Nor does it assume that members of a nuclear family will be a positive basis of care, though it always attempts to nurture caring in families. It does not assume that members of the extended family will be caring and effective problem-solvers. It does assume one thing: if a group who cares about both the offender and victim cannot be assembled, this means the conference coordinator is incompetent, not that these human beings are devoid of caring relationships.

The challenge for a conference coordinator is to find the people in an offender's life who really care about him or her, wherever they are. One example of the handling of a male teenager in Wagga Wagga illustrates this point. The boy had been thrown out of his home. The coordinator discovered that his community of concern was the football team where he enjoyed respect and affection. At the football club, the coordinator asked whether the parents of other team members would be prepared to take him in for a time. Several offered. The boy chose the one he liked best but then found he did not like living there; he moved on to another set of football team parents and seemed to be happy at the second try.

Another important feature is that the conference approach is geared to a multicultural society. Anglo-Saxon liberal legalism has crushed the communitarian justice of the Celtic peoples, the Maoris, Aboriginal Australians, Native Americans, and Asian ethnic groups, with a univocal imperial system that sacrifices diversity in problem-solving strategies to belief in equal treatment under one standard strategy. The community conference, in contrast, empowers particular communities of citizens who care about particular people to come up with unique solutions in ways that seem culturally appropriate to those people and circumstances. Western liberal legalism does have a valuable role in plural problem-solving: constitutionalising it and providing citizens with guarantees that certain human rights cannot be breached in the name of cultural integrity. Hence, when conferences are established, advocates can ring alarm bells to engage court intervention when sanctions are imposed beyond the maximum allowed according to more universal state laws. There must be methods of reviewing decisions to ensure that offenders are not coerced into admitting guilt for offences they claim not to have committed. The New Zealand state has attended to these issues in its reform agenda (Office of the Commissioner for Children 1991; Ministerial Review Team 1992). What we might aspire to is a creative blend of empowered legal pluralism constrained by Western universalist legal principles.[8]

Community Conferences in the Regulatory Pyramid

How would the community conference be used in responding to men's violence against women? We shall consider men who assault intimates, an estimated 10 to 33 per cent of whom also rape them (Frieze and Browne 1989: 186-90). To do so, we first sketch how community conferences articulate with other forms of state intervention including powers to arrest and punish.

Republican criminology gives up on prison as the best way of responding to or containing men's violence towards women. It advocates minimalism in the use of imprisonment (Braithwaite and Pettit

1990), but it does not advocate abolitionism. Like Dobash and Dobash (1992: 210-12), we are wary of an abolitionist agenda of returning men's violence towards women to an ill-defined 'community', since power imbalances would reinforce patriarchal power. We are interested in the possibilities for communitarian institutions to empower victims 'to use the criminal justice process to negotiate their own security with suspects/ spouses' (Fagan and Browne 1990: 190; see also Mugford and Mugford 1992). Both mandatory arrest and abolitionism deprive victims of the discretion necessary for such negotiation. Some feminist abolitionist proposals (e.g., Meima 1990) do contain an incipient conference strategy, but they do not allow for any accommodation of communitarian ideals with the option of imprisonment. If non-carceral approaches fail and if imprisonment of a violent man offers more protection of republican liberty than doing nothing, then the man should be imprisoned.

We envisage the regulatory ideal in the form of an enforcement pyramid (see Figure 9.1). The existence of imprisonment at the peak of the pyramid channels the regulatory action down to the base of the pyramid. Regulatory institutions can be designed such that state power enfeebles community control or, as in the pyramid model, so that it enables it. The republican does not call for an informalism that replaces formalism, but for a formalism that empowers and constitutionalises informalism. The preference is to solve problems at the base of the pyramid, but if they cannot be solved there, they are confronted at higher levels. By signalling a societal capability of escalating through these levels, we communicate to a violent man that he should respond by bringing his violence under control. Otherwise, he will face one escalation after another of intervention in his violent life.

At the pyramid's base, the theoretical assumption is that violence within families is least likely when family members have internalised an abhorrence of violence, when masculinity does not depend on domination to persuade, when women are not socially subordinated, and when caring for others is valued. A long historical process of community and state involvement in shaming acts of intimate violence can create a society in which most citizens internalise the shamefulness of violence. The great historical agent of this process is not families or the police, but an active women's movement. Thus, most social control can occur at the pyramid's base by self-sanctioning with pangs of conscience.

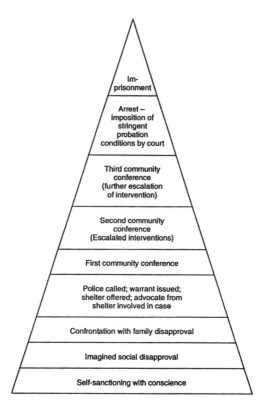

Figure 9.1 Domestic Violence Enforcement Pyramid

If self-sanctioning fails, the history of community shaming of violence can persuade an abusive man that others will disapprove of him and his violence. No one has to confront the man with shame at this level; a man who understands the culture will know that those who learn about his violence will gossip disapprovingly. When gossip hits its target, it will do so without being heard by the target; it will be effective in the imagination of a culturally knowledgeable subject (Braithwaite 1989). But if a man is incapable of imagining the disapproval others feel, then someone must confront him with that disapproval. If family members are too intimidated, then public intervention is required. Consequently, the next rung in the pyramid involves the police being called and a warrant for arrest being issued.

Warrant for arrest is preferred over actual arrest at this level because there is evidence that arrest warrants may be effective in reducing subsequent violence (Dunford 1990). Sherman (1992) interprets this as a 'sword of Damocles' effect. It is identical to the theory of the pyramid: automatic punitiveness is inferior to signalling the prospect of future enforcement, hence channelling the regulatory game towards cooperative problem-solving (for the underlying game theory, see Ayres and Braithwaite 1992: Chapter 2). Issuing an arrest warrant, even if the man is present,[9] is the first intervention.[10] When the warrant is issued, the police may advise the woman to move to a shelter and seek the advice and support of a shelter advocate. The man has time to think about the 'sword of Damocles' that the warrant has put in place.[11]

The design, meaning, and results of the original Minneapolis police field experiment and subsequent replications continue to be debated (Sherman and Berk 1984; Lempert 1989; Sherman 1992; Dunford 1990; Lerman 1992; Bowman 1992; Frisch 1992). It is important to recall that the experiments randomly assigned different police 'treatments' in responding to domestic violence calls: arrest, separation, and mediation. The original Minneapolis study (Sherman and Berk 1984) revealed significant effects of arrest over separation in reducing subsequent violence. The accumulated evidence from recent research suggests a simple deterrence model of arrest is inaccurate. Sherman (1992) now rejects the pro-arrest conclusions drawn from his previous research. For a subset of violent men in four of the Minneapolis replications, those white and employed, he concludes that arrest seemed to have a shaming effect that reduced subsequent violence (see also Hopkins and McGregor 1991: 125-30; Williams and Hawkins 1989). But for another subset of men, those black (in three of the studies) and unemployed (in four), arrest seemed to promote rage or defiance rather than shame. For this group, arrest was another stigmatic encounter with the justice system, which increased the men's anger and violence. The stigmatic effect of arrest for the latter group was stronger than the positive shaming effect of arrest for the former; thus, across-the-board pro-arrest policies may cause more violence than they prevent. This is why we favour arrest warrants as the first state intervention; these would be followed by community conferences before moving up the enforcement pyramid to arrest.[12]

Although arrest may subsequently escalate an abuser's violence, at the time of the incident, taking a violent man into police custody may provide an abused woman a measure of safety. There can be ways to achieve such safety without arrest. While the man is issued a suspended warrant by one police officer, another could take the woman aside and suggest moving to a shelter until a community conference is convened.[13] Such a policy would mean shifting resources from police lock-ups under pro-arrest policies to community shelters. Although shelters are expensive, they are less costly to build and run than lock-ups. Another key benefit of encouraging shelters is that shelter staff are made available to abused women as caring advocates for community conferences.

The next rung of the pyramid is the conference. Several unsuccessful conferences might be held before warrants for arrest were acted upon, in the worst cases leading to prosecution and incarceration. Some may recoil at the thought of one conference failing, more violence, another failed conference, more violence still, being repeated in a number of cycles before the ultimate sanction of incarceration is invoked. But there can be considerable intervention into a violent man's life when moving from one failed conference to another. For example, there could be escalation from weekly reporting by all family members of any violent incidents to the man's aunt or brother-in-law (conference 1), to a relative or other supporter of the woman moving into the household (conference 2), to the man moving to a friend's household (conference 3).

There are many other possible ways to intervene. For example, agreement might be reached on a restructuring of the family's bank accounts so that the woman is economically empowered to walk out if she faces more violence. The conference might agree that the man move out for a month and participate in a pro-feminist counselling programme (for evidence on the effectiveness of such programmes, see Dutton et al. 1992; for violent men's reactions to such programmes, see Ptacek 1988; Warters 1993). When conference intervention escalates to taking away the man's home and handing it over to his wife, some will object that this amounts to a six-figure fine, higher than the fine any court would impose after due process. But if the man feels an injustice is being done, he can walk away from the conference, allow his warrant(s) to be activated and face any punishment a criminal court may impose. Agreement at a conference to hand over a house is therefore viewed as a consensual civil remedy to the breakdown of a violent relationship rather than as a criminal punishment.

Contrast our regulatory pyramid with what a pro-arrest or mandatory arrest policy yields: routine perfunctory criminal justice processing. One problem with contemporary police practices, noted in Sherman

(1992), is that the police tend not to process any differently cases of domestic violence that are the first or the most recent in a repeated pattern of violence. Thus, if the incident is judged not to have caused significant physical injury to the victim, it will be treated similarly, whether it is the first or fifteenth time an incident has been reported. The idea behind the enforcement pyramid is that intervention is responsive to patterns of offending, where communities of care monitor those patterns with state back-up.

Men who repeatedly batter may ultimately have to be removed from their homes or imprisoned. But to repeat perfunctory arrests while waiting for the victim's luck to run out, waiting for the day when her arrival in the hospital emergency room or the morgue will justify locking him up, is a deplorable policy. Equally, locking up all assailants is unworkable: there are too many for our prisons to accommodate. A policy based on the enforcement pyramid is more practical and more decent.

Community Conferences and the Pyramid as a Response

We propose that a response to men's violence against women which places a heavy, though not exclusive, reliance on community conferences, can address some of the failures in justice system responses. Let us consider each of the three problems.

Problem 1: Most men are not made accountable for acts of rape or violence against intimates. Women do not report rape or intimate violence because they feel ashamed and responsible for the violence; they fear family disintegration, physical reprisal, and being degraded in the courtroom. Institutionalising community conferences provides a means of exposing men's violence without re-victimising women. It is a route of crime control that is not dependent solely on the courage or tenacity of victims. The proposal is unreservedly for net-widening, except it is nets of community rather than state control that are widened. It is important that a court processing option is kept in place; indeed, the community conference option can be managed in such a way as to increase rather than reduce the number of prosecuted rape cases. How could this be?

When a woman is concerned with one or more of the above consequences of a criminal trial, she will not continue with the case. But she may be persuaded by police to go with the more private, quicker and less traumatic option of a community conference. At the same time, the police pressure the man to cooperate with the conference, proposing that he may do better and get the matter handled more quickly than if it goes to trial. The conference can proceed without any admission of guilt on the man's part, and he has the right to stop the conference at any point, insisting on his right to have the matters of dispute argued in court. The conference proceeds on the woman's allegations; the man may choose 'not to deny' the allegations, though initially he may decline to admit guilt. If the conference goes well, it might conclude with the man's admitting guilt and agreeing to sanctions that are less than a court would have imposed, yet more than an absence of sanctions, had the complaint been withdrawn. The empirical experience of New Zealand and Australian conferences is that defendants are mostly willing to admit guilt to secure the gentler justice of the conference in preference to the uncertain consequences of a criminal trial. If the conference goes badly (e.g., the man refuses to admit his guilt and nothing is settled), the support the woman receives at the conference might embolden her to press charges.

The availability of a community conference option can encourage more women to come forward and to be supported in their victimisation. It can also encourage many women who do report offences, but who do not want to proceed with criminal prosecution, to do something to confront the offender with responsibility for his wrongdoing at a conference. Whether by community conference or trial, increasing numbers of men would be made accountable for their violence against women.

Problem 2: The men who are arrested and prosecuted for violence against women have likely got away with it any number of times before and may well have entrenched patterns of raping and assaulting women. When we consider the callousness of some men prosecuted for rape, we may question the plausibility of affecting them through reasoned dialogue and shaming. Equally, we may question the plausibility of deterring them through prison sentences. The objective should be to intervene earlier in these men's lives before they have reached a hardened state. Evidence suggests that abusive men were violent towards family members such as sisters, brothers and mothers when they were young (Straus and Gelles 1990).[14]

In the New Zealand and Wagga Wagga juvenile programmes, the aim is to communicate shame to male adolescents for their very earliest acts of violence. When community conferences become well established, forums are made available to families and concerned citizens for bringing violence and exploitation to light at early stages. The psychologists who dominated criminological thinking until the 1950s were strong advocates of early intervention, a position discredited by 1960s labelling theorists. On balance, we should be pleased that early intervention driven by psycho-therapeutic models was defeated.

Republican criminology incorporates the labelling theory critique by calling for a radically different justification for and modality of early intervention: community intervention. One patriarchal legacy of labelling theory is a squeamishness about shaming, a 'boys will be boys' approach to violent masculinity. We must distinguish between harmful and productive early intervention. We can and must be early interveners again: we can use the power of shaming to avert patterns of exploitation and degradation of women. This power will be sustained and amplified by a strong women's movement and pro-feminist men's groups.

A conference at Wagga Wagga illustrates the potential for early intervention. It concerned a teenage boy's assault of a teenage girl. Out of the dialogue among participants, it was revealed that the boy had assaulted other girls and had viciously assaulted his mother. Australia has a major problem of teenage boys assaulting their mothers, although one would not know this from media accounts or the scholarly literature, which focus on spouse abuse. While there has been a 'breaking of the silence' with spouse assault, this has not occurred for son-mother assault. In a patriarchal culture, it is mothers not sons who feel shame and responsibility for these assaults. Traditional courts and justice system responses offer little chance to break the silence of maternal shame and maternal protectiveness of sons from a punitive justice system. A problem-solving dialogue among people who care for both victim and offender, such as occurred at this Wagga Wagga conference, offers a way to break the silence and to confront a violent boy before his patterns become entrenched.

Another recent Wagga Wagga conference concerned the sexual assault of a 14-year-old girl in a swimming pool by a 14-year-old boy.

The victim was most upset by the way the boy had been bragging to his mates, within the victim's hearing, that he had 'got one finger in her'. The victim was not only re-victimised by this humiliation, but was also labelled as a 'dobber' (a 'tattle-tale') by boys at her school after she reported the incident. Gossip among her classmates was that she 'deserved what she got'. Dialogue at the conference clarified that this was not the case. It also made it impossible for the offender's father to believe, as he had before the conference, that his son had been singled out unfairly for a bit of 'horseplay'. Participants at the conference affirmed her 'courage' for coming forward in the face of such social pressures. The offender not only apologised to the victim in a meaningful way, but undertook, together with five other classmates (one male, four female) who attended the conference, to spread the word among their peers that her conduct was blameless in every respect, while he took responsibility for his totally unacceptable conduct. In this conference, an exploitative masculinity of 14-year-old boys and an excusing 'boys will be boys' fatherly masculinity was confronted by six teenagers and the parents of the victim. Our hypothesis is that this is a better way to confront a misogynist culture than a criminal trial ten years later.

Problem 3: Women victimised by men's violence are re-victimised by engaging an the criminal process. One reason rape victims are re-victimised at trial is that criminal trials are transacted in the discourse of stigma.[15] Winning is the objective, and each side tries to win through maximum efforts to blacken the adversary's character. The rape trial is a ceremony that puts a highly trained practitioner at the defendant's disposal to deny responsibility, to deny injury, and to deny the victim (we draw from Sykes and Matza's 1957 'techniques of neutralisation' formulation here and below). The rape trial institutionalises incentives for a defendant to reinforce his denials, denials which he believed before the trial, and denials that may have encouraged the rape in the first place (see, e.g., Scully and Marolla 1984, 1985). Faced with prosecutorial vilification of his character, the trained competence to exaggerate evil, the transforming of a partially flawed person into a demon devoid of any redemptive potential, the defendant is ever more equipped to condemn his condemners. If he started the criminal trial in a mood of moral ambivalence towards the victim, he may end up holding the victim and prosecution in utter contempt. The discourse of stigma in rape trials reinforces misogynist masculinities (see also Bumiller 1990 on this point). Even if a man is convicted and imprisoned, he will be released eventually, perhaps a more deeply committed and angry misogynist.

When fact-finding processes are allowed to stigmatise, disputants slide into a vortex of stigma: stigmatisation is mutually reinforcing. More generally, as Lewis (1971), Scheff (1987), Scheff and Retzinger (1991), and Lansky (1984, 1987) find, when human institutions are designed to foster the by-passing or denial of shame, shame-rage spirals are likely. Justice system procedures promote such spirals.

The community conference is based on different principles. It is designed to minimise stigma. Participants are selected based on their capacity to provide maximum support to victims and offenders, not as in criminal trials, to exert maximum damage to the other side. The aim of community conferences is to reintegrate victim and offender, not to stigmatise.

Compared to the offender-centred criminal trial, community conferences, if managed well, are victim-centred. The victim can confront the offender in her own words in her own way with all the hurt she has suffered, and victim supporters add more. Offenders often admit there were effects they denied or had not realised. The aim of the process is to confront the many techniques of neutralisation offenders use. It is to engage in an unconstrained dialogue that leaves responsibility as a fact that is admitted, regretted rather than denied.

Victim reintegration can be accomplished by sub-ceremonies following the formal conference. For example, at a conference concerning two boys who had assaulted a boy and girl, the girl said she did not want the offenders to come around to her house to offer a more formal apology because she was still afraid of them. The coordinator asked the girl's family to stay, and in a post-conference session, the coordinator discussed what had been said, suggesting that the boys would not come after her or the other victim again. This session ended with the girl agreeing she was no longer afraid. Later, a minister at the girl's church confirmed that the victim reintegration session helped to allay fears and distrusts the girl harboured up until the conference.

In contrast to the rape trial, from which a victim can emerge more afraid, frustrated at not having any degree of control, and suffering more reputation damage than the offender, community conferences are designed to empower victims with voice and control. Victims and their supporters have the right to veto the plan of action proposed by offenders and their supporters.

Conferences typically conclude with an apology by the offender. This is important for relieving the victim of any taint of blame. The apology can be a much more powerful ceremony than punishment in affirming moral values that have been transgressed, as the contrast between American and Japanese culture attests (Braithwaite 1989; Tavuchis 1991). When an offender rejects any suggestion that the victim may have been at fault and openly condemns the wrongfulness of the act, the censure of crime is reinforced and the cultural support for techniques of neutralisation is eroded.

One wonders how the Clarence Thomas hearings might have gone if American political culture would have allowed Anita Hill's allegations of sexual harassment to be handled in a community conference format. Would it not have been better for women if Thomas could have admitted his abusing Hill and apologised for his acts without his being stigmatised and professionally destroyed (Daly 1992)? If after he apologised and stated his commitment to upholding anti-discrimination law, Thomas was then appointed to the court, one wonders whether we would have had a less misogynist US Supreme Court.[16]

When institutions trade in stigma and rule out apology- forgiveness sequences as outcomes, forces of exploitation are uncensured, reinforced, and legitimated. The community conference strategy attempts to break the shame-rage spiral, to intervene early in transgressors' lives, and to reintegrate rather than stigmatise victims and offenders.

Questions About the Conference-Pyramid Enforcement Model

We are advocating an alternative way of responding to men's violence against women. We are not tied to a standard ordering of the pyramid levels, only to the preference for a dynamic problem-solving model. Although our arguments are meant to be suggestively sketched, there are vexing questions about the conference strategy that should be addressed.

Question 1:
**Is this just another form of mediation
with all of its attendant problems?**

Traditional mediation has been criticised for failing to take violence seriously, lacking procedural accountability, 'bar[ring] abused women from access to courts for enforceable protection' (Lerman 1984: 72), neutralising conflict by individualising and privatising grievances (Abel 1982), and failing to deal with the unequal bargaining power of the parties. Balance of power questions will be addressed under Question 2.

Community conferencing is not like family counselling and traditional victim-offender mediation. The participation of other community members on the basis of special relationships of care[17] for victims and offenders has a transformative effect on the nature of the interaction and on the agreed action plans. David Moore's research on the Wagga Wagga process (private communication with the authors) concludes that 'more is better' with regard to participants beyond the nuclear family, so long as they are participants who have a relationship of genuine caring with one of the principals.

We agree that traditional mediation hands unaccountable power to mediation professionals whose 'assumptions about the nature and seriousness of family violence' (Lerman 1984: 72) should be open to public scrutiny. We agree that it is wrong to bar women from access to courts for enforceable protection. Accountability to the courts should be guaranteed for both sides. Victims, like defendants, should have the right to withdraw from a conference and insist on activating an arrest warrant. Accountability to courts is not the most important accountability, however. Accountability to those citizens who have concern for victims and offenders is the more deeply democratic form of accountability (Barber 1984; Dryzek 1990). The traditional justice process 'steals conflicts' from citizens (Christie 1977), keeping victims and offenders apart. The community conference requires victims and offenders to confront their conflict, without neutralising their emotions.

We agree that traditional mediation risks a limited, privatised justice. Scutt (1988: 516) argues that privatisation of justice is detrimental to the interests of the disadvantaged when it 'shuts off from public view the very nature of the inequality from which the individual and group suffer' (see also Allen 1985; Hatty 1985). In contrast to mediation, conferences are designed to encourage community dialogue on intimate violence.

Private justice does risk rendering 'the personal apolitical' in the traditional dyadic form of offender and victim, mediated by a professional. Traditional public justice hardly does better in grappling with domination: it silences communities of concern by the disempowering roles of legal professionals (Snider 1990). The important question is not whether private or public justice is the bigger failure in communicating censure. It is how to redesign both, and the dynamic interplay between them, so that incidents of violence become occasions for community debates about brutalising masculinities and inequalities spawning violence.

Question 2:
Can we expect 'communities of concern' to be any less sexist or misogynist than traditional justice system responses or state intervention?

Some will think it naïve that communitarian dialogue can work in places like Australia, where one-fifth of survey respondents agree that it is acceptable under some circumstances for a man to hit his wife (Public Policy Research Centre 1988). It is not naïve precisely because four-fifths do not find such violence acceptable. The problem is that one-fifth are able to erect walls around the private space of the family to protect themselves from the disapproval of the four-fifths. Even if many of these four-fifths 'condemn wife beating, and yet at the same time actively support the type of marital relationship that encourages it' (Dobash and Dobash 1979: 179), at least their condemnation can be harnessed in conferences.

Voices in defence of exploitation and brutality will be heard in community conferences. But exploitation and brutality flourish more in secretive settings, when they go unchallenged and unnoticed (Hopkins and McGregor 1991: 127). When intimate violence is noticed and challenged, rationalisations sustained in secret settings are opened to dialogue. It would not be possible to have regulatory institutions where only feminist voices were heard and misogynist voices were completely silenced. However, dialogic institutions favour parties who are on the moral high ground, and feminists are clearly on the high ground. So we suspect that conferences can create spaces to advance struggles for feminist voices to be heard against those of misogynists.

As a flexible process of community empowerment, conferences permit more latitude for redressing power imbalances than the inflexible procedures of the court. Balance can be restored by the collective might of a victim's supporters (as in the case of the Wagga Wagga teenagers who supported their friend after she was sexually assaulted). It can be restored by powerful men, for example, a doctor, a brother, an uncle, a teacher, a neighbour, who subscribe to an anti-violent masculinity and who are more than a match for a domineering husband. Women can create institutions that give male allies a chance to show their mettle. Power imbalance can be most effectively restored by organised feminists who work as shelter advocates. Here, one strength of our proposal is that a shift in resources from police lock-ups to shelters can provide a base for feminist organisation. Improved criminal justice institutions are no substitute for a stronger women's movement as the keystone to controlling violence against women. In the meantime, we can design criminal justice institutions to enfranchise voices from the women's movement, coupled with those of abused women and caring men.

Conference coordinators need training to be effective in organising conferences that are responsive to men's violence against women. Training could include speakers from the women's movement and shelters, and role playing of conference scenarios subject to feminist interpretations. Coordinators can readily be required to hear feminist voices during in-service training, while it may take longer to require judges to do so.

Question 3:
Do conferences work? Are participants satisfied?

Evaluation of conferences for juvenile cases in New Zealand (Maxwell and Morris 1993; Morris and Maxwell 1991) suggests 'there is much that is positive and novel about [this] system of youth justice' (Morris and Maxwell 1991: 88), including the diversion of most juveniles away from courts and institutions, involvement of families in decisions and taking responsibility and acknowledgment of differences in cultural groups. The authors cite these problems, however: professionals often took over the process; adolescent offenders often did not feel involved; and just half of victims said they were satisfied with the outcome. Levels of satisfaction with conference outcomes were substantially higher for offenders and family members (85 percent) than for victims (51 percent) (Maxwell and Morris 1993: 115-20). Victim dissatisfaction was explained by 'inadequate conference preparation . . . about what to expect . . . and unrealistic expectations [for] likely . . . outcomes, especially with respect to reparation' (Morris and Maxwell 1991: 86). More research is needed and more is under way. In particular, we need methodologically sound outcome evaluations (from both juvenile and adult samples) on whether violence falls following conferences more than it does following criminal trials.

We do not wish to hide implementation failures of conferences in New Zealand or Wagga Wagga or the difficulties of struggling against domination and stigma, nor would we suggest that conferences are a panacea even when perfectly implemented. We are suggesting that community conferences open an avenue for addressing the failures of contemporary justice processes which leave misogynist masculinities untouched by shame and victims scarred by blame.

Conclusions

Men's violence against women is a crime enabled by men's domination (Daly and Wilson 1988; Dobash and Dobash 1979; Evason 1982; Yllo and Straus 1990). Republican and feminist theory (Braithwaite 1991, 1993; Yllo and Bograd 1988; MacKinnon 1983) argue that a reduction in men's violence towards women will occur when gender inequality is reduced and when human social bonds are more caring. There are many ways of causing cracks in patriarchal structures that have barely been discussed here. Among the most central are transforming economic power, familial and sexual relations towards greater gender equity and strengthening the political power of the women's movement and pro-feminist elements in other liberation movements.

Contemporary criminal justice practices may do more to cement over cracks in patriarchal structures than prise them open. Current practices leave patriarchal masculinities untouched and victims more degraded and defeated; and to continue with more of the same policies may make things worse. This is not to deny a role for the criminalisation of violence and state intervention of the kind envisaged in the enforcement pyramid.

We have proposed an alternative way of thinking about responding to men's violence against women that is based on these ideas: (1) the threat of escalated state intervention (formalism) can empower more effective communitarian intervention (informalism); (2) ceremonies can centre on reintegrative shaming of offenders and reintegrative caring for victims; (3) communities of care can devise their own preventive strategies, and can be motivated to implement them by their affection and attachment to particular victims and offenders; and (4) dialogue can be sustained within communities of care about the rejection of violent masculinities and, more optimistically, about the search for non-violent masculinities. While non-exploitative masculinities have the potential to emerge in community conferences, their expression is largely foreclosed in courtrooms and prisons. The creation of institutions that require men to listen to women and open spaces for apology and dialogue might clear the way for a collective wisdom to emerge. That communal wisdom may re-define masculinities beyond the wit of our individual imaginings. Though it may not be possible to design criminal justice institutions that prevent violence, we can fashion institutions that generate less violence.

Notes

1. Thanks to Susan Brennan for research assistance and to Lawrence Sherman and Iris Young for helpful comments on the paper.

2. Our remarks centre on expressions of hetero-masculinity. We note, for example, that men's caring and compassionate responses towards other men have been recently evidenced in response to AIDS. For an early review and critique of the 'men's studies' literature, see Carrigan et al. (1985), and more recently, Connell (1987).

3. Statistics for rape arrests and convictions are clearer than those for domestic assaults for several reasons. Domestic assaults are a sub-set of assaults, and researchers have focused more on police than court actions (see Ferraro and Boychuk 1992 for an exception). In the US, rates of reporting rape to the police vary by victim-offender relation (Williams 1984) and whether women viewed the incident as 'rape' (Estrich 1986: 1164-8). Rates of report vary from 7 to 30 per cent (for known and stranger, respectively, Russell 1984) to 50 per cent (National Crime Surveys). Some 20 to 32 per cent of arrests for rape lead to conviction; these percentages are similar to other violent offences and are not unique to rape (Estrich 1986: 1161-71).

4. The same facts cause not only the failure of rehabilitation, but the failure of deterrence and incapacitation as well. Deterrence fails in the face of these long histories of offending followed by non-conviction. Incapacitation fails for the string of victims prior to the first conviction, for the men in prison who are raped by those who have learnt to dominate the vulnerable and for the women who suffer post-release violence at the hands of men who emerge from the degradation of prison with a deepened hatred of women. Even under the toughest of incapacitative regimes in the Western world, for example the incarceration of men convicted of rape in the US, the incapacitation is very partial. In the US, 90 per cent of rape convictions lead to incarceration; of those receiving prison sentences, the average sentence length is twelve years (Bureau of Justice Statistics 1987: 8,16). A man in prison from age 20 to age 32 can victimise a lot of women in his teens, forties and beyond.

5. For a more detailed description of New Zealand's youth justice system and the relationships among police, court, and FGC, see Maxwell and Morris (1993: Chapter 1).

6. Except when we discuss men's abuse of women, we shall not assume a generic 'he' for the offender or 'she' for victim.

7. The variety of modalities of implementation is dazzling in the states of New South Wales, South Australia, Western Australia, Victoria and the Australian Capital Territory. Some programmes are coordinated by the police, others by state welfare departments (as in New Zealand), others by the Juvenile Court, others by Aboriginal elders. Some are pre-court diversionary initiatives; others involve courts using conferences as an alternative to traditional sentencing. These programmes have varying success at empowering victims. Research is currently under way to assess the strengths and limits of different conferencing models.

8. Republican theory requires unbreachable upper limits on any discretionary exercise of the power to punish. It is opposed to any constraining minimum levels of punishment, however (Braithwaite and Pettit 1990).

9. That is, the police for the moment choose to use their discretion not to activate the warrant, even in the presence of the alleged offender. This may require law reform to render the activation of warrants discretionary.

10. In the Charlotte replication (Hirschel et al. 1990), one condition was citation. This meant issuing a citation to the offender, usually in the presence of the victim, which the offender signed. The couple was advised of a court date, although the victim was not asked if she wished to go to court. Citation increased subsequent violence about as much as did arrest. Citation is more like arrest than the arrest warrant we propose because of its non-discretionary channelling of the case onto a courtroom track.

11. We recognise that for some men, an arrest warrant (like a restraining or protection order) will be merely viewed as a 'piece of paper' (Chaudhuri and Daly 1992), especially for men who have been arrested before. When this is true, the remedy is escalation up the pyramid. Note also a key difference between a criminal arrest warrant and a civil restraining order. The restraining order enables escalation to enforcement action in the face of further misconduct; the arrest warrant enables prosecution for the violence that has already occurred in addition to enforcement directed at the further misconduct.

12. Another relevant empirical finding that justifies a preference for the dialogue of the conference before any further escalation is from the Milwaukee experiment. Arrestees who said (in lock-up) that police had not taken the time to listen to their side of the story were 36 per cent more likely to be reported for assaulting the same victim over the next six months than those who said the police had listened to them (Bridgeforth 1990: 76; Sherman 1993).

strich, S. (1987). *Real Rape*, Cambridge, Massachusetts: Harvard University Press.

vason, E. (1982). *Hidden Violence*, Belfast: Farset Press.

agan, J. and Browne, A. (1990). 'Violence towards intimates and spouses', report commissioned by the Panel on the Understanding and Control of Violent Behavior, National Research Council, National Academy of Sciences, Washington, DC.

erraro, K. J. (1989). 'Policing woman battering', *Social Problems* 36: 61-74.

erraro, K. J. and Boychuk, T. (1992). 'The court's response to interpersonal violence: a comparison of intimate and nonintimate assault' in Buzawa, E. S. and Buzawa, C. G. (eds), *Domestic Violence: The Changing Criminal Justice Response*, Westport, CT: Auburn House.

ineman, M. (1991). *The Illusion of Equality: The Rhetoric and Reality of Divorce Reform*, University of Chicago Press, Chicago.

rieze, I. H. and Browne, A. (1989). 'Violence in marriage' in Ohlin, L. and Tonry, M. (eds) *Family Violence*, Chicago: The University of Chicago Press.

risch, L. A. (1992). 'Research that succeeds, policies that fail', *Journal of Criminal Law and Criminology* 83: 209-16.

rohmann, L. (1991). 'Discrediting victims' allegations of sexual assault: prosecutorial accounts of case rejections', *Social Problems* 38: 213-26.

Gagnon, A. G. (1992). 'Ending mandatory divorce mediation for battered women', *Harvard Women's Law Journal* 15: 272-94.

Hatty, S. (1985) 'On the reproduction of misogyny: the therapeutic management of violence against women' in Hatty, S.E. (ed.) *National Conference on Domestic Violence*, vol. 1, Canberra: Australian Institute of Criminology.

Hatty, S.E. (1988) 'Male violence and the police: an Australian experience', working paper, School of Social Work, University of New South Wales, Sydney.

Hirschel, J.D., Hutchinson, I.W. III, Dean, C., Kelley, J.J. and Pesackis, C.E. (1990) *Charlotte Spouse Assault Replication Project: Final Report*, National Institute of Justice, Washington, DC.

Hopkins, A. and McGregor, H. (1991) *Working for Change: The Movement Against Domestic Violence*, Sydney: Allen & Unwin.

Kalven, H. and Zeisel, H. (1996) *The American Jury*, Chicago: University of Chicago Press.

Katz, J. (1988) *The Seductions of Crime: Moral and Sensual Attractions of Doing Evil*, New York: Basic Books.

Lansky, M. (1984) 'Violence, shame and the family', *International Journal of Family Psychiatry* 5:21-40.

Lansky, M. (1987) 'Shame and domestic violence', in Nathanson, D. (ed.) *The Many Faces of Shame*, New York: Guilford.

Lasch, C. (1977) *Haven in a Heartless World*, New York: Basic Books.

Lempert, R.O. (1989) 'Humility is a virtue: On the publicization of policy-relevant research', *Law and Society Review* 23: 145-61.

Lerman, L.G. (1984) 'Mediation of wife abuse cases: the adverse impact of informal dispute resolution on women', *Harvard Women's Law Journal* 7:57-113.

Lerman, L.G. (1992) 'The decontextualization of domestic violence', *Journal of Criminal Law and Criminology* 83: 217-40.

Lewis, H.B. (1971) *Shame and Guilt in Neurosis*, New York: International Universities Press.

Luckenbill, D.F. (1977) 'Criminal homicide as a situated transaction', *Social Problems* 26: 176-86.

MacKinnon, C. (1983) 'Feminism, Marxism, method, and the state: an agenda for theory', *Signs: Journal of Women in Culture and Society* 8: 635-58.

MacKinnon, C. (1987) *Feminism Unmodified: Discourses on Life and Law*, Cambridge Mass: Harvard University Press.

Maxwell, G.M. and Morris, A. (1993) 'Family victims and culture: youth justice in NZ' Institute of Criminology, Victoria University of Wellington, Wellington.

Meima, M. (1990) 'Sexual violence, criminal law and abolitionism' in Rolston, B. and Tomlinson, M. (eds) *Gender, Sexuality and Social Control*, Bristol, England: The European Group for the Study of Deviance and Social Control.

Miedzian, M. (1991) *Boys Will Be Boys: Breaking the Link Between Masculinity and Violence*, New York: Doubleday.

Ministerial Review Team to the Minister of Social Welfare (1992) Review of the Children Young Persons and their Families Act, 1989, Minister of Social Welfare, Wellington.

Morris, A. and Maxwell, G.M. (1991) 'Juvenile justice in New Zealand: A new paradigm', *Australian and New Zealand Journal of Criminology* 26: 72-90.

Morrison, T. (ed.) (1992) *Race-ing Justice, En-gendering Power: Essays on Anita Hill Clarence Thomas, and the Construction of Social Reality*, New York: Pantheon Books.

Mugford, J. and Mugford, S. (1992) 'Policing domestic violence' in Moir, P. and Eijkman H. (eds), *Policing Australia: Old Issues, New Perspectives*, Melbourne: Macmillan

Newby, L. (1980) 'Rape victims in court: the Western Australian example' in Scutt, J.A (ed.) *Rape Law Reform*, Canberra: Australian Institute of Criminology.

Office of the Commissioner for Children (1991) 'A briefing paper: An appraisal of the first year of the Children, Young Persons and Their Families Act 1989', Office of the Commissioner for Children, Wellington, New Zealand.

Polk, K. and Ranson, D. (1991) 'Patterns of homicide in Victoria' in Chappel, D. Grabosky P. and Strang, H. (eds) *Australian Violence: Contemporary Perspectives*, Canberra: Australian Institute of Criminology.

Ptacek, J. (1988) 'Why do men batter their wives?' in Yllo, K. and Bograd, M. (eds) *Feminist Perspectives on Wife Abuse*, Newbury Park CA: Sage.

Public Policy Research Centre (1988) Domestic Violence Attitude Survey, conducted for the Office of the Status of Women, Department of Prime Minister and Cabinet Canberra.

Real Rape Law Coalition (1991) 'Sexual assault: the law v. women's experience' in Law Reform Commission of Victoria, Rape: Reform of Law and Procedure, Appendices to Interim Report No. 42, Melbourne.

Retzinger, S.M. (1991) *Violent Emotions: Shame and Rage in Marital Quarrels*, Newbury Park: Sage.

Rifkin, J. (1989) 'Mediation in the justice system: a paradox for women', *Women and Criminal Justice* 1: 41-54.

Russell, D.E.H. (1984) *Sexual Exploitation*, Beverly Hills: Sage.

Scheff, T.J. (1987) 'The shame-rage spiral: a case study of an interminable quarrel', in Lewis, H.B. (ed.) *The Role of Shame in Sympton Formation*, Hillside, NJ: LEA.

Scheff, T.J. and Retzinger, S.M. (1991) *Emotions and Violence: Shame and Rage in Destructive Conflicts*, Lexington: Lexington Books.

About the Authors

John Braithwaite is Professor in the Law Program, Research School of Social Sciences, Australian National University. His current research projects are on restorative justice, nursing home regulation and the globalization of business regulation. He is interested in the interface between explanatory and normative theories of the regulation of social life.

Stephanie R. Bush-Baskette is Assistant Professor of Criminology and Criminal Justice at Florida State University. She received her JD from American University in Washington, DC, in 1978 and her MA from Rutgers University in Criminal Justice in 1996. She is currently completing research for her dissertation investigating the impact of the war on drugs on Black females. Prior to entering graduate school, she practiced law, was elected to the New Jersey State Legislature for three terms, and was appointed to the Governor's Cabinet as commissioner of the New Jersey Department of Community Affairs. Her research interests include the impact of public policies, girls in the juvenile justice systems, and the effects of race, gender, and class in the administration of justice.

Teresa A. Carlo is a PhD candidate in the Department of Sociology at Western Michigan University. She received her MS in Criminal Justice from the College of Law Enforcement at Eastern Kentucky University. Her research interests are drug courts and other alternatives to incarceration.

Lynn S. Chancer is Assistant Professor of Sociology at Barnard College. She is the author of *Sadomasochism in Everyday Life* (1992) and a forthcoming volume titled *Reconcilable Differences: Confronting Beauty, Pornography, and the Future of Feminism*. Her research interests include gender and crime, social theory, race, and inequality.

Kathleen Daly is Associate Professor in the School of Justice Administration at Griffith University, Queensland, Australia. She received her PhD from the University of Massachusetts in 1983, taught at the State University of

198

New York at Albany, was a member of the faculty at Yale University from 1983 to 1992, and was a Visiting Associate Professor of Sociology at the University of Michigan. She is interested in applying feminist, sociological, and legal theories to problems of crime and justice. Her book *Gender, Crime, and Punishment* received the Hindelang Award from the American Society of Criminology in 1995.

Mona J. E. Danner is Assistant Professor and Graduate Program Director in the Department of Sociology and Criminal Justice at Old Dominion University. Her interests are in social control, inequalities (class, race-ethnicity, gender, and nation), and women globally. She is currently engaged in research on gender and the process of negotiating the academic contract and in the cross-national investigation of the relationship between gender inequality and criminalization mechanisms in the social control of women. In 1995, she was in Beijing, China, where she presented research on Social Indicators of Gender Inequality at the NGO Forum held in conjunction with United Nations Conference on Women. She received the New Scholar Award in 1997 from the American Society of Criminology, Division on Women and Crime.

James Massey is Director of the University Honors Program at Northern Illinois University (NIU) and Associate Professor in the NIU Department of Sociology. His scholarly interests are in historical criminology and the use of law and judicial process for purposes of repressive social control.

Susan L. Miller is Associate Professor in the Department of Sociology and Criminal Justice at the University of Delaware. She received her PhD in Criminology from the University of Maryland. Her research interests include victimology and victims' rights, woman battering, social control, and criminal justice policy. Her work has been published in various journals, such as *Law & Society Review, Justice Quarterly, Women & Criminal Justice,* and *Violence & Victims.* She received the New Scholar Award in 1994 from the ASC Division of Women and Crime. She is currently working on a book about gendered power and social-occupational relations among foot patrol and traditional rapid-response police officers.

Merry Morash holds a PhD from the Institute of Criminology and Criminal Justice at the University of Maryland. Prior to receiving her degree, she worked in a number of criminal justice settings, including the juvenile court in Maryland, a street work program in Massachusetts, and the Virginia prison system. Much of her research has been focused on women, and she has done research on wife battering in Latino neighborhoods in Detroit and of Korean and Korean American women. She also has done extensive research on women in policing. She has recently completed a study of

management and programming for incarcerated women, and she is currently doing an evaluation of two especially promising programs for women
offenders.

Claire M. Renzetti is Professor and Chair of Sociology at St. Joseph's
University. She also chairs the Board of Directors of the National Clearing-
house for the Defense of Battered Women. She is editor of *Violence Against
Women: An International, Interdisciplinary Journal* and the Gender, Crime,
and Justice book series. With Jeffrey Edleson, she coedits the Violence
Against Women book series. She is the author or editor of 10 books and
numerous book chapters and scholarly articles.

Lila Rucker, a criminologist, is Associate Professor in the Criminal Justice
Studies Program at the University of South Dakota. Most of the classes she
teaches relate to the question of violence: Family Violence; Drugs, Violence,
and Gangs; Exploring Nonviolence. She facilitates the Alternatives to
Violence Project conflict resolution workshops in all of the South Dakota
prisons. Her current research interests include the contexts in prison
environments within which rape does or does not occur and batterers' belief
systems.

Zoann K. Snyder-Joy is Assistant Professor in the Department of Sociology
at Western Michigan University. She received her PhD from the School of
Justice Studies at Arizona State University in 1992. Her recent publications
address the use of risk need instruments in probation supervision and
self-determination in American Indian justice.

Elizabeth A. Stanko, Reader in Criminology, Lecturer in Criminology,
Department of Law, Brunel University, United Kingdom, received her PhD
in sociology from the City University of New York Graduate School in
1977. She taught sociology and women's studies at Clark University (U.S.)
before moving to London in 1990 to take the position of Director, Centre
for Criminal Justice Research, and Convenor, M.A., in Criminal Justice.
She is the author of *Everyday Violence* and *Intimate Intrusions,* editor of
texts on gender and crime (most recently, *Just Boys Doing Business: Men,
Masculinities, and Crime,* coedited with Tim Newburn) and has published
widely on issues of prosecutorial discretion, violence, violence against
women, and crime prevention. She is currently writing a book tentatively
titled *The Good, The Bad and the Vulnerable: Victims, Victimization and
Gender.*

Anna Wilhelmi received her JD from Northern Illinois University (NIU)
School of Law and is completing her MA in the NIU Department of
Sociology. She is currently a staff attorney with the Kane County, Illinois,
Public Defender's Office.

cully, D. and Marolla, J. (1984) 'Convicted rapists' vocabulary of motive: excuses and justifications', *Social Problems* 31: 530-44.

cully, D. and Marolla, J. (1985) 'Riding the bull at Gilley's: convicted rapists describe the rewards of rape', *Social Problems* 32: 251-63.

cutt, J. (1983) *Even in the Best of Homes: Violence in the Family*, Melbourne: Penguin.

cutt, J. (1988) 'The privatization of justice: power differentials, inequality, and the palliative of counselling and mediation', *Women's Studies Forum* 11: 503-20.

Sherman, L.W. (1992) *Policing Domestic Violence: Experiments and Dilemmas*, New York: Free Press.

Sherman, L.W. (1993) 'Defiance, deterrence and irrelevance: a theory of the criminal sanction', *Journal of Research in Crime and Delinquency* 30.

Sherman, L.W. and Berk, R.A. (1984) 'The specific deterrence effects of arrest for domestic assault', *American Sociological Review* 49: 261-272.

Smart, C. (1989) *Feminism and the Power of Law*, London: Routledge.

Smart, C. (1990) 'Law's truth/women's experience' in Graycar, R. *Dissenting Opinions: Feminist Explorations in Law and Society*, Sydney: Allen & Unwin.

Smith, M.D. (1990) 'Patriarchal ideology and wife beating: a test of a feminist hypothesis', *Violence and Victims*, 5: 257-73.

Snider, L. (1990) 'The potential of the criminal justice system to promote feminist concerns', *Studies in Law Politics and Society* 10: 143-72.

Snider, L. (1992) 'Feminism, punishment and the potential of empowerment', submitted to *Canadian Journal of Law and Society*.

Stanko, E.A. (1982) 'Would you believe this woman? Prosecutorial screening for 'credible' witnesses and a problem of justice' in Rafter, N.H. and Stanko, E.A. (eds) *Judge, Lawyer, Victim, Thief*, Boston: Northeastern University Press.

Stanko, E.A. (1985) *Intimate Intrusions*, London: Unwin Hyman.

Stanko, E.A. (1989) 'Missing the mark? Policing battering' in Hanmer, J., Radford, J. and E.A. Stanko, E.A. (eds) *Women, Policing, and Male Violence: International Perspectives*, London: Routledge & Kegan Paul.

Stith, S.M. (1990) 'Police response to domestic violence: the influence of individual and familial factors', *Violence and Victims* 5: 37-49.

Straus, M.A. and Gelles, R.J. (1990) *Physical Violence in American Families*, New Brunswick, N.J.: Transaction Publishers.

Sykes, G. and Matza, D. (1957) 'Techniques of neutralization: a theory of delinquency', *American Sociological Review* 22: 664-70.

Tavuchis, N. (1991) *Mea Culpa: A Sociology of Apology and Reconciliation*, Stanford: Stanford University Press.

Temkin, J. (1987) *Rape and the Legal Process*, London: Sweet and Maxwell.

Warters, W.C. (1993) 'Collisions with feminism: perspectives of abusive men who've been challenged to change', unpublished manuscript, Department of Sociology, Syracuse University.

Williams, C.S. (1984) The classic rape: when do victims report?', *Social Problems* 31: 459-67.

Williams, K.R. and Hawkins, R. (1989) 'The meaning of arrest for wife assault', *Criminology* 27: 163-81.

Wilson, P. (1978) *The Other Side of Rape*, St. Lucia, Queensland: University of Queensland Press.

Yllo, K.A. and Bograd, M. (eds) (1988) *Feminist Perspectives on Wife Abuse*, Newbury Park: Sage.

Yllo, K.A. and Straus, M.A. (1990) 'Patriarchy and violence against wives: the impact of structural and normative factors', in Straus, M.A. and Gelles, R.J. (eds) *Physical Violence in American Families*, New Brunswick, N.J.: Transaction Publishers.

Zaretsky, E. (1976) *Capitalism, the Family, and Personal Life*, New York: Harper & Row.

Zorza, J. (1992) 'The criminal law of misdemeanour domestic violence', *Journal of Criminal Law and Criminology* 83: 46-72.

CHAPTER TEN

Connecting the Dots

Women, Public Policy, and Social Control

Claire M. Renzetti

◆ When I began reading the chapters of this book, my 7-year-old son positioned himself next to me on the couch and worked studiously on one of his favorite activity books. I found myself staring at his hands as he slowly and carefully drew a line from one number to the next in consecutive order until he had completed a picture. He felt my gaze and without looking up from the page, he said, "I like connecting the dots because you don't know when you start what it's going to be, but when you're done you have a big picture."

A big picture. *The* big picture. Suppose I connect the major themes of these chapters, I thought, and see what picture emerges. So I invite you to join me as I connect the dots, so to speak. I must warn you that I may add some extra dots along the way—research, anecdotes, issues, questions—that I think might help bring the picture into sharper focus. And you should feel free to add dots, too; after all, this is a complicated picture and one that I suspect will take a long time and much collective effort to complete.

Controlling Women

The chapters in this book address various means of social control, both formal and informal. Social control is not inherently bad. To the contrary, it's a necessary part of organized social life. Social control makes social order possible and imbues our everyday interactions with a degree of predictability. But what struck me when I read this book is the extent to which controls over women are proliferating—multiplying and extending into women's lives like tentacles that grasp prey and squeeze it into submission. And I couldn't help wondering if it isn't more than coincidental that efforts to impose more far-reaching control over women have followed a period during which women as a group have struggled successfully for greater autonomy and self-determination. It's hardly surprising, as Miller (this volume) points out in the introductory chapter, that many of the proponents of "get-tough" crime policies are also outspoken leaders of the antifeminist backlash. But we must be careful not to dismiss their views as more ramblings from the radical Right. Not everyone on the get-tough bandwagon identifies as politically conservative. Fear is a powerful motivator—and a useful political ploy—such that even many who see themselves as liberal feminists have added their voices to the litany of crime-fighting rhetoric without carefully considering the effects of specific policies and practices on women or children. Indeed, as many authors in this book (e.g., Danner, this volume; Miller, "The Tangled Web," this volume; Morash & Rucker, this volume) repeatedly show, anything other than a tough-on-crime stance is derided as weak, ineffective, coddling—in a word, feminine.

To be sure, the metaphors of get-tough crime control policies are decidedly masculine. Most common are military metaphors: for example, crime control policies are *weapons* in the *war* on crime or in the *theater* of illegal narcotics (Massey, Miller, & Wilhelmi, this volume.). Of course, the military metaphors are most direct in boot camp corrections programs. Morash and Rucker (this volume) deftly point out the dangers of applying the traditional boot camp model—designed to transform young men into unemotional, calculating soldiers willing to kill "enemies"—to a correctional setting, where we supposedly wish to teach offenders *not* to be aggressive, ruthless, and antisocial. In reading Morash and Rucker's chapter, and the others that highlight the military metaphors of get-tough crime control policies, I was reminded of another article I read recently by Zvi Eisikovits and Eli Buchbinder (1997). Eisikovits and Buchbinder discovered in their interviews with men who had abused their wives or girlfriends that batterers typically use military metaphors to describe their intimate relationships and the reasons for their abusive behavior. The men spoke of feeling "embattled," of "digging in and fighting it out," and of not "surrendering." Their descriptions of intimate relationships as an ongoing war between men and women are not unlike the descriptions of punitive crime control policies, policies that in their consequences constitute a war *against* women.

The connection between the militaristic metaphors of crime control and woman battering is not trivial. The military represents organized, legitimized violence, and a common theme throughout these chapters is the violence in women's lives—violence imposed by male intimates (fathers, boyfriends, husbands) and institutionalized violence in a variety of forms, some quite insidious. Consider, for example, the forfeiture laws that Massey and his colleagues (this volume) discuss. The innocent owners who try to save their homes and other property are mostly women, many of whom testify that they feared their husbands or were physically abused by their husbands. The courts, as Massey et al. show, rarely consider such arguments adequate and award the property in question to the government. The women and their children are twice victimized—first, by their husbands and then again by the court. Some readers may object that my definition of violence is too broad, that the courts' decisions are not really "violent." But I submit that the loss of one's home, which represents for most of us not only a considerable financial investment but also feelings of security and attachment, is as traumatic as many forms of outright physical abuse. Moreover, because a home is for most people their greatest financial asset—most American families do not have substantial savings but do have some equity in their homes—forfeiture may propel women and children into poverty and homelessness, increasing their vulnerability to other, more familiar forms of violence, such as street crime.

Stanko (this volume) is quite right in arguing for recognition of a continuum of violence against women. She urges us not to parcel out and divide violence against women into separate and discrete categories. Her point is well illustrated by not only her own chapter but by the other chapters in this book as well. I was surprised, for example, by

Danner's statement (this volume) that a discussion of entitlements to the poor is to some extent a debate separate from the debate over Three Strikes and similar crime control policies. I see these two issues as fundamentally connected. Danner acknowledges that the poor are disproportionately represented among prison populations and that much of the crime committed by poor people is an outgrowth of economic deprivation and the stressors that accompany it. Chesney-Lind (1997) has convincingly argued that women's crime, in particular, is directly related to their disadvantaged economic position. It is also often, as Richie (1996) shows, a product of the violence in women's everyday lives. Some of the women Richie interviewed in prison were there because they had defended themselves against an abuser, but others had been compelled to commit other crimes (e.g., drug trafficking, prostitution, theft) by intimate partners who intimidated, threatened, and abused them.

Who are these women? Many of them are the same women who politicians and the public are demonizing in the welfare reform debates. As Bush-Baskette (this volume) points out, they are typically young, minority women with children. They are depicted by politicians and others as promiscuous, lazy, undeserving. The political rhetoric in welfare reform, like the rhetoric surrounding Three Strikes and other get-tough crime control policies, calls for these women and the men in their lives to take responsibility for their behavior. Taking responsibility means not accepting public assistance; getting a job that does not pay enough to lift you and your children out of poverty; trying to keep your children safe and well cared for while you work, even though affordable, quality child care is unavailable. And in some states, taking responsibility may soon mean being forced to marry the man who fathered your child. This latter version of responsibility is especially dangerous in light of research that shows that most fathers of children of teenage girls are older men; the majority are over 20. The younger the mother, in fact, the greater the difference is likely to be between her age and the father's age (Robinson, 1996). These findings in themselves should be sufficient testimony as to the level of abuse and powerlessness in many of these women's lives.

One of the underlying goals of welfare reform legislation, presented in the guise of individual responsibility, is to make women more dependent on men (Fineman, 1995). Yet at the same time, the consequences of Three Strikes laws and similar get-tough crime control policies is to put more of those men—and increasingly, more women (Bush-Baskette, this volume)—behind bars. Indeed, the authors in this volume highlight the many contradictions inherent in get-tough crime control. Snyder-Joy and Carlo (this volume), for example, point out the contradiction between the rhetoric of "saving the family" and punitive prison policies that tear families apart and exacerbate family problems that predate incarceration. But these contradictions should force us to also ask, Whose family do the "family values" proponents wish to save? Their disapproval of all but the traditional patriarchal nuclear family is hardly disguised. Perhaps there really is no contradiction after all: If the family does not conform to the traditional patriarchal nuclear form, it's not worth saving.

Certainly, many of the policies and practices discussed in this book are predicated on a specific image of the ideal family. For instance, Massey et al. (this volume) show how women's claims of lack of knowledge of their partners' illegal behavior are typically disbelieved by the courts, who assume, "She must have known. How could a wife not know what her husband was doing in their own home?" Such assumptions are predicated on an idealized image of marriage as characterized by mutuality, reciprocity, equality, and openness. The reality, however, is that few marriages fit this bill. Studies of married couples consistently show that secrecy is common, and rarely, if ever, are partners equals in the marriage (Blumstein & Schwartz, 1983; Rubin, 1991). Even if they manage to establish equality in their interactions with one another, they will not be regarded as equals by others, including the legal system (Lindgren & Taub, 1993). At the same time, the courts assume in forfeiture cases that if the wife was aware of her husband's illegal activity and did not do everything "reasonably" possible to stop it, she gave her implicit consent and, therefore, cannot be regarded as innocent. As I noted earlier, this position overlooks the intimidation, abuse, and violence that characterize many marriages. But if you hold the idealized image of marriage that apparently informs these judicial decisions, intimate violence doesn't exist anyway. Stanko (this volume) and Chancer (this volume) also remind us that a corollary of the idealization of marriage is the notion that the women most vulnerable to attack (of various kinds) are those who step outside the bounds of normative femininity, be they women who choose to live alone, single mothers, or white women who date minority men. In contrast, Bush-Baskette (this volume) maintains that Black women do not conform to normative femininity by virtue of their race, but instead of being viewed as vulnerable, Black women are considered immune from attack because they are stereotyped as violent, dangerous, and immoral.

Lest I be misunderstood and accused of male-bashing—a popular charge against feminists—allow me to add that I am not arguing that women never willfully commit crimes or that all women offenders are really just innocent victims of violent men and therefore should not be held responsible for their crimes. What I am saying is that contemporary get-tough crime control policies do not take into account the complex circumstances surrounding much female criminality *and* victimization nor do they reflect the diversity of women's lives. To make this point clearer, let me shift the discussion a bit by turning to a feminist model for evaluating public policy.

Feminism and Public Policy

The get-tough crime control rhetoric often appeals directly to women, playing on our fears and promising us safety. Given the nature of women's fear of crime (Madriz, 1997; Stanko, 1987), it is not difficult to understand why many women, including feminists, have openly or covertly supported more punitive crime control legislation. My concern is that the support may be forthcoming without a careful feminist analysis of a specific policy. What questions should such an analysis entail?

The most fundamental question that must be asked about any policy is, What are its consequences? To frame the question more specifically, we must ask, "Who wins and who loses if this policy is adopted?" Though the questions may seem obvious to some readers, the process of answering them is not as easy as it first appears. Rarely will there be a single or unequivocal answer to either question (Davies, Lyon, & Monti-Catania, in press). This is because women are not a homogeneous group. Women differ in many ways, including, among the most important, their races and ethnicities, social classes, sexual orientations, ages, marital statuses, parenting statuses, and physical abilities or disabilities. As Chancer (this volume) and Bush-Baskette (this volume) rightly argue, these factors are not competing oppressions but rather intersecting inequalities. In considering how a specific policy affects women, feminists must analyze this *intersectionality* (Crenshaw, 1994), and the analysis must be inclusive of the voices of diverse women. Only by *listening* to the concerns of diverse groups of women will the differential impact of a policy be revealed. Of course, some standard must be adopted for deciding whether or not to support a specific policy, and I cannot pretend to know what that standard should be because I believe it will vary from policy to policy. But I would argue vehemently against a "majority rules" standard. If the safety of even a small group of women is seriously threatened in some way by a particular policy, the policy does not deserve feminist support.

In undertaking policy assessment, we should also be wary of policies touted as gender neutral. Some policies that appear gender neutral are actually discriminatory or harmful in their effects. Danner (this volume) writes about Virginia's "right to carry" law, which ostensibly "benefits" women and men by allowing them to carry concealed weapons for personal protection. But although proponents of the law portrayed it as especially beneficial to women, it is men, not women, who are most likely to carry concealed firearms. Moreover, such a law increases women's risk of victimization at the hands of violent intimate partners.

Policy assessment, then, requires us to consider not only what a policy is *supposed to do,* but also how it will be *implemented.* I remember one of my favorite professors in graduate school, Bill Chambliss, telling his students over and over again that there is usually a disparity between the written law and the law in action. Policy evaluation, therefore, cannot end with policy enactment, for experience tells us that even policies written to benefit women may not be beneficial when they are implemented and may sometimes be used against women. For example, Stanko (this volume) notes how many of the reforms in sexual assault legislation, for which feminists lobbied to improve the treatment of rape victims, have been used by law enforcement and government to shift responsibility for crime prevention from the state to the individual. Public awareness and women's safety campaigns show that the state is "doing something" for women, so if some women fall victim to assault, it must be their fault. "Don't say we didn't warn you!"

Similarly, Danner (this volume) mentions how women were regarded as the "quiet winners" in the 1994 federal crime bill because of the inclusion of the Violence Against Women Act (VAWA). Certainly, passage of the VAWA should be applauded, but implementation of specific aspects of the law have not always benefited women. For instance, mandatory arrest policies, which are explicitly encouraged by the VAWA, are resulting in the arrest of an increasing number of women who defend themselves against their violent partners. Subsequently, these women have criminal records and are often mandated for treatment in batterers' programs (Hamberger & Potente, 1996). Crime control policies designed to cast a wider net are ensnaring a greater number of women, many of whom are not criminal offenders.

Last, in analyzing public policy, feminists must be clear about our goals. Morash and Rucker (this volume) argue, for instance, that if our correctional goal is to develop a more humane, caring, and benevolent society, then the boot camp model is not the best means for achieving this goal. However, I have strong doubts about whether building a more humane, caring, and benevolent society is really a national goal at the present time. As Miller (this volume) emphasizes in her chapter on community policing, the promise and potential of a police model based on an ethic of care are undermined by the rules and structure of policing as a masculinist, paramilitary organization (see also Miller, in press). At the same time, the public climate, which policy makers have quickly picked up on, appears to be one obsessed with punishment and exacting revenge. The popular American ethos is one of making any and all offenders pay for their misdeed through suffering—the more, the better. Although feminists often claim a "different voice," a voice of benevolence and caring, support for some punitive crime control policies, especially those aimed at batterers, indicates otherwise. Braithwaite and Daly's chapter (this volume) is illustrative. In a personal conversation, John Braithwaite told me that the family conferencing model for handling domestic violence was often denounced by members of the battered women's movement who see it as failing to adequately hold men accountable for their violence. Could another translation of this objection be "for failing to adequately *punish* men for their violence?" It is interesting that in other conversations I have had with battered women, especially battered women of color and battered lesbians, the family conferencing model is thought to be worth a try. These are women who are reluctant to turn for help to a criminal justice system that is racist and homophobic, and they do not wish their partners to be subjected to the abuses and brutality that the police and courts have historically inflicted on minorities and homosexuals. In identifying feminist goals with respect to public policy, we must once again listen to diverse voices.

The Big Picture

At the conclusion of this chapter, I had hoped to present a coherent picture of gendered social control. But as I read and reread my words, I saw so many dots connected by multiple lines criss-crossing the page that I could hardly celebrate an artistic masterpiece. Instead, I must conclude that a single picture is impossible and, indeed, not even desirable. What we need are multiple pictures that can be viewed and analyzed as a collage—a work with unifying lines and themes but one that highlights the complexity and diversity of women's lived experiences. I recognize the task is daunting, but I believe that only by undertaking it can we hope to see the big picture. This collection is a first step toward achieving that goal.

References

Blumstein, P., & Schwartz, P. (1983). *American couples.* New York: William Morrow.

Chesney-Lind, M. (1997). *The female offender.* Thousand Oaks, CA: Sage.

Crenshaw, K. W. (1994). Mapping the margins: Intersectionality, identity politics, and violence against women of color. In M. A. Fineman & R. Mykitiuk (Eds.), *The public nature of private violence* (pp. 93-118). New York: Routledge.

Davies, J., Lyon, E., & Monti-Catania, D. (in press). Complex lives/difficult choices: Safety planning with battered women. Thousand Oaks, CA: Sage.

Eisikovits, Z., & Buchbinder, E. (1997). Talking violent. *Violence Against Women, 3,* 482-498.

Fineman, M. A. (1995). Masking dependency: The political role of family rhetoric. *Virginia Law Review, 81,* 501-534.

Hamberger, L. K., & Potente, R. (1996). Counseling heterosexual women arrested for domestic violence: Implications for theory and practice. *Violence & Victims, 9,* 125-138.

Lindgren, J. R., & Taub, N. (1993). *The law of sex discrimination.* St. Paul, MN: West.

Madriz, E. (1997). *Nothing happens to good girls: Fear of crime in women's lives.* Berkeley: University of California Press.

Miller, S. L. (in press). *Negotiating masculine space: A feminist analysis of the gendered nature of community policing.* Boston: Northeastern University Press.

Richie, B. (1996). *Compelled to crime.* New York: Routledge.

Robinson, R. A. (1996). Bearing witness to teen motherhood: The politics of violation of girlhood. In D. Dujon & A. Withorn (Eds.), *For crying out loud: Women's poverty in the United States.* Boston: South End Press.

Rubin, L. (1991). *Erratic wars.* New York: Harper & Row.

Stanko, E. (1987). Typical violence, normal precaution: Men, women, and interpersonal violence in England, Wales, Scotland, and the USA. In J. Hanmer & M. Maynard (Eds.), *Women, violence and social control* (pp. 122-134). London: Macmillan.

Index